W9-AHM-740

BATTLEFIELD
HARDLINE

INTRODUCTION

Following in the tradition of *Battlefield 2142* and the *Bad Company* series, *Battlefield: Hardline* offers a new take on the beloved franchise, introducing players to the high-stakes world of cops vs. criminals. Instead of high-intensity military conflicts, prepare yourself for bank heists, high-speed chases, and hostage rescues set across a wide range of urban and rural environments. Whether you're new to *Battlefield* or not, *Hardline* has something for everyone and this guide offers everything you need to know to gain the upper hand during each intense engagement.

WHAT'S NEW?

Before you jump into the game and start delivering your own brand of justice, take a moment to review some of the new features introduced by *Battlefield: Hardline*. From an engaging single-player campaign to a revamped and fast-paced multiplayer mode, there's rarely a moment to catch your breath. Use this time to familiarize yourself with *Hardline's* unique vision of *Battlefield* before the bullets start flying.

CAMPAIGN

Hardline's single-player campaign takes place over ten action packed episodes, following the newly promoted vice detective, Nicholas Mendoza. Objectives offer varied gameplay with multiple ways to achieve success. Points are awarded for non-lethally taking down the criminals and most times stealth is a viable option, but there are times when survival is your only goal. Nearly the entire game can be played with more direct tactics though, if that is more your style.

New skills and gadgets give the player the ability to stealthily move through the environment, taking down oblivious bad guys while leaving others none the wiser. Equip the Scanner and survey the area for possible threats, plotting a course for success. Freeze perps with a flash of the badge and arrest them without incident. Always stocked with plenty of shell casings, use distraction to lure criminals to an easy takedown or simply sneak past them. Between fights, the Scanner allows the player to find evidence, unlocking improved gear once Case Files are complete.

The single-player section offers a full walkthrough with detailed, tried and tested strategies for every objective along with maps that display locations for all evidence and suspects with warrants. Comprehensive listings point out how to acquire every weapon and gadget in the campaign.

MULTIPLAYER MAPS AND GAME MODES

When it comes to multiplayer, *Hardline* doesn't disappoint, offering nine new maps and seven game modes. While fan-favorites like Conquest and Team Deathmatch have returned, *Hardline* introduces five completely new game modes, providing a welcome change of pace. Whether attempting to escape with the loot in Heist or speeding through city streets in a boosted car in Hotwire, the new game modes demand new tactics and strategies if you hope to lead your team to victory. The guide provides a detailed breakdown of every map and game mode, providing useful hints and tips directly from the game's developers at Visceral.

NON-LETHAL TAKEDOWNS

Each encounter doesn't have to end with someone's death. By using a variety of blunt melee weapons and the new T62 CEW stun gun, it's possible to incapacitate your target. Once down, an incapacitated foe can be interrogated, giving up vital intel useful for hunting down their teammates. Intel derived from interrogations is shared with your whole team, making non-lethal takedowns a crucial tactic, particularly in the new competitive Crosshair and Rescue game modes.

GAME-CHANGING GADGETS

The new grappling hook and zipline gadgets give players unparalleled mobility, allowing them to ascend to new heights and traverse great expanses in a matter of seconds. But these aren't the only new gadgets available. Deploy the new laser tripmine or sabotage to booby-trap choke points and objectives. Or, take advantage of the improved first aid packs and ammo boxes. Interact with a gadget-enabled operator or enforcer to take health or ammo directly from your teammates.

ECONOMY AND PLAYER-DIRECTED PROGRESSION

In *Hardline*, cash is king—and that doesn't just apply to cash-centric game modes like Heist and Blood Money. As you earn points during your multiplayer career, you're also awarded with cash. Use this cash to purchase new weapons, attachments, grenades, gadgets, and vehicle enhancements. The in-game economy and this player-directed approach to progression is all-new to *Hardline*, allowing *you* to choose what weapons and gear you unlock next.

ENHANCED VEHICLE GAMEPLAY

Offering a mix of police and civilian cars, trucks, and helicopters, vehicle combat is more frantic than ever. Passengers can now lean out of a vehicle's windows, firing at targets in all directions. Whether driving a getaway car or chasing down a van full of criminals, drivers finally get the respect they deserve, racking up points for roadkills, jump bonuses, and boosting Hotwire cars. Although these vehicles are less durable than those found in previous games, this only makes high-speed chases all the more intense. Expect plenty of memorable *Battlefield* moments as vehicles crash, flip, and explode in spectacular fashion.

THE ACADEMY

The Academy covers the basics of *Battlefield Hardline* including, weapons, gadgets, techniques, and expert score. This section assumes familiarity with first-person shooters and only covers that which is unique to Hardline.

DIFFICULTIES

When starting a new game, you must select a difficulty. This can also be changed at any time through the pause menu. Raising the difficulty increases enemies' damage output and makes them tougher to take down. The only other change is on Veteran and Hardline where button prompts are missing.

Prologue

CADET
OFFICER
VETERAN
HARDLINE

> DIFFICULTY
> This difficulty level is built to offer a challenging and rewarding experience for casual gamers and newcomers to the genre. If you are familiar with shooters, consider making the jump to Veteran difficulty.

CADET	Recommended if you haven't played a shooter before. It's the full *Battlefield Hardline* experience, but enemies are easier to defeat, and their weapons have decreased damage output.
OFFICER	This difficulty is built to offer a challenging and rewarding experience for casual gamers and newcomers to the genre. If you are familiar with shooters, consider making the jump to Veteran difficulty.
VETERAN	The way VISCERAL prefers to play *Battlefield Hardline*. We encourage all experienced players to do the same. Enemies have increased damage output. The challenge is greater, but so is the sense of accomplishment.
HARDLINE	An uncompromising difficulty level for the truly battle-tested. Aiming is unassisted and you will have no recovery time between bullet hits. Plan your encounters strategically and remain in stealth as long as possible to survive.

TACTICAL GEAR

Before beginning an Episode, customize your equipment by selecting Tactical Gear. Choose a primary weapon, secondary weapon, two gadgets, and a melee weapon from an increasing amount of equipment. Arrest suspects, collect evidence, scan your environment, perform non-lethal takedowns, and complete objectives to unlock better equipment. Refer to the Unlocking Weapons & Gadgets chapter for full details on how to unlock it all.

Keep an eye out for Tactical Gear cases and lockers that are set up in various locations throughout the campaign. These allow you to change your loadout mid-episode. Specific objectives greatly change the way the game is played and different gadgets must be swapped in and out to achieve each. Better weapons that are unlocked while progressing through an objective can be selected at the next Tactical Gear. The Episode maps show the locations of all cases and lockers.

TACTICAL GEAR

WEAPONS

With the exception of one Episode, you carry two guns at all times: a primary and a secondary. The former is selected from a variety of versatile pistols, hard-hitting revolvers, and automatic / burst fire machine pistols. This is your lightweight, quick select alternative to your more powerful weapon—great for finishing off a weakened foe.

The secondary weapon is the bigger, heavier weapon with, for the most part, higher damage and range than your primary. A huge variety of automatic rifles, up-close shotguns, long-range sniper rifles, and more are available for any situation. The Hardline single-player campaign is mostly about being stealthy, non-lethally taking down the criminals. There are times though where the player must escape a hairy situation, survive an onslaught of enemies, or a direct approach is desired. An accurate, high damage weapon is a must for these situations. Select the one that best suits your playstyle.

As you reach certain Expert Levels, you unlock attachments for your weapons. Improve primary and secondary weapons by giving them an Optic, Accessory, Muzzle, and/or Grip. Attachments such as infrared scopes, the Suppressor, and

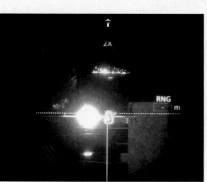

Extended Magazine are big game changers. The Suppressor should be considered in any stealth situation while the nighttime, infrared scope is vital in the smoke of Episode 6 and lights-out fight in 9. Play around with different setups to find the one you like best.

Some accessories, such as the Laser Sight, can be toggled on and off by pressing Up on the digital pad. Guns are either single-shot, semi-auto, automatic, or burst fire. When a weapon has multiple fire rates or a distance setting, it can be altered by pressing Down.

GADGETS

The player starts the game out with one gadget, the T62 CEW. By increasing Expert Level and progressing through the story, more are unlocked—offering you a wide variety in how you complete objectives. On the bottom of your HUD, available gadgets are shown on the left and right. Press that direction on the digital pad to equip the item.

T62 CEW

The T62 CEW is an electroshock weapon that non-lethally knocks a target out and it is the only gadget available at the start of a game. The range is extremely short, but a direct hit with this weapon scores 100 points toward Expert Score. It also goes unheard by nearby enemies, keeping the player undetected.

Whether firing from the hip or ADS, wait for two circles to appear in the gun's sights before firing. Reload is relatively slow, so be sure to duck behind cover if there are nearby enemies aware of your location.

GRAPPLING HOOK

The Grappling Hook can be used to reach rooftops and out of reach platforms. If a ledge is climbable, it is indicated by a glowing effect when the gadget is equipped. It is vital when first received in Episode 3 to complete an objective. There are also a few items in the Everglades that cannot be reached without it. Otherwise, it is only used to find alternate paths through the environment.

The device is aimed and fired just like any weapon. When aiming, a circle with a line through it means the hook cannot be fired. Line it up with an edge until it changes to a square and fire. Now, walk into the rope to grab on.

Continue pushing forward to climb to the next level. A fully loaded Grappling Hook holds four hooks, but looking at a used hook and pressing the Reload button can recover them. Note that if there are any obstacles in your way as you climb the rope, you are knocked to the ground.

ZIPLINE

The zipline, used in the same manner as the Grappling Hook, is great for reaching lower areas very quickly. Aim until the square is shown in the sights and fire the rope. Jump onto the line or press the Reload button while looking at the post to slide down. This is required for an objective and to reach a few items in Episode 3. Otherwise, it is only needed to quickly move to a lower location.

ARMORED INSERT

The Armored insert is a passive Gadget, protecting the user from ballistic damage to the torso. This is a good selection for tough gunfights, especially the "Survive!" objectives.

FIRST AID PACK / AMMO BOX

First Aid Pack tosses out a red bag that heals any player nearby. A green plus icon is shown next to the health bar when receiving the benefit. Ammo Box throws out a small crate that refills ammunition for all weapons and gadgets. Select the gadget and press the Fire button to use both of these. These are great alternatives when facing a tough fight.

With an AI partner following the player, additional help is occasionally given when low on health. Your partner can passively heal you when in close proximity. A green plus icon next to the health bar in the lower-right corner indicates the player is being healed. Note that the enemy can still take you out while healing, so take cover if possible. This benefit should not be relied on, but it is nice when it happens.

LASER TRIPMINE

When stealth is the priority, the Laser Tripmine is not a good choice for one of your gadgets. But there are times where a location must be defended. If there is time to set up, place a couple of these explosives in known routes to weaken the onslaught. These are also fun to use when stealth is not a concern. Place the mine on a wall and then lure a criminal to the other side to cause mayhem.

Look at a desired location for placement and a green highlight appears. Press Fire to place the mine. You can carry two at a time with a maximum of two placed at one time. Return to Tactical Gear to restock or replace with another gadget. The explosive is detonated as an enemy runs through the line. It does not go off when a player trips it, though harm is done when caught in the blast. You can pick up an undetonated mine by pressing the Reload button.

BREACHING CHARGE

The only other explosive in the single player campaign is the Breaching Charge. Unlike the tripmine though, it must be detonated remotely. Press the Aim button to throw down a charge. You can carry two at a time and both can be deployed at once. From a safe distance and with enemies near the explosive, press the Fire button to detonate. This allows you to set traps and ambushes. Press the Reload button to pick one up.

GAS MASK

Starting in late Episode 2, criminals start throwing Gas Grenades. These explode on contact, filling the immediate area with a damaging, green gas. This can be avoided by moving away from the smoke. Or, you can equip the Gas Mask, negating the effects of the Gas Grenade. There are only a handful of battles where these explosives are used, so for the most part this gadget is best saved for times where these grenades make a fight too difficult.

DROPPED AND FOUND WEAPONS

Approach a weapon dropped by a criminal to display the gun and stats on the right side of the HUD. Hold the Interact button to pick it up. This unlocks the gun in your Tactical Gear. Now you can grab your original weapon or go with the new one.

Some weapons can be found lying around the environment. The M/45 SMG and Scout Elite Sniper Bolt Action are only available by finding them in the Everglades.

POLICE TRAINING

SCANNER

In Episode 1, the player is introduced to the Scanner, an extremely valuable tool in the fight against crime. Pressing the Scanner button equips the device. This is used to tag suspects and objects within view. This allows the player to know where tagged enemies are even when behind a barrier. Suspects with warrants, high-value targets, and evidence within the reticle can be analyzed further by holding down the Jump button.

Survey an area with the Scanner whenever possible. Not only does this give the player valuable insight into the situation, but points are scored for tag subjects and objects.

ALARM

Starting in Episode 3, alarms protect many of the locations. When scanning the criminals in each area, keep an eye out for these devices. An alarm box, usually hanging on a central wall, is connected to a series of loudspeakers. If the player is spotted, a criminal goes for the button. Once pushed, reinforcements join the bad guys—making your fight that much tougher. It is best to reach the switch first and disable it, which can also be done by shooting it. Destroying all of the sirens can also turn off the alarm. Use a suppressor to hide your location.

Counter the toxic gas with the Gas Mask gadget. Both continue to do damage over time as the player remains in the area of effect. It is best to clear out when one is incoming.

DESTRUCTIBLE ENVIRONMENTS

Much of the environment in *Battlefield Hardline* is destructible. Crates, windows, thin walls, and more are blown to pieces with gunfire. Use this to your advantage when an enemy hides around a corner or behind weak cover.

AVOIDING GAS AND FIRE GRENADES

Some criminals in the single-player campaign are equipped with grenades, but they are limited to gas and fire. Upon impact, a Gas Grenade produces a cloud of green smoke that hurts a nearby player. The Fire Grenade releases fire in the immediate area that is even more damaging. A grenade icon indicates an incoming explosive. You can avoid these by simply moving away.

SUSPECT AWARENESS

Suspect awareness is indicated in two ways: an Alert Meter that fills as suspects become more dangerous and white vision cones on the minimap which vary based on your stance. The Alert Meter appears as an arc that fills in white as an enemy becomes more aware of your presence. As long as the player can get

out of sight or take down the criminal who notices the detective, the awareness goes away. If it fills completely, the bad guys go on high alert. At that point, it becomes a gunfight.

Vision cones display the area in which each criminal spots the player. When going for stealth, avoid making contact with these cones. If the player is spotted, these turn yellow to indicate awareness. Crouching makes these cones smaller. When enemies are investigating, they are able to spot the player from further away.

LAST KNOWN POSITION

Flee an area after being spotted to avoid making contact with the enemy. Hide from or evade them while they search and they eventually look elsewhere. An orange circle on the map indicates the last place the player was seen or heard.

FREEZE

Freezing suspects with the detective badge is a great way to take down one to three bad guys in a non-lethal manner. A white shield icon with an exclamation point indicates the person will put up his hands with a flash of the badge. Keep an eye on the criminals, since they go after their gun if left uncovered. Move the reticle between all of the suspects as you approach. If possible, move in from the side before flashing the badge. With the suspects in line, they are easier to keep an eye on.

THROW DISTRACTION

Distracting an enemy with a shell casing is great for separating a specific guy from a group or stealthily sneaking through an area. The casing is tossed straight ahead. Aim the center of your screen where you wish the item to hit. A white circle on the minimap shows the distraction radius. If someone is within this earshot, a yellow circle appears on the minimap and vision cones turn yellow, indicating that person is investigating. A question mark also appears above his head.

Distracted by the item, he moves to that location, giving the player a great opportunity to non-lethally take him down or move through the area undetected.

If more than one criminal hears the noise, only one investigates while the others remain in an alert state. This may make it impossible to arrest the first guy, since it would be in view of the second enemy. Another shell casing can be tossed further away to separate them more.

Toss too many shell casings in a short period and enemies go on high alert. Try to limit successive throws to two. This should be enough to isolate the enemy you want from a group. If an enemy is hit with the shell or it is tossed between the player and target, the player is detected.

WARRANTS

Starting in the first episode, some bad guys have warrants out for their arrest. Use the scanner to tag the enemies. If a bust icon appears above the guy, he is wanted. Analyze him further to find out an identity. This must be done to get credit for the arrest.

Handcuff the guy or use the T62 CEW to take him down non-lethally. Doing this is optional, but you score big points for identifying the guys and taking them down. You also earn two Achievements / Trophies along the way.

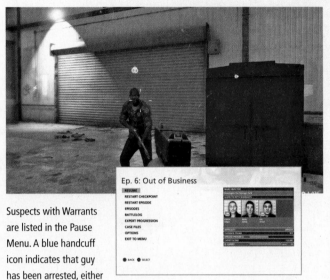

Suspects with Warrants are listed in the Pause Menu. A blue handcuff icon indicates that guy has been arrested, either during the current playthrough or a previous game. A skull icon is shown when that suspect was killed instead of arrested.

CASE FILES AND EVIDENCE

Starting in Episode 1, you can examine the environment for potential evidence to be added to on-going Case Files. With the Scanner equipped, the upper-left corner of the HUD lets you know how many pieces have been found and the total number in the current area, as well as the distance to the nearest item. The controller also vibrates when the player is near evidence. Note that an item can be shown as nearby, but it is actually on a different level. Be sure to keep that in mind when searching an area.

When evidence is viewed through the Scanner, it turns green. Hold the Jump button to analyze the item and add it to the appropriate Case File. Complete Case Files to unlock new weapons and Battlepacks.

Collecting the evidence is optional beyond the first episode, but it does earn valuable expert points as well as three Achievements / Trophies. The Case Files screen contains an overview of all of your cases and the rewards you receive for completing them. You can dive into a case in more detail by selecting a piece of collected evidence. Refer to our Case Files chapter for full details on where to find them all.

EXPERT SCORE AND LEVEL

You earn points by completing specific actions. These points go toward your Expert Score, which in turn increases your Expert Level. Refer to the Unlocking Weapons and Gadgets chapter to find out required points and what is unlocked at each level.

ACTION	POINTS
ARREST SUSPECT WITH WARRANT	1000
TAKEDOWN SUSPECT WITH WARRANT	500
COMPLETE OBJECTIVE	500
MAKE AN ARREST	250
TAKEDOWN	100
FIND EVIDENCE	200
DISARM ALARM BOX	200
IDENTIFY SUSPECT WITH WARRANT WITH SCANNER	150
TAG SUSPECT WITH WARRANT WITH SCANNER	25
TAG SUBJECT OR OBJECT WITH SCANNER	20

PROLOGUE

As Nicholas Mendoza, a newly promoted Vice detective for the Miami Police Department, the player sets out to fight the drug war that plagues the city. Following orders from his Captain, Julian Dawes, Nick takes to the streets with his partner to investigate the trail of evidence. It becomes clear that not everyone is on the level and he must decide whom to trust.

The single-player campaign of *Battlefield Hardline* is presented in an introductory Prologue and ten Episodes. Each chapter covers every objective, confrontation, bust, and piece of evidence. Maps give key points of interest as well as all evidence and suspect with warrant locations.

LOCATION:
MIAMI

 DETECTIVE:
NICHOLAS MENDOZA

 PARTNER:
CARL STODDARD

CASE FILE(S):
NONE

 EVIDENCE

 SUSPECTS WITH WARRANTS:
SHEA DORSETT

MAIN OBJECTIVE:
RAID THE HOTEL.

After an introductory scene with Nicholas Mendoza being taken to prison on a bus, we flash back three years to a drug bust at a Miami hotel. This mission introduces you to some of the features of *Battlefield Hardline*.

A RAID THE HOTEL

Press the Interact Button to knock on the door as voices can be heard panicking on the other side. Press it again to kick it in. Aim the flashlight at the right perp's face and when prompted, click the Melee Button to arrest him. Do the same to the left criminal. At this point, things get out of hand fast. Crouch behind the table and quickly take out the other three.

> "You might wanna secure that weapon, Deputy, before one of these 'gentlemen' takes it off you."
> — Nicholas Mendoza

B GATHER EVIDENCE

Move over to the woman's body, crouch down and pick up the object that sits nearby.

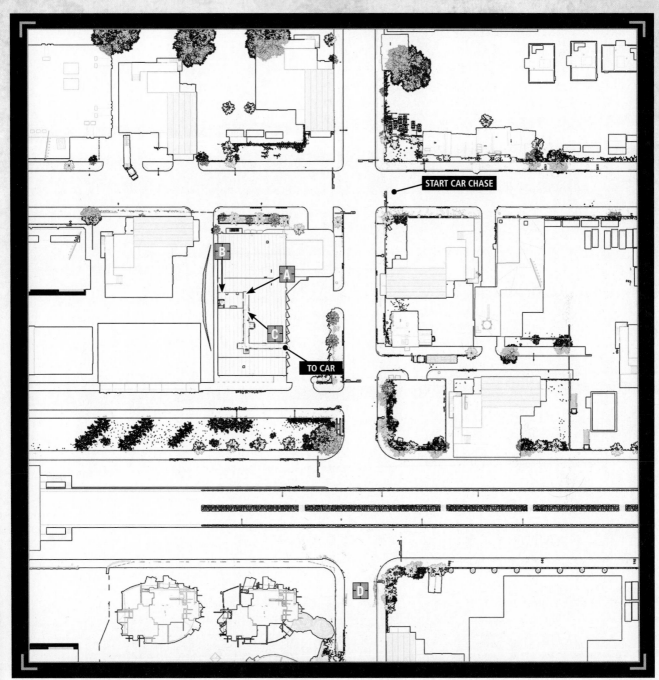

C CHASE THE SUSPECT

A sixth suspect enters the room, but immediately takes off when he spots the detectives. Run after him, down the hall. At the dead end, he is spotted taking off in his car.

"Yeah. Maintain distance. Try not to kill anyone."
— Nicholas Mendoza

Once behind the wheel, hold down the accelerator and follow the criminal around the city streets—cutting any corner you can. Keep your eyes trained down the street as traffic and other obstacles get in your way at the most inopportune times.

If the player falls too far behind, the game starts the current objective over. As long as the suspect's automobile is kept in view, things are okay. After the police cars cut the guy off and force a left turn, Stoddard fires out the window at the car, causing the vehicle to crash in spectacular fashion.

▣ MAKE THE ARREST

Once the player is out of the car, approach the driver and arrest him. This completes the Prologue.

VEHICLE CONTROL

There are several vehicles used throughout the single-player campaign and they all control in a similar manner. Hold the Fire button to accelerate. The Aim button slows the vehicle down or backs up when stopped. The left stick steers while the right allows the driver to look around.

SHEA DORSETT

Arresting a suspect with a Warrant gains you extra points toward your Expert Score. This one was easy. Others need to be found, identified, and taken down in a non-lethal manner.

ON THE JOB
Complete the Prologue in single-player

EPISODE
BACK TO SCHOOL

With new partner, Khai Minh Dao, Nick Mendoza heads out on assignment to find Tyson Latchford. After a tour of a Miami neighborhood, Khai comes to a stop near the projects. No need to spook the locals, the detectives will hoof it from here.

LOCATION:
MIAMI

 DETECTIVE:
NICHOLAS MENDOZA

 PARTNER:
KHAI MINH DAO

CASE FILE(S):
THE HOT SHOT FILE

3 EVIDENCE

 SUSPECTS WITH WARRANTS:
LAWRENCE KENT

MAIN OBJECTIVE:
INVESTIGATE TYSON LATCHFORD.

OBJECTIVES

A FIND BRIX

B INTERROGATE BRIX

C GET TO THE PROJECTS

D AVOID DETECTION

E INTERROGATE TAP

F SCAN AND ANALYZE TAP

G FOLLOW TAP TO FIND TYSON

H SAVE TYSON

I INVESTIGATE THE ROOM

J GET TO THE CAR

"You're gonna get along great. Dismissed."
—Julian Dawes

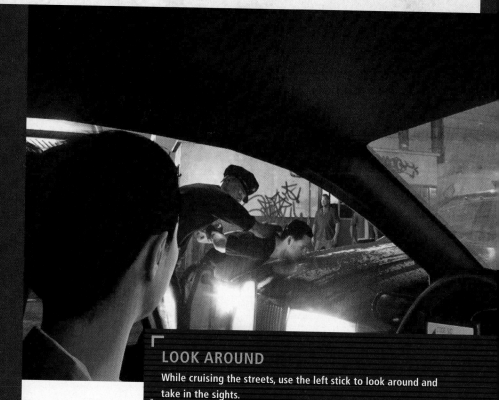

LOOK AROUND
While cruising the streets, use the left stick to look around and take in the sights.

A FIND BRIX

Exit the vehicle and follow Khai through the old neighborhood. Once Brix is spotted across the street, approach the trio of men.

Freeze the suspect by holding down the Show Badge button as you train your taser on him. His friends flee the scene as Mendoza asks some questions.

FREEZE

Freezing suspects with the detective badge is a great way to take down one to three bad guys in a non-lethal manner. A white shield icon with an exclamation point indicates the person will put up his hands with a flash of the badge. Keep an eye on the criminals, since they go after their gun if left uncovered. Move the reticle between all of the suspects as you approach.

B INTERROGATE BRIX

When instructed to do so, approach and cuff him. The detectives find out what they need through some quick questioning.

> "Okay. Let's jump right to Worse Cop."
> —Khai Minh Dao

C GET TO THE PROJECTS

Continue down the sidewalk toward the Arcola Projects before spotting Tap's crew to the right.

D AVOID DETECTION

Follow Khai across the street, taking cover behind the wall alongside her. The way is blocked ahead, so follow the detective up the driveway and through the small gate.

AVOIDING DETECTION

Watch the vision cones on the minimap. They clue you in on where you can go without being seen. Alert Meters above suspects' heads also let the player know when the situation is getting more dangerous.

Approach a bigger gate on the right and open it. Click the Sprint button to keep up with your partner, vaulting the fence when the prompt appears.

SPRINT

By default, clicking the Sprint button switches to a run. This can be changed in the Gameplay menu in Options. Switch Agent Sprint to Hold button, to require the button to be held to sprint. Let go, and the character walks.

Run to the right and crouch through the busted fence. Continue behind Khai until you find a few of Tap's guys. Crouch down, let the first pass, and then weave around the dumpster ahead. Move quietly, but quickly, to avoid detection. Alert Meters appear, but as long as you move silently, everything is fine.

To the right, a thug blocks the path. Aim further down the alley and tap the Throw Distraction button to toss a shell casing. Follow Detective Dao as she cuts through the apartments on the left.

THROW DISTRACTION

Be sure to place the reticle where you wish the shell casing to go. If you throw it between the detectives and the criminal or hit him with it, you are detected. A question mark above his head indicates he is investigating the noise.

Toss a shell casing to the left and the thug looks that way. Now you can sneak around to the right and get behind the other guy. Perform a melee attack when within range to quietly knock him out. Now approach the first guy and take him down in the same manner.

E INTERROGATE TAP

Continue along the path until you find Tap, as his buddy ditches him.

F SCAN AND ANALYZE TAP

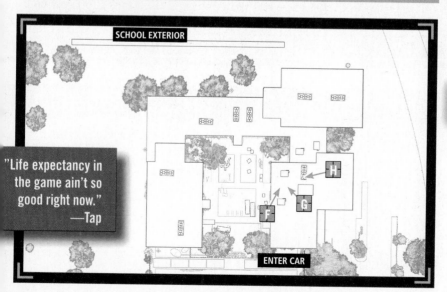

SCHOOL EXTERIOR

H

G

F

ENTER CAR

"Life expectancy in the game ain't so good right now."
—Tap

As the detectives keep watch over Tap from a nearby rooftop, you are introduced to a valuable piece of equipment, the Scanner. Tap the Scanner button to equip the device.

Move the reticle onto Tap, standing next to a dumpster on the left, to tag him. This allows the detective to follow the suspect. Hold the Jump button to analyze him. A full analysis of a tagged person identifies suspects with warrants or high-value targets.

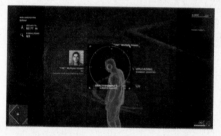

G FOLLOW TAP TO FIND TYSON

Once Tap enters the school, scan as many criminals as you can—inside and out. Look for the blue diamonds and simply move the reticle over each one.

After Tap and Tyson's short conversation, two vehicles pull into the courtyard on the left. Scan the criminals inside each one.

MOTLEY CREW

Tag all criminals visible from the rooftop in Episode 1: Back to School. Here is a list of all 17 guys:

- Two guarding entrance
- Three just inside the school
- One upstairs to the right
- Three upstairs near the windows on the left
- Eight inside the two vehicles that pull up

Crouch as you near the courtyard ahead, as you spot two men to the right. They block the path and must be separated, so that they can be taken down one at a time.

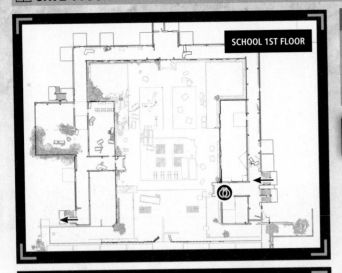

SCHOOL 1ST FLOOR

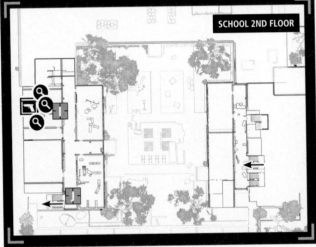

SCHOOL 2ND FLOOR

G17 PISTOL

Some of the criminals inside and out of the school drop a G17 Pistol. Be sure to pick one up to add it to Tactical Gear.

10 👤 BY THE BOOK

Use a non-lethal takedown on 10 criminals to earn this Achievement / Trophy. If played correctly, this is easily obtainable during the first episode.

Descend another set of stairs and approach the guy at the next doorway. He has a warrant, so quietly arresting him gives extra rewards. Flash the badge to freeze him and then cuff the criminal.

Follow Khai into the nearby roof access and run down the stairwell. Two thugs hide behind cover ahead. Flash your badge to cause them both to freeze. Keep them both frozen as you approach and cuff them. There is no way around it, the second guy goes after his gun and your partner takes him out.

LAWRENCE KENT

As the two vehicles enter the school courtyard, scan the right, rear passenger in the first car to find Lawrence Kent. Take him down in a non-lethal manner to gain Expert Score points. As long as you scanned him, a handcuff icon indicates his position. Quietly approach him from behind and arrest him.

As you enter the courtyard, as long as the criminals were scanned, their positions should all be shown with chevrons. Quietly move to the far right, flash the badge at the lone thug, and cuff him.

FREEZE MULTIPLE TARGETS

An Alert Meter slowly fills as a suspect gets more dangerous. Do not let this meter fill completely before aiming your weapon at the agitated thug. Move your reticle between the criminals to keep them all under control.

EXPERT LEVELS

Taking down criminals non-lethally gives the player points toward his or her Expert Score. Completing objectives, capturing suspects with warrants, and scanning evidence / objects also earns the user points. Earn enough points and your Expert Level rises to a maximum of 15. Each time you reach a level new items are unlocked in Tactical Gear. On top of that, three Achievements / Trophies are earned at Levels 5, 10, and 15.

Weave through the obstacles in the courtyard as you move toward the school entrance. Freeze the two guards and arrest them before entering the building.

There is only one guy in the first floor; approach his location just inside and handcuff the suspect. Meet up with your partner at the stairs on the left side of the school and move up to the next level, where four more guys hold out.

USE THE SCANNER

Bringing up the Scanner gives a better idea where the criminals are than the chevrons. Use it to see how they are grouped.

Take care of the lone criminal in the right room. Turn around and flip a shell casing across the hall to attract the attention of the nearby thug. Arrest him before quietly moving down the hallway into the central area.

Take cover behind the right wall and toss a shell into the room across the hall. Handcuff the guy who comes to investigate. Move into the classroom on the right and take down the final suspect.

INVESTIGATE THE ROOM

Enter the room across the hall and equip the Scanner. Analyze the document on the nearby desk to log the first piece of evidence. Another document can be scanned on the right counter, next to the printer.

THE HOT SHOT FILE EVIDENCE

Scanning the three pieces of evidence for The Hot Shot File Case File is part of the first episode. Later on, evidence is tougher to find, though assistance is given. The controller rumbles when one is nearby. Equipping the scanner gives you the distance to the closest evidence, as well as how many remain in the current area. Completing the Case Files gains the player valuable Expert Score and better gear so be sure to keep an eye out for evidence.

Interacting with the case on the table ahead gives you access to your Tactical Gear—in case you wish to make any changes.

Finally, move into the next room and analyze the trace on the table to complete The Hot Shot File. At this point, Khai opens a nearby door. Move inside and open the laptop.

> "Yeah, that's not something you're typically told ahead of time!"
> —Tyson Latchford

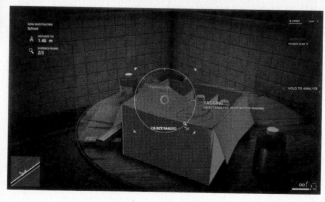

GET TO THE CAR

Return to the staircase and head downstairs. Three thugs chat at the hall intersection. Quietly, but quickly, walk toward them until all three are within range of a badge flash—indicated by the white exclamation points above their heads. Use it to freeze them until you can cuff each one.

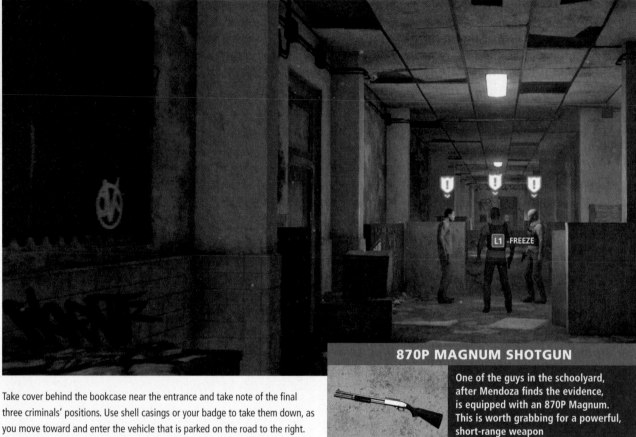

Take cover behind the bookcase near the entrance and take note of the final three criminals' positions. Use shell casings or your badge to take them down, as you move toward and enter the vehicle that is parked on the road to the right.

870P MAGNUM SHOTGUN

One of the guys in the schoolyard, after Mendoza finds the evidence, is equipped with an 870P Magnum. This is worth grabbing for a powerful, short-range weapon

Once control is regained, knock on the door and then kick it open. When directed to do so, hold the left stick Up to apply pressure. At this point, you are only able to fire your handgun. Bad guys enter through the doorway and the windows. Quickly take them all down as they approach until the episode is complete.

PRESSURE APPLIED

Complete Episode 1: Back to School.

> "Oh, him? He does spreadsheets."
> —Nicholas Mendoza

EPISODE
CHECKING OUT

2

As Leo flees the meeting, take off behind him—sprinting up to the next floor of the parking garage. Two nearby criminals are easily taken down with a flash of the badge.

LOCATION:
MIAMI

 DETECTIVE:
NICHOLAS MENDOZA

 PARTNER:
KHAI MINH DAO

CASE FILE(S):
THE ELMORE HOTEL INVESTIGATION,
HOT SHOT SUPPLY CHAIN

6 **EVIDENCE**

SUSPECTS WITH WARRANTS:

 JAVIER ROSADO

 GARY VOLKER

MAIN OBJECTIVE:
BRING IN LEO RAY.

OBJECTIVES

A APPREHEND LEO

B ESCAPE THE LOBBY

C GET IN THE TRUCK

D MEET DAWES

TACTICAL GEAR

By this time, you should have several new weapons in Tactical Gear. Before each episode, and at any Tactical Gear case, weapons, gadgets, and attachments can be swapped in and out. Grab a primary and secondary weapon that best suit your playstyle and add attachments to improve stats or give them added features.

A APPREHEND LEO

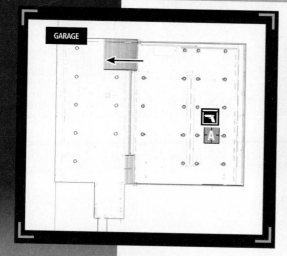

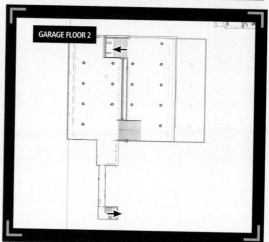

Just ahead, Leo abandons his car and runs inside the building. Meanwhile, several criminals have entered the garage and hinder the pursuit. It is possible to cuff the closest suspect, but at that point, it becomes a firefight. Use the vehicles as cover and work your way through the open door.

"It might not be any more secure inside this shop than it is on the street. Am I clear?"
—Julian Dawes

MAC-10 MACHINE PISTOL

Some of the criminals in this episode drop the Mac-10 Machine Pistol. This gives you the option of an automatic primary weapon, if preferred.

YOU TAZED HIM, BRO!

Zap five criminals with the T62 CEW in single-player. It shouldn't take too long to find five suspects within range. In fact, you may already have this one.

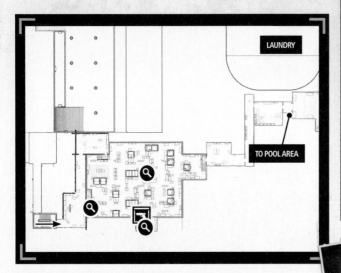

LAUNDRY

TO POOL AREA

Follow Leo up the stairwell, down the hall, and into the laundry facility. Tag the five enemies inside. These guys can be dealt with in three ways: straight on with a gunfight, stealthily with well-placed shell casings and non-lethal take downs, or not at all with distraction. Non-lethal take downs net the player the most points, so whenever possible, that is the way to go.

USING THE T62 CEW ELECTROSHOCK WEAPON

In a gunfight such as this, it is tempting to just pull out your favorite weapon and mow down the criminals. This does not net the player any Expert Score though. Any time you can get within range, take an enemy down with an electroshock from the T62 CEW. Two circles appear in the gun's sights when your target is within range. With its slow reload time, it is wise to quickly take cover or switch weapons if the situation is still dangerous. This non-lethal take down earns 100 points toward the Expert Score. This is not necessary to max out your Expert Level, but it can get you there quicker.

BOX OF HOT SHOT

From the entrance to the laundry room, search the far-right corner. A Box of Hot Shot sits on the floor near the steps. Scan it to log the evidence.

CARE INSTRUCTIONS MEMO

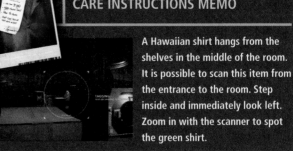

A Hawaiian shirt hangs from the shelves in the middle of the room. It is possible to scan this item from the entrance to the room. Step inside and immediately look left. Zoom in with the scanner to spot the green shirt.

DRUG PURCHASE LIST

Enter the break room adjacent to the laundry facility. Resting on the center table is a piece of evidence for The Elmore Hotel Investigation.

After some time passes, two criminals patrol the previous hall. Hurry through the room to avoid the reinforcements or grab more points by taking them down. A Tactical Gear case sits inside a small break room up the side steps.

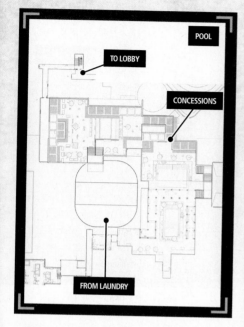

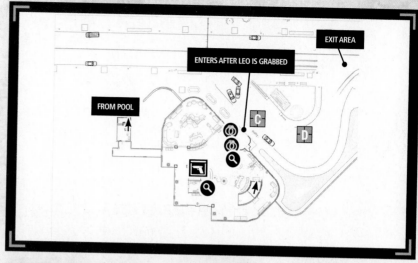

Exit out the far side and follow Leo out to the hotel's pool. Around every turn, use the Scanner to spot upcoming hostiles. As you pass the first two pools and concession area, the criminals can be arrested with stealthy movement.

As you approach the final outdoor area, you see a gunfight in the lower level. Until noticed, the combatants pay no attention to the detective. If Expert Score is not a concern, pick them off from the upper vantage point. It is possible to hop down and take cover behind the nearby planters. From there, the T62 CEW can be used as criminals near your location. It becomes necessary though to leave the safety of this protection and hunt the baddies down. Whatever strategy you use, the goal is to exit out the door in the far-right corner.

Follow the hallway to the right and descend the stairwell to the first floor. Enter the door to the left to find the hotel lobby. Seven men search the room with an eighth found on the street outside.

Immediately upon entering, flash your badge at the two men just inside. Keeping them both in check, cuff them before using the Scanner to tag the criminals near the front door.

JAVIER ROSADO

After taking down the first two guys inside the lobby, scan the criminals who guard the exit ahead to find Javier Rosado on the right. Clear out more of the enemies in the room before approaching the duo and cuffing the suspect.

Walk around to the right and arrest two more suspects as they begin to move away. A lone hostile walks the circular staircase. Use shell casings to draw him closer to your position in the hallway and arrest him as he investigates. Now it is safe to freeze and arrest the two men at the hotel entrance. Cuffing the final criminal outside maximizes the possible points.

VIAL OF HOT SHOT

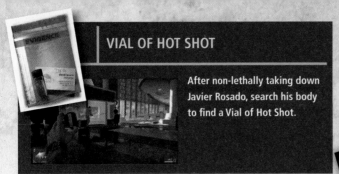

After non-lethally taking down Javier Rosado, search his body to find a Vial of Hot Shot.

Before heading upstairs, explore the first floor. A Tactical Gear case rests behind the reception desk.

TABLET WITH IM CLIENT

Behind the reception desk, a tablet rests on top of the photocopier. Analyze it with the Scanner to register the evidence.

ANSWERING MACHINE

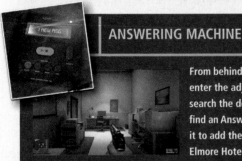

From behind the reception desk, enter the adjacent office and search the desk on the left to find an Answering Machine. Scan it to add the evidence to The Elmore Hotel file.

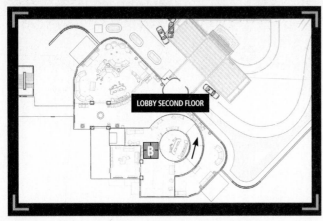

LOBBY SECOND FLOOR

After finishing up downstairs, run up the stairs and enter the manager's office to find Khai and Leo.

B ESCAPE THE LOBBY

Look over the left railing as a new group of enemies enters the hotel. These guys are already on high alert so be careful taking them on.

GARY VOLKER

5'8"
5'6"
5'4"
5'2"
5'

Scan the new group of hostiles as they enter the hotel to find Gary Volker. The quickest way to him is to wait until he passes down below and hop down behind him. Be sure he is alone before attempting this. Otherwise, the other criminals need to be taken care of as you make your way to him. Note that Volker can be taken down with the T62 CEW to get credit for the bust.

In order to remove Leo from the hotel, these guys must be taken care of. This can be done with a big gunfight from the balcony above or by stealthily taking each one down. Using non-lethal means can be tough as there is usually another suspect nearby. Use distraction to move them around and flee to another location if spotted. The downstairs office is a great place to hole up and it allows the player to zap incoming hostiles with the T62 CEW.

C GET IN THE TRUCK

More criminals pull up in a truck outside. Once everyone has been taken care of, enter the driver seat.

D MEET DAWES

Drive the truck left to the second stoplight, turn right, and follow the road onto the highway. Criminals continually attempt to bring your vehicle to a stop. Avoid what you can, but do not be afraid to plow through them. When you reach

the trailer that spans the width of your lane, keep the accelerator pressed and drive right through. Just ahead, the detectives meet up with Dawes.

BUMPY RIDE
Complete Episode 2: Checking Out.

EPISODE
GATOR BAIT

3

Nick and Khai are sent to Everglades National Park to investigate drug bales that are being dropped in the wetlands.

LOCATION:
EVERGLADES NATIONAL PARK

DETECTIVE:
NICHOLAS MENDOZA

PARTNER:
KHAI MINH DAO

CASE FILE(S):
INTERNAL AFFAIRS,
HOT SHOT SUPPLY CHAIN

12 EVIDENCE

SUSPECTS WITH WARRANTS:

UIS MINGUEZ   THOMAS BELL   NATHAN BROWN

MAIN OBJECTIVE:
TAG BALES DROPPED IN EVERGLADES AND INVESTIGATE.

OBJECTIVES

A FIND THE DRUG BALE

B FIND THE DRUG BALE #2

C FIND THE DRUG BALE #3

D TAG THE FINAL BALE

E GET ACROSS THE FENCE

F INVESTIGATE THE BOATHOUSE

G INVESTIGATE THE LEADS

H INVESTIGATE THE GATOR FARM

I RETURN TO THE AIRBOAT

J INVESTIGATE THE SAW MILL

K GET TO THE STADIUM

L IDENTIFY NELTZ

M APPREHEND NELTZ

AIRBOAT

The airboat is driven in the same manner as the vehicles in earlier Episodes. The Fire button moves the boat forward and Aim goes in reverse. Guide the watercraft with the left stick. A flag icon on the map and HUD indicates a location where the airboat can be docked. Hold the Reload button as you approach to disembark.

A FIND THE DRUG BALE

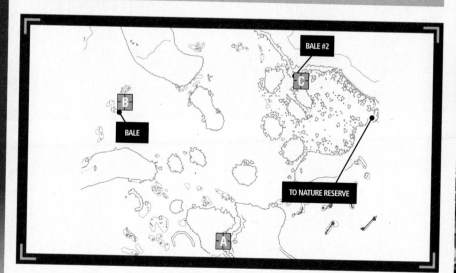

Drive the airboat ahead along the narrow path as an icon appears on the map. Once out in the open, guide the boat toward the marker until Khai is able to hit it with a tracker.

$10,000

B FIND THE DRUG BALE #2

Turn right and again, an icon shows the location of another bale. Drive between the islands until Khai marks the second bale.

C FIND THE DRUG BALE #3

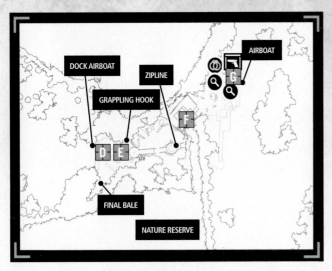

Continue along the left side until you reach a dock. Exit the boat to find the third bale.

D TAG THE FINAL BALE

Look to the right to spot the final bale. Wade through the water and tag it. At this point, an alligator attacks Mendoza. Press the analog sticks in the indicated directions to fight it off. Perform the following motions.

- WHEN THE GATOR FIRST GOES UNDERWATER, PRESS LEFT STICK RIGHT + RIGHT STICK LEFT.

- ONCE BACK ABOVE WATER, PRESS LEFT STICK DOWN + RIGHT STICK UP.

- AS IT TURNS ON ITS SIDE AGAIN UNDERWATER, AGAIN PRESS LEFT STICK RIGHT + RIGHT STICK LEFT.

> "Look at all those pretty points of light. All up and down the lake."
> —Khai Minh Dao

E GET ACROSS THE FENCE

Move up the bank toward the observation tower where Khai drops a Grappling Hook. Pick it up, fire a hook at the platform above, and climb the rope.

GRAPPLING HOOK

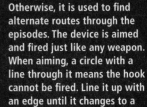

The Grappling Hook must be selected in Tactical Gear and it takes up a Gadget slot. During this episode, this item is necessary to reach a few items. Otherwise, it is used to find alternate routes through the episodes. The device is aimed and fired just like any weapon. When aiming, a circle with a line through it means the hook cannot be fired. Line it up with an edge until it changes to a square and fire. Now, walk into the rope to grab on. Continue pushing forward to climb to the next level. A fully loaded Grappling Hook holds four hooks, but looking at a used hook and pressing the Reload button can recover them.

Move toward the second tower, firing another hook at the upper platform any time along the way. Use the rope to climb onto the upper landing.

10 CAPE AND EARS NOT INCLUDED

Climb a total of 10 meters with the grapple gun in single-player. This is achieved by the time you reach the top of the second tower.

Atop the second tower, Khai sets a bag on the ground that holds a zipline crossbow. Pick it up, aim at the wooden deck below, and fire the zipline. Hop on to reach the other side of the fence.

ZIPLINE

The zipline, used in the same manner as the Grappling Hook, is great for reaching lower areas very quickly. Aim until the square is shown in the sights and fire the rope. Jump onto the line or press the Reload button while looking at the post to slide down.

FAST ROPE EXPERT

Travel a total of 90 meters with the zipline crossbow in single-player. It takes a few uses to reach this distance, but it's easily obtainable within Episode 3.

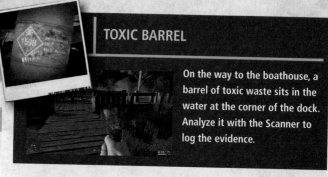

TOXIC BARREL

On the way to the boathouse, a barrel of toxic waste sits in the water at the corner of the dock. Analyze it with the Scanner to log the evidence.

F INVESTIGATE THE BOATHOUSE

Equip the scanner and tag the three men who enter the area ahead. Walk toward the group and once they are all within range, flash your badge to freeze them. Be sure to calm each one down as they are handcuffed.

G INVESTIGATE THE LEADS

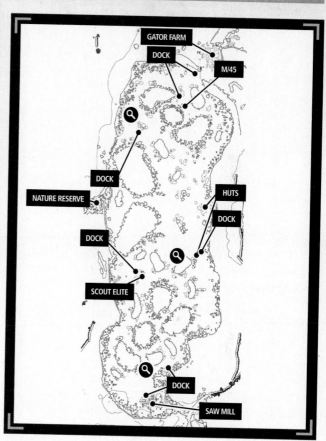

With new leads to investigate, hop into the nearby airboat, which holds its own Tactical Gear case. Before pursuing these clues, explore the lake. There are a number of docks that allow the player to get out of the craft and look around. A couple of these locations require the Grappling Hook and zipline, though these can be grabbed at any time from the boat.

LUIS MINGUEZ

Use the Scanner on the three criminals ahead to find Luis Minguez. Freeze the trio with your badge and cuff them to score the arrest.

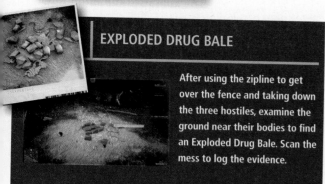

EXPLODED DRUG BALE

After using the zipline to get over the fence and taking down the three hostiles, examine the ground near their bodies to find an Exploded Drug Bale. Scan the mess to log the evidence.

Use a crowbar to enter the nearby boathouse to find a Tactical Gear case and a radio. Interact with the latter to continue the episode.

REGIONAL ZONING MAP

Head north from the nature reserve and steer right as a dock comes into view. Hop out of the airboat and use the Grappling Hook on the open side of the nearby tower. From there, look north to spot another, lower platform. Fire the zipline at the back wall and slide down the line to find a map hanging inside. Log the evidence before returning to the boat.

M/45 SMG

From the gator farm, take the airboat southwest to a nearby dock. Use the Grappling Hook to climb onto another wooden tower. Look southeast to spot a lower platform and use the zipline to reach it. Sitting on the workbench is the M/45 SMG. Pick it up to add it to Tactical Gear.

CHEMICAL BARREL

South of the gator farm, directly east of the nature reserve, are a group of huts that can be explored. South from that location is another structure that is still considered the huts. Hop out at the dock and find the Chemical Barrel that sits nearby. Analyze the container to add the evidence.

SCOUT ELITE SNIPER BOLT ACTION

Drive the airboat south from the nature reserve until a dock is spotted next to a small island. Use the Grappling Hook to reach the wooden ledge above and then use the zipline to reach another platform to the east. A Scout Elite rifle rests on a table there.

KILO OF COCAINE

On the south end of the lake, near the saw mill, is another dock. Disembark and use the Grappling Hook to reach the top of a tower. Scan the Kilo of Cocaine that sits on the table.

TWO LEADS

There are two separate leads that can be investigated next. On the north side of the lake is a gator farm and to the south is a saw mill. I does not matter which you do first.

INVESTIGATE THE GATOR FARM

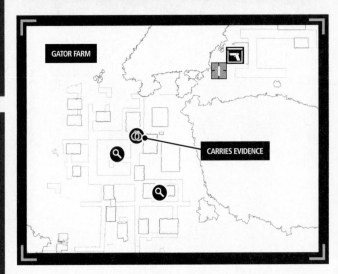

To reach the gator farm, drive to the far north and park at the dock. You can get a great view of the area by climbing the tower straight ahead, but it's not necessary. Instead, follow the walkway past the windmill and sign to a slanted roof on the right. From there scan the criminals who have gathered in the middle of the area. They soon disperse, so move swiftly.

SINGLE PLAYER

| PROLOGUE | EPISODE 1 BACK TO SCHOOL | EPISODE 2 CHECKING OUT | EPISODE 3 GATOR BAIT | EPISODE 4 CASE CLOSED | EPISODE 5 GAUNTLET | EPISODE 6 OUT OF BUSINESS | EPISODE 7 GLASS HOUSES | EPISODE 8 SOVEREIGN LAND | EPISODE 9 INDEPENDENCE DAY | EPISODE 10 LEGACY |

AKM ASSAULT RIFLE

Some of the criminals in the Everglades carry the AKM assault rifle. This is the first chance to grab this weapon, so be sure to pick one up to add it to Tactical Gear.

TORTURE TRACES

These guys patrol around the boardwalk ahead and through the buildings on the right. The area is plenty big enough to move the felons around and take them down one at a time. The structures are great for separating the enemies. Toss shell casings to move them in or out, leaving their cuffed bodies out of sight.

Enter the longer building on the right and find the pair of boots on the floor inside. Analyze them to register the evidence into the case file.

DEAD GATOR

In the middle of the gator farm is an open, viewing area with a Dead Gator lying within. Scan the corpse to add it to the Internal Affairs file.

Once the area is clear of enemies, follow a path on the far side of the gator farm to reach the fuel dock. Enter the building to complete the investigation of the gator farm.

NEWSPAPER STORY

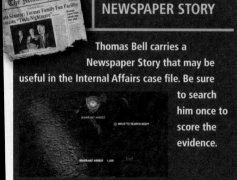

Thomas Bell carries a Newspaper Story that may be useful in the Internal Affairs case file. Be sure to search him once to score the evidence.

THOMAS BELL

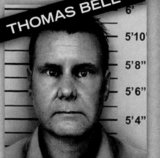

6'
5'10"
5'8"
5'6"
5'4"

If the group of criminals were scanned in the middle of the gator farm, the suspect was spotted. With distraction and non-lethal takedowns, handcuff or zap each hostile until you've taken care of Thomas Bell.

RETURN TO THE AIRBOAT

Return to the airboat and drive it to the far south of the lake to find the saw mill.

29

NATHAN BROWN

6'2"
6'
5'10"
5'8"
5'6"

One of the criminals hangs out near the big barn in the back. This is Nathan Brown, a suspect with a warrant. As you move around the saw mill and take the enemies down, be sure to use a non-lethal method on this guy.

This area can be treated similarly to the gator farm, but this time it is protected by an alarm. Run up the steps on the right to the water tower and use the vantage point to scan the hostiles and alarm system.

STAINED FANBOAT

This piece of evidence is hard to miss. A fanboat is propped up under a shelter in the middle of the saw mill. It is possible to analyze it from the water tower; just zoom in with the Scanner.

ALARM

From this point on, alarms protect many of the locations. When scanning the criminals in each area, keep an eye out for these devices. An alarm box, usually hanging on a central wall, is connected to a series of loudspeakers. If the player is spotted, a criminal goes for the button. Once pushed, reinforcements join the bad guys—making your fight that much tougher. It is best to reach the switch first and disable it, which can be done by shooting it. Destroying all of the sirens can also turn off the alarm. Use a suppressor to hide your location.

WATER SAMPLING EQUIPMENT

Exit out the left side of the big barn and equip the Scanner to spot Water Sampling Equipment sitting on a workbench inside a small shack. Analyze it to log the evidence.

NOTE PINNED WITH SWITCHBLADE

Look for a log pile located just east of the big barn. A note is pinned to the far side with a switchblade. Analyze the letter to enter it into evidence.

The delinquents are scattered throughout the area with plenty of room to work with. Using distraction, it is possible to sneak past everyone in the area, but to score maximum Expert Score, non-lethal takedowns are the way to go. Work your way from one side to the other, pulling the guys away from each other.

Once everyone has been taken care of, enter the cargo container on the far side of the saw mill to find an office. On the desk, you find a mobile phone with another clue.

Run up the ramp until you spot a lone bad guy ahead. Arrest him and then equip the Scanner. Tag the enemies below until you find Neltz on the far left. Analyze his face to confirm his identity.

MANILA ENVELOPE

Inside the office, equip the Scanner and search next to the computer on the far desk. Analyze the documents to log them into the Internal Affairs file.

APPREHEND NELTZ

The least resistance to Neltz is along the middle level of the stadium. This is also where the alarm is. Take care of these guys first, in order to eliminate the chance of reinforcements. Be careful as some of the men may patrol up the steps from their lower location.

If going for maximum points, move down to the bottom level and arrest the criminals next to the water. Make your way to the far left side and pursue Neltz into the first building.

GET TO THE STADIUM

Exit the office and follow the path to the right to find a dock. Three criminals have generously delivered an airboat. Walk up to them, flash your badge, and arrest them. Hop onto the vehicle and drive it away.

DAMN THING DOESN'T WORK

Disarm two alarm boxes in single-player. If you disabled the alarms at the saw mill and stadium, you earned this Achievement / Trophy.

IDENTIFY NELTZ

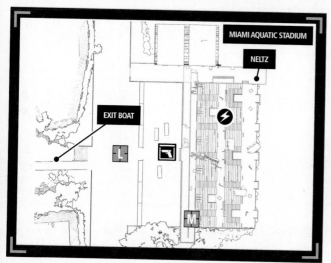

MIAMI AQUATIC STADIUM

NELTZ

EXIT BOAT

L

M

START

TO 2ND FLOOR

A tough gunfight is forthcoming, so swap out your equipment at the Tactical Gear case in the trunk of the car. The Armored Insert, First Aid Pack, and Ammo Box are all good choices for Gadgets. The criminals begin using Gas Grenades, so the Gas Mask is also a wise choice.

You track Neltz down to a warehouse. Once inside, take cover to the left of the crates. Several felons attempt to keep the detectives from their boss using high-powered weapons along with gas grenades. It is possible to get close enough to a couple of these guys to zap them with the T62 CEW. Otherwise, this is a good old-fashioned gunfight.

DESTRUCTIBLE ENVIRONMENTS

Do not stand around during this battle, even if you think it safe behind a pile of crates. These boxes and the drywall are no match for the barrage of bullets from the bad guys. Unless it is metal or concrete, do not rely on an object to protect you. By tagging the criminals with the Scanner, you can use this to your advantage. If an enemy hides around a corner, shoot out the wall to take him out.

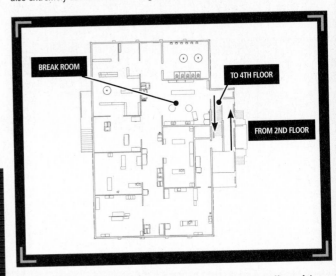

Climb the steps in the corner to reach the second floor. Hostiles pour in from the opening on the right side of the room. Rows of shelves offer moderate protection from their bullets as they close in on your location. Some of the guys use the far walkway to get a straight shot at the detectives.

GAS GRENADES

This fight is the reason a Gas Mask was recommended before. A grenade icon indicates an incoming explosive. Once detonated, a green gas fills the immediate area and damages any detective within. You can ignore this if the mask is equipped. If not, clear out of the area to avoid losing health.

45T HEAVY PISTOL

The criminals in this warehouse give the player the first opportunity to pick up a 45T Heavy Pistol. Nab one to add it to Tactical Gear.

Use the chevrons that indicate a criminal's location as well as the mini-map. Knowing the enemy position is key to getting out alive. Damage indicators are also extremely useful in determining where attacks originate.

Once the room has been cleared out, access the Tactical Gear case in the far office to top off your ammo. If the Gas Mask is equipped, swap it out for another Gadget that is more beneficial in gunfights. The Gas Grenades are not used from this point on.

FIRST AID FROM PARTNER

With an AI partner following the player, additional help is occasionally given when you're low on health. Look for her to toss out a First Aid Pack and get close to regain health at a quicker rate. A green plus icon next to the health bar in the lower-right corner indicates the player has found it. Note that the enemy can still take you out while you're healing, so take cover if possible. You shouldn't rely on this benefit, but it is nice when it happens.

Fight your way to the doorway and ascend to the next level. The offices of the third floor offer many hiding spots, but the thin walls are not very protective. Use this to your advantage when a criminal's position is known behind a wall.

Hide around a corner and the enemy often comes to your position. This allows you to use the T62 CEW to score some extra points. Take out the hostiles, moving between the offices and then through the break room. Find the staircase and move up to the fourth floor.

DEAL? WHAT DEAL?
Complete Episode 3: Gator Bait.

EPISODE
CASE CLOSED

Despite an incoming hurricane, Mendoza and Dao are sent back to the warehouse to look for any leads. This is the same location as the end of Episode 3, but the rear stairwell is completely open and the second floor is closed off.

LOCATION:
MIAMI

DETECTIVE:
NICHOLAS MENDOZA

PARTNER:
KHAI MINH DAO

CASE FILE(S):
INTERNAL AFFAIRS, THE ELMORE HOTEL INVESTIGATION, HOT SHOT SUPPLY CHAIN

10 EVIDENCE

SUSPECTS WITH WARRANTS:

 PHILIP EVANS

 LEONARD MILLER

 FRANKIE DIAZ

 XAVIER GONZALEZ

MAIN OBJECTIVE:
INVESTIGATE CORRUPT COP.

OBJECTIVES

A INVESTIGATE NELTZ' WAREHOUSE
B MEET KHAI
C ENTER THE BUILDING
D APPREHEND STODDARD
E ESCAPE THE BASEMENT
F ESCAPE TO THE CAR
G ENTER THE MALL
H FIND KHAI
I GET TO DAWES

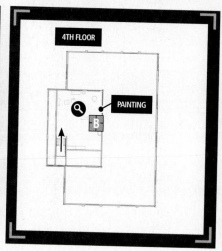

A INVESTIGATE NELTZ' WAREHOUSE

To progress in the episode, run up to the fourth floor office using the rear stairwell. Though, there are a few pieces of evidence to collect along the way.

BARRELS OF DYE

On the first floor of the warehouse, search along the back wall for the blue Barrels of Dye. Scan them in to add them to the case file.

GYM BAG OF MONEY

Still on the first floor, enter the office to the right and analyze the Gym Bag of Money that sits on the table. This is added to the Hot Shot Supply Chain Case File.

BURNER CELLPHONES

Run up to the third floor and from the central hallway, enter the middle left office. Search the trashcan ahead to find Burner Cellphones.

TALKING TAMU-TAMU STUFFY

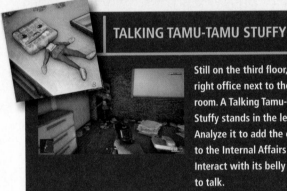

Still on the third floor, enter the right office next to the break room. A Talking Tamu-Tamu Stuffy stands in the left corner. Analyze it to add the evidence to the Internal Affairs file. Interact with its belly to get it to talk.

ELMORE PLAZA BUSINESS CARD

Take the steps in the break room to reach the manager's office. Lying on the desk is an Elmore Plaza Business Card. This is added to The Elmore Hotel Case File.

Interact with the painting that hangs on the back wall to find a safe. Analyze the keypad with the Scanner to get the numbers to the access code. Drop the Scanner and use the keypad to find out what is inside.

B MEET KHAI

Return to the first floor and find Khai inside the storage container on the right.

> "My advice? Don't go in through the front door."
> —Khai Minh Dao

C ENTER THE BUILDING

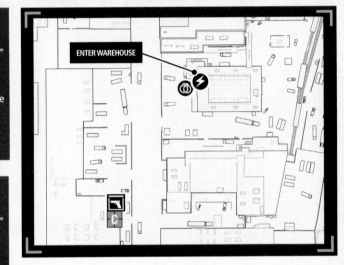

From the vantage point across the street, the player gets a good view of the area. Guards patrol all around the Domo Roboto building including the two adjacent rooftops. An alarm is spotted on the front and is guarded by two men. The objective is to get inside the middle warehouse through a door on the left side, located on the second floor.

There are many ways to get this done. It is possible to sneak around the left side, move a couple guys with distraction, and slip into the building. The direct approach can be taken, but a pulled alarm results in more enemies to take care of. Strategic, non-lethal takedowns are a good choice as they earn the most points toward your Expert Level. Grab the Grappling Hook from the nearby Tactical Gear case and let's try the latter option.

Hop down and use the grappling hook on the right side of the building ahead to reach the rooftop. Find the lone criminal ahead, pull him away from the edge with a shell casing, and arrest him. Move around to the right where four more guards can be tagged below.

You can take care of these criminals in almost any order. Be careful of the two who stand guard on the rooftops on the other side of the warehouse. These two should be arrested out of sight from the other and before the two in front of the building. Be sure to disable the alarm when the chance arises. Once everyone has been taken care of, climb the steps on the left side of the Domo Roboto building and enter the door behind the air conditioner unit.

APPREHEND STODDARD

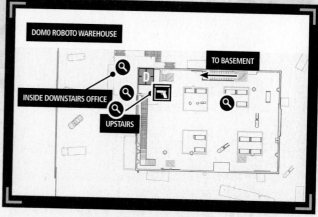

DOMO ROBOTO WAREHOUSE

TO BASEMENT

INSIDE DOWNSTAIRS OFFICE

UPSTAIRS

Tag the criminals on the warehouse floor from inside the office before going downstairs. Draw the men away from the center of the room with shell casings and arrest them out of view of the others.

PHILIP EVANS

Philip Evans stands guard next to the alarm box in front of the Domo Roboto warehouse. Be sure to tag him before taking him down with non-lethal measures.

POSTER FOR TAMU-TAMU

Just after entering the Domo Roboto warehouse, look under the Tactical Gear case for a Poster for Tamu-Tamu. Analyze it to register it as evidence.

TAMU-TAMU DVDS

Step out of the upstairs office, and use the Scanner to spot a box of Tamu-Tamu DVDs on a central shelving unit below. Zoom in and analyze the evidence from the walkway.

LETTER FROM NELTZ'S BUSINESS MANAGER

Just below where you entered the building is a bigger office. Search the desk in the back of the room to find a Letter from Neltz's Business Manager.

CRATE OF HOT SHOT

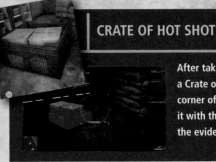

After taking out the guard, find a Crate of Hot Shot in the back corner of the room. Analyze it with the Scanner to log the evidence.

FLYER FOR TAMU-TAMU

In the downstairs office of the warehouse, search the bookshelf next to the water cooler to find a Flyer for Tamu-Tamu. Analyze it to enter the evidence into the Internal Affairs file.

3. TRUE DETECTIVE

Complete three case files in single-player. Once all of the evidence for The Hot Shot File, The Elmore Hotel, and Internal Affairs has been found, you earn True Detective.

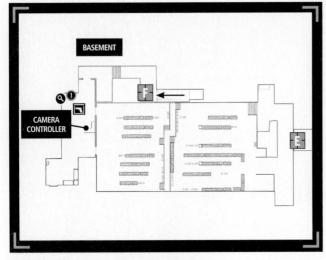

With the room clear, take the stairs down to a locked door. Force it open to enter the basement. Follow the corridor to an open door and arrest the guard inside who mans the security system. Access the camera controller to spot your objective.

Move into the grow house, where criminals tend to the plants. It is possible to crouch down and sneak through this room without confronting anyone until you reach the other side. To get those extra points though, simply walk down the aisles and arrest the guys who work on the herbs. Ignore their vision cones as they are too focused on their work to notice what is going on. A guard in the middle does pose more of a risk, but a flash of the badge takes care of him.

Two men block the door on the other side. Freeze them with your badge and cuff the suspects before entering the office.

E ESCAPE THE BASEMENT

M16A3 ASSAULT RIFLE

Before attempting to escape the basement of the Domo Roboto warehouse, a criminal drops the M16A3 Assault Rifle. This is the first opportunity to get this secondary weapon, so be sure to pick it up.

The enemies are now after the detective as the basement is set on fire. With guns at the ready, run out of the office into the grow house. Enemies litter the

basement and they are all gunning for the detective. Take cover whenever possible and kill the criminals who get in the way.

UMP-45 SMG

Inside the basement of the Domo Roboto warehouse, some criminals drop the UMP-45 SMG. Be sure to pick it up when the opportunity arises to make it available in Tactical Gear.

The detectives park on the second floor of the parking garage, across the street from Palm Court mall. Look out the window and tag the enemies who patrol

in front of the mall. A better view can be had from the third and fourth floors of the garage, but it's not necessary. Once ready, take the stairs down to the ground floor and walk out onto the street.

🅵 ESCAPE TO THE CAR

Retrace your steps out of the basement and into the warehouse. To the left of the office, press the button to raise the garage door and escape to the car.

🅶 ENTER THE MALL

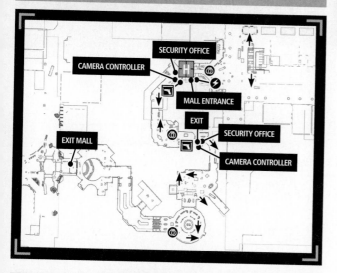

LEONARD MILLER

5'10"
5'8"
5'6"
5'4"

Among the guys patrolling in front of the mall is Leonard Miller, who has a warrant. Scan him from the parking garage before moving outside. The criminals are fairly spread out, so isolating him for an arrest is fairly straightforward.

An alarm hangs on the far left wall, so starting from that side is advisable. Work your way through the handful of enemies until you reach the entrance to the mall.

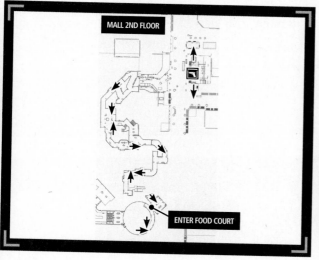

🅷 FIND KHAI

Enter the security office just ahead and use the camera controller to get an idea of what is in store ahead. Back in the mall, take one of the escalators up to the

second floor. Pull the first criminal away from the edge of the balcony with a shell casing and cuff him. Use this opportunity to scan the first floor and balconies, tagging the guards who patrol the mall.

FRANKIE DIAZ

6'
5'10"
5'8"
5'6"
5'4"

Amongst the men who hang out in the mall is Frankie Diaz, who has a warrant. He is located on the first floor with guards patrolling the balconies above. It is a good idea to eliminate the threats on the upper level first, analyze the suspect from above, and then move down to the first floor, where this suspect can be taken down non-lethally.

Stealthily walk around the balcony and take down the criminals who patrol the second floor, preferably away from the ledge. On the far side, ride the escalator down and separate the remaining group with distraction. Once they have been taken care of, continue through the mall by going through the exit.

GET TO DAWES

Return to the mall and follow your partner up to the second floor. Pry open the right door to reach the food court. The final group of Neltz's men awaits the

detectives below. As the winds get stronger though, they don't plan to stick around too long. Quickly tag them and then drop down to the first floor.

XAVIER GONZALEZ

5'10"
5'8"
5'6"
5'4"

Awaiting the detectives at the mall food court is the final group of Neltz's men including Xavier Gonzalez. From the balcony, analyze the guy on the left to find the suspect. Quickly hop down and arrest him if possible or hit him with a non-lethal shot from the T62 CEW.

Another security office is just ahead. Access the camera controller to find Khai and the four guys keeping her there. Take the nearby escalator to the second

floor and pick the criminals off from above. Survivors ride up to your level, so be ready for them. After disposing of them, head back downstairs and enter Domo Roboto at the other end.

WATCHED, DAWG

Use the scanner to identify 10 suspects with warrants to earn this reward. The fourth suspect in Episode 4 is the tenth in the game.

Take out the criminals that get in your way while continuing through the mall. After the left turn, move to the right side to miss a rolling "O" and then sidest

left to miss the "P." R◼ up the left steps and c◼ the exit.

> "More of Neltz's guys are coming. We might need him to get out of here."
> —Khai Minh Dao

GOOD GUYS
Complete Episode 4: Case Closed

EPISODE
GAUNTLET

For Episode 5, Mendoza is alone with no weapons or gadgets, for the moment. The first objective is to elude the search party and reach the water tower, which can be seen on the hill in the distance. It doesn't matter how you get there, just stay out of the cones of vision and helicopter search lights to remain undetected.

LOCATION:
UNKNOWN

 DETECTIVE:
NICHOLAS MENDOZA

PARTNER:
NONE

CASE FILE(S):
NONE

 EVIDENCE

SUSPECTS WITH WARRANTS:
NONE

MAIN OBJECTIVE:
ESCAPE.

OBJECTIVES

A GET TO THE WATER TOWER

B OPTIONAL: CREATE A DISTRACTION

C OPTIONAL: LEAVE THE METHLAB

D MEET UP WITH THE CONTACT

...and you definitely don't wanna know where it's been." —"Tap"

A GET TO THE WATER TOWER

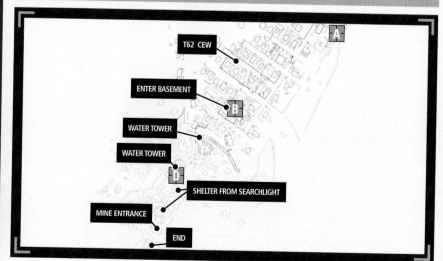

Once you gain control of Mendoza, sprint across the lot ahead, following your fellow escapees. Separate from them as they head the wrong way and cut through the opening on the right. Cut through the backyards ahead, hopping the dividing fence. Turn left after the house and stop at the wagon. Two men search the street ahead. Wait for one to pass and the other to turn, then cut through the garage ahead.

Use the nearby ramp to clear the chain-link fence and pause before the next road. Wait for the vehicle to drive by before crossing the street. Quietly move behind the two officers and to the right of the house, hopping over the picket fence to reach the neighboring property.

Quickly take cover at the patio ahead as a member of the search party turns around and looks right over Mendoza. As the cone of vision passes, immediately step into the backyard and walk through the opening on the right. Two guys search the next property. Crouch behind the side-by-side chairs until the first man moves into the building. Walk up to the second and take him down from behind.

Hop the wall and step up to the concrete barrier on the left. Let the two guys pass as well as a helicopter with a searchlight. Hide in shadows to avoid the spotlight. If the spotlight catches you all nearby cops are alerted to your location. If caught, run and hide until the helicopter resumes its patrol. Once the chopper is gone, follow the officer to the squad car on the left. Perform a takedown on him and then grab the T62 CEW from the trunk.

Follow the fence line to the right and enter the adjacent backyard. An officer searches for fugitives ahead. Sneak around him or grab the easy points with a non-lethal takedown. Continue over the picket fence and around the playground equipment. Walk straight toward the lone man ahead and zap him.

Another fugitive surveys the situation ahead and decides to make a run for it. Take advantage of the distracted police and sprint across the street and through the small building. Continue up the ramp, through the storage container, and down the dirt road to the right.

At the dead end, climb over the concrete blocks and enter the first building.

> "It's a great place to kick a cocaine habit.
> Believe me, I know."
> —Tyson Latchford

THEIR OWN MEDICINE
Steal a T62 CEW from the back of a police cruiser in Episode 5: Gauntlet.

B OPTIONAL: CREATE A DISTRACTION

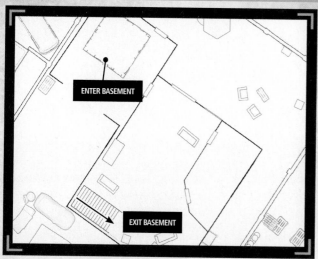

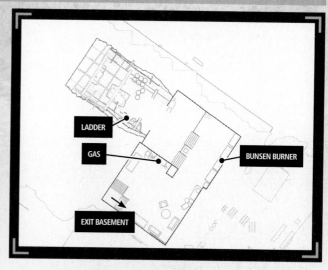

OPTIONAL OBJECTIVE

This objective is completely optional, but it does distract the search party and, more importantly, it earns an Achievement or Trophy.

Climb down the ladder on the right into the basement to find a meth lab. Around the corner to the right is a container of gas and straight ahead is a Bunsen burner. Interact with both to complete the optional objective.

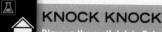

KNOCK KNOCK

Blow up the meth lab in Episode 5: Gauntlet. Complete this optional objective to earn an Achievement or Trophy.

C LEAVE THE METHLAB

Run up the staircase located opposite the gas, go through the left door, and exit out the garage door. Quickly, run through the opening in the wall, across the street, past the playground, and out onto another dirt road. Drop into the concrete tunnel to the right and crawl up the sewer pipe to a construction site. Run up the hill to reach the water tower.

D MEET UP WITH THE CONTACT

The final objective of Episode 5 is to get to the bottom of the hill without being spotted by the helicopters or officers. Run along the left edge until a helicopter

is spotted ahead. Duck under the rock formation until the chopper passes on the other side. Follow the light to the right, zapping the police officer that gets in the way.

Cut between the trees, drop off the cliff, and duck under another rock shelter. When someone comes to investigate, lure him in with a shell casing and take him down or simply wait for him to move on. Move out toward the trailer on the right and then follow the left rock wall to a mine. Run through the tunnel to complete the episode.

GRACEFUL EXIT

Don't get spotted in Episode 5: Gauntlet. Make it through the entire episode without being seen by the search party, including the helicopters. Restarting a checkpoint does not affect this Achievement. Be careful just before the mine. An officer stands to the right and even if he spots you as you escape into the shaft, the reward is spoiled.

YOU PROBABLY HAVE QUESTIONS

Complete Episode 5: Gauntlet.

OUT OF BUSINESS

A Los Angeles car dealership serves as a front for the Korean Mafia. Mendoza and Latchford are going in to find out how it all connects to their investigations.

LOCATION:
LOS ANGELES

 DETECTIVE:
NICHOLAS MENDOZA

PARTNER:
TYSON LATCHFORD

CASE FILE(S):
HOT SHOT SUPPLY CHAIN, POWER PLAY

9 **EVIDENCE**

SUSPECTS WITH WARRANTS:

 EDGAR KWOK

 JAMES MUN

 JI-HUN OH

MAIN OBJECTIVE:
INVESTIGATE NEW LEADS AT DEALERSHIP.

OBJECTIVES

A INVESTIGATE THE DEALERSHIP

B TRANSFER THE DATA

C RETRIEVE THE DRIVE

D GET BACK TO CAR

E STEAL A CAR

F DRIVE TO THE SALVAGE YARD

G INVESTIGATE THE SALVAGE YARD

H FIND THE LAPTOP

I MEET UP WITH TYSON

J ESCAPE IN CAR

K INVESTIGATE THE CHOP SHOP

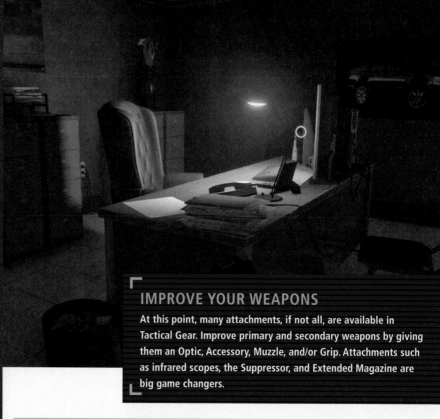

IMPROVE YOUR WEAPONS

At this point, many attachments, if not all, are available in Tactical Gear. Improve primary and secondary weapons by giving them an Optic, Accessory, Muzzle, and/or Grip. Attachments such as infrared scopes, the Suppressor, and Extended Magazine are big game changers.

A INVESTIGATE THE DEALERSHIP

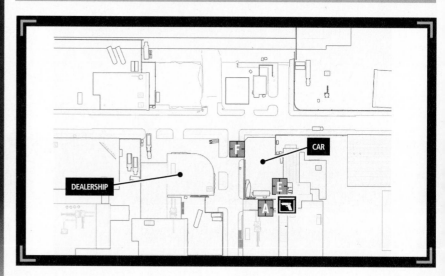

Once parked in the alley, cross the street and enter the dealership, either through one of the front doors or shoot up the side window for the quickest route. Find the computer in the right office. Interact with it to initiate download.

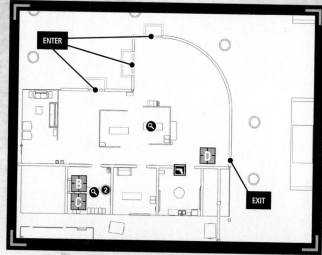

The next group of men is a bit more fierce—literally entering the building with guns blazing. An SUV equipped with a minigun joins the battle. Dig in inside one of the offices and fight the men off. The walls are very thin and don't offer much protection. Move around to avoid being pinned down. It is possible to take the guy out on the minigun, but another one eventually shows up.

PURCHASE ORDER FOR BIANCHI

Inside the dealership, a Purchase Order for a Bianchi sits on the left, front desk. Analyze it to begin the Power Play Case File.

TACTICAL GEAR

A Tactical Gear locker is available in the break room. If ammo runs low or you desire a different weapon, pay the cabinet a visit. When first entering the dealership, it is a good idea to grab a couple of gadgets for the gunfight, such as the Armored Insert and First Aid Pack.

LETTER FROM KANG'S WIFE

Inside the dealership, find the unconnected computer in the back office. A Letter from Kang's Wife sits on the other side of the desk.

C RETRIEVE THE DRIVE

Letting some of the men into or near the offices allows for non-lethal takedowns with the T62 CEW, though it really isn't worth the trouble. Once the data transfer is complete, grab the drive.

B TRANSFER THE DATA

Progress toward transferring the data is shown in the upper-right corner. Once it reaches 100/100, you can grab the thumb drive. Unfortunately, a silent alarm has been tripped and four thugs pull up out front.

ONE GOOD COP
Reach Expert Level 15 in single-player. If you used non-lethal takedowns whenever possible, Expert Level 15 is easily achieved during Episode 6. Once you reach this level, you don't need points, and making arrests is less important.

D GET BACK TO CAR

Quickly jump out the far right window and sprint to the car, still parked in the alley. Arcing the run to the right does limit the damage taken from the minigun.

These guys are aware of your presence, but they still must find you. They split up with two entering the building while the others search the parking lot. Flash your badge when the first two are within range and arrest them. The guys outside can be taken down individually with relative ease.

"Between prison and this...I'll take this."
—Nicholas Mendoza

E STEAL A CAR

The escape is halted as your vehicle flips into a neighboring property. You must find another car and a nice candidate sits in the middle of the lot. Four thugs

attempt to keep the detective from it. Take cover and kill them or make a run for the vehicle. The higher the difficulty, the tougher the latter plan becomes. Watch out for incoming fire grenades.

F DRIVE TO THE SALVAGE YARD

Enter the car and bust through the gate. Drive straight ahead into the riverbed and follow it to the left. Drive up the ramp on the right, cross the tracks, and head into the parking lot of the salvage yard.

G INVESTIGATE THE SALVAGE YARD

Exit the vehicle, follow Tyson up the steps inside the warehouse, and use the Scanner to tag the criminals and alarm system across the street. Hop over the railing and step into the street.

There are a few ways to get into the salvage yard and begin taking down the criminals. The building on the right can be scaled with the Grappling Hook. From there, shoot the alarm box and take the enemy on with a direct approach. Or, drop off the other side and stealthily take them down.

A second option is to run around the left side, entering the area near the trailer. Start out by taking out the guy inside and then make your way around

the garage. Be careful. Starting out this far away from the alarm box means more time to get caught before the system can be disabled.

If the direct approach is preferred, go in through the front entrance and take the bad guys head on. It is best to get a shot at the alarm box before getting caught or reinforcements are called in.

JAMES MUN

WARRANT IDENTIFIED   150

5'10"
5'8"
5'6"
5'4"

Hanging out behind the salvage yard garage is James Mun, a suspect with a warrant. Be sure to analyze him from one side or the other as he hides out of view from the initial warehouse. Use a non-lethal takedown on him to get credit for the arrest.

BOOMER PHOTO

Search James Mun to find a photo of Boomer. This adds the evidence to the Power Play Case File.

Use the card at the gate to reach the salvage yard warehouse. You can enter on the left, straight ahead, or up the steps on the right. This last choice gives a good

view of the ground level, so climb to the second floor. Take down the lone guy inside and tag the criminals below.

DESIGNER LUGGAGE

With the criminals taken care of, search inside the garage to find Designer Luggage sitting on a side table. Analyze it to log the evidence.

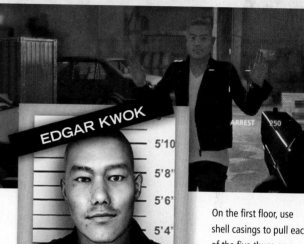

EDGAR KWOK

5'10"
5'8"
5'6"
5'4"

From the upstairs office, scan the criminals on the first floor, including Edgar Kwok, who stands near the far wall. Use shell casings to pull each thug to the sides and arrest them.

Once everyone has been taken care of, run over to the crane in the far-right corner and push the lever forward to lower the car. Interact with the trunk to find Boomer. He graciously hands over his key card.

On the first floor, use shell casings to pull each of the five thugs away from the group, arresting them out of view from the others. Once the building is clear, exit out the back door.

🅷 FIND THE LAPTOP

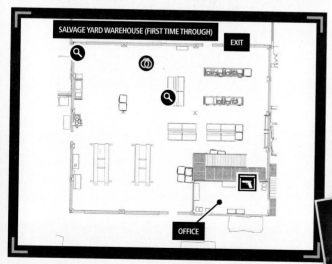

SALVAGE YARD WAREHOUSE (FIRST TIME THROUGH)

EXIT

OFFICE

K-POP ALBUM

With the warehouse clear of enemies, search the corner opposite the office to find a K-Pop Album next to a boom box. Analyze the case and insert to add it to the Power Play file.

REMOTE DETONATOR

A Remote Detonator sits on a workbench near one of the cars. Use the Scanner to find and enter it into evidence.

"Ok...I heard gunshots...and, uh...I'm not dead so that means...you're not one of them! You wanna pop this thing please? Come on, man!"
—Marcus "Boomer" Boone

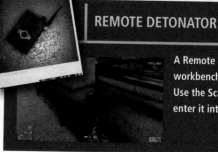

Search the trunk ahead to find the laptop. An attacker jumps the detective. While fighting the guy off, press the Fire button when you have the shot.

I MEET UP WITH TYSON

An explosion attracts five more thugs to the warehouse as it fills up with smoke. These guys actively search for the detective, but they can still be moved around with distraction. Exit out the front or side door and take cover behind the car.

Reinforcements have reoccupied the scrapyard, including one guy who fires from atop the garage. The criminals come after the detective very aggressively, so be ready. More men show up during the battle. Make your way out to the street and jump into the car.

After you switch to the passenger seat, the car comes to a stop. As soon as an enemy vehicle enters the construction site, begin firing at the passenger. The primary or secondary weapon can be used and ammunition is unlimited without the need to reload. Continue to take out any passenger that leans out of the window until a car flies overhead. Inside the metro, one last car attacks from the left tracks. Fire at the vehicle until it plows into the wall.

"Let's talk about why an army was guarding a salvage yard."
—Nicholas Mendoza

J ESCAPE IN CAR

Accelerate down the street, turning left and then right when forced to do so, ending up back in the riverbed. Stay out of the river while avoiding the attacking vehicles. Attempt to take them out with PIT maneuvers whenever possible.

A van enters the chase ahead, showing the way to the other side. Follow the van as it fires rockets your way. Weave left and right to minimize the damage. Eventually, a path opens up to the right.

K INVESTIGATE THE CHOP SHOP

CHOP SHOP

Run down the alley, under an overpass, and turn left at the wall. A Tactical Gear case sits inside a cardboard box in case you need to make a change to your equipment. Just ahead, use the Scanner to survey the situation on the other side of the train tracks.

The big warehouse is the chop shop and your objective is to get inside and investigate. There are many ways to enter the building, but first you should take care of the guards around the outside.

One way to eliminate the outside criminals is as follows.

1. MOVE AROUND THE LEFT SIDE OF THE LOCOMOTIVE, WALK UP TO THE LONE GUY IN BACK, AND ARREST HIM.

2. TAKE COVER BEHIND THE DUMPSTER AS ANOTHER GUY HEADS YOUR WAY. STEP OUT AND CUFF HIM.

3. WALK AROUND THE CORNER FROM WHICH HE CAME AND ARREST THE THREE CRIMINALS WHO ARE GROUPED TOGETHER.

4. RETURN TO THE TRACKS, AND WALK UNDER THE WALKWAY. WHEN YOU FIND THE SINGLE ENEMY NEXT TO THE TRUCK, TAKE HIM DOWN.

5. ONE FINAL MAN STANDS GUARD OUTSIDE THE BUILDING. LURE HIM AWAY FROM THE GARAGE DOOR AND DROP HIM AROUND THE CORNER.

Getting inside the chop shop can be as easy as entering through the back office or through one of the garage doors. Or, use the Grappling Hook to climb onto the rooftop and slip into the open window to reach the walkway inside.

The garage door that the lone offender guarded is the best option since an alarm box hangs on the wall just inside. Press the button to open it up and duck behind the barrel. This gets the attention of the guy inside. Take him down as he investigates.

Immediately disable the alarm and then head up the steps to eliminate the criminal on the walkway. Take out anyone who remains in the garage.

PHOTO OF LILY KANG AND ROARK

Use the door on the backside of the chop shop, next to the tracks. This leads to the back office. Search on the left desk to find a Photo of Lily Kang and Roark and scan it in.

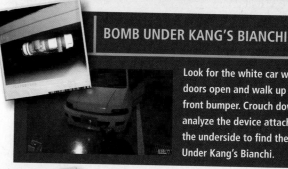

BOMB UNDER KANG'S BIANCHI

Look for the white car with its doors open and walk up to the front bumper. Crouch down and analyze the device attached to the underside to find the Bomb Under Kang's Bianchi.

PALLET OF HOT SHOT

Find a Pallet of Hot Shot against the wall opposite the back office. It lies under the walkway. Analyze it to log the evidence.

Once you are ready to move on, return to the area near the alarm box. Two doors lead to another small garage area. Open one up and take out the four guys inside. Continue through the exit ahead to complete Episode 6.

JI-HUN OH

Inside the chop shop, Ji-hun Oh wanders the area near the alarm box. With the outdoor guards out of the way, open the garage door and wait for him to investigate. Lure the guy outside and analyze him before taking him down.

SNOW BLIND
Complete Episode 6: Out of Business.

EPISODE
GLASS HOUSES

7

You find an invitation for a party in the ritzy Los Angeles neighborhood of Mount Olympus. The address list makes it worth checking out, so Nicholas and Khai decide to crash the celebration.

LOCATION:
MOUNT OLYMPUS, LOS ANGELES

 DETECTIVE:
NICHOLAS MENDOZA

 PARTNER:
KHAI MINH DAO

CASE FILE(S):
POWER PLAY

9 **EVIDENCE**

 SUSPECTS WITH WARRANTS:
CAMERON BRILLER

 MARVIN THOMAS

MAIN OBJECTIVE:
CHECK OUT PARTY ON MOUNT OLYMPUS.

OBJECTIVES

A ENTER THE HOUSE

B BUG THE ROOM

C GET TO THE POOL HOUSE

D PLANT THE PHONE

E SURVIVE!

A ENTER THE HOUSE

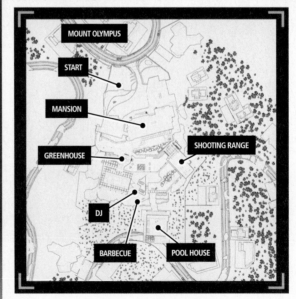

First, the detectives must break into the mansion. As soon as the power goes out, there are three options: a small window on the left side gives access to the gym, a door on the right allows the detective to enter the utility room, or fire a Grappling Hook onto the balcony above and walk through the open sliding-glass door.

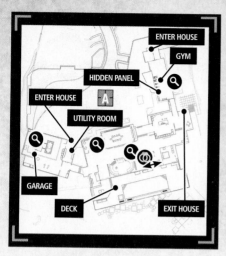

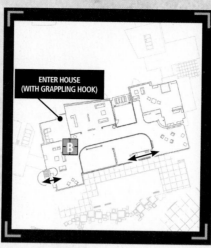

Your objective requires climbing to the second floor, but it is a good idea to collect the evidence inside the house first, which involves exploring the lower level too.

> "I'm not much of a party girl, but…all right."
> —Khai Minh Dao

B BUG THE ROOM

WHITE VAN

Enter the garage located next to the utility room. Approach the white van parked on the far side and scan the torn label on the side. This adds evidence to the Power Play file.

SHIPPING LABELS

Located on the first floor, next to the dining room, is an office. Analyze the Shipping Labels that are spread around the desk to log the evidence.

WALL OF PHOTOS

Enter the gym on the opposite side of the mansion from the garage and carefully examine the right wall, opposite the weight bench. Open the panel and then interact with the keypad to open the secret door. Photos are pinned to a corkboard on the left wall. Analyze to enter them into evidence.

HOLLYWOOD HIDEAWAY

Find Roark's hidden room in Episode 7: Glass Houses. Use the keypad inside the gym to find the hidden security room.

Take the staircase in the living room up to the second story, circle around the balcony, and climb the corner steps up to the meeting room on the upper floor. Interact with the statue on the coffee table to plant the bug.

> "It worked in Miami, so I'd like nothing better than to see our own local luminaries start thinking like actual businessmen."
> —Neil Roark

49

ⓒ GET TO THE POOL HOUSE

A Tactical Gear case sits just outside the room. If you are carrying the Grappling Hook, this is a good time to exchange it for another gadget. Return to the second floor where criminals have made themselves comfortable throughout the mansion.

Four thugs occupy this level. They can each be taken down with a flash of the badge or avoided altogether by hugging the left wall and exiting out to the balcony. On the first floor, two men sit in the living room, another pair starts out in the gym, one guy patrols the deck, and three guys stand out front in the driveway. They all move at some point, so be careful leaving bodies lying around in the open.

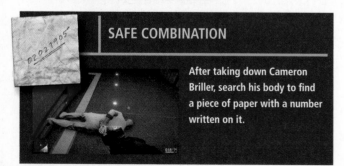

Two guys sit downstairs in the living room. Analyze them with the Scanner to identify one as Cameron Briller. Approach them from the steps or the front door and flash your badge to get them to freeze. Take them down to score the arrest.

SAFE COMBINATION

After taking down Cameron Briller, search his body to find a piece of paper with a number written on it.

Once satisfied with the work done in the mansion, exit through the side door, just beyond the kitchen. Descend the steps and flash your badge at the guy ahead and arrest him.

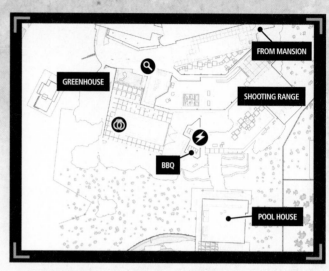

There is evidence to collect, a suspect with a warrant, and two Achievements / Trophies in between here and the objective. If all of that has already been taken care of, then it is possible to reach the pool house without confronting anyone.

Hop over the railing and drop to the ground to the left of the shelter. Move down the steps, cut through the shooting range, and hug the left side all the way to the pool house door.

Walk all the way to the right and hop over the railing. Enter the greenhouse and arrest the lone guy inside. Exit out the other side and run around the wooden fence ahead. Two criminals mess with a ball machine on the tennis court. Flash your badge and take them down. Return to the greenhouse and continue onto the terrace.

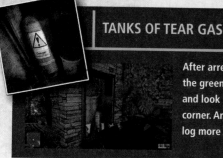

TANKS OF TEAR GAS

After arresting the lone guy in the greenhouse, turn around and look inside the closet in the corner. Analyze the Tear Gas to log more evidence.

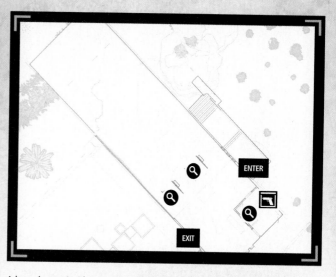

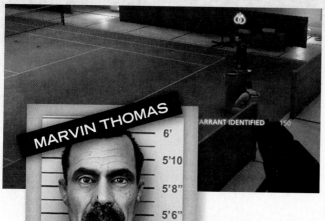

MARVIN THOMAS

6'
5'10"
5'8"
5'6"
5'4"

At the tennis courts, analyze the two men before flashing your badge to find out that one is Marvin Thomas, who has a warrant out for his arrest. Perform a non-lethal takedown on him.

Four criminals ahead are oblivious to your presence and they are spaced far enough apart that a flash of the badge takes care of each one. At the far end, descend the steps and enter the shooting range.

A lone shooter inside is an easy takedown, as he cannot hear your approach. Feel free to spend some time using the range to test out a weapon or two. Press one of the buttons to cycle a target in or out. There is a Tactical Gear locker inside the building. This is a good time to exchange out gadgets and improve your weapons. Three good gadget choices at this point are the Armored Insert, First Aid Pack, and/or Ammo Pack.

BOX OF SS190 CARTRIDGES

At the booth left of the lone shooter, find a Box of SS190 Cartridges sitting on the shelf. Analyze it to log it into evidence.

RIFLE SUPPRESSORS

At the booth right of the shooter, Rifle Suppressors lie on the floor. Scan them in to add them to the Power Play Case File.

SWAT FLAK JACKETS

Search inside the small corner room to find SWAT Flak Jackets sitting on the metal shelf. Scan them in to log the evidence.

Exit the shooting range and approach the building ahead. Toss a shell casing at the right opening to lure the DJ outside and take him down. Disable the alarm box that hangs on the exterior wall and then take care of the grill cook.

BYOB

Use the BBQ to take out the chef in Episode 7: Glass Houses. After exiting the shooting range, lure the DJ out of the building ahead, take him down, and disable the alarm. Step back and shoot the grill to cause an explosion that kills the cook.

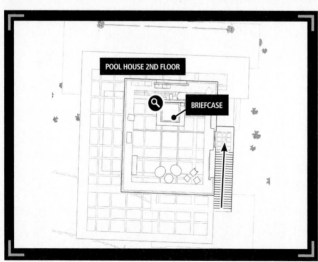

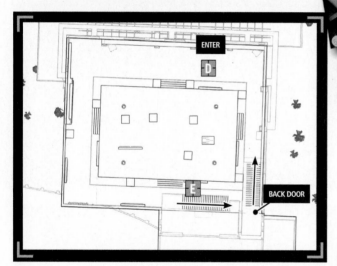

One last criminal stands guard at the pool house, unless he was taken out in the BBQ blast. Take him down and enter the building.

D PLANT THE PHONE

CREATE MORE SPACE

Before going upstairs, spend some time destroying the back windows and opening the backdoor. This gives more space and cover for the survival fight.

Climb to the upper floor and enter the bedroom. Interact with the briefcase on the bed to plant the phone.

FILE INSIDE SAFE

Before planting the phone, open the safe on the left side of the bed to find a file. Scan the file to log the evidence.

> "I just pushed a button, which means about a dozen coked-up psychopaths with automatic weapons are heading your way."
> —Neil Roark

E SURVIVE!

Criminals pour into the pool house. On higher difficulties, this fight gets tough. Take cover behind the displays, but don't stay long as bullets tear through them. Slip out to the back deck where there is more space to recover. Defeat the enemies to complete Episode 7.

HOLLYWEIRD
Complete Episode 7: Glass Houses.

EPISODE
SOVEREIGN LAND

8

Boomer informs the group of a device called The Brute that can help in their next objective, though it requires a trip to a Nevada Desert. Mendoza joins him on a trip to meet an old friend.

LOCATION:
NEVADA DESERT

DETECTIVE:
NICHOLAS MENDOZA

PARTNER:
MARCUS "BOOMER" BOONE

CASE FILE(S):
HOT SHOT SUPPLY CHAIN,
BOOMER CONNECTION

9 **EVIDENCE**

SUSPECTS WITH WARRANTS:
JIM PRESTON

MAIN OBJECTIVE:
COLLECT SAFECRACKER.

OBJECTIVES

A DRIVE TO THE COMPOUND

B ESCAPE THE SILO

C GET YOUR GEAR

D GET TO THE CAR

E SURVIVE!

F DRIVE TO THE AIRFIELD

G GET THE BRUTE

H DEFEND THE AIRFIELD

I DEFEAT TONY ALPERT

J ESCAPE IN THE PLANE

A DRIVE TO THE COMPOUND

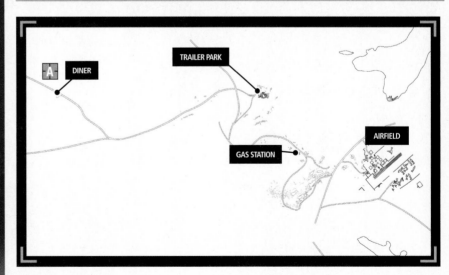

Turn right and follow the road until the intersection. Continue straight onto the dirt path until you reach the compound.

"Now, I used to hang with some folks that have an autodialer, it's like a safecracking robot."
—Marcus "Boomer" Boone

B ESCAPE THE SILO

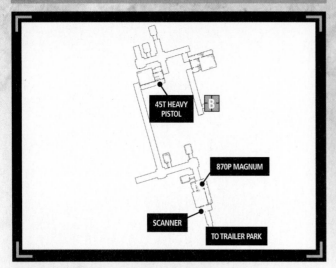

45T HEAVY PISTOL

B

870P MAGNUM

SCANNER

TO TRAILER PARK

Boomer and Mendoza end up locked in an old silo. Fortunately Marcus has secured a lock pick. Follow the narrow corridors to an intersection, turn left, enter the doorway, and locate a worker to the far left. Take him down to get his handgun.

Proceed through the door ahead, turn left, left again, and drop the guy oblivious to your escape. At the end of the hall, make a right turn before running into more of Tony's followers and an 870P Magnum sitting on the table ahead.

Take care of the guy in the left room first. Lure the first away from the others and constrain him. Then move into the living quarters and freeze the last three enemies. Pick up your Scanner off the table on the way to the silo exit.

C GET YOUR GEAR

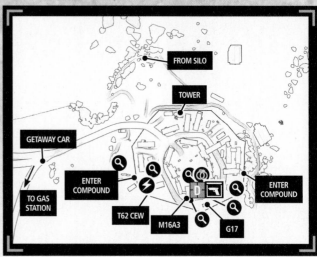

FROM SILO

TOWER

GETAWAY CAR

ENTER COMPOUND

TO GAS STATION

T62 CEW

M16A3

D

G17

ENTER COMPOUND

Your gear must first be acquired from the trailer park below before leaving. A discussion with Boomer covers three options for entering the compound. Boards and panels on the far left side allow for easy entry onto the tops of the trailers. It is possible to stealthily walk all the way to the objective without being spotted, though watch out for the guys who patrol just below the path.

A ditch on the right goes under the fence at a convenient location, next to an alarm box and a T62 CEW. A third option is to enter at the front gate and take them head on. Note that unless you can disable the alarm first, reinforcements join the fight.

We will crawl under the fence as it is convenient for getting all of the evidence, the suspect with a warrant, and a bonus Achievement / Trophy. Before heading out, tag as many of the followers inside the compound as possible along with the alarm system. Then find the entry point to the right, beyond the communication trailer.

BOMB BLUEPRINT

Join Boomer inside the communication trailer, located outside of the compound. Scan the Bomb Blueprint that sits on a table to the left.

Duck under the fence and immediately take down the two guys inside. Disable the alarm on the right and grab the T62 CEW that sits on the picnic table. Toss a shell casing into the adjacent trailer to attract the guy from the other side and drop him inside.

HOT SHOT LAB

After disabling the alarm, enter the trailer to the left. Sitting on the stove and cabinet is a Hot Shot Lab. Analyzing it completes the Hot Shot Supply Chain Case File.

Exit out the other side and continue around the perimeter of the compound to the mobile home with the front patio. Inside, your gear sits atop the cabinet on the right. A quick way to flee the trailer park requires the Grappling Gun and Zipline, so equip yourself accordingly.

A CRAFTSMAN'S TOOLS

Find your weapons in Episode 8: Sovereign Land before instigating combat in the trailer park. Enter the compound over the fence on the left or under on the right and carefully make your way to the trailer that props another up on its roof. Inside, a Tactical Gear case holds your weapons. Distraction and non-lethal takedowns are both great ways to avoid combat.

JIM PRESTON

5'10"
5'8"
5'6"
5'4"

Before heading into the compound, use the Scanner to tag the guys inside, including Jim Preston, who has a warrant. He patrols inside the inner-circle of trailers. After grabbing your gear, lure him into or around the outside of the mobile home and cuff him.

ATF AGENT'S BADGE

After arresting the suspect with a warrant, Jim Preston, search him to find the ATF Agent's Badge. This is logged into The Boomer Connection file.

D GET TO THE CAR

Some of Tony's followers patrol inside the inner-circle of trailers. Lure them your way with distraction and quietly take each one down. Watch the vision cones, being careful to not be spotted.

TORTURE ROOM

From your gear, exit into the interior of the compound and find the ladder on the side of the trailer. Climb onto the mobile home and enter the upper home ahead. Analyze the table, chair, and torture equipment to add to The Boomer Connection Case File.

CELL PHONE

Inside the trailer with the torture equipment, find a Cell Phone sitting on a cabinet in the far corner. Analyze the device to log the evidence.

BOOMER DOSSIER

Inside Tony's compound, find the mobile home in the southeast corner—the furthest point away from the silo. Scan the Boomer Dossier that sits on a table toward the front.

You can exit the trailer park through any of the three spots mentioned before as entry points. Another way out, especially good if enemies are left behind, is via the concrete watchtower near the front gate. Fire the Grappling Hook to the upper platform and climb up. Look out beyond the front gate to a bunch

of boulders on the left side of the road. Fire the zipline between the road and these rocks and slide down to find Marcus, Dune, and a getaway car.

Follow the road until the vehicle comes to a stop at a gas station. Take cover inside the building, where you can find a Tactical Gear case in the

back room. Access it immediately and select weapons and gadgets for another tough "survival" gunfight.

Miniguns mounted on the back of off-road vehicles present the biggest danger. They eat away at the building, leaving very little for protection. Target the guy

operating the weapon immediately and knock him off. Armed men also join the fight. Be careful not to get too distracted by the miniguns and forget about the other enemies.

If you're taking too much damage, duck into the small room and go prone until you recover health. Continue to fight off the attack, using the gas pumps

and explosive barrels against nearby foes whenever possible.

Once it is safe to do so, exit the building and hop into the vehicle inside the garage.

⊞ SURVIVE!

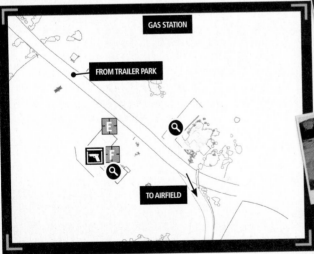

GAS STATION

FROM TRAILER PARK

E

F

TO AIRFIELD

LICENSE PLATE

Before leaving the gas station, run around to the far side of the building and analyze the rear License Plate on the sedan.

ATF AGENT'S GRAVE

From the gas station, cross the street to the burnt out building and find the mound of dirt on the left side. Analyze it to find the ATF Agent's Grave.

> "Well, at least it's being used for a noble cause."
> —Dune Alpert

F DRIVE TO THE AIRFIELD

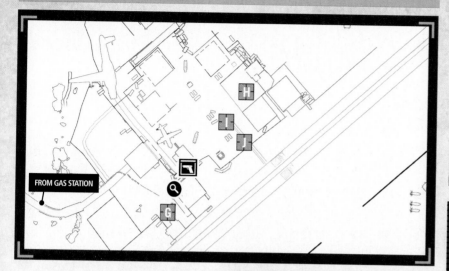

Turn right out of the gas station and follow the road all the way to the airfield, turning in at the Bissell Air Base sign and coming to a stop next to the parked van.

G GET THE BRUTE

Enter the hangar, separate from Boomer, and exit out the far side. Tactical Gear can be accessed outside, but there isn't any need to do so. Climb the stairs to the rooftop.

RICIN BOMB

Turn left once inside the hangar and approach the workbench in the corner. Analyze the Ricin Bomb to complete The Boomer Connection Case File.

Nicholas takes control of a 105MM minigun on a nearby aircraft as Alpert's men attack. Start out by taking out the men ahead. Jeeps, a van full of soldiers, and helicopters assault your position. Shoot them as they approach, using the explosive tanks when enemies are nearby.

AIRCRAFT TURRET

The Fire button shoots the minigun while the right stick aims the reticle. Hitting a red explosive tank takes out nearby enemies in its explosion. Aim just ahead of the helicopters to hit them with the minigun.

Once the choppers have been shot down, exit the turret and run straight across the airfield. Enter the open door and pick up the Brute that sits on a desk in the back.

H DEFEND THE AIRFIELD

Exit the warehouse, enter the tank, and drive into the airfield. Helicopters approach from ahead and behind. Shoot them down before Tony Alpert shows up in his own tank.

TANK

The tank controls much like other vehicles in the game. The cannon is fired with the fire button while the right stick aims. A message on the bottom of the HUD informs the player when an AP shell is ready. Fire ahead of a moving target to score the hit.

I DEFEAT TONY ALPERT

Hit him with as many cannon shots as possible as it passes by. Eventually he releases a smoke screen. At that point, make sure a metal storage container is between your tank and his.

Two more choppers enter the area, but they can be ignored as you focus attention on the enemy tank. As he peeks out from behind the container, take a shot and hide again as your AP shell reloads. Continue this until he has been defeated.

J ESCAPE IN THE PLANE

Exit the tank and meet Boomer on the runway.

FROM THEIR COLD, DEAD HANDS

Complete Episode 8: Sovereign Land.

INDEPENDENCE DAY

The supplies have been gathered and a plan has been hatched. As the group cleans out their hideout, two thugs bust in. Quickly take them down with your handgun. When the opportunity arises, put a couple of bullets in a third guy.

LOCATION:
FOSTER KEY, MIAMI

 DETECTIVE:
NICHOLAS MENDOZA

 PARTNER:
KHAI MINH DAO

CASE FILE(S):
PREFERRED OUTCOMES,
POWER PLAY

8 EVIDENCE

SUSPECTS WITH WARRANTS:

 DEREK KELLY

 JOHN STARNES

MAIN OBJECTIVE:
BREAK INTO PREFERRED OUTCOMES HEADQUARTERS.

OBJECTIVES

A MEET CREW AT THE VAN

B GET TO THE ELEVATOR

C GIVE EXPLOSIVES TO TYSON

D FIND THE PRIVATE ELEVATOR

E LET TYSON IN

F FIND THE VAULT

G SURVIVE!

H GET TO THE BOAT

"Radios, uniforms, C4...scuba gear, harnesses, cable trolley, and...one safecracking robot."
—Khai Minh Dao

A MEET CREW AT THE VAN

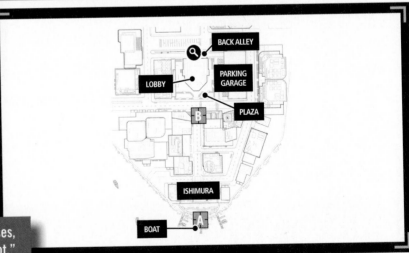

Follow Khai and Marcus up the dock, around Ishimura, and up the street to the parked van.

B GET TO THE ELEVATOR

The plan calls for accessing the penthouse through its private lift, which can be reached through the 19th floor. First the public elevator must be unlocked and ridden up to that point. Two men across the street pose little threat. Freeze them with a flash of the badge and perform non-lethal takedowns on them.

Step up to the plaza and tag any lobby guards and the alarm system visible from outside while avoiding vision cones. The upper floors of the adjacent parking garage offer a better view, but peering through the window from ground level does the job.

There are five doors to the front lobby, a side entrance to the second floor, and a way in through the rear loading area. This latter option takes you right to a camera controller and the alarm box.

DEREK KELLY

Among the guards inside the lobby is Derek Kelly, who has a warrant out for his arrest. Lure him away from the others with distraction or stealthily make your way through the enemies from behind as described here.

Run around to the back alley and take care of two guards with a flash of the badge. Enter the building via the loading dock.

BOX OF BOOKS

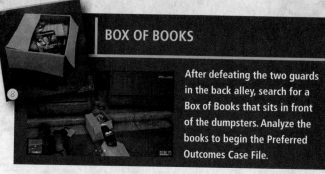

After defeating the two guards in the back alley, search for a Box of Books that sits in front of the dumpsters. Analyze the books to begin the Preferred Outcomes Case File.

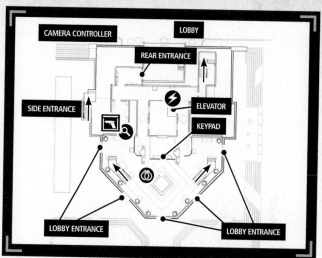

CAMERA CONTROLLER · LOBBY · REAR ENTRANCE · SIDE ENTRANCE · ELEVATOR · KEYPAD · LOBBY ENTRANCE · LOBBY ENTRANCE

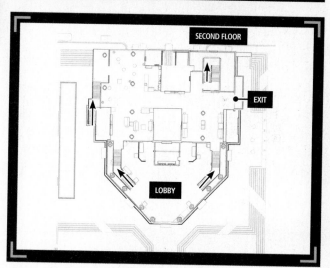

SECOND FLOOR · EXIT · LOBBY

Continue through the next door and enter the security room ahead. Perform a takedown on the lone guy inside and use the camera controller to see what is going on in the lobby.

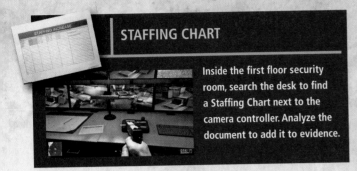

STAFFING CHART

Inside the first floor security room, search the desk to find a Staffing Chart next to the camera controller. Analyze the document to add it to evidence.

While keeping an eye out for any incoming enemies, return to the hallway and disable the alarm box that hangs on the wall ahead. In order to take care of the

upper guard first, climb the stairwell ahead to the second floor and cross over to the far side. Pull the guy away from the ledge with a shell casing and take him down.

Return to the first floor, next to the alarm box, and lure one of the security guards into the hallway and drop him. If two guys respond to the noise, pull

the first one further into the corridor or wait for them to forget. Eliminate another bad guy in the same manner. Now two guards remain.

WALK-THROUGH METAL DETECTORS

Two metal detectors sit on the sides of the security console in the lobby. An alarm sounds if someone walks through them, so be careful.

Walk out to the lobby and quietly perform a non-lethal maneuver on the man with his back turned. Before going after the final guy, scan the keypad on the

security console and then interact with it to unlock the elevator. Step over to the right metal detector, flash your badge at the last guard, and arrest him.

C GIVE EXPLOSIVES TO TYSON

19TH FLOOR

TO 21ST FLOOR

D

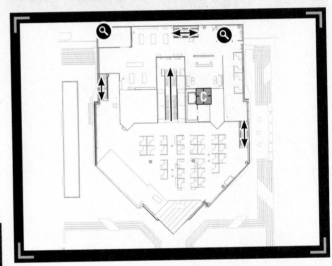

C

Join Khai at the elevator and take it to the 20th floor. Walk into the hallway behind the reception desk and take down the patrolling guard. The only other guy on this floor is around the glass wall. Lure him away from the edge before eliminating him.

"Guys, I'm on the nineteenth floor, but it's a guard party up here."
—Tyson Latchford

SINGLE-PLAYER

| PROLOGUE | EPISODE 1 BACK TO SCHOOL | EPISODE 2 CHECKING OUT | EPISODE 3 GATOR BAIT | EPISODE 4 CASE CLOSED | EPISODE 5 GAUNTLET | EPISODE 6 OUT OF BUSINESS | EPISODE 7 GLASS HOUSES | EPISODE 8 SOVEREIGN LAND | EPISODE 9 INDEPENDENCE DAY | EPISODE 10 LEGACY |

LETTER FROM CHICAGO POLITICIAN

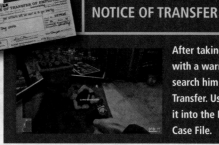

Enter the corner office near the reception desk. Scan the tablet that lies on the desk to find a Letter from a Chicago Politician.

NOTICE OF TRANSFER

After taking care of the suspect with a warrant, John Starnes, search him to find the Notice of Transfer. Use the Scanner to log it into the Preferred Outcomes Case File.

REVENUE SKETCH

In the far corner from the elevator is a meeting room. Analyze the whiteboard to find a Revenue Sketch that is added to evidence.

Duck into one of the cubicles on the right and lure the two guards, one at a time, away from the office and handcuff them. Now it is possible to walk up to the

three remaining guys, flash your badge, and arrest them. Enter the corner office to meet up with Tyson.

Descend the back steps to the 19th floor and get rid of the guard as he walks away. Arrest two more guys who patrol the nearby cubicles. This leaves six

guys on the far end of the floor. Two guard the door to the corner office while three watch the fireworks out the window.

⬛ FIND THE PRIVATE ELEVATOR

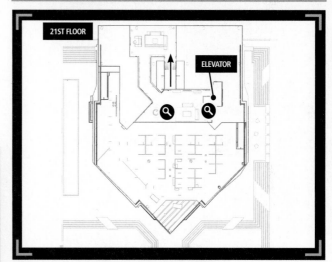

21ST FLOOR

ELEVATOR

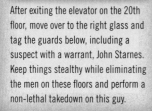

JOHN STARNES

After exiting the elevator on the 20th floor, move over to the right glass and tag the guards below, including a suspect with a warrant, John Starnes. Keep things stealthy while eliminating the men on these floors and perform a non-lethal takedown on this guy.

Exit the room and follow the staircase straight ahead up to the 21st floor. Proceed through the waiting area and follow the hallway to the main office.

EMAIL FROM DAWES'S COMPUTER

Enter the main office on the 21st floor and analyze the monitor on the desk. An open email completes the Power Play Case File.

PHOTOGRAPH OF DAWES' WIFE

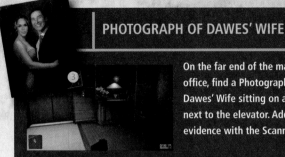

On the far end of the main office, find a Photograph of Dawes' Wife sitting on a shelf next to the elevator. Add it to evidence with the Scanner.

BANK WEBSITE

In the penthouse, enter the office which is located left of the vault. An open laptop displays a Bank Website. Analyze the screen to add it to evidence.

Use a crowbar to enter the private elevator. When the opportunity arises, press the button and swim up the elevator shaft to the penthouse.

E LET TYSON IN

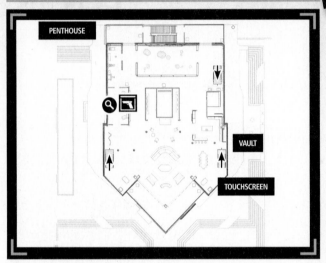

PHOTO OF DAWES' DYING WIFE

Climb the stairs just outside of the office to find a bedroom. Sitting on a shelf next to the bed is a Photo of Dawes' Dying Wife.

F FIND THE VAULT

Before putting The Brute to work, you must find the vault. This is a good time to take a look around the penthouse and make sure your gadgets and weapons are

suitable for an upcoming survival fight. Tactical Gear can be found in the office. Once ready, interact with the bust on the fireplace mantle to proceed.

G SURVIVE!

After a short while, bad guys move into the penthouse. Dig in behind a window on the terrace and pick them off as they approach. Continue to scan left and right to make sure nobody gets too close.

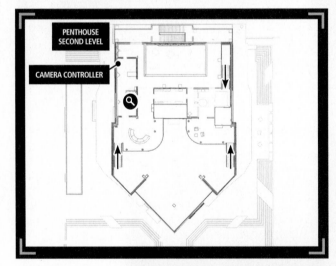

Move forward to the living room and interact with the touchscreen to open the terrace and let Tyson in.

"Hey, you know I haven't actually robbed a place in probably eight days."
—Tyson Latchford

GADGETS

Security guards flood into the penthouse, cutting through the rooms and hallways. A couple Laser Tripmines can be placed in these locations to weaken the assault. Breaching Charges can also be used, but be sure to detonate them when enemies are nearby. These take up vital gadget slots though. The Laser Tripmines can be placed and then switched out for an Armored Insert or First Aid Pack. The Breaching Charges must be equipped to use. Gas Grenades are used during the attack, though their effect barely reaches the terrace. Move away if taking damage from one.

REAL ACTION HERO

Kill a criminal in Episode 9: Independence Day from mid-air after escaping the penthouse. As Mendoza swings back toward the high-rise, he gains control of his primary weapon. This allows the player to fire at the men on the balcony. The reticle immediately targets the nearest guard. Unload your clip into the center of the light to kill him.

Once you've taken care of the first group, run into the office and access the Tactical Gear. If you haven't already, attach infrared, night vision scopes to the Primary and Secondary weapons. The guards cut the power to the penthouse, so these make the fight much easier. When not ADS, look for their flashlights. Once the objective is complete and the vault is open, move inside and interact with the console table in the back.

After touching down in the street, take cover behind the car and shoot the approaching bad guys. Any time there is a lull, run down the street—ducking behind a vehicle when more show up. Sprint around Ishimura to the boat to escape.

SOME DAMN FINE FIREWORKS
Complete Episode 9: Independence Day.

GET TO THE BOAT

Meet up with Khai on the terrace, where the crew links up with a cable and slides toward the boat. It does not work out as planned and the detective begins to flail around.

"I have no idea if this is gonna work."
—Nicholas Mendoza

EPISODE
LEGACY

This is it, the final showdown with Dawes. Nicholas Mendoza takes on an island full of thugs in a quest to get revenge against his old boss.

LOCATION:
SANTA ROSATA ISLAND

DETECTIVE:
NICHOLAS MENDOZA

PARTNER:
NONE

CASE FILE(S):
PREFERRED OUTCOMES

4 EVIDENCE

SUSPECTS WITH WARRANTS:

HOWARD WHITE

LYLE FELDMAN

CRAIG FOSTER

MAIN OBJECTIVE:
GET THE BOSS.

OBJECTIVES

A GET DAWES

B OPEN THE PASSAGE

> "There's no walking away after everything
> we've done."
> —Nicholas Mendoza

A GET DAWES

The island is split into four sections: the roadblock, the cabanas, the utility complex, and the mansion. Each contains a piece of evidence, while the first three hold a suspect with a warrant. The four locations can be explored in any order, except that the ending is found at the mansion, so that should be done last.

The first three locations are all teeming with bad guys and alarms can be used to call in reinforcements. A tower sits just outside each spot, so you can scope out the scene ahead of time, including the suspects with warrants. Feel free to slide into each locale with the zipline, shoot up the camps from a safe distance, or sneak your way through. No matter the method, remember that the warrants must be taken down non-lethally and a piece of evidence resides at each.

THE QUICK WAY

If this is your second playthrough and evidence and warrants have already been collected, this episode can be done in a few minutes while only confronting six foes. Wind around the roadblock, cabanas, and utility complex and head to the left side of the mansion. From that point follow our walkthrough to complete the episode. With a few shell casings and a T62 CEW, the time spent against the foes can also be minimized.

Take down the two-man greeting party and follow the road to the left to the roadblock. Picking off the outside guys first lowers the number of guards with little effort. Next, lure more outside the walls with distraction. Once it has been reduced to the two guys next to the alarm, freeze them with a flash of the badge and handcuff them. Follow the dirt road out the far side.

HOWARD WHITE

Be sure to tag the guys in the middle of the roadblock area. Howard White hangs out near the alarm box. Work your way around the outside, eliminating the guards with distraction and silent takedowns. With the number of enemies down to two, freeze them with your badge and arrest them.

FAX FROM NEIL ROARK

At the roadblock, enter the back building where the alarm box hangs. Approach the desk and scan the paper that still sits on the fax machine to log it into evidence.

At the next fork, the left path leads to the cabanas and the right goes to the utility complex. We will head left first. Move down to the beach and take down a lone guard who stands next to the water and enter the resort. An alarm box hangs on a pole in between the first two buildings.

Continue along the outside perimeter, eliminating anyone who gets in your way. Follow another guard onto the pedestrian bridge and cuff him. Only one other guy patrols this separated area. Walk up to him on the right and take him down before disabling another alarm that hangs on a utility pole.

SUMMONS FROM THE IRS

Enter the hut next to the second alarm box and walk behind the bar. Sitting on a shelf is a Summons from the IRS. Scan it in to add it to the case file.

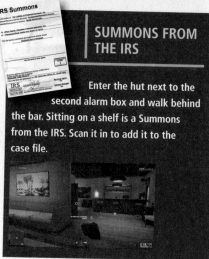

Return to the beach and resume your removal of the outer bad guys. Lure them into the bungalows or to the outside path before disposing of them. With

two men remaining in the center of the resort, cross one of the bridges, flash your badge, and perform non-lethal takedowns on the criminals.

CRAIG FOSTER

6'
5'10"
5'8"
5'6"
5'4"

Craig Foster roams around the northeast quadrant of the utility complex. Analyze him from outside the fence. He is easily reached from the northeast. To be safe, lure him outside the compound before non-lethally taking him down.

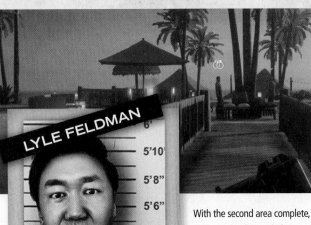

LYLE FELDMAN

6'
5'10"
5'8"
5'6"
5'4"

When tagging the bad guys around the cabanas, a suspect with warrant is found in the very center. Dispose of the guards around the outside until the two in the middle remain. Freeze them with your badge and take them down non-lethally.

With the second area complete, return to the dirt road. The utility complex can be accessed to the left or right. A tall tower sits to the southwest and a construction site sits high above to the south, though two men guard it. Both offer a great view of the service area. It is fenced-in with three entry points, though a zipline can get you there in a hurry from above.

BRING 'EM TO JUSTICE

Capture all warrants alive in single-player. If all of the suspects with warrants have been taken down non-lethally up to this episode, you earn this award once all three are captured on Santa Rosata Island.

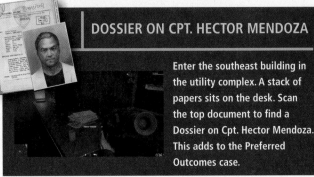

DOSSIER ON CPT. HECTOR MENDOZA

Enter the southeast building in the utility complex. A stack of papers sits on the desk. Scan the top document to find a Dossier on Cpt. Hector Mendoza. This adds to the Preferred Outcomes case.

With the three areas fully explored, it is time to head for the mansion on the far east end of the island. The grounds can be entered through the front gate,

where the guards can be disposed of stealthily or with a more direct approach. There is a better way of accessing the home though.

The area is fairly compact with three big buildings. The guards can be lured into these structures and taken down out of sight from the others. Two things should

be taken care of sooner than later. The alarm box sits on the north side of the southeast structure and one guy patrols from the rooftop in the southwest.

DARE DEVIL

Jump the dirt bike into the mansion grounds in Episode 10: Legacy. Look for the wooden walkway, east of the utility complex. Drop off the far end to find a dirt bike. Hop on and ride it down the path and into the mansion grounds. This causes a scene, so either fight it out, run and hide, or restart at previous checkpoint.

Instead, follow the dirt path out the northeast corner of the utility complex until it splits. Turn left and then right. At a dead end, two guards patrol near a Tactical Gear case on the north side of the mansion. Dispose of them and then grab the Grappling Hook and zipline, if they are not already equipped.

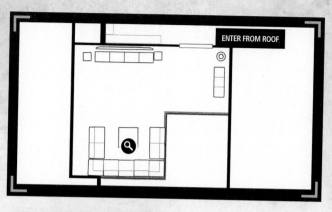

ENTER FROM ROOF

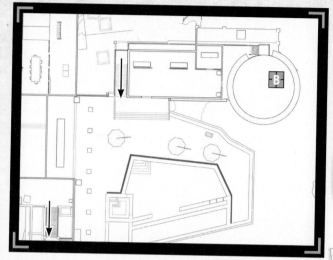

Look straight up to spot a balcony. Use the Grappling Hook to climb to the ledge. Do this again with another platform high above. Quickly take down the lone guard and approach the mansion. Two more hooks allow access to the rooftop.

 SOCIAL CLIMBER

Find the hidden access to the mansion grounds in Episode 10: Legacy. Using the suggested, quick, route into the mansion earns this Achievement / Trophy.

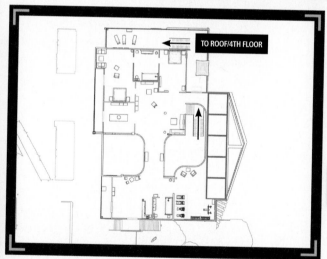

TO ROOF/4TH FLOOR

SURVEILLANCE LOG

Use the Grappling Hook to access the mansion rooftop and enter the room ahead that makes up the fourth floor. Sitting on the coffee table is a Surveillance Log. This evidence completes the Preferred Outcomes Case File.

WORLD'S GREATEST DETECTIVE

Complete all case files in single-player. If every piece of evidence has been found to this point, World's Greatest Detective is earned.

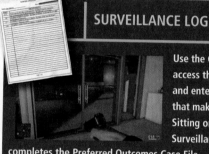

Return to the rooftop and approach the east railing. Fire a zipline this side of the helipad and use it to reach the lower level. Turn around and descend the steps to the first floor, disposing of the guard if he gets in your way. Enter the circular office at the end of the hallway.

B OPEN THE PASSAGE

Interact with the letter on the desk and then walk over to the bookshelf on the right. Turn the bookend to open the hidden passage and descend the steps.

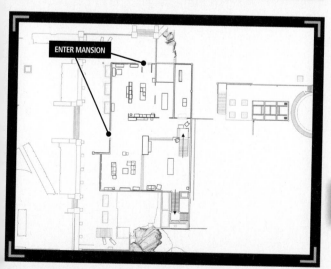

ENTER MANSION

SERVED COLD

Complete Episode 10: Legacy. Achievements / Trophies can be earned at this point if playing on Officer, Veteran, or Hardline difficulties.

UNLOCKING WEAPONS AND GADGETS

At the start of the single-player game, the following items are available:

PISTOLS	92FS, P226
GADGET	T62 CEW ELECTROSHOCK WEAPON
MELEE WEAPONS	NIGHTSTICK, POLICE BATON, COLLAPSIBLE BATON

Complete the Episodes and Case Files, using non-lethal means against the criminals, to unlock more weapons and gadgets.

WEAPON AND INVENTORY UNLOCK PROGRESSION

Arrest suspects with warrants, scan objects and evidence, take down criminals non-lethally, and complete objectives to earn points toward the expert score. As this score grows, Expert Levels are reached. Weapons, gadgets, and attachments are unlocked at these levels according to the following table.

EXPERT LEVEL / EXPERT SCORE REQUIRED	WEAPONS / GADGETS / ATTACHMENTS UNLOCKED
Expert Level 1 2,000	CZ-75 Pistol M1911A1 Heavy Pistol
Expert Level 2 3,000	37 Stakeout Shotgun
Expert Level 3 3,000	Armored Insert First Aid Pack Ammo Box Gas Mask
Expert Level 4 4,000	MP5K SMG MPX SMG P90 PDW
Expert Level 5 4,000	New "Cop" Primary Weapon Attachments
Expert Level 6 5,000	R700 LTR Sniper Bolt Action SOCOM16 Sniper Semi-Auto SR-25 ECC Sniper Semi-Auto
Expert Level 7 5,000	New "Cop" Secondary Weapon Attachments
Expert Level 8 6,000	.40 Pro Heavy Pistol Bald Eagle Heavy Pistol .410 Jury Revolver .44 Magnum Revolver
Expert Level 9 6,000	Laser Tripmine Breaching Charge
Expert Level 10 6,000	New "Criminal" Primary Weapon Attachments
Expert Level 11 6,000	TEC-9 Machine Pistol Blackjack Melee Baseball Bat Melee Lead Pipe Melee Golf Club Melee
Expert Level 12 7,000	SPAS-12 Shotgun Double-Barrel Shotgun
Expert Level 13 7,000	New "Criminal" Secondary Weapon Attachments
Expert Level 14 7,000	AKS-74U Carbine G36C Carbine
Expert Level 15 7,000	300 Knockout Sniper Bolt Action AWM Sniper Bolt Action SAIGA .308 Sniper Semi-Auto PTR-91 Sniper Semi-Auto

CASE FILE UNLOCKS

Keep on the lookout for evidence that can be scanned for the seven case files. Each completed file unlocks the listed weapons as well as a Silver Battlepack.

CASE FILE	WEAPON UNLOCKED
The Hot Shot File	.38 Snub Revolver .357 RS Revolver Silver Battlepack
Hot Shot Supply Chain	SCAR-H Battle Rifle HCAR Battle Rifle Silver Battlepack
The Elmore Hotel Investigation	93R Machine Pistol G18C Machine Pistol Silver Battlepack
Internal Affairs	M416 Assault Rifle RO933 Carbine SG533 Carbine Silver Battlepack
Power Play	HK51 Battle Rifle SA-58 OSW Battle Rifle Silver Battlepack
The Boomer Connection	K10 SMG UZI SMG FMG-9 SMG Silver Battlepack
Preferred Outcomes	M240B LMG Silver Battlepack

FOUND AND DROPPED WEAPONS

Some weapons can be picked up off downed enemies or found lying around. The player must pick the weapon up to add it to Tactical Gear. The original gun can be grabbed again if preferred. The following table lists how to find each.

	WEAPON / GADGET	FOUND IN
	870P Magnum Shotgun	Found in Episode 8: Sovereign Land, sitting on a table inside silo. First dropped by Criminals in Episode 1: Back to School
	45T Heavy Pistol	First dropped by Criminals in Episode 3: Gator Bait.
	AKM Assault Rifle	First dropped by Criminals in Episode 3: Gator Bait
	G17 Pistol	Found in Episode 8: Sovereign Land, sitting next to a truck inside the trailer park. First dropped by Criminals in Episode 1: Back to School
	M16A3 Assault Rifle	Found in Episode 8: Sovereign Land, sitting on a couch on top of the trailer with Nick's gear. First dropped by Criminals in Episode 4: Case Closed in basement of Domo Roboto warehouse.
	M/45 SMG	Found in Episode 3: Gator Bait. From the gator farm, take the airboat southwest to a nearby dock. Use the Grappling Hook to climb onto the wooden tower. Look southeast to spot a lower platform and use the Zipline to reach it. Pick up the M/45 SMG to add the gun to Tactical Gear.
	MAC-10 Machine Pistol	First dropped by Criminals in Episode 2: Checking Out
	Scout Elite Sniper Bolt Action	Found in Episode 3: Gator Bait. Drive the airboat south from the nature reserve until you spot a dock next to a small island. Use the Grappling Hook to reach the wooden ledge above and then use the Zipline to reach another platform to the east. A Scout Elite rifle rests on a table there.
	UMP-45 SMG	First dropped by Criminals in Episode 4: Gator Bait in basement of Domo Roboto warehouse.
	Grappling Hook	Given to player in Episode 3: Gator Bait
	Zipline	Given to player in Episode 3: Gator Bait

CAMOUFLAGE UNLOCK

A variety of camouflage is unlocked as you complete the single player episodes, at which point it can be added to any weapon in Tactical Gear.

COMPLETE EPISODE	WEAPONS / ATTACHMENTS UNLOCKED
Default Camo	Default, Zebra Bliz, Zebra Blaz, Zebra, Circuit, Rattlesnake, Visceral Dev.
Ep. 1: Back to School	Solid Camos (Black, FDE, Green, Grey, Navy, Olive, Tan)
Ep. 2: Checking Out	Forest Camos (Splinter, Digital, ERDL, Hexagon, Spray, Tiger)
Ep. 3: Gator Bait	Aviator Camos (Splinter, Digital, ERDL, Hexagon, Spray, Tiger)
Ep. 4: Case Closed	Snow Camos (Splinter, Digital, ERDL, Hexagon, Spray, Tiger)
Ep. 6: Out of Business	Hunter Camos (Splinter, Digital, ERDL, Hexagon, Spray, Tiger)
Ep. 7: Glass Houses	Desert Camos (Splinter, Digital, ERDL, Hexagon, Spray, Tiger)
Ep. 8: Sovereign Land	Urban Camos (Splinter, Digital, ERDL, Hexagon, Spray, Tiger)
Ep. 9: Independence Day	Jungle Camos (Splinter, Digital, ERDL, Hexagon, Spray, Tiger)
Ep. 10: Legacy	Exotic Camos (Splinter, Digital, ERDL, Hexagon, Spray, Tiger)
Complete all Episodes on Cadet Difficulty	Bronze Plated
Complete all Episodes on Officer Difficulty	Silver Plated
Complete all Episodes on Veteran Difficulty	Gold Plated

MULTIPLAYER: GETTING STARTED

While the single player campaign offers a great story and plenty of memorable moments, it's only a small part of *Battlefield: Hardline*. Playing against others and working together as a team with members of your squad adds an entirely new dimension of intensity and fun. Plus, earning new ranks and unlocks is incredibly addictive, making hours melt away.

HARDLINE FUNDAMENTALS

Are you new to *Battlefield*? If so, don't worry about it. *Hardline* is different than previous entries in the series, making the game a learning experience for rookies and veterans alike. Regardless of your experience or skill level, there's a role for everyone in *Hardline*. In fact, this is one of the only online shooters where you can post a big score without even firing a shot. In this chapter we take a look at the basic gameplay mechanics as well as the different multiplayer game modes, helping you get up-to-speed before spawning into your first match.

INTERFACE

The heads up display, or HUD, is the way that vital information is displayed on your screen. None of the items on your HUD are there for aesthetics alone. They are there to help you accomplish your objectives and keep you alive. Here's a brief explanation of every major item on the HUD.

RETICLE: The reticle is always located in the center of the HUD. The reticle is the aiming point for your selected weapon. To hit a target, place the reticle over it and fire. The reticle may change based on the weapon you're using (shotguns have ring-shaped reticles, for example). When firing at an enemy, watch for diagonal lines flashing around the perimeter of the reticle—these are hit markers. Hit markers appear when your weapon is hitting the target. There are different types of hit markers in *Hardline*. White hit markers indicate a standard hit on-target while red hit markers represent headshots. Bracketed hit markers indicate a successful hit on an enemy vehicle.

CASH TO SPEND: Every time you score points, you're awarded with cash, shown here. Use this money to purchase new weapons, grenades, gadgets, attachments, and vehicle enhancements.

AWARDS AND PROMOTIONS: Each time you rank-up or complete the criteria necessary for a coin, bounty, or assignment, you're notified here.

MINIMAP: Located in the bottom left corner of the screen, the minimap provides a top-down, 360-degree view of the environment through which you are moving. The minimap rotates as you change direction so that the top of the minimap is always the direction you are currently facing—make note of the compass headings on the perimeter of the map. In addition to showing the terrain, the minimap also shows the location of all detected enemies, appearing as red triangles or red vehicle icons. Teammates show up as blue icons, while squad members are green. Empty vehicles and Battle Pickups are represented by white icons. It is a good idea to constantly refer to the minimap to keep track of all detected enemies. Even if you can't see them visually, the minimap lets you know where they are located, whether behind a hill or inside a building. Finally, blue and red icons show you the location of objectives. These same objective icons also appear on the HUD. The color of the ground on the minimap also has meaning. The shaded area behind the red line is out of bounds. If you move into this area, you have ten seconds to get back on the map before you die.

GAME MODE INFORMATION: The icons and meters above the minimap relate to the current game mode. All game modes have slightly different configurations, but most have a ticket meter and a timer. The ticket meter indicates how many reinforcements your team has. When your team runs out of tickets, you lose.

OBJECTIVES: The colored icons on the HUD represent objectives. Blue-colored icons are held by your team while orange-colored icons are held by the opposing team. Beneath each of these icons is a number showing the distance to each objective, measured in meters.

HEALTH: By default your health is at 100%. But if you take damage, your health drops. If it reaches 0%, you die. You can slowly regenerate health by staying behind cover and avoiding injury, but the fastest way to heal is with a First Aid Pack dropped by an operator. Stand close to a First Aid Pack to rapidly restore your health.

AMMO: Your ammo is represented by two numbers. The large number to the left is the number of rounds you currently have loaded in the weapon's magazine while the small number to the right is the amount of ammo available in unloaded magazines.

GRENADES: This number represents how many grenades you have. By default you can only carry one M67 Frag grenade, but you can purchase other grenades which allow you to carry multiples. The Extra Grenade reputation perk allows you to carry one extra grenade of any kind.

FIRE MODE: Some weapons allow you to switch fire modes, choosing from single shot, automatic, and burst modes. The weapon's current fire mode is shown here.

KILL NOTIFICATIONS: The text in the top right corner of the screen reports recent deaths, showing who killed whom and with what weapon or vehicle.

SCORE NOTIFICATIONS: Every time you earn points, text appears in the middle of the screen describing what action you're being rewarded for and how many points you gain.

REPUTATION PERKS: This meter represents progression toward your next reputation perk. Score squad-based actions to progress through the four levels of upgrades. If your squad is eliminated, you lose progress.

SQUAD LIST: Shown in green text on the right side of the minimap, the squad list shows every member of your squad as well as the kit and specialization they currently have equipped. The squad leader appears at the top of the list with a star icon next to their name.

DEPLOYMENT SCREEN

When you first join a game, the deployment screen is where it all begins. Before immediately jumping into the game, take a few seconds to choose your class. But if you want to make more adjustments to your kit, choose the loadout option. This opens a new screen allowing you to make even more tweaks to your loadout, including weapon attachments and camo. Once you're finished adjusting your loadout, return to the deployment screen and figure out where you want to join the fight. If you're in a squad, you can spawn on any living squad member. Or if a mechanic squad member has deployed a satellite phone, you can spawn at its location. Depending on the game mode, there are also bases, deployment areas, and control points at which you can spawn. You can also spawn directly into the seat of a vacant vehicle belonging to your team. As you can see, the spawning options are numerous.

In most instances you should spawn on or close to your squad so you can provide support. But if your squad is in a tense firefight, sometimes it's safest to spawn at a less dangerous location, otherwise you may get killed as soon as you spawn into the game. Study the small video monitor in the bottom left corner of the deployment screen before spawning on a squad member. This live video feed allows you to see if the selected squad member is under fire. When you've determined your spawn location, choose the deploy option to enter the game. By simply choosing safe spawn locations you can improve your kill-death ratio significantly, as many deaths occur due to poor spawn choices.

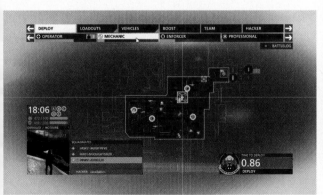

Before spawning on a squad member, monitor their view in the video monitor, located in the bottom left corner of the deployment screen.

MOVEMENT

Congratulations, you've made it onto the battlefield. Now what? Moving your character around the map is simple, especially if you've played the earlier *Battlefield* installments or other first person shooters. When standing, your soldier jogs at a moderate pace, ideal for getting around areas where threats are minimal. While crouched, you move more slowly, and while prone your speed is literally reduced to a crawl. However, since you are lower, you make a smaller target for the enemy to hit and you can more easily duck behind cover. When advancing against an enemy position, it is best to move while crouched or prone, as it is harder for the enemy to detect you. Weapon accuracy is also increased while you are crouched or prone, so make a habit of dropping to a knee or down on your belly before firing a shot.

At times, it is better to move fast, by sprinting. You can't use weapons or gadgets while sprinting, but you are much more difficult for the enemy to hit. Sprint when you have to cross a dangerously open piece of ground, dashing from one piece of cover to another. Never sprint in tight, confined spaces where you're likely to encounter enemy troops. If you encounter an enemy at close-range while sprinting, chances are you won't have time to stop, raise your weapon, and fire before your opponent does. Don't give in to the temptation to sprint. You're better off moving at a slower speed with your weapon raised and ready to fire.

In Hardline, you can sprint faster when equipping a handgun or melee weapon. Switch to you sidearm when rushing to objectives at the start of a match.

SWIMMING

If you encounter deep water, like in Riptide or Everglades, it's possible to swim. Swimming works just like moving on land, but at a significantly slower pace. Just as on land, you can sprint in the water. This is called sprint swim, a quick freestyle stroke. Sprint swim is the fastest way to cross deep bodies of water. Swim to shore as fast as possible and seek cover. You can also dive and swim underwater, using the water to conceal your movements. Simply crouch while in deep water to dive beneath the surface. Swimming underwater is a good way to stay out of sight, but you're not invincible to incoming fire. Bullets still penetrate the surface of the water and can injure or kill you. Furthermore, you can only hold your breath so long. If you remain underwater for an extended period of time, you begin losing health at a steady rate. Get to the surface before you drown! For the most part, it's best to avoid swimming when possible. While in the water your ability to defend yourself is greatly diminished, literally making you a sitting duck for enemy troops. While you're incapable of accessing your primary weapon or gadgets while swimming, you can equip your sidearm and some gadgets, like breaching charges. Firing a pistol while swimming is highly inaccurate, but it's better than nothing.

While in deep water, you can't access your primary weapon. Switch to your sidearm until you can swim to shore or hop on a boat.

PARACHUTES

Whether jumping out of a damaged helicopter of hopping off a tall building, you can avoid cratering into the ground by deploying your parachute. While in free fall, press the jump button/key once to open your parachute. You can steer the parachute with standard movement inputs. Unless you're parachuting from dizzying heights, don't expect to travel great distances, as the descent is rapid. It's possible to fire your weapons during the descent, but your accuracy is greatly diminished. If you're descending directly over an enemy position, consider dropping grenades or breaching charges—just make sure they explode before you reach the ground. But the longer you're in the air, the more attention you're likely to attract. For this reason, free fall as long as possible and open the parachute just before you reach the ground. This is a great way to sneak into enemy-held locations.

Instead of looking for ladders or ziplines, simply jump off rooftops and parachute safely to the ground.

COMBAT BASICS

While moving about the battlefield is a major part of gameplay, the sole purpose of movement is to place you in a position where you can deploy your weapons, engaging and eliminating the enemy. When it comes to weapons, *Hardline* has you covered, offering a wide range of knives, firearms, grenades, and anti-vehicle options.

SPOTTING

Before attacking your first enemy, you must learn how to spot them. When you have an enemy player or vehicle in your sight, press the spot button/key to highlight it for your team. This places a red icon on the HUD and minimap, showing your entire team where the enemy unit is located. Enemy players show up as red triangle icons while enemy vehicles are represented by red vehicle icons. Targets only remain spotted for approximately five seconds, but that's usually more than enough time for your team to take notice of the threat. Also, once the icon disappears, you can spot the target again as long as you've maintained a line of sight. If a teammate kills the target you tagged, you earn a Spot Bonus worth 25 points. Consider playing as a professional with a high-powered scope and simply spot enemy units for your team. Even if you don't fire a shot, you can still rack-up a decent score by spotting enemies. Spotting is crucial for your team's helicopters, making it easier for pilots to perform strafing runs against enemy players and vehicles. If nobody is spotting vehicles for your team's pilots, don't complain about a lack of close air support.

See an opponent? Spot them so your teammates can assist you in taking them out.

CAUTION!

While spotting enemies is a good habit, sometimes this extra step can cost you, particularly in close quarter engagements. If you've been seen and come under fire, focus on eliminating the threat or taking cover. It's always better to stay alive than to take the time to spot.

> Don't forget to spot enemies. This is helpful to yo[u]
> squad and team overall. Having an enemy spotted ca[n]
> be the difference between life and deat[h]
> —Brian McKelvey, Quality Analy[st]

MELEE COMBAT

Don't want to give away your position? Out of ammo? Consider taking out your unsuspecting opponent with a silent melee attack. The police baton or baseball bat are the standard-issue weapons available to law enforcement and criminal players, respectively. New melee weapons can be purchased, unlocked, or obtained from Battlepacks. There are two types of melee weapons in *Hardline*: blunt and sharp. Sharp weapons, like knives, are always lethal. Blunt weapons can be used to incapacitate opponents, but only when attacking from behind. If you attack an enemy head-on, it takes at least two swipes with your melee weapon to score a kill. If an enemy is looking in your direction, think twice before attempting a melee attack. They are likely to shoot you in the face before you can get within striking range. Instead, always look for opportunities to flank, sneaking up behind unsuspecting opponents and striking them from behind. In addition to scoring stealthy kills, the melee weapons are great for bashing through fences and other light obstacles.

Incapacitated opponents can be interrogated, revealing the locations of their teammates.

Always approach opponents from behind before initiating a melee attack. Opponents who are prone are particularly vulnerable.

NON-LETHAL TAKEDOWNS AND INTERROGATIONS

Non-lethal takedowns are new to *Hardline*, allowing you to incapacitate opponents. When using a blunt weapon, like the police baton or baseball bat, performing melee attacks from behind an opponent results in an instant non-lethal takedown. The T62 CEW stun gun, a secondary weapon purchase, can also incapacitate an opponent. Incapacitated players are down for the count and forced to redeploy. But before their body disappears, you can interrogate them. Interact with the incapacitated enemy at close range, holding down the corresponding button/ key to complete the interrogation. This takes a few seconds, leaving you vulnerable. But once the interrogation is complete, the locations of the opponent's teammates appear on your minimap. This information is relayed to your entire team, offering a brief tactical advantage. Use this intel to hunt down nearby enemies. Their positions only appear on the minimap for a few seconds.

FIREARMS

Battlefield: Hardline offers a wide range of firearms at your disposal. But it's up to you to pick the best weapon for the job, taking into account your chosen class and preferred style of play. Unlike previous *Battlefields*, weapon unlocks aren't tied to linear progression. Rather, most weapons can be purchased, allowing you to invest your hard-earned cash into the weapons you want. Let's take a quick look at the types of firearms available.

ASSAULT RIFLES: Carried exclusively by the operator class, assault rifles are well-rounded full-auto weapons best deployed when engaging targets at intermediate ranges.

CARBINES: Also exclusive to the operator class, carbines offer the versatility and functionality of an assault rifle in a smaller, compact frame, allowing them to perform admirably at both close and intermediate ranges.

SUBMACHINE GUNS (SMGS): These are the primary weapons of the mechanic class. SMGs are compact, fully automatic weapons known for their high rate of fire, making them ideal during close quarter engagements.

SHOTGUNS: These close quarter beasts are available to the enforcer class. While extremely lethal at close-range, shotguns are largely ineffective beyond 25 meters.

BATTLE RIFLES: When the enforcer class needs better long-range performance they can rely on battle rifles to get the job done. These function similar to the assault rifles, yet with improved damage and range.

BOLT-ACTION SNIPER RIFLES: The professional class' bolt-action sniper rifles offer extreme power and precision, intended for long-range engagements—due to their low rate of fire, these are best deployed by marksman experts.

SEMI-AUTO SNIPER RIFLES: Also exclusive to professionals, these semi-auto rifles offer a great balance of precision and stopping power, putting them somewhere in between the assault rifles and bolt-action sniper rifles.

HANDGUNS: Every player is equipped with a sidearm, serving as a backup to their primary weapon. Sidearms include a variety of pistols including the mechanic's hard-hitting revolvers and the professional's automatic machine pistols.

As you earn money in multiplayer matches, don't forget to shop for new weapons.

BASIC OPERATION

As mentioned earlier, the reticle in the center of the screen is your aiming point for using weapons. Most of the weapons you use are direct fire, meaning that the projectile you fire travels in a straight line from your weapon to the target. However, when engaging targets at long range, be prepared to aim high to compensate for "bullet drop," gravity's pull on the bullet which causes it to drop over distance. Using these weapons is simple. Place the reticle directly over the target and then squeeze the trigger. This is called firing from the hip. Firing from the hip isn't accurate, but it gets the job done at close range. Attach a laser sight to your weapon to increase hip fire accuracy.

Most weapons in *Hardline* have selectable fire modes, allowing you to choose from single-shot, burst, and automatic modes. For semi-automatic or single-shot weapons such as pistols, shotguns, and sniper rifles, each time you press the fire button/key, you fire a single round. However, automatic weapons, such as submachine guns, assault rifles, carbines, and battle rifles, continue to shoot as you hold down the fire button/key until they run out of ammo. So experiment with each weapon's fire modes in an effort to increase accuracy and reduce recoil.

The hit markers on the HUD indicate a successful hit with your weapon. A red hit marker indicates a headshot.

RECOIL COMPENSATION

Recoil is unavoidable, but it can be reduced with attachments like muzzle brakes, compensators, and foregrips.

The first round you fire with any weapon exhibits the most recoil. As the muzzle climbs after the first shot, follow-up shots may miss the intended target completely. When firing automatic weapons, the longer the burst, the less accurate your fire. Therefore, to maintain greater accuracy and still put a lot of lead on-target, fire in short bursts. You are more likely to kill your target, especially at medium- to long-range, with a few accurate rounds rather than spraying an entire magazine over a wide area. If recoil is still a problem, consider switching to burst or single-shot mode. While attachments like the compensator, muzzle brake, angled grip, and vertical grip help reduce recoil, they don't eliminate it entirely.

As you get more comfortable with the weapons, compensate for muzzle climb by applying slight downward pressure, using either your mouse or controller's analog stick. This allows you to fight the recoil, helping keep the weapon on-target.

> As always, it's good to pump on the trigger to maintain optimal control
> —Salvador Ruiz Jr., Animator

AIMING DOWN SIGHTS

When you fire a weapon using the reticle on the HUD to aim, you are firing from the hip. Hip fire is not accurate and should only be employed when engaging targets at close range. To increase your accuracy, press the zoom button/key to aim down the weapon's sights. This brings up the iron sights view, where you are actually looking through the weapon's sight to aim. The butt of the weapon is brought up to your shoulder, giving you greater stability and accuracy. If your weapon is equipped with an optic attachment, the zoom button/key provides a view through the optic rather than iron sights. It is a good idea to get in the habit of pressing the zoom button to bring up your iron sights before firing. This not only is more accurate, but it also provides a zoomed-in view of the target. To further increase accuracy, crouch or drop prone and remain stationary while firing. When peering through high-powered scopes, found on bolt-action sniper rifles, there is noticeable sway, making it difficult to aim. You can temporarily reduce this sway by holding your breath. To do this hold down the sprint button/key, but you can only hold your breath for a few seconds. Be ready to fire after holding your breath to deliver a precise shot on-target.

Take aim through your weapon's iron sights or optic for improved shot placement.

OPTIC GLINT

High-powered optics (6X and higher) emit a white glint while the player is aiming. This can give away a sniper's location. When using one of these scopes, limit the time you spend peering through the optic to avoid giving away your position. Alternately, switch to a lower-powered 4X optic. These emit no glint and exhibit no scope sway, meaning you don't have to hold your breath to fire a precise shot.

RELOADING

At some point you need to reload your weapon. While reloading, you're very vulnerable, so make an effort to find cover or have a squadmate watch your back. For most weapons, rounds are loaded in detachable box magazines which are then inserted into the firearm. The capacity of magazines differs greatly based on the type of weapon you're using. Some sniper rifle magazines only hold five rounds while the LMG Battle Pickups can hold 100 rounds.

It's best to reload your weapon after each major engagement, when you have a few rounds left in a magazine. This means a round is already chambered in the weapon, significantly reducing the duration of the reload animation. If you fire a weapon until it runs dry, a reload animation automatically begins. But this time, the weapon's chamber is empty, requiring your character to load a fresh round after seating a new magazine. While this extra action may only take a second longer, one second can make all the difference during a heated firefight. Sometimes you can't avoid firing all the rounds in a magazine. If a threat is still active and your magazine is empty, instead of reloading your primary weapon, switch to your secondary weapon. It's always faster to draw your handgun than it is to load a new magazine in your primary weapon. Shots fired from a pistol may be just enough to finish off your opponent.

For faster reloads, don't run a magazine dry; leave one round chambered to streamline the process.

UNIQUE RELOADS

The developers at Visceral have created some unique reload animations which occur randomly. Consider yourself lucky if you see one.

Reloading should be a conscious decision and not a reaction. Many players get in the bad habit of reloading after each kill, leaving them open to retaliation by their victim's teammates, who are usually lurking around the next corner. So quickly analyze the situation before initiating a reload, ensuring you're in a relatively safe, covered location.

TOP OFF YOUR SHOTGUN

The enforcer's pump-action shotguns are a bit tricky to reload, requiring you to load one shell at a time. Load these shotguns frequently, inserting new shells at your earliest convenience until the weapon is full.

ATTACHMENTS

All firearms can be equipped with a variety of attachments, allowing you to customize your weapon to meet the demands of any tactical situation. By default, most weapons have minimal attachments equipped—you must purchase the rest. Before attachments can be purchased, you must score several kills with the weapon. The number of kills required differs based on weapon and desired attachment. For example, you need to score 30 kills with the mechanic's MP5K before you can purchase any of the optic attachments. Once the 30-kill threshold for optics has been met, you can then purchase any of the optics available for the MP5K.

Most firearms have five customization categories; here's a brief description of each:

OPTIC: Here you can choose from three categories of optics from close-range red dot sights to long-range, high-magnification ballistic scopes.

ACCESSORY: Choose from a variety of lights and canted iron sights for your weapon. You can also purchase an extended magazine for some weapons.

MUZZLE: Swap out your weapon's barrel for a heavy barrel or attach a muzzle brake, flash hider, or suppressor.

GRIP: The grips available here help dampen recoil, making the weapon easier to control.

CAMO: Select a camo pattern for your weapon to help blend in with your environment. Some camos can be purchased, others are unlocked in Battlepacks.

As you purchase more and more attachments for your weapons, experiment with different configurations until you find one that best matches your style of play. Like weapons, attachments are largely subjective. So don't be afraid to try out new configurations, taking into account the type of weapon you're customizing. A favorite configuration for an assault rifle might not feel the same when applied to a carbine or battle rifle. This is why it's important to keep experimenting.

WEAPON SPECIFIC ATTACHEMENTS

Attachments purchased for one weapon cannot be applied to another. Each weapon has its own set of available attachments. For more information on attachments, reference the Weapon Customization section in the next chapter.

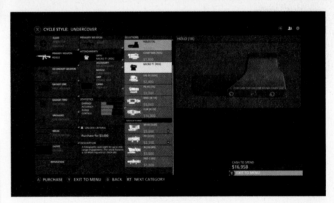

Before you can purchase attachments, you must first score several kills with the weapon you wish to customize.

VOUCHERS

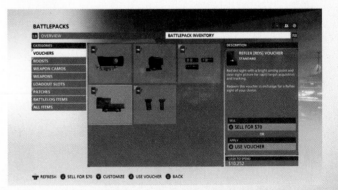

Vouchers, awarded in Battlepacks, are new to *Hardline* and allow you to acquire specific attachments for unlocked weapons. After receiving a voucher in a Battlepack, go to your Battlepack Inventory. Here you can see everything you've unlocked. In the Vouchers section you can see all of the attachments you've unlocked. Select one and then choose which weapon you want to apply it to. For example, if you have a voucher for a Reflex (RDS) optic, select it and then use the pop-up menu to apply it to one of the weapons in your arsenal. This unlocks the optic, even if you haven't met the kill prerequisite to purchase other optics. This is a great way to add attachments to newly purchased weapons. If you don't want to use a voucher, you can sell it, adding in-game cash to your account.

GRENADES

Battlefield: Hardline has a fresh line-up of grenades, allowing you to further customize your loadout to meet the needs of your squad and team. Although these grenades perform different functions, they're all deployed the same way—by throwing them. Use your weapon's reticle on the HUD to best judge where you want to throw a grenade. One press of the grenade button/key causes the grenade to be thrown. But grenades have limited range, so you may need to aim high to get them near your intended target. The farther your target, the higher you should aim your throw. Grenades have a short time-delayed fuse, detonating within five seconds of being thrown. As a result, you can bounce grenades around corners or roll them down inclines. Like your own grenades, enemy grenades show up as white grenade icons on the HUD. So if you see one of these icons nearby, sprint in the opposite direction before it explodes.

Incendiary devices and Molotov cocktails are great for denying the enemy access to objectives

CAUTION!

Unless playing on Hardcore mode, most grenades do not harm your teammates. However, they can still harm you. Be extra careful, particularly when tossing frag grenades. Gas grenades harm everyone, so be considerate when deploying these near teammates.

GRENADE LAUNCHERS

Hand grenades aren't the only option. Grenades can also be launched from the mechanic's M320 HE and M79 grenade launchers. Unlike a bullet or rocket which travels in a straight line, launched grenades travel in a parabolic arc due to their lower speed and the effect of gravity. Therefore, the farther away you are from the target, the higher you need to aim. That is why the reticle for a grenade launcher has several horizontal line aiming points. For a short-range shot, use the top line or aim directly at the target with the weapon's iron sights. The farther away your target, use the lower lines on the reticle. By using a lower aiming point, you are essentially aiming the weapon up higher to lob the grenade towards the target. All launched grenades explode on impact, much like a rocket or missile. So take this into account, particularly when launching grenades at nearby targets. The splash damage may injure or kill you.

The grenade launchers are now exclusive to the mechanic class. They are especially handy for taking out vehicles in the new Hotwire game mode.

BATTLE PICKUPS

Battle Pickups are weapons and gadgets scattered across each map. In *Hardline* there are several different types of Battle Pickups: the MG36 and M240B light machine guns, the RPG-7V2 and MK153 SMAW rocket launchers, the FIM-92 Stinger anti-air missile launcher, grappling hooks, ziplines, defibrillators, first aid boxes, and ammo lockers. These items can be equipped by any player lucky enough to grab one. They're not necessarily hidden; look for the white icons on the HUD, minimap, or deployment screen to find their locations. Battle Pickups function similarly to vehicles. They spawn at designated spots on the map, allowing any player to pick them up. Due to their power, the weapon Battle Pickups have very limited ammo, and they can't be replenished with an ammo box, so make each shot count. Don't be surprised if players flock around Battle Pickup spawn points, eager to grab a weapon or ambush those running for it.

But be aware, Battle Pickups can be booby-trapped with the mechanic's new Sabotage gadget.

The SMAW rocket launcher is the most powerful Battle Pickup, capable of destroying any vehicle with one hit.

VEHICLES

Vehicles have always been a huge part of the *Battlefield* experience, and this tradition continues with *Hardline*. Obviously, the game's law enforcement vs. criminals theme has necessitated some changes as the game shifts away from military-style vehicles to police and civilian cars, vans, trucks, and helicopters. With less armor than their military counterparts, the new vehicles require greater skill on behalf of the driver and passengers, particularly in the new Hotwire game mode. A vehicle crew that communicates and works together can be a formidable threat, sometimes turning the tide in a close match.

TRANSPORTATION

In *Hardline*, the roles of vehicles are different in each game mode. But the primary role of every vehicle is to transport teammates around the map. Use vehicles to get around whenever possible, making an effort to pick-up teammates along the way. There are several types of vehicles in the game, yet they all are driven with similar controls. All vehicles have more than one seat. When you get into a vacant vehicle, you are placed in the driver's seat by default. However, you can move to another position inside the vehicle with the press of a button/key, cycling through all seats. The driver has control of a vehicle's movement and, in the counter attack trucks and attack helicopters, also controls the vehicle's primary weapon. Some vehicles even have gunner positions, allowing teammates to man vehicle-mounted weapons and machine gun-equipped gun ports. Passengers can help defend the vehicle too, firing their weapons and gadgets out of windows. In some vehicles, passengers can even lean out of windows for a better perspective, but this also makes them more vulnerable to incoming fire.

VEHICLE DAMAGE

With the exception of the heavily armored counter attack trucks and mobile command centers, all of vehicles in *Hardline* are light-skinned, meaning they can be damaged by all weapons, even small-caliber firearms. Furthermore, only a few of the vehicles have bulletproof windows, leaving the driver and occupants vulnerable to incoming fire. If you want to stop a car, simply shoot the driver. This requires a more defensive mindset on behalf of the driver and passengers. When you're driving a sedan, coupe, utility van, or motorcycle do your best to avoid hazardous areas occupied by opponents, as you're likely to come under attack. All it takes is one lucky shot or a hit from a grenade or rocket launcher to send you back to the deployment screen. Light damage can be patched up by a mechanic equipped with a repair tool. Instead of stopping the vehicle to repair it, have a passenger conduct repairs while you keep driving. Weapons aren't the only threat. Collisions with other vehicles can also quickly erode a vehicle's health, visible just above your health bar in the bottom right corner of the HUD. Avoid head-on collisions with oncoming vehicles.

Most of the vehicles in Hardline are vulnerable to small arms fire. If your ride catches fire, get out!

UPGRADE YOUR RIDE

The stunt driver gadget, available to all classes, and the reinforced chassis vehicle upgrade can greatly increase the durability of your vehicle. The stunt driver gadget also adds a beneficial nitrous oxide boost.

"JUNK IN THE TRUNK"

Light machine guns, rocket launchers, and Stingers aren't exclusive to Battle Pickups. By purchasing the LMG armory, anti-armor armory, or anti-air armory upgrades for the sedan or coupe, you can retrieve these hard-hitting weapons from the trunk of your car. The developers like to refer to these weapons as "junk in the trunk." The LMG armory places a MG36 light machine gun (with 200 rounds of ammo) in your car's trunk. An RPG-7V2 (with two rockets) is waiting in your trunk if you have the anti-armor armory upgrade equipped. Or if enemy helicopters are present, choose the anti-air armory upgrade to acquire a Stinger missile launcher (with two missiles) in your car's trunk. Since these weapons are relatively rare, they can give you and your team a significant advantage. If you're driving, let one of your passengers have the weapon in your trunk so they can help defend your vehicle. These armory upgrades are extremely expensive, but in a tight match, the heavy weapons provided can be a game-changer.

Passengers can now lean out of a vehicle's window, providing better defensive coverage.

KILL CAM

Every time you die you get a brief glimpse of your killer through the kill cam. This screen appears immediately after your death, providing a shot of the player who killed you as well as their name, rank, health, patches, kit, weapon, and attachments. It's a nice touch, but the kill cam has larger implications for how the game is played. Snipers can't camp one spot and kill from an undisclosed location throughout the entire match. Through the kill cam, victims can see approximately where an enemy player is camping and enact revenge once they respawn. Make a habit of moving frequently, or else you're likely to face one of your angry victims sneaking up behind you.

SQUAD PLAY

If you've played past installments of *Battlefield*, you know the benefits of joining a squad. A squad is a five-player unit that can communicate with each other over headsets. Being able to talk to the other players in your squad allows you to discuss each situation and respond as a single unified fighting force. Beyond the obvious tactical advantages, being in a squad allows you to earn the squad bonus points, boosting your score and fast-tracking promotions. But if you're new to *Battlefield* and the squad system, let's take a look at how they work.

JOINING A SQUAD

Upon joining a match, you're automatically assigned to a squad. Chances are your new squadmates are complete strangers, so say hi and discuss loadouts before the match starts. If you prefer playing with friends, you can create a squad from your friends list before even joining a game. You don't need five players to form a squad, so feel free to join a game once you have at least one friend on your side. However, if you have less than five players in your squad, the extra slots could be filled by strangers. Once formed, squads can be locked, preventing others from joining without an invite.

Your squadmates have green name tags above their heads; don't wander too far from your buddies.

SQUAD SPAWN

One of the huge benefits of playing in a squad is the ability to spawn on any squadmate. In the deployment screen you can see a number of spawning options, including your team's base and vehicles. If you don't want to spawn at one of those static locations, select one of your squad members, represented by a green icon on the deploy screen. As you select their icon, the camera view in the left corner of the deployment screen switches to the selected squad member's perspective. Before spawning on a squad member, make sure they're in a safe location. The last thing you want to do is spawn in the middle of an enemy kill zone. You can also spawn on any squad member who is in a vehicle with unoccupied seats. Satellite phones, deployed by mechanics, can also serve as spawn points. These gadgets can be placed almost anywhere on the map and serve as forward spawn points for your squad. This is a great way for attackers to maintain a presence close to an objective, especially during Heist matches. But don't let enemies see where your satellite phone is placed, otherwise they may camp nearby and pick-off your squadmates as they enter the game.

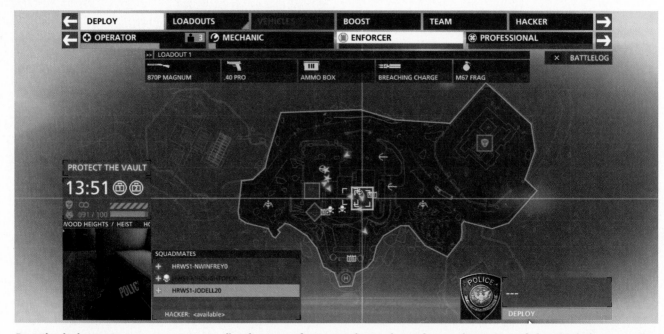

From the deployment screen, you can spawn directly on any of your squadmates, but make sure they're in a safe location before spawning.

SQUAD LEADER

Each squad has one squad leader tasked with issuing attack and defend orders. The first player to form a squad is the squad leader. When you've been selected as the squad leader, a message appears on the screen informing you of your new job. Your name also appears at the top of the squad list on the left side of the HUD, marked with a star icon. Serving as squad leader you can better direct your squad by placing attack or defend orders on objectives. Once an order has been placed at a location, any kills that occur within a wide radius of the given order results in points for both you and your squad. It's a simple mechanic, but it's a great way to keep your squad focused on one objective. And if promotions and scoreboard placement is important, a squad that uses orders effectively will easily out-score those who don't.

When serving as a squad leader, don't forget to issue orders to your squad; aim at an objective and press the spot button/key to issue an order.

> Be sure to give out orders when you're the squad leader so everyone gets more points.
> —Brian Paoloni, Quality Designer

TEAMWORK

Once in the game, you can identify your squadmates by the green name tags above their heads accompanied by their kit icon. They also show up as green triangles on the minimap. Other teammates have blue name tags above their head, while enemies appear as red. Stay close to your squad so you can support one another, but don't cluster around each other too tightly or all five of you can be eliminated by an explosive attack. Instead, try to stay within each other's line of sight. By simply communicating and working together you can gain a huge advantage over your opponents, especially those that wander off by themselves.

In addition to talking to each other over your headsets, use the target spotting system to tag enemies and issue attack/defend orders. Only the squad leader can issue orders so watch for blinking boxes around objectives like vaults, money piles, Hotwire vehicles, and control points. If no order has been issued, ask your squad leader to place an order on an objective. Kills performed within close proximity of an objective marked with an attack/defend order result in a squad order bonus, worth 50 additional points. So if you're the squad leader, don't forget to issue orders to help your squad's scores. Otherwise you're just leaving points on the table.

You'll score more points when assisting members of your squad. So stay together so you can support one another.

PROGRESSION AND ECONOMY

Every action performed in a multiplayer match earns you points. But unlike previous *Battlefields*, points also earn you money. The amount of cash you score is equal to the amount of points earned. For example, if you score a kill, worth 100 points, you also get $100. You can then use money to purchase new weapons, gadgets, grenades, attachments, and vehicle accessories in the loadout screen or on Battlelog. The better you perform, the faster you move up the ranks and the more money you earn. So at the end of a round, check out your overall performance in the End of Round screens. These screens show your current rank as well as your progress toward achieving the next rank. It also has statistical breakdowns of your score, showing how many points were earned with each class and vehicle. The scoreboard shows where you ranked among teammates and opponents. Your progress toward completing assignments is also shown.

After a match, review the End of Round screens for a detailed overview of your performance.

AWARDS

AWARD	NAME	DESCRIPTION
	Ranks	New ranks are achieved at regular intervals by earning points. Some ranks offer Battlepacks as a reward.
	Coins	You earn a coin when you accomplish an in-game objective such as getting a certain number of kill assists or headshots. coins are earned on a per-match basis and can be received multiple times.
	Bounties	You are awarded with a bounty once you have collected a certain amount of coins of the same type. Bounties represent milestones for good performance and can be earned multiple times.
	Assignments	Similar to coins and bounties, assignments have multiple criteria which must be met before they are completed. Upon completion you're awarded with a patch or weapon.
	Patches	Every player in Hardline has a left and right patch, providing a way to customize your character. These function like dog tags from previous Battlefields. You can collect new patches by completing assignments or opening Battlepacks. You can also get your opponents' patches by taking them down with a melee weapon.
★★★	Service Stars	Bronze, silver, and gold service stars are awarded for each class, weapon, vehicle, and game mode. Each service star nets you points, allowing you to rank-up faster.
	Battlepacks	Battlepacks contain random combinations of new camos, patches, melee weapons, XP boosts, and vouchers for attachments. These items are designed to add customization options and give you some personalization on the battlefield. Battlepacks are earned through progression or promotion. They can also be purchased for in-game cash.

REPUTATION PERKS

The field upgrade system from *Battlefield 4* has been overhauled, allowing players to choose their own in-game perks, providing a variety of enhancements. All classes have four reputation levels, each with two perks per level. Just like field upgrades, reputation perks are tied directly to your performance in a round. The more points your score, the more reputation levels you unlock. At each level you're prompted to choose from one of two perks. For example, at reputation level one, the operator can choose from the Extra Magazines or Fast Climb perks. Make a habit of choosing your perks as soon as they're available. Otherwise you don't benefit from their enhancements. At the end of the round your reputation perks are reset, requiring you to start over. If you have a good round, you should have no problem reaching level two, but you may need some help from your team's hacker to achieve the higher levels. The hacker's Squad Upgrade ability awards squads with one reputation level. The reputation boosts, awarded in Battlepacks, can also help you reach those higher levels.

An on-screen notification appears when you have reached a new reputation level, prompting you to choose a new perk.

SCORE!

For complete information on the game's scoring system and awards, flip to the Appendix at the back of the guide. There you can find scoring details for each action as well as criteria for every coin, bounty, and assignment.

BOOSTS

Boosts are back, but they function a little differently than they did in *Battlefield 4*. There are now seven different kinds of boosts, each providing a unique benefit. Boosts are unlocked through Battlepacks and can be applied during a match from the Boost tab. Here you can choose a class for which you wish to apply a boost—this boost is only active while playing the assigned class. Boosts remain active for 30 minutes and provide an XP multiplier for specific actions. For example, the elimination boosts provide a multiplier for kills you score. Boosts are offered in 25%, 50%, and 100% variants—special 200% boosts are awarded during special community events. Make a habit of applying boosts at the start of a match. Remember, the more points you score, the more cash you earn.

Before starting a match, apply any boosts you've received from Battlepacks; these can really increase your score/cash.

> Watch for your squadmates! Squadmates are players with green text. You get massive bonus points for coordinating with teammates when attacking/defending objectives.
> —James Berg, User Experience Researcher

BOOSTS

BOOST	NAME	DESCRIPTION
100	Quick Draw	Boost any score from a kill modifier by 25%, 50%, or 100%.
100	Assistant	Boost any score from an assist by 25%, 50%, or 100%.
100	Elimination	Boosts scores from kills by 25%, 50%, or 100%.
100	Gearhead	Boost any score from vehicle activities by 25%, 50%, or 100%.
100	Objective	Boosts objective scores by 25%, 50%, or 100%.
100	Reputation	Boost how fast perks are earned on the Reputation track by 25%, 50%, or 100%.
100	Teamplay	Boost any score from team-aiding actions or gadgets by 25%, 50%, or 100%.

> Apply boosts to your favorite class frequently to maximize your earning power.
> —Julian Beak, Senior Producer

PURCHASING WEAPONS AND GEAR

After playing only a few rounds of multiplayer, you probably have accumulated several thousand dollars. Instead of admiring your growing pile of cash, spend it on new weapons and gear. From the game's multiplayer menu, choose the customize option to bring-up the loadout screen. This can also be accessed during a match, from the deployment screen. Here you can purchase new primary and secondary weapons as well as gadgets, grenades, and melee weapons. Select any of these categories and browse through the available options. It's important to note that the law enforcement and criminal factions have slightly different weapons and gear. Some weapons are exclusive to each faction. For example, if you buy a law enforcement exclusive weapon, like the M16A3 assault rifle, it won't be available when playing as the criminals. However, this is only the case with weapons. Gadgets and grenades are shared across both factions. You can also purchase vehicle enhancements including weapons, upgrades, countermeasures, and optics. So no matter how much

you play *Hardline*, you're unlikely to run out of things to buy. For complete pricing information and analysis of each item reference the Class and Weapons and Vehicles chapters.

New purchases can be made directly from the loadout screen or from Battlelog.

MULTIPLAYER TACTICS

Tactics is the combining of maneuvers and firepower to achieve an objective. Both movement and weapons have already been covered, so this section focuses on using the two together in an effort to gain an advantage over your opponents.

PLAY THE OBJECTIVE

There is an old saying that those who fail to plan, plan to fail. You need to come up with a plan before the bullets start flying. The best place to start is to look at your game mode's objectives, since those determine victory or defeat. While killing the enemy is helpful, it is often a means to an end. Instead, focus on the objectives. Do you have to destroy a target, defend a position, or just get to a certain point on the map?

Once you know what you must do, look at the map and examine the terrain. Where are you located? Where is the objective? How will you get there? Are there any vehicles you can use? These are all questions you need to ask yourself. Once you have determined how to get to the target, you must then consider how to accomplish your orders. Will you need to get in close and set a charge on a vault door? If so, how will you secure the perimeter? Finally, you need to take into account your opposition. What does the enemy have and where are they located? Usually you will not know that type of information until you get in close to the target and can see the enemy with your own eyes. Therefore, planning continues on the fly as you learn new information about enemy positions and actions.

When playing as the criminals in Heist mode, you need to find a way into a vault. Discuss your plan of attack with your squad before the match begins.

> Concentrate on the objective. Playing the objective always gives you more reward than having a high Kill/Death ratio.
> —Brian McKelvey, Quality Analyst

COVER

Aim down your weapon sights when standing behind cover. This allows you to peek around or over the piece of cover.

Combat is very dangerous. Bullets and other deadly projectiles fly through the air and can kill you outright if they make contact. The concept of cover is to place something solid between you and the enemy that stops those projectiles and keeps you safe. The multiplayer maps are filled with objects that you can use as cover: buildings, walls, trees, rocks, earthen mounds, and so on. Some types of cover stop small arms fire such as rifle bullets, but does not stop the heavier weapons. Most walls stop machine gun fire, but not rockets or grenades. Therefore, pick cover that protects you from the current threat. Objects constructed from wood or flimsy sheet metal don't stop a bullet.

Cover should become ingrained in your combat thinking. In addition to looking for enemies, you also need to be looking for cover. During a firefight, always stay behind cover. The only reason to leave cover is to move to another position with cover. If the cover is low, you may need to crouch down or drop prone to get behind it, standing only to fire over it. When moving from cover to cover, sprint to get there quicker. If carrying a compact weapon, you can lean around corners, allowing you to peek out and return fire while keeping most of your body behind cover.

While you want to stay behind cover, you also want to try to deny the benefit of cover to your enemies. Destroying their cover is a way to do that. Another way is to reduce the effect of their cover by moving to hit them from a direction for which they have no cover. This is called flanking. For example, if an enemy is taking cover behind a wall, move around to the side of the wall so that the wall is no longer between you and your target. Or, if you have an explosive weapon, you can simply blow a hole in the wall, taking your target out in the process.

DESTRUCTIBLE ENVIRONMENTS

One of the awesome features in *Hardline* is that many of the structures and objects can be damaged or outright destroyed. This presents a large range of possibilities and opportunities that affects the tactics you use. For example, if the enemy is holed up in a house on Dust Bowl and taking shots at you from the windows, you could try to throw a grenade through the window or rush into the house via the doorway and clear the threat out with close-range combat. However, with destruction as an option, you can launch a rocket at a wall of the structure and blow a hole in it. If an enemy was on the other side of the wall, that threat might be killed. Otherwise, you can then use direct fire to kill the enemy, since you destroyed the wall providing cover.

The interior of the mansion on Hollywood Heights is highly destructible. Use gunfire and grenades to punch holes through walls.

Often structures can funnel you into a kill zone the enemy has set up. But you can blast your way through walls or other objects and come at the enemies from different directions that they might not expect. While this may seem to favor the attacker, the defender can also use this as an advantage. Destroy potential cover the attacker may use to approach your position.

As a result, you can create your own kill zones which the enemy must traverse while exposed to your team's fire.

Use grenades and other explosives to knock down walls and other barriers, opening new paths and lines of sight.

CLOSE QUARTER COMBAT

The mechanic's submachine guns and the enforcer's shotguns are ideal for close quarter firefights.

In close quarters, such as in a town or even within a building, you don't have a lot of time to aim before shooting. However, at such short ranges, accuracy is not really a factor. Instead, you need a weapon that puts out a lot of firepower with some spread so you are more likely to get a hit while moving. Shotguns and SMGs are great for close-quarters combat. Your minimap is also an important tool, especially if teammates have spotted targets. Since you can see where enemies are located, use this info to set up shots while strafing around corners. Your weapon will already be aimed at the target as it appears on the minimap, which saves you just enough time to have the advantage and make the kill rather than be killed. Don't forget to use grenades, which can be thrown around corners or over walls to hit enemies who think they are safe behind cover.

LONG-RANGE COMBAT

If possible, it is best to try to attack the enemy at long-range before they're even aware of your presence. While sniper rifles work great for this type of combat, you can even use assault rifles, battle rifles, or rocket launchers to hit targets at long-range. The key to winning at long-range is to take your time. Drop prone, stay still, and use iron sights or optics to increase your magnification and accuracy. As always, make sure you have some good cover in case the enemy decides to shoot back—if you can see them, they can see you. Also, when firing an automatic weapon, fire in short bursts to ensure that more of your bullets hit the target. For greater accuracy and precision, switch to semi-auto mode.

When sniping with a high-powered optic, remember to hold your breath to steady your aim by holding down the sprint button/key.

GAME MODES

There are a total of seven game modes, and five of them are completely new to *Hardline*. Heist, Blood Money, Hotwire, Crosshair, and Rescue are completely new modes requiring a different tactical mindset than the more traditional Conquest and Team Deathmatch modes.

HEIST

Heist is all about pulling off that big job or that perfect score. The criminals are trying to infiltrate a cash-filled vault, and the cops must regulate them. Once the criminals break in, they have to nab two bags of cash and jam out with them back to each of the two base points.

There's more than one way into a vault. Use secondary breach points, like the roof on Bank Job, to create alternate routes.

OVERVIEW

Battlefield: Hardline has a great number of brand new modes that are major game-changers in the *Battlefield* franchise; Heist is just one of them. Allowing for many of the same tactics classic game modes require, such as running and gunning, mid- to long-range sniping, full lockdown defense, teamwork and communications, and tactical aerial assault. In Heist, your team is tasked with either protecting the vault holding all of the cash or stealing the cash from said protected vault. Each team must work with their squads at all times in order to win a round of Heist. Your team can have the best shooters, but if every man is out for himself, failure is inevitable.

BLOOD MONEY

A huge pile of loot has been intercepted in transit. The criminals are fighting to steal the money, while the cops are trying to secure it as evidence. Each team is trying to secure the money in their team's vault, but it's not safe there. Raid the enemy's vault to help your team score the most money.

Scan the area for enemy activity while interacting with the money pile or an enemy vault. You can aim and fire your weapon while stuffing your pockets with cash.

HEIST TACTICS

- As the squad leader, work with your team's hacker to cover your sector and time your attacks accordingly to fight alongside your friendly squads cooperatively.

- Find the high ground on any Heist map and use the zipline to escape to any extraction point much quicker than any conventional method.

- Always remember, there is probably another way. Most Heist maps have three or more entrances to a money vault, and opening every possible route makes the criminal team's job much easier. For those maps with two separate cash locations and one way each to pick up the bags, they are always separated by some obstruction or distance and protecting both is not quite as simple as it sounds. Go for one then change it up to keep the enemy guessing. The separate bag locations are usually out in the open, leaving the attacking team the opportunity to clear the area around a money bag before running in to pick it up.

- Winning a firefight in *Battlefield: Hardline* sometimes takes a lot more tactical thinking than just skill with your weapon. When defending a vault, do not stand immediately in the general location of any single bag. The enemy will be running into the vault looking for the cash. Make them work to find you and use their greed as a distraction to kill them before they can make any type of escape.

- When a criminal drops a bag, a return timer automatically starts. This timer is slow, but piling your entire police squad around a dropped bag dramatically speeds up this timer. If you keep criminals from touching the bag, it is returned to the vault.

- Once the vault is breached and the criminals are beginning their push to extract the cash, the police deploy in what seems like the farthest point away from the extractions, making them incredibly difficult to defend. Drop a satellite phone near the center of the map or close to the extraction your squad is tasked to defend, making your deployments much more useful in a pinch.

> When playing as criminals in Heist, concentrate on moving the bag closer to the extraction point above all else. If you know you cannot possibly pick it up without getting killed immediately, it is worth it to pick up the bag to keep it from being returned to the vault. Every inch counts
> —Brian McKelvey, Quality Analyst

OVERVIEW

Blood Money is the ultimate culmination of tactful striking and competition-based intense warfare packed into one single game mode. This game mode puts your thievery skills to the test, letting you choose from a virtually unlimited range of tactics and possibilities on defeating the enemy team. Each team is tasked with stealing money from a neutral location and bringing it back to their own vault. At the neutral money pile there is an unlimited amount of money separated into stacks of cash. A player can hold up to ten stacks of cash, but gathering a single stack at a time leaves you vulnerable the longer you wait and the more money you wish to take. You can leave and take the money you have gathered at any time, but the choice is yours whether you choose to risk your neck and fill your pockets or slowly build your vault by running one or two stacks at a time.

> Robbing enemies returning to their vault with loot is the easiest way to gain money—depending on who is carrying it!
> —Brian Carden, Quality Analyst

The money pile isn't the only place your team can gather cash from—in fact you shouldn't rely on the money pile alone. If a player is holding an amount of cash, that player can then be killed and drop all of their money for anyone with room in their pockets to run by and pick up. In some ways, killing enemy players for their cash is far more efficient than taking from the money pile because simply running over the cash automatically picks it up. Each team's vault can also be raided, meaning the enemy team can run in and start stealing from your vault, thus depleting your team's collection. Communicate with your team and make sure that the money you are gathering isn't going straight to the enemy's collection.

BLOOD MONEY TACTICS

- Once your team has a small lead, order a couple of squads to begin stealing from the enemy vault. This distracts the enemy from stealing from the money pile as well as depletes their cash count, extending your lead whether the cash makes it all the way back to your vault or not.

- Communicate with your team when attacking the enemy vault. Players at the money pile may be able to spot any enemies retreating back to their base and give you a heads up before they get there.

- Use vehicles whenever possible. An enemy on foot can't catch you running away with money that they need. Helicopters and mobile command centers make for quick money collection and a stronger defense.

- Play the midfield when the money pile is too hot. Live to fight another day and take down enemies running away with money. Don't be afraid to let the other team do the hard work.

- Make sure you're safe and protected before getting too greedy at the money pile. It's already a high-risk, high-reward situation so why not lower the risk by keeping your friends close?

- Never leave your vault unprotected. A single squad can enter your vault and take most, if not all, of your money in a single raid.

Always have someone defending the team vault in Blood Money—unless you want to lose.
—Jeff Zaring, Lead MP Map Designer

HOTWIRE

The nitrous oxide boost provided by the stunt driver vehicle upgrade is great for putting some distance between your Hotwire car and any pursuers.

The criminals are trying to steal a list of marked cars while the cops are trying to repossess them. Use your driving skills to catch up with the enemy, and bring a friend riding shotgun to take them down.

OVERVIEW

Hotwire is the culmination of everything that is cops and robbers. Chase down the criminals and repossess those stolen vehicles, or play as the criminals and get the job done by stealing every vehicle on the list and make sure the cops stay off your back. A lot like Conquest, Hotwire is all about capturing the five control points spread out all around the map. Your team can bleed the other's tickets if you control more points than them, except there is a twist. These control points are ground vehicles of all types. They're fast and highly destructible which makes good drivers essential to winning a round of Hotwire.

The objective of this game mode is to take one of the Hotwire vehicles and get it to maximum speed. The control point does not begin to capture until the vehicle is going at a fast enough speed to start the process. Once the Hotwire vehicle is captured, it must stay at a high rate of speed to keep control of the point. Once the car slows down, it begins to un-capture, turning the vehicle back into a neutral point until you regain enough speed to recapture it. Since these control points need to gain speed, they need to continue moving around the map, and as long as they are within the map's general boundaries, they can go anywhere. However, Hotwire vehicles can be destroyed, but they spawn back in their original position.

HOTWIRE TACTICS

- Communicate with your team. If your team is close to destroying an enemy Hotwire vehicle, you or someone listening can quickly get to the original spawn point of that vehicle and capture it as soon as it spawns again.

- You can deploy in a controlled Hotwire vehicle, granted there is room. Doing so, and protecting the vehicle, is one of the more useful actions you can take for your team.

- Work with your squad and your team's hacker to call out enemy locations. Knowing about an upcoming ambush makes it avoidable, saving the lives of everyone inside the Hotwire vehicle, and more importantly, the objective itself.

- Grenade launchers and rocket launcher Battle Pickups are the most effective items for destroying an enemy-controlled Hotwire vehicle.

- Destroying enemy Hotwire vehicles slows down the enemy team from winning the round, but it means nothing unless your team is capturing control points. Capture Hotwire cars while the rest of your team goes for the kills. If there are uncaptured vehicles on the map, you're missing out on a big opportunity.

Invest in upgrading your vehicles for extra protection in Hotwire.
—Ryan Murphy, Level Designer

CONQUEST

A *Battlefield* staple, Conquest is based on the idea of controlling a base. Capture a base by standing near a flag on foot, in a vehicle, or in the skies. If your team owns more flags than the enemy you slowly reduce their tickets, which are their ability to respawn. The first team to run out of tickets loses.

Pay attention to the highlighted zone on the minimap. This is the control point's capture zone.

OVERVIEW

The classic *Battlefield* game mode is back, but this time it's on tighter, faster, more intense maps. Conquest is all about dominating the other team by controlling more key locations than they do and shooting them along the way. Gain control of a control point by standing near the flares on the ground in the center of the key location. Instead of flags, *Battlefield: Hardline* uses flares and shows the objective's area of control by designating it on your minimap as a red, white, or a blue highlighted area. Stand in this area to either gain control or prevent the enemy from gaining control. The more teammates you have in the area causes the control point to be captured faster. If there is an even number of players from each team in the area, the control point is contested and is not captured by either team. Pay attention to your ticket count because no matter which team controls what, the first team to run out of tickets loses.

CONQUEST TACTICS

- Even if your team holds a control point, it is best to defend it from inside the area of control. Whether you see an attacker or not, they don't begin to gain control until you are outnumbered.

- Spawn on your squad leader and set up satellite phones to keep your squad intact and prevent yourself from being attacked without help.

- Work with your team's hacker to make sure each squad has orders. Following orders not only gets you bonus points, it also keeps your team from getting flanked or losing a control point. For best results, assign one squad to each control point. For the duration of the match it's their job to attack/defend that single point.

- Pick your spawns carefully. Except at the start of a match, it costs your team one ticket to spawn. Spawning directly into the line of fire (and dying) unnecessarily wastes tickets.

- Balance your squad and make sure they are equipped with first aid packs, defibrillators, and ammo packs to keep everyone full and healthy. A self-sufficient squad can operate a long time without being wiped.

> Waiting just outside a control area can put you in position to control it without tipping the enemy off to your location.
> —Brian Carden, Quality Analyst

TEAM DEATHMATCH

Team Deathmatch is infantry only and has the easiest objective to understand: Shoot the enemy team more than they shoot you.

Get out of the streets and find a good location to lockdown during Team Deathmatch.

OVERVIEW

Team Deathmatch is simple, kill the enemy more times than they kill you. The team who runs out of tickets or the team with the least amount of tickets by the end of the round loses. However, just because this is a simple concept does not mean it is a simple strategy. While taking into account the plethora of gadgets, grenades, and Battle Pickups, you must develop ways to outsmart the enemy as well as outshoot them. Each map, while being located in a much smaller area than the entire map, is very different which means you and your team must outfit yourselves in a manner that complies with your surroundings. Keep your eyes open, watch your squad's back, and then aim and shoot in order to win a round in Team Deathmatch.

TEAM DEATHMATCH TACTICS

- Outfit your squad with first aid packs and defibrillators. The name of the game is to keep your ticket count high, so by bringing your team back to life and keeping them alive you lose far fewer tickets.

- Equip weapons that are made for the ranges at which you are fighting. Shotguns are no good if your strategy is to move through the wide open spaces of the map, and sniper rifles are debilitating when you're fighting indoors at close-quarters.

- Find a stronghold and stay there. If the enemy knows where you are, they will most likely come to you. If you are holed up in a stronghold, like a building or a well-protected corner of the map, you have the upper hand.

- Set up satellite phones so that your squad can spawn in a well-guarded and sheltered area, keeping them protected while they get familiar with the area they just spawned in. Spawning near your team also allows for better fortification of an area.

- When on the run, check corners and rooftops for enemy campers and snipers waiting for you to walk into their sights. Don't give them your head to shoot at too easily.

RESCUE

Rescue is one of the two competitive modes. This is a cop-centric mode that lets you step into the boots of a SWAT operative tasked with saving innocent lives from the hands of criminals. Lead your team carefully into dangerous environments and get the hostages back to safety. Be careful though, because there are no second chances in this mode.

The professional's gadgets are very useful during Rescue. Use cameras to detect the enemy team and decoys to lure them into traps.

OVERVIEW

Rescue is a game mode that requires an intense amount of cooperation and strategy because unlike any of the previous modes, there's no respawning here. The police must infiltrate the area in which two hostages are located and carry at least one of them out and back to the extraction area, located near their deployment area. It is up to the criminals to keep the hostages secure and tied up for collateral. The premise of Rescue is simple. It's the knowledge of the map, communication with your team, and being able to outsmart the enemy that wins each three minute round of this brand new game mode.

RESCUE TACTICS

- Strike as a team. Simply bombarding the enemy doesn't work in this game mode because of the fact that you simply can't respawn. So once the five members on your team are dead, the round is over and you lose.

- Equip a gas mask and gas the immediate area of the hostages. You can't kill the hostages so don't worry about them. Gas the area and clear the enemy out so you can swoop in and rescue the hostage.

- Never bunch up! Moving too close to a teammate or two makes you an easy target for the enemy to kill multiple players in one move, which can be detrimental any single round.

- There are only three minutes in a round, so be careful but don't delay. The police have a seemingly daunting task. Paying attention to how many enemy players are left alive helps you make quick tactical decisions.

- You only need one hostage to win, so pick the one that is the easiest to rescue. Or if given the opportunity, take both and go separate ways to split the criminals' forces as they search for you.

Gas Grenades do not harm Hostages and trigger a hit marker that can be used to detect enemies.
—Brian Carden, Quality Analyst

CROSSHAIR

In this second competitive mode, a former criminal turned state's witness is on the run from his former crew. The criminals are trying to erase the VIP while the cops are trying to get him out safely. Once again, there are no second chances—one death and you are out for the match.

Grappling hooks and ziplines are very effective for the law enforcement team in Crosshair. Use grappling hooks to quickly access rooftops then zipline down to the extraction point.

OVERVIEW

Crosshair is very much like the second phase of Rescue, but both teams have a full set of players. The twist is, one of the players on the police team is the VIP and this player must be protected at all costs. The VIP is armed with only a Bald Eagle pistol and is dressed very differently than the police. He also has special information and knows exactly where to find Battle Pickups on any given map. The objective of Crosshair is to get the VIP to one of the two possible extractions. It doesn't matter how many police are left alive, if the VIP gets killed the round is over and the police lose. However, if the criminal team is killed the police automatically win. There's no need to reach the extraction point if all opponents are dead.

CROSSHAIR TACTICS

- The VIP should never be left alone. Armed with only a pistol, the VIP should always be under the protection of at least one police officer.

- Use distractions and deterrents when attempting to extract the VIP. It only takes a few seconds once the VIP has begun the extraction, so distracting the enemy at the opposite extraction could give you just the amount of time you need to win.

- Don't give your position away on defense. Stay hidden and let the police pass by while you keep your eye out for the VIP.

- Pick a leader to call the shots and communicate with the VIP to coordinate the path and direction your team should take in order to succeed.

- With only three minutes in each round, you need to move fast but don't rush in blindly. The police can't win if the VIP is dead, so check your corners then move out before you run out of time.

Spotting enemies is more important than ever in Crosshair and Rescue.
— Jeff Zaring, Lead MP Map Designer

EXTENDED PLAY

With the additions of Hacker Mode, Spectator Mode, and Battlelog, there's plenty to do, and you don't even have to be in front of your PC or console to take part. Whether taking command of your team and leading them to victory, or simply watching a battle unfold from the sidelines, these features offer more ways to experience and make new *Battlefield* moments.

HACKER MODE

Hackers are vigilantes, above the war on the streets and helping whichever side of the law suits them. Their arsenal consists of subroutines, used to gain access to useful systems such as GPS tracking on phones, CCTV cameras in buildings, and many others. With their plethora of subroutines, an expert hacker has as many actions per minute as their agent counterparts on the streets below. To become a hacker, select a server from the server browser then select the Join as Hacker option.

Order friendly squads to engage points of interest and objectives that you can see are most important. Try to keep your squads organized and spread out.

HACKER SUBROUTINES

SUBROUTINE	NAME	DESCRIPTION
	Trojan	Speed friendly interaction and slow enemy interaction; nullify enemy subroutines instantly.
	GPS Jamming	Eliminate passive spotting by scrambling your team's GPS coordinates.
	GPS Spotting	Reveal enemy locations by gaining access to their GPS devices.
	Backdoor	Gain control of an automated in-world object by exposing a backdoor vulnerability.
	Trace	Reveal High Value Targets and enemy Hacker subroutines with an area scan.
	Overclock	Decrease the cooldown on all subroutines. WARNING: some subroutines may overheat after use.
	Point of Interest	Highlight an important objective for one of your Squads through an AR overlay.
	Squad Upgrade	Boost the Reputation of every Squad member to the next tier by upgrading their firmware.
	Fast Deploy	Decrease the deploy time for a Squad by rerouting traffic.

OVERVIEW

Knowledge is power, and this truth is obvious when playing as the hacker in *Battlefield: Hardline*. You are the most powerful weapon on your team because you can see more than anyone on the streets. You must work together with your team's squad leaders and support them in any way possible.

Lead them to points of interest that they may not have the ability to see from their point of view. Upgrade squads to raise their reputation, giving them

valuable bonuses or granting them fast deploy when they're in a pinch for reinforcements.

Sever hacker connections by destroying enemy hacked in-world objects. This helps your team against the enemy hacker and makes the friendly hacker's job a little easier.

When you're not coordinating with your team you have the ability to trace the battlefield for major hotspots or vehicles racing around the objectives. Use this information and drop a GPS spotter which allows you to hack their GPS devices in a small area of the map, revealing their location to anyone nearby. The more you use the hacker abilities, the more you can do with them once they are upgraded based on your performance.

JAM IT!

If you don't have the ability to backdoor an enemy controlled camera, jam their GPS near it to prevent the camera from showing anything on the nearby enemy's radar.

Use the surveillance feed to get a better view of the battlefield, helping you judge the best plan of action in each area.

The third major feature that you should pay attention to is insulating yourself and your team against the enemy hacker. Yes, there is someone else with the same abilities on the other team, attempting to support their team and keep you from supporting yours. As the hacker, you have special abilities which allow you to hack into items and fixtures all around the map. This includes security cameras that automatically spot enemies, gas systems that are essentially proximity gas grenades that explode when an enemy gets close, and power transformers which are proximity based and temporarily blind enemies nearby, just like a flashbang.

You have access to all of these map objects, however, so does the enemy hacker. It is like a chess match as you work to outsmart the enemy, based on timing and which objects are most important for your team to have on their side.

If you see the enemy hacker using the backdoor to take a valuable object, use the Trojan to nullify the enemy subroutine.

Hacker abilities like GPS jamming, overclock, and Trojan are your most valuable abilities when battling the opposing hacker. Pay attention to your team's locations. If they are doing something that should desperately stay hidden, drop a GPS jamming device right on top of them to keep the enemy team from being able to spot them. Use overclock when your team is in a pinch and you need your subroutines to come back up as quickly as possible. Overclock is also a good move when your timing is slightly behind the enemy hacker, allowing you to push ahead and be able to counter anything the other team can use. Finally, you have the Trojan, something that can really jam a monkey wrench into the enemy hacker's operation. Be ready to give everything you've got once you activate the Trojan. This is when you have the most opportunity as it speeds up all of your subroutines while also slowing the enemy's at a detrimental rate. Use the Trojan carefully because it has a long cooldown and you don't want the enemy to counter it.

Friendly hacked in-world objects appear with a blue icon above them indicating that they are working for you. Do not destroy these objects, but keep your distance so that when they are activated you can jump in and take down the affected targets.

The hacker's job is to support the team in any way possible. Your teammates must be the ones to kill enemy forces and take over the objectives, but in a large number of situations your team can't finish the job without your help. Keep those fingers busy and hack away as you outsmart the enemy and defeat them.

SPECTATOR MODE

Spectator Mode returns in *Hardline*, offering players the opportunity to simply watch a match unfold. Each server supports up to four spectators per match. To start Spectator Mode, open the server browser and select a server you'd like to spectate. You must access the Server Info screen to join the server as a spectator. Like playing as the hacker, joining as a spectator does not count against the server's maximum player count, so neither team will be short players. Once in Spectator Mode you have four camera perspectives to choose from. The Table Top view looks similar to the deployment screen, giving you a broad view of the map, complete with the ability to zoom all the way in and watch pitched battles from a satellite-like perspective.

With the first-person camera, you can switch to the perspective of any player on the map, seeing exactly what they see in real-time. The third-person perspective puts you behind any player on the map, along with a player card which shows their current weapon, attachments, health, and ammo. Finally there's the free cam, tied to no single perspective. Instead, you can simply fly around the battle and choose any perspective you like. This is perfect for those seeking to make videos. Whichever perspective you choose, Spectator Mode offers a unique way to experience *Battlefield*. Consider sitting-in on some matches and watch how others play. You may learn something new.

Use Spectator Mode's third-person perspective to follow players around the map.

BATTLELOG

Battlelog extends your *Battlefield* experience by enhancing your gameplay, tracking your progression throughout your multiplayer career, and allowing you to compete with millions of *Battlefield* players around the world. Battlelog is available in-game, on the web, and through tablet and smartphone apps. Battlelog can track all rounds you have played, your unlocks, stats, awards, assignments, and much more. You can complete missions and compete with your friends to see who the best driver is, or use the Geo Leaderboards to compete against people in your city or country. You can even customize your loadout and find a server in the Server Browser that is right for you. You can always bring up Battlelog in-game too. You can check your stats, your friends' stats, see how your suggested or tracked unlocks are progressing, create and join missions, see how you are doing in the Geo Leaderboards, and much more.

Battlelog's overview page provides a wealth of statistical data at a glance.

EMBLEMS

The emblem is a feature that gives you an additional identity marker. The emblem is displayed on vehicles, weapons, and characters. You can even use your emblem as a spray tag, marking your territory in-game. Create your unique emblem with the Emblem Editor on Battlelog. Use the provided shapes and symbols to create complex designs; more symbols can be unlocked through Battlepacks. You can create several emblems and then choose between them before entering a server.

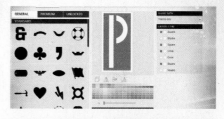

Design a custom emblem on Battlelog then use it as a spray tag in-game.

COMMUNITY

The *Battlefield* community is very active, and always a good source of information for game news, software updates, patch notes, and even unorthodox tactics. Here's a few good sources to check-out for the latest *Battlefield* news:

OFFICIAL BATTLEFIELD TWITTER
@Battlefield

Get the latest tweets from the game's developers.

BATTLEFIELD BLOG
blogs.battlefield.ea.com

This is the official blog maintained by employees of DICE and Visceral. Go here for all the latest information on the game straight from the developers.

PRIMAGAMES.COM
primagames.com

Check back with the Prima team for blogs and videos, offering even more insight on classes, weapon, vehicles, and evolving tactics.

CLASSES AND WEAPONS

Succeeding during *Hardline*'s multiplayer often comes down to choosing the right tools for the job. That's where the classes come in, also known as troop kits. Before spawning into a game you're prompted to choose which class you wish to play. If you're a team player your choice should be based on what is needed as opposed to which kit you prefer. Although there are only four classes to choose from, the customization options allow you to mix and match weapons, gadgets, and reputation perks to create a completely unique kit that complements your style of play and meets the demands of any tactical situation.

> "*Battlefield* veterans: *Hardline* plays differently, so take a good look through the kits to learn what your options are, and what your opponents' strengths and weaknesses are going to be."
> —James Berg, User Experience Researcher

➕ OPERATOR

UNDERCOVER	SWAT	BANGERS	THIEVES

STARTING LOADOUT

SLOT	EQUIPMENT
PRIMARY WEAPON	RO933
SECONDARY WEAPON	92FS
GADGET ONE	FIRST AID PACK
GADGET TWO	—
GRENADE	M67 FRAG
MELEE	POLICE BATON/BASEBALL BAT

STRENGTHS: WELL-ROUNDED KIT; HEAL/REVIVE TEAMMATES
WEAKNESSES: LIMITED ANTI-VEHICLE CAPABILITY

If you're familiar with the assault class from other *Battlefield* games, then you'll feel right at home with the operator. Thanks to its versatility, this is a great class to choose when starting out, or playing a new map or game mode for the first time. The assault rifles and carbines available to the operator are excellent choices at any range, with great damage output and impressive rates of fire. Beyond its impressive offensive capabilities, the operator class is responsible for healing injured teammates with their First Aid Pack and reviving downed teammates with the police Defibrillator or criminal Revive adrenaline shot. But the Defibrillator and Revive adrenaline shot gadgets aren't immediately available—they must be purchased. Consider making these essential gadgets your first purchases for the operator. Reviving teammates isn't only a huge help to your team, but it's also a great way to rack-up some points.

REPUTATION PERKS

	PERK	NAME	DESCRIPTION
LEVEL 1		Extra Magazines	Increases the number of primary weapon magazines carried.
		Fast Climb	Climb ropes, ladders, and walls faster.
LEVEL 2		Fast Ready	Practice allows you to bring your weapons to bear faster after sprinting.
		Healing Upgrade	An improved First Aid Pack increases the rate of healing.
LEVEL 3		Fast Aim	All that time on the firing range has paid off—you can bring your weapon to bear faster when aiming down sights.
		Revive Upgrade	Advanced training allows you to revive teammates at full health without needing a full charge.
LEVEL 4		Fast Reload	Practice makes perfect—you can reload your weapons much faster.
		Fast Swap	Knowing your equipment and practicing transitions allows you to rapidly swap between weapons and gadgets.

OPERATOR WEAPONS

CARBINES

FIRE MODES
I = Semi-Auto
II = Burst
III = Full-Auto

Carbines bridge the gap between assault rifles and SMGs, ideal for a variety of situations. Their compact design makes them easy to maneuver in tight quarters. The shorter barrel length mean, less muzzle velocity, accuracy, and range than their assault rifle counterparts, but they still have the stopping power to take down opponents quickly.

RO933 — $0

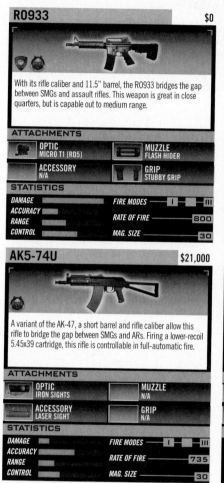

With its rifle caliber and 11.5" barrel, the RO933 bridges the gap between SMGs and assault rifles. This weapon is great in close quarters, but is capable out to medium range.

ATTACHMENTS

OPTIC	MUZZLE
MICRO T1 [RD5]	FLASH HIDER
ACCESSORY	GRIP
N/A	STUBBY GRIP

STATISTICS

DAMAGE	FIRE MODES	I II III
ACCURACY		
RANGE	RATE OF FIRE	800
CONTROL	MAG. SIZE	30

SG553 — $21,600

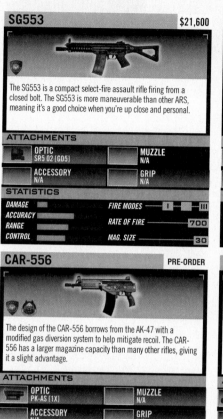

The SG553 is a compact select-fire assault rifle firing from a closed bolt. The SG553 is more maneuverable than other ARS, meaning it's a good choice when you're up close and personal.

ATTACHMENTS

OPTIC	MUZZLE
SR5 02 [GD5]	N/A
ACCESSORY	GRIP
N/A	N/A

STATISTICS

DAMAGE	FIRE MODES	I II III
ACCURACY		
RANGE	RATE OF FIRE	700
CONTROL	MAG. SIZE	30

ACWR — PRE-ORDER

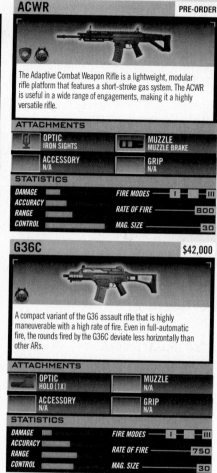

The Adaptive Combat Weapon Rifle is a lightweight, modular rifle platform that features a short-stroke gas system. The ACWR is useful in a wide range of engagements, making it a highly versatile rifle.

ATTACHMENTS

OPTIC	MUZZLE
IRON SIGHTS	MUZZLE BRAKE
ACCESSORY	GRIP
N/A	N/A

STATISTICS

DAMAGE	FIRE MODES	I II III
ACCURACY		
RANGE	RATE OF FIRE	800
CONTROL	MAG. SIZE	30

AK5-74U — $21,000

A variant of the AK-47, a short barrel and rifle caliber allow this rifle to bridge the gap between SMGs and ARs. Firing a lower-recoil 5.45x39 cartridge, this rifle is controllable in full-automatic fire.

ATTACHMENTS

OPTIC	MUZZLE
IRON SIGHTS	N/A
ACCESSORY	GRIP
LASER SIGHT	N/A

STATISTICS

DAMAGE	FIRE MODES	I II III
ACCURACY		
RANGE	RATE OF FIRE	735
CONTROL	MAG. SIZE	30

CAR-556 — PRE-ORDER

The design of the CAR-556 borrows from the AK-47 with a modified gas diversion system to help mitigate recoil. The CAR-556 has a larger magazine capacity than many other rifles, giving it a slight advantage.

ATTACHMENTS

OPTIC	MUZZLE
PK-AS [1X]	N/A
ACCESSORY	GRIP
N/A	N/A

STATISTICS

DAMAGE	FIRE MODES	I II III
ACCURACY		
RANGE	RATE OF FIRE	700
CONTROL	MAG. SIZE	40

G36C — $42,000

A compact variant of the G36 assault rifle that is highly maneuverable with a high rate of fire. Even in full-automatic fire, the rounds fired by the G36C deviate less horizontally than other ARs.

ATTACHMENTS

OPTIC	MUZZLE
HOLO [1X]	N/A
ACCESSORY	GRIP
N/A	N/A

STATISTICS

DAMAGE	FIRE MODES	I II III
ACCURACY		
RANGE	RATE OF FIRE	750
CONTROL	MAG. SIZE	30

ASSAULT RIFLES

Assault rifles are the most versatile primary weapons available, useful in a variety of situations. Although bulkier and slightly less maneuverable than the compact carbines, the assault rifles benefit from greater stopping power, particularly when engaging targets beyond intermediate range. When engaging targets at long range, switch to semi-auto mode. A 4X optic can also help.

M16A3 — $37,500

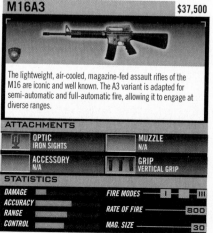

The lightweight, air-cooled, magazine-fed assault rifles of the M16 are iconic and well known. The A3 variant is adapted for semi-automatic and full-automatic fire, allowing it to engage at diverse ranges.

ATTACHMENTS

OPTIC	MUZZLE
IRON SIGHTS	N/A
ACCESSORY	GRIP
N/A	VERTICAL GRIP

STATISTICS

DAMAGE	FIRE MODES	I II III
ACCURACY		
RANGE	RATE OF FIRE	800
CONTROL	MAG. SIZE	30

M416 — $43,800

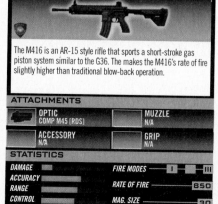

The M416 is an AR-15 style rifle that sports a short-stroke gas piston system similar to the G36. The makes the M416's rate of fire slightly higher than traditional blow-back operation.

ATTACHMENTS

OPTIC	MUZZLE
COMP M45 [RDS]	N/A
ACCESSORY	GRIP
N/A	N/A

STATISTICS

DAMAGE	FIRE MODES	I II III
ACCURACY		
RANGE	RATE OF FIRE	850
CONTROL	MAG. SIZE	30

AKM — $12,000

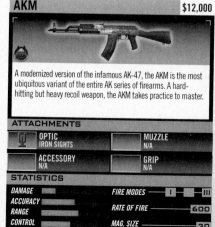

A modernized version of the infamous AK-47, the AKM is the most ubiquitous variant of the entire AK series of firearms. A hard-hitting but heavy recoil weapon, the AKM takes practice to master.

ATTACHMENTS

OPTIC	MUZZLE
IRON SIGHTS	N/A
ACCESSORY	GRIP
N/A	N/A

STATISTICS

DAMAGE	FIRE MODES	I II III
ACCURACY		
RANGE	RATE OF FIRE	600
CONTROL	MAG. SIZE	30

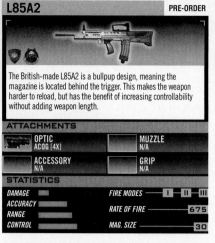

L85A2
PRE-ORDER

The British-made L85A2 is a bullpup design, meaning the magazine is located behind the trigger. This makes the weapon harder to reload, but has the benefit of increasing controllability without adding weapon length.

ATTACHMENTS

OPTIC ACOG [4X]	MUZZLE N/A	
ACCESSORY	GRIP N/A	

STATISTICS

DAMAGE	FIRE MODES	I — II — III
ACCURACY		
RANGE	RATE OF FIRE	675
CONTROL	MAG. SIZE	30

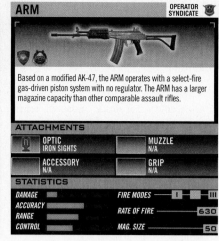

ARM
OPERATOR SYNDICATE

Based on a modified AK-47, the ARM operates with a select-fire gas-driven piston system with no regulator. The ARM has a larger magazine capacity than other comparable assault rifles.

ATTACHMENTS

OPTIC IRON SIGHTS	MUZZLE N/A	
ACCESSORY	GRIP N/A	

STATISTICS

DAMAGE	FIRE MODES	I — III
ACCURACY		
RANGE	RATE OF FIRE	630
CONTROL	MAG. SIZE	50

⌐ NOTE

Some weapons are exclusive to the law enforcement or criminal factions. However, if you score 300 kills with a faction-exclusive weapon, you earn a weapon license. This allows you to equip the weapon as either faction. For example, scoring 300 kills with M16A3 when playing as law enforcement, unlocks the weapon license, allowing you to use the M16A3 in your criminal loadouts.

HANDGUNS

The handguns available for the operator class serve as solid back-ups to their carbines and assault rifles. When your primary weapon runs dry, switch to one of these capable sidearms to finish the fight. Each handgun has a relatively large magazine capacity, giving you more than enough ammo to neutralize nearby threats.

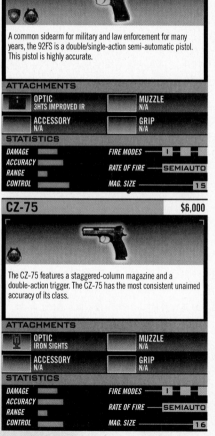

92FS
$0

A common sidearm for military and law enforcement for many years, the 92FS is a double/single-action semi-automatic pistol. This pistol is highly accurate.

ATTACHMENTS

OPTIC 3HTS IMPROVED IR	MUZZLE N/A	
ACCESSORY N/A	GRIP N/A	

STATISTICS

DAMAGE	FIRE MODES	I
ACCURACY		
RANGE	RATE OF FIRE	SEMIAUTO
CONTROL	MAG. SIZE	15

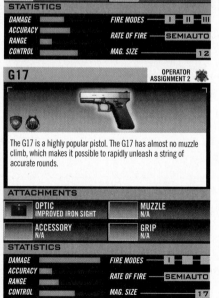

P226
$17,400

Ergonomics and balance make this pistol easy to handle. High damage and stability make this weapon a great choice for accuracy during medium- and close-range combat.

ATTACHMENTS

OPTIC IRON SIGHTS	MUZZLE N/A	
ACCESSORY N/A	GRIP N/A	

STATISTICS

DAMAGE	FIRE MODES	I — II — III
ACCURACY		
RANGE	RATE OF FIRE	SEMIAUTO
CONTROL	MAG. SIZE	12

CZ-75
$6,000

The CZ-75 features a staggered-column magazine and a double-action trigger. The CZ-75 has the most consistent unaimed accuracy of its class.

ATTACHMENTS

OPTIC IRON SIGHTS	MUZZLE N/A	
ACCESSORY N/A	GRIP N/A	

STATISTICS

DAMAGE	FIRE MODES	I
ACCURACY		
RANGE	RATE OF FIRE	SEMIAUTO
CONTROL	MAG. SIZE	16

G17
OPERATOR ASSIGNMENT 2

The G17 is a highly popular pistol. The G17 has almost no muzzle climb, which makes it possible to rapidly unleash a string of accurate rounds.

ATTACHMENTS

OPTIC IMPROVED IRON SIGHT	MUZZLE N/A	
ACCESSORY N/A	GRIP N/A	

STATISTICS

DAMAGE	FIRE MODES	I
ACCURACY		
RANGE	RATE OF FIRE	SEMIAUTO
CONTROL	MAG. SIZE	17

OPERATOR GADGETS

FIRST AID PACK
$0

Deployable First Aid Pack. Nearby combatants slowly heal to full health, even in combat. Teammates can interact with anyone carrying a First Aid Pack for healing.

FIELD NOTES

The First Aid Pack is the default gadget available to the operator class, and costs nothing to unlock. The law enforcement and criminal teams have slightly different looking packs, but they function identically. Simply drop these on the ground near wounded teammates to heal them. The longer you (or an injured teammate) stands next to a First Aid Pack, the more health you receive. The First Aid Pack has a small healing radius, requiring players to stand very close to it.

Healing team and squadmates earns you a healing bonus. Critically injured teammates have a white cross icon flashing above their head—the same icon appears on the minimap. These icons are only visible to friendly assault players so look for them to locate and heal teammates before they die. All teammates have a life meter below their name, allowing you to see exactly how much health they have. Even if a teammate isn't critical, offer them a First Aid Pack to fully replenish their health. When deployed, a First Aid Pack can heal multiple teammates at once. However, players must stay within the pack's healing radius, potentially making them vulnerable if the gadget is deployed in a dangerous location. Pay close attention to where you drop these. You don't want teammates rushing out into incoming fire just to access your First Aid Pack in the middle of a street. Make a habit of dropping them at corners or behind other pieces of cover. However, new to *Hardline*, you no longer have to drop a First Aid Pack to heal teammates. Simply interacting with an operator carrying a First Aid Pack gives a wounded teammate health.

SURVIVALIST — $7,800

You'll be given the opportunity to revive yourself from a roadkill or explosive attack. It does not bring you back from deaths caused by bullets, fire, gas, melee, stun, or falling damage.

FIELD NOTES

The Survivalist is a new gadget to *Hardline*, giving operators a second chance at life when they've been downed by an explosion or speeding vehicle. When the Survivalist occupies one of your gadget slots and you get knocked to the ground by one of these events, you're given the opportunity to accept a revive or return to the deployment screen. This interaction is identical to being revived by a teammate using a Defibrillator or adrenaline shot. If you accept the revive, your character automatically plunges the Survivalist into their arm, and returns to their feet. However, after reviving yourself with the Survivalist, your health is reduced to 10%, making you extremely vulnerable. Get to cover and heal yourself with a First Aid Pack. Given the limited application of this gadget, it probably isn't a priority purchase unless you're playing a lot of Hotwire, where roadkills are common. But in most game modes, your deaths are caused by gunfire. The Survivalist cannot bring you back from those wounds.

DEFIBRILLATOR — $14,400

The AED (Automated External Defibrillator) is a portable electronic device that can bring downed teammates back into the fight. Spending time preparing the AED brings teammates back with increased health. Fully charged, it can also take down an enemy.

FIELD NOTES

The Defibrillator, available only to law enforcement, functions a little differently than it did in *Battlefield 4*. You're no longer limited to three charges. You can now use the Defibrillator continuously, with no cooldown period. However, there is a cooldown period when reviving the same teammate, preventing players from spamming revives. To use the Defibrillator, hold down the trigger to charge it, then release the trigger to deliver an electrical jolt to your target at pointblank range. A partially charged Defibrillator restores only partial health to a downed teammate. Hold down the trigger to give the Defibrillator full power before deploying to revive a teammate with 100% health. A full charge is also necessary to score a kill with the Defibrillator. Defibrillator kills are still as satisfying (and hilarious) as they've always been. If your operator is also equipped with a First Aid Pack, consider using partial charges to get your teammates back in the action. Once your teammate is revived, drop a First Aid Pack nearby to get them back to full health. While it takes your teammate a bit longer to reach full health, using a partial charge is much faster than charging the paddles, allowing you to switch back to your weapon.

REVIVE — $14,400

The adrenaline shot has a wickedly long needle and can be used to bring downed teammates back into the fight. Spending time preparing the adrenaline shot brings teammates back with increased health. Once prepared, it can be used to take down an enemy as well.

FIELD NOTES

The adrenaline shot is the criminal team's answer to the Defibrillator and it functions the same way. Jab this long needle into downed teammates to revive them. The longer you hold down the trigger, the more health your teammate receives. You can also turn this gadget against opponents, but you need a full dose from this gadget to score a kill. Like the Defibrillator, the adrenaline shot is very effective when combined with the First Aid Pack. Use quick, partial doses from the shot to revive teammates with partial health, then drop a First Aid Pack to heal them. Partial doses are much faster to deliver than the long wind-up a full dose. This gets your teammate back to their feet while allowing you to quickly swap back to your primary weapon. If you purchase the Defibrillator for law enforcement or the Revive adrenaline shot for the criminals, both are unlocked—you only need to buy one.

OPERATOR TACTICS

☆ The operator is a great class for players of all levels. Keep the First Aid Pack equipped as often as possible and support your team when they get hit, you save your team tickets, and possibly determine whether an objective is captured or lost.

☆ Purchase an assault rifle as soon as they are unlocked, because they provide you with a more stable weapon for shooting at a much wider variety of distances, while still doing enough damage to drop enemies in a timely manner.

☆ The operator is best at a medium range, so don't get too close to your enemy if given the choice. Your primary weapons do far more damage than the mechanic's SMGs or the enforcer's shotguns at this distance and have a better rate of fire than any battle rifle, making the medium range, the Operator's sweet spot.

☆ Playing as an operator, you are doing most of the running around and taking down ground forces, reviving fallen teammates, and unloading your rifle into enemy vehicles. On game modes such as Hotwire, Conquest, and Blood Money, consider taking the Survivalist gadget with you because you get run over or bombarded by a wide range of explosives at some point. This gadget pops you right back on your feet and you'll be back in the fight without a moment's delay.

☆ As one of the main foot-mobile classes, the operator's role is not to charge into danger looking for some bad guys to kill. Use your armament and optics to scope out the situation before making your move. Equipped with 3.4X and 4X scopes, you are able to see what's going on while staying hidden at a distance.

> If you want to be a lone wolf and are tired of "helping the team" or "playing the objective," deploy as an operator with a first aid pack and Survivalist. You can heal yourself, survive explosions, and use the best all-around weapons in the game. And remember, the First Aid Pack is for when *you're* injured, not you're allies!
> —William Bordonaro, Quality Analyst

UNDERCOVER	SWAT	BANGERS	THIEVES

STARTING LOADOUT

SLOT	EQUIPMENT
PRIMARY WEAPON	MP5K
SECONDARY WEAPON	.38 SNUB
GADGET ONE	M320 HE/M79
GADGET TWO	—
GRENADE	M67 FRAG
MELEE	POLICE BATON/BASEBALL BAT

STRENGTHS: **CLOSE-QUARTER SPECIALIST; VEHICLE REPAIR**
WEAKNESSES: **WEAK LONG-RANGE PERFORMANCE**

If you're expecting the mechanic to play just like engineers from previous *Battlefield* games, then you're in for a few surprises. For one, the mechanic relies solely on submachine guns as their primary weapon. This significantly limits the range at which the mechanic is effective, making them best suited for close quarter combat, where the SMGs really shine. Instead of carrying a rocket launcher, the mechanic comes equipped with a grenade launcher, maintaining some decent anti-vehicle capability. Light-skinned vehicles can be destroyed with one hit. In addition to demolishing vehicles, the mechanic can also repair them with the Repair Tool gadget. Repairing occupied friendly vehicles earns you repair points, a great way to supplement your score. The mechanic also has access to a Satellite Phone, which functions as a spawn beacon, ideal for keeping your squad near the action. Or equip the new Sabotage gadget and booby-trap objectives and other strategic areas, surprising your opponents with a fiery explosion. So while the mechanic is slightly different than the engineer, once you find the mechanic's niche there's no denying its effectiveness in any squad.

REPUTATION PERKS

	PERK	NAME	DESCRIPTION
LEVEL 1		Extra Grenade	You can carry an additional grenade, whether it's a frag, flashbang, or other throwable.
		Flak Jacket	Reduces explosive damage, allowing the wearer to survive an otherwise lethal blast.
LEVEL 2		Extra 40mm Grenades	Increases the amount of carried 40mm grenade launcher ammunition.
		Fast Repair	Increases the effectiveness of the Repair Tool.
LEVEL 3		Fast Aim	All that time on the firing range has paid off—you can bring your weapon to bear faster when aiming down sights.
		Delayed Trigger	Laser Tripmines and Sabotage have an extra delay before triggering, giving you a chance to avoid them.
LEVEL 4		Fast Reload	Practice makes perfect—you can reload your weapons much faster.
		Fast Swap	Knowing your equipment and practicing transitions allows you to rapidly swap between weapons and gadgets.

MECHANIC WEAPONS

SUBMACHINE GUNS

The submachine guns associated with the mechanic class are designed for close quarter combat. In fact, many of these SMGs outperform the larger carbines and assault rifles at close range, hitting harder and killing faster, with blistering rates of fire. But the SMGs are quickly outclassed by their larger counterparts when engagement ranges increase beyond 20 meters. So make an effort to avoid wide-open spaces when carrying an SMG.

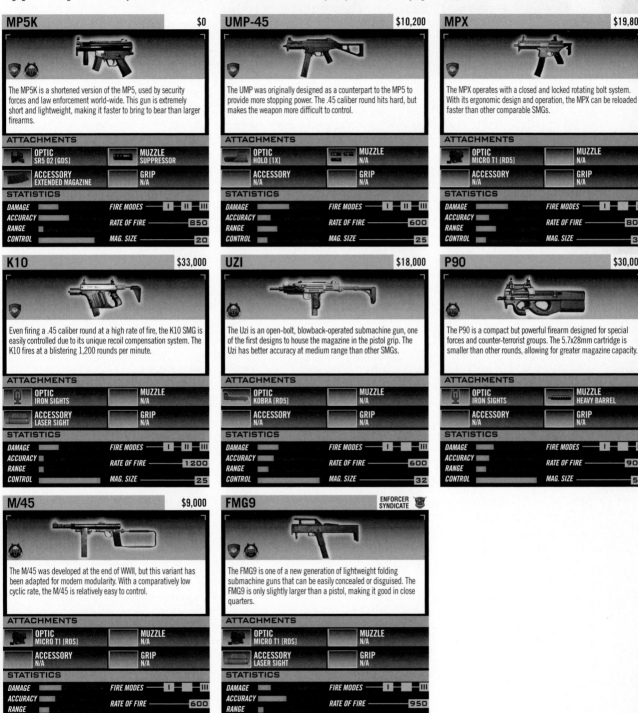

MP5K — $0

The MP5K is a shortened version of the MP5, used by security forces and law enforcement world-wide. This gun is extremely short and lightweight, making it faster to bring to bear than larger firearms.

ATTACHMENTS

OPTIC	MUZZLE
SR5 02 [GDS]	SUPPRESSOR
ACCESSORY	GRIP
EXTENDED MAGAZINE	N/A

STATISTICS

DAMAGE	FIRE MODES I II III
ACCURACY	
RANGE	RATE OF FIRE 850
CONTROL	MAG. SIZE 20

UMP-45 — $10,200

The UMP was originally designed as a counterpart to the MP5 to provide more stopping power. The .45 caliber round hits hard, but makes the weapon more difficult to control.

ATTACHMENTS

OPTIC	MUZZLE
HOLO [1X]	N/A
ACCESSORY	GRIP
N/A	N/A

STATISTICS

DAMAGE	FIRE MODES I II III
ACCURACY	
RANGE	RATE OF FIRE 600
CONTROL	MAG. SIZE 25

MPX — $19,800

The MPX operates with a closed and locked rotating bolt system. With its ergonomic design and operation, the MPX can be reloaded faster than other comparable SMGs.

ATTACHMENTS

OPTIC	MUZZLE
MICRO T1 [RD5]	N/A
ACCESSORY	GRIP
N/A	N/A

STATISTICS

DAMAGE	FIRE MODES I III
ACCURACY	
RANGE	RATE OF FIRE 800
CONTROL	MAG. SIZE 30

K10 — $33,000

Even firing a .45 caliber round at a high rate of fire, the K10 SMG is easily controlled due to its unique recoil compensation system. The K10 fires at a blistering 1,200 rounds per minute.

ATTACHMENTS

OPTIC	MUZZLE
IRON SIGHTS	N/A
ACCESSORY	GRIP
LASER SIGHT	N/A

STATISTICS

DAMAGE	FIRE MODES I II III
ACCURACY	
RANGE	RATE OF FIRE 1200
CONTROL	MAG. SIZE 25

UZI — $18,000

The Uzi is an open-bolt, blowback-operated submachine gun, one of the first designs to house the magazine in the pistol grip. The Uzi has better accuracy at medium range than other SMGs.

ATTACHMENTS

OPTIC	MUZZLE
KOBRA [RD5]	N/A
ACCESSORY	GRIP
N/A	N/A

STATISTICS

DAMAGE	FIRE MODES I III
ACCURACY	
RANGE	RATE OF FIRE 600
CONTROL	MAG. SIZE 32

P90 — $30,000

The P90 is a compact but powerful firearm designed for special forces and counter-terrorist groups. The 5.7x28mm cartridge is smaller than other rounds, allowing for greater magazine capacity.

ATTACHMENTS

OPTIC	MUZZLE
IRON SIGHTS	HEAVY BARREL
ACCESSORY	GRIP
N/A	N/A

STATISTICS

DAMAGE	FIRE MODES I III
ACCURACY	
RANGE	RATE OF FIRE 900
CONTROL	MAG. SIZE 50

M/45 — $9,000

The M/45 was developed at the end of WWII, but this variant has been adapted for modern modularity. With a comparatively low cyclic rate, the M/45 is relatively easy to control.

ATTACHMENTS

OPTIC	MUZZLE
MICRO T1 [RDS]	N/A
ACCESSORY	GRIP
N/A	N/A

STATISTICS

DAMAGE	FIRE MODES I III
ACCURACY	
RANGE	RATE OF FIRE 600
CONTROL	MAG. SIZE 35

FMG9 — ENFORCER SYNDICATE

The FMG9 is one of a new generation of lightweight folding submachine guns that can be easily concealed or disguised. The FMG9 is only slightly larger than a pistol, making it good in close quarters.

ATTACHMENTS

OPTIC	MUZZLE
MICRO T1 [RDS]	N/A
ACCESSORY	GRIP
LASER SIGHT	N/A

STATISTICS

DAMAGE	FIRE MODES I III
ACCURACY	
RANGE	RATE OF FIRE 950
CONTROL	MAG. SIZE 32

REVOLVERS

The revolver sidearms carried by the mechanic stand in stark contrast to the SMGs, making them an excellent backup weapon, balancing some of the class's deficiencies. What they lack in magazine capacity and rate of fire, the revolvers make up for in range, accuracy, and stopping power. When operating in large, open areas, consider switching to your revolver. These handguns are more effective at intermediate ranges than the SMGs.

.38 SNUB $0

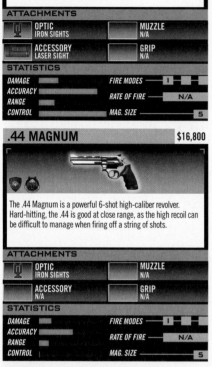

With a barrel length of fewer than 3" the Snub .38 is a popular firearm with law enforcement. The .38 Snub fires as fast as you can work the trigger.

ATTACHMENTS

| OPTIC | IRON SIGHTS | MUZZLE | N/A |
| ACCESSORY | LASER SIGHT | GRIP | N/A |

STATISTICS

DAMAGE		FIRE MODES	I
ACCURACY			
RANGE		RATE OF FIRE	N/A
CONTROL		MAG. SIZE	5

.357 RS $16,800

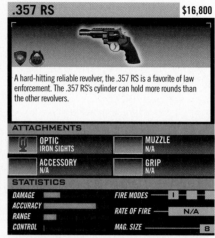

A hard-hitting reliable revolver, the .357 RS is a favorite of law enforcement. The .357 RS's cylinder can hold more rounds than the other revolvers.

ATTACHMENTS

| OPTIC | IRON SIGHTS | MUZZLE | N/A |
| ACCESSORY | N/A | GRIP | N/A |

STATISTICS

DAMAGE		FIRE MODES	I
ACCURACY			
RANGE		RATE OF FIRE	N/A
CONTROL		MAG. SIZE	8

.44 MAGNUM $16,800

The .44 Magnum is a powerful 6-shot high-caliber revolver. Hard-hitting, the .44 is good at close range, as the high recoil can be difficult to manage when firing off a string of shots.

ATTACHMENTS

| OPTIC | IRON SIGHTS | MUZZLE | N/A |
| ACCESSORY | N/A | GRIP | N/A |

STATISTICS

DAMAGE		FIRE MODES	I
ACCURACY			
RANGE		RATE OF FIRE	N/A
CONTROL		MAG. SIZE	5

.410 JURY   MECHANIC ASSIGNMENT 2

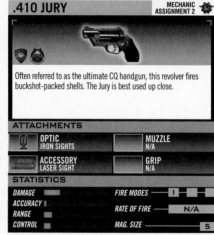

Often referred to as the ultimate CQ handgun, this revolver fires buckshot-packed shells. The Jury is best used up close.

ATTACHMENTS

| OPTIC | IRON SIGHTS | MUZZLE | N/A |
| ACCESSORY | LASER SIGHT | GRIP | N/A |

STATISTICS

DAMAGE		FIRE MODES	I
ACCURACY			
RANGE		RATE OF FIRE	N/A
CONTROL		MAG. SIZE	5

MECHANIC GADGETS

M320 HE $0

It's not exactly clear how law enforcement got ahold of this baby. A breach-loading launcher, it fires a 40mm high-explosive grenade that is effective against light vehicles and agents.

FIELD NOTES

The M320 HE grenade launcher, available only to law enforcement, fires explosive 40mm rounds, perfect for destroying vehicles, punching holes in walls, or hitting distant opponents with indirect fire. The horizontal marks superimposed on the HUD help determine barrel elevation prior to firing. Unlike traditional firearms, the M320 HE is an indirect fire weapon, meaning rounds are lobbed toward distant targets, flying an arc-like trajectory. Aim high to hit distant targets. As a result, the weapon isn't very accurate beyond 100 meters. However, with practice, the M320 HE is a very formidable weapons platform. You only get four shots, though, so make them count. More ammo can be retrieved from an enforcer's Ammo Box.

M79 $0

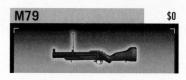

The surplus grenade launcher was probably not obtained through legal channels. A breach-loading launcher, it fires a 40mm high explosive grenade that is effective against light vehicles and agents.

FIELD NOTES

It may be an older design, but the criminals' M79 grenade launcher still packs a punch, performing just like the police M320 HE. When engaging targets at close range, aim down the weapon's sights for direct fire. But when lobbing grenades at distant targets, zoom out and use the horizontal marks on the HUD to gauge the proper angle before firing. Watch where the grenade falls, then make adjustments. Lower your aim if the grenade overshot the target, or aim higher if the grenade fell short. But with only four shots, you want to stay close to an enforcer with an Ammo Box.

REPAIR TOOL $5,400

Hand-held oxy-fuel welding and cutting torch that repairs friendly vehicles and damages enemy vehicles and agents.

FIELD NOTES

The mechanic's Repair Tool is the only way to repair disabled vehicles. To deploy, simply stand next to a damaged vehicle (while aiming at it) and hold down the trigger. Watch the circular meter in the center of the HUD fill in a clockwise fashion. Once the meter is completely filled, the vehicle is fully repaired. You're vulnerable while using this tool, so make sure you have adequate cover. Put the vehicle between yourself and incoming fire while conducting repairs. Some vehicles allow you to use a repair tool while sitting in a passenger seat, letting you conduct repairs while within the confines of the vehicle. This is a great tactic when riding around in a transport helicopter. Repairing vehicles manned by a team or squadmate earns you repair points—a great way to boost your score. The Repair Tool can also be turned against enemies. Torching an occupied enemy vehicle causes it to lose health rapidly, but be careful when using the Repair Tool on an enemy vehicle. If the vehicle's health is completely depleted, it explodes, potentially killing you. In addition to damaging enemy vehicles, the repair tool is also lethal against enemy infantry. All it takes is a quick hit with this torch to send your opponent back to the deployment screen.

SATELLITE PHONE $27,000

The Satellite Phone provides a new spawn location for you or members of your squad.

FIELD NOTES

It isn't cheap, but the Satellite Phone can make all the difference during close matches, allowing your squad to spawn close to the action or hotly-contested objectives. This unit is approximately the size of a laptop computer and must be placed on a flat surface. When equipped, a green flashing image of the satellite phone appears on the ground when you've found a suitable location. Press the fire button/key to deploy it. This gadget provides a new spawn point on the deployment screen, accessible only by you and members of your squad. When spawning on the Satellite Phone, you automatically appear right next to the gadget. Unlike spawn beacons in previous *Battlefield* games, you never parachute in. While the Satellite Phone is handy, it can be exploited by your opponents. Instead of destroying the gadget, enemies may simply camp it, mowing down your squad as they spawn. Be mindful of enemy activity around the Satellite Phone before spawning into the game. You can retrieve and move your Satellite Phone to a new location if spawning issues persist. Each mechanic can deploy one at a time. Your squad can have multiple Satellite Phones deployed simultaneously, as long as they were deployed by separate mechanics.

SABOTAGE $30,000

Sabotage bomb that can be used to trap vehicles, objectives, and interaction points. Detonates when used by an unsuspecting enemy. Look for the blinking light! Can be disarmed by the Repair Tool, shot, or exploded.

FIELD NOTES

This sneaky little device is new to *Hardline*, giving the mechanic the ability to booby-trap objectives and other key locations. But when it comes to deployment, Sabotage isn't as versatile as the enforcer's breaching charges. Sabotage can only be placed in predetermined locations on any given map or game mode. When equipped, look for the white explosive charge icon on the HUD to locate areas where Sabotage can be placed. When you see this icon, press the fire button/key to deploy Sabotage. Place this gadget directly on objectives like the money pile in Heist or on Hotwire vehicles in Hotwire. Sabotage can also be used to Booby-Trap battle pickups like the LMGs, rocket launchers, and Stingers. Once placed, you don't have to do anything. Sabotage explodes automatically when an enemy interacts with the booby-trapped object. So before interacting with these objects, look for the flashing red light to locate Sabotage gadgets placed by your opponents. Take a step back and shoot the gadget to detonate it.

> Use Sabotage on Hotwire objective vehicles for the laughs.
> —Jeff Zaring, Lead MP Map Designer

ARMORED INSERT $33,000

Armored Insert offers a layer of protection from ballistic damage to the torso, giving the wearer extra time to respond to a threat.

FIELD NOTES

The Armored Insert is a passive gadget, worn by the mechanic to reduce gunfire damage dealt to the front and back of your character's torso. You don't have to do anything to activate it. Given the chaotic close quarter engagements the mechanic is likely to participate in, this gadget can be an absolute lifesaver during one-on-one duels, but keep your expectations in-check. This is by no-means an invincibility upgrade. Instead, it simply buys you a bit more time during firefights, giving you a slight advantage. It does not reduce damage dealt to your character's head or limbs. It also doesn't protect you from explosions, fall damage, or roadkills. But since most players aim for center mass, this gadget reduces the damage of most incoming rounds that strike you, giving you slightly more time to retaliate or escape.

MECHANIC TACTICS

☆ Playing as a mechanic means you are right in the middle of the action. Move fast, watch your back, and try not to get surrounded as you push through enemy lines. Be sure to set up satellite phones to make sure your squad is always deploying near you to keep the pressure on the enemy.

☆ Keep your grenade launcher close and be ready to bring it out at any moment. *Battlefield: Hardline's* fast paced maps don't give you much time to react and get ready for an oncoming vehicle. Equipping your grenade launcher without hesitation saves your life and gives you the chance to rack up multiples kills at a time when a fully loaded sedan or utility van comes racing at you at full-speed.

☆ Any combination of having the satellite phone, sabotage, and/or the armored insert equipped gives you the ability to barricade any room or hallway and protect yourself from more or less an entire squad, as long as you bottleneck them as they come for you.

☆ Sitting in the passenger seat with a repair tool is more than just useful for keeping yourself alive. As long as you don't get hit by a rocket launcher you can keep your Hotwire cars up for a significant amount of time, granting you several Hotwire Cruising coins. Collect 50 of those and you've earned yourself the Hotwire Cruising Bounty.

☆ The mechanic's primary weapon is a close-ranged SMG, so use the zipline and M18 smoke grenades to get close to your opponent then unload your magazine in rapid succession to riddle them with bullets.

| UNDERCOVER | SWAT | BANGERS | THIEVES |

STARTING LOADOUT

SLOT	EQUIPMENT
PRIMARY WEAPON	870P MAGNUM
SECONDARY WEAPON	45T
GADGET ONE	AMMO BOX
GADGET TWO	—
GRENADE	M67 FRAG
MELEE	POLICE BATON/BASEBALL BAT

STRENGTHS: VERSATILE ANTI-PERSONNEL PERFORMANCE; AMMO RESUPPLY
WEAKNESSES: LIMITED ANTI-VEHICLE CAPABILITY

While there are some residual similarities, the enforcer class plays differently than the support class in other *Battlefield* games. For one, light machine guns are now exclusively limited to Battle Pickups and the LMG armory upgrade affiliated with sedans and coupes. Instead, the enforcer has access to shotguns and battle rifles. This gives the enforcer solid close quarter performance when using shotguns and greater long range versatility when equipped with a battle rifle. Before spawning into a match, take into consideration the size of the map and environmental features before settling on a shotgun or battle rifle.

The iconic ammo box makes its return, allowing the enforcer to distribute ammo to teammates. Ammo can also be retrieved directly from an ammo box-equipped enforcer. It's also possible to equip a Ballistic Shield, great for deflecting small arms fire when defending your team in close quarters. The enforcer is also home of the powerful breaching charge, perfect for knocking down doors, blowing holes in walls, booby-trapping objectives, or ambushing opponents. Whether racking-up kills or assisting teammates, there's plenty of ways for enforcers to support their team.

REPUTATION PERKS

	PERK	NAME	DESCRIPTION
LEVEL 1	✋	Fast Throw	Keeping your grenade accessible means you can deploy it in the heat of battle much faster.
		Reduced Fall	Your agility allows you to survive falling longer distances than others.

	PERK	NAME	DESCRIPTION
LEVEL 2		Fast Ready	Practice allows you to bring your weapons to bear faster after sprinting.
		Upgraded Ammo Box	You carry two ammo boxes into battle, allowing you to resupply yourself and other teammates.

	PERK	NAME	DESCRIPTION
LEVEL 3		Fast Aim	All that time on the firing range has paid off—you can bring your weapon to bear faster when aiming down sights.
		Extra Charges	Carry and deploy more breaching charges at one time.

	PERK	NAME	DESCRIPTION
LEVEL 4		Increased Suppression	Experience with suppressive fire increases the effect of suppression on opponents.
		Reduced Suppression	Confidence under fire reduces the effects of suppression on you.

SHOTGUNS

Nobody misses with a shotgun. Although these weapons lack the accuracy and finesse of the other weapons, their brutal power is a worthwhile trade-off. At close range, these weapons are unmatched, capable of killing with one devastating shot. But at ranges beyond 10-15 meters, the shotguns are outclassed by almost every weapon in the game, including handguns. So only equip a shotgun when operating in close quarter environments where you can get the jump on your opponents.

870P MAGNUM — $0

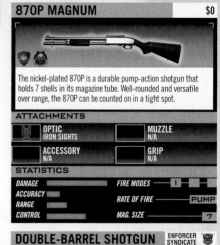

The nickel-plated 870P is a durable pump-action shotgun that holds 7 shells in its magazine tube. Well-rounded and versatile over range, the 870P can be counted on in a tight spot.

ATTACHMENTS

OPTIC IRON SIGHTS	MUZZLE N/A
ACCESSORY N/A	GRIP N/A

STATISTICS

DAMAGE		FIRE MODES	I
ACCURACY			
RANGE		RATE OF FIRE	PUMP
CONTROL		MAG. SIZE	7

37 STAKEOUT — $6,000

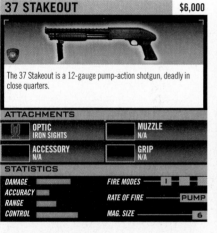

The 37 Stakeout is a 12-gauge pump-action shotgun, deadly in close quarters.

ATTACHMENTS

OPTIC IRON SIGHTS	MUZZLE N/A
ACCESSORY N/A	GRIP N/A

STATISTICS

DAMAGE		FIRE MODES	I
ACCURACY			
RANGE		RATE OF FIRE	PUMP
CONTROL		MAG. SIZE	6

SPAS-12 — $50,000

The SPAS-12 is a combat shotgun adopted by civilian markets and police forces worldwide. The SPAS-12 is a semi-automatic weapon, meaning the pump is not operated between shots.

ATTACHMENTS

OPTIC PK-AS [1X]	MUZZLE N/A
ACCESSORY N/A	GRIP N/A

STATISTICS

DAMAGE		FIRE MODES	I
ACCURACY			
RANGE		RATE OF FIRE	PUMP
CONTROL		MAG. SIZE	9

DOUBLE-BARREL SHOTGUN — ENFORCER SYNDICATE

This shotgun would look more at home over somebody's fireplace, but this one's been modified into a combat weapon. Two barrels of 12-gauge are bound to wreck someone's day.

ATTACHMENTS

OPTIC IRON SIGHTS	MUZZLE N/A
ACCESSORY N/A	GRIP N/A

STATISTICS

DAMAGE		FIRE MODES	I
ACCURACY			
RANGE		RATE OF FIRE	PUMP
CONTROL		MAG. SIZE	2

BATTLE RIFLES

When you're not sneaking around a building's interior or lurking about in cramped alleyways, consider choosing one of these battle rifles for improved intermediate- and long-range performance. These are essentially larger assault rifle variants capable of firing higher caliber rounds. The end result is more stopping power with increased recoil. Given their limited magazine capacities and harsh recoil, consider switching to semi-auto mode, particularly when engaging targets at long range.

SCAR-H — $26,400

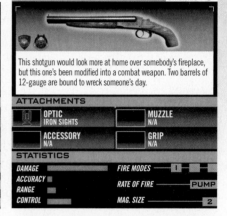

This modular battle rifle firing 7.62 NATO is setup in the Close Quarters Combat variation. In the right hands, the SCAR-H is effective from close all the way out to long range.

ATTACHMENTS

OPTIC IRON SIGHTS	MUZZLE N/A
ACCESSORY N/A	GRIP N/A

STATISTICS

DAMAGE		FIRE MODES	I	III
ACCURACY				
RANGE		RATE OF FIRE	625	
CONTROL		MAG. SIZE	20	

HCAR — $37,200

The HCAR is a modernized version of the WWII-era BAR. Firing a high-power .30-06 round, the HCAR has a lot of stopping power, but comes with heavy recoil to manage during full-automatic operation.

ATTACHMENTS

OPTIC M145 [3.4]	MUZZLE N/A
ACCESSORY N/A	GRIP N/A

STATISTICS

DAMAGE		FIRE MODES	I	III
ACCURACY				
RANGE		RATE OF FIRE	450	
CONTROL		MAG. SIZE	30	

SA-58 OSW — $25,000

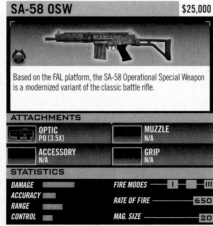

Based on the FAL platform, the SA-58 Operational Special Weapon is a modernized variant of the classic battle rifle.

ATTACHMENTS

OPTIC PO [3.5X]	MUZZLE N/A
ACCESSORY N/A	GRIP N/A

STATISTICS

DAMAGE		FIRE MODES	I	III
ACCURACY				
RANGE		RATE OF FIRE	650	
CONTROL		MAG. SIZE	20	

HK51 — $34,800

A cut-down G3A3 which has been modified to take MP5 furniture and accessories. Smaller size makes this weapon maneuverable in tight quarters, but recoil is more difficult to manage.

ATTACHMENTS

OPTIC IRON SIGHTS	MUZZLE N/A
ACCESSORY STOCK	GRIP N/A

STATISTICS

DAMAGE		FIRE MODES	I	II	III
ACCURACY					
RANGE		RATE OF FIRE	500		
CONTROL		MAG. SIZE	20		

HANDGUNS

The enforcer's arsenal of semi-automatic handguns performs much like those affiliated with the operator class. But while those fire smaller 9mm rounds, these handguns are chambered in .40 caliber and up, resulting in superior damage. But these handguns also exhibit heavier recoil and the large rounds lead to smaller magazine capacities. Still, if you manage to hit your target, you should have no problem dropping a threat with these hard-hitting handguns.

45T $0

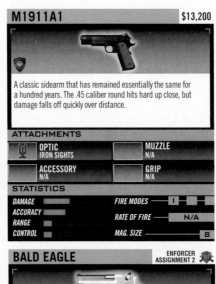

The 45T is a polymer-framed handgun with great control due to its ergonomics. It has high recoil but skilled users can master this sidearm.

ATTACHMENTS

OPTIC MINI [RD5]	MUZZLE N/A
ACCESSORY N/A	GRIP N/A

STATISTICS

DAMAGE		FIRE MODES	I
ACCURACY		RATE OF FIRE	N/A
RANGE			
CONTROL		MAG. SIZE	10

M1911A1 $13,200

A classic sidearm that has remained essentially the same for a hundred years. The .45 caliber round hits hard up close, but damage falls off quickly over distance.

ATTACHMENTS

OPTIC IRON SIGHTS	MUZZLE N/A
ACCESSORY N/A	GRIP N/A

STATISTICS

DAMAGE		FIRE MODES	I
ACCURACY		RATE OF FIRE	N/A
RANGE			
CONTROL		MAG. SIZE	8

.40 PRO $7,200

The .40 Pro is a popular sidearm in the civilian market. The .40 caliber round makes a decent trade off of damage for accuracy.

ATTACHMENTS

OPTIC IRON SIGHTS	MUZZLE N/A
ACCESSORY N/A	GRIP N/A

STATISTICS

DAMAGE		FIRE MODES	I
ACCURACY		RATE OF FIRE	N/A
RANGE			
CONTROL		MAG. SIZE	15

BALD EAGLE   ENFORCER ASSIGNMENT 2

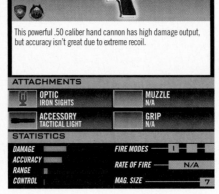

This powerful .50 caliber hand cannon has high damage output, but accuracy isn't great due to extreme recoil.

ATTACHMENTS

OPTIC IRON SIGHTS	MUZZLE N/A
ACCESSORY TACTICAL LIGHT	GRIP N/A

STATISTICS

DAMAGE		FIRE MODES	I
ACCURACY		RATE OF FIRE	N/A
RANGE			
CONTROL		MAG. SIZE	7

ENFORCER GADGETS

AMMO BOX $0

Deployable ammo box. Nearby combatants resupply ammo for all weapons, gadgets, and explosives. Anyone near the ammo box carrier can interact with him to resupply.

FIELD NOTES

The ammo box contains ammo for all weapon types. Simply stand next to one of these boxes for a few seconds to replenish the ammo for all of your weapons and gadgets, including grenades. When playing as an enforcer, drop these boxes around clusters of teammates. Each time someone retrieves ammo from a box you earn a resupply bonus. This is a great way to supplement your score while supporting your team and squadmates. If a team or squadmate is low on ammo, an icon depicting three bullets appears above their head. Get them some ammo fast! By default you can only drop one ammo box at a time, but with the Upgraded Ammo Box reputation perk you can deploy up to two ammo boxes at a time, greatly increasing your resupply score. For best results, drop these boxes in areas where multiple teammates are pinned or defending choke points. New to *Hardline*, ammo can be retrieved directly from an enforcer outfitted with an ammo box—you no longer have to jump up and down to get their attention. Simply interact with the enforcer at close range to grab some ammo.

BALLISTIC SHIELD $18,000

The ballistic shield is designed to block bullets and explosive damage. After absorbing a certain amount of damage, the shield is destroyed. The shield can be used to perform a vicious bash attack.

FIELD NOTES

This large rectangular shield can block any bullet, even those fired by high-powered rifles and heavy machine guns. But you must have the shield deployed, placing it between you and the incoming rounds, to benefit from its life-saving capability. Both of the enforcer's hands are required to hold this heavy shield, meaning you have no way to shoot back, so use this gadget when working with your squad. Lead the way while they follow and provide supporting fire. This works well when entering rooms or maneuvering down narrow hallways. For best results, crouch while inching forward. Otherwise, your ankles and feet are exposed, giving opponents an opportunity to inflict damage. At close range it's possible to smack opponents with the shield. Press the fire button/key to perform a melee strike, but it takes at least two solid hits to produce lethal results. When the shield is not equipped, it is worn on the enforcer's back, deflecting incoming rounds from the rear.

AMMO BOXES

The law enforcement and criminal ammo boxes look slightly different, but they perform identically. The criminal ammo box has a white label. Take note of an enemy team's ammo boxes, as there's likely a hostile enforcer lurking nearby.

> If you see a teammate with a ballistic shield, use that to your advantage and back them up.
> —James Berg, User Experience Researcher

BREACHING CHARGE $23,400

Plastic explosives that stick to most surfaces. The remote detonator allows for traps and ambushes.

FIELD NOTES

Just like C4 from other *Battlefield* games, the breaching charge gives the enforcer enough explosive firepower to destroy almost anything.

Initially, up to three breaching charges can be placed at a time and detonated simultaneously with a remote detonator. The enforcer can replenish their charges using an ammo box. When attacking vehicles, no matter the size, always plant at least two charges to guarantee destruction. One breaching charge is enough to take out most vehicles, but armored vehicles may require two. Charges can also be used as booby traps, placed around critical high-traffic areas like control points, money piles, and vaults, but it's up to you to detonate them when there are enemies nearby. Don't overlook the opportunity to use breaching charges on walls too. If you suspect enemies are on the other side of a wall, plant a charge and detonate it. If the wall is destructible, the charge blows a hole in it, killing opponents on the other side. You can also experience some success by tossing charges out of moving vehicles, ideal in Hotwire game modes. This is a very rewarding way to detonate enemy vehicles pursuing your getaway car. Or have your driver pull alongside an enemy vehicle so you can slap a charge on it. But in any situation, make sure you're far away from these charges when they go off. Otherwise you run the risk of blowing yourself up.

> Place breaching charges on objects that are explosive for maximum effect. Gas stations or fuel tanker trucks are a great example. If you have a truly dedicated teammate, a suicidal fuel tanker with breaching charges can cause massive damage.
> —Ethan Solak, Video Editor

ENFORCER TACTICS

☆ Playing as the enforcer, you carry a big gun. To compensate for the small amount of gadgets to choose from you have two completely different classes of primary weapons: shotguns and battle rifles. Choose the weapon class that balances out your squad. Choose something that fits the area of operation and you have the most useful weapon around.

☆ Drop ammo boxes near health packs in strongholds to create an area for your teammates to recoup after a firefight.

☆ Equip the ballistic shield and step in front of VIPs and objectives to protect everyone behind you as they shoot around you, giving your team extra cover that they wouldn't have otherwise.

☆ Enforcers are highly defensive, making them incredibly useful on game modes like Heist and Rescue. Point your shotgun into a bottleneck piece of the map you're on and wait to aim down the sights until you have to move forward. Having the widest field of view is essential when defending a specific location.

☆ Use the breaching charge to set up ambush points on Hotwire maps to destroy cars as they pass through popular narrow checkpoints. These points are avoidable, but sometimes the enemy just doesn't have a choice but to fall right into your trap.

⊕ PROFESSIONAL

| UNDERCOVER | SWAT | BANGERS | THIEVES |

STARTING LOADOUT

SLOT	EQUIPMENT
PRIMARY WEAPON	SCOUT ELITE
SECONDARY WEAPON	G18C
GADGET ONE	LASER TRIPMINE
GADGET TWO	—
GRENADE	M67 FRAG
MELEE	POLICE BATON/BASEBALL BAT

STRENGTHS: LONG-RANGE SPECIALIST; RECONNAISSANCE
WEAKNESSES: LIMITED CLOSE-QUARTER AND ANTI-VEHICLE CAPABILITY

Like the recon class from other *Battlefield* games, the professional is the master of long-range combat. This class has access to a mix of powerful bolt-action rifles and fast-firing semi-auto rifles. While the bolt-action rifles offer the best damage output, they have a very slow rate of fire and limited magazine capacities. These drawbacks are addressed by the semi-auto rifles, trading damage for greater versatility. Beyond sniping opponents, the professional can assist their team with a host of unique gadgets. Use the laser tripmine to catch unsuspecting opponents off-guard. Or deploy cameras around objectives and other high-traffic areas to relay enemy movements to your teammates. Divert attention away from your team or lure opponents into an ambush by using a decoy, a device which simulates gunfire. Or equip the stealth training hood to sneak around the map without being detected. The professional class can be tricky to play on smaller maps. But with some practice and careful customization, the professional can perform admirably in any situation.

REPUTATION PERKS

LEVEL 1	PERK	NAME	DESCRIPTION
		Fast Climb	Climb ropes, ladders, and walls faster.
		Reduced Fall	Your agility allows you to survive falling longer distances than others.

LEVEL 2	PERK	NAME	DESCRIPTION
		Advanced Spot	Your targets stay spotted for a longer duration.
		Fast Unspot	Your evasive nature reduces the time you stay spotted by opponents.

LEVEL 3	PERK	NAME	DESCRIPTION
		Hold Breath	You can hold your breath for longer, giving you a longer window of time to steady your scope.
		Low Profile	Undetected by cameras and security cameras, except when sprinting.

LEVEL 4	PERK	NAME	DESCRIPTION
		Fast Reload	Practice makes perfect—you can reload your weapons much faster.
		Delayed Trigger	Laser tripmines and Sabotage have an extra delay before triggering, giving you a chance to avoid them.

PROFESSIONAL WEAPONS

BOLT-ACTION RIFLES

SCOUT ELITE $0

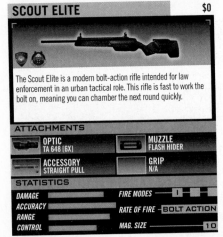

The Scout Elite is a modern bolt-action rifle intended for law enforcement in an urban tactical role. This rifle is fast to work the bolt on, meaning you can chamber the next round quickly.

ATTACHMENTS

OPTIC TA 648 (6X)		MUZZLE FLASH HIDER	
ACCESSORY STRAIGHT PULL		GRIP N/A	

STATISTICS

DAMAGE	FIRE MODES	I
ACCURACY		
RANGE	RATE OF FIRE	BOLT ACTION
CONTROL	MAG. SIZE	10

The bolt-action sniper rifles offered by this kit require the greatest amount of skill and patience of any weapon type, best reserved for players willing to put in the practice to master them. Unless you score headshots every time, it takes at least two hits to down an opponent with these powerful weapons. To increase stability while peering through a high-powered scope, hold your breath. This makes it much easier to steady your aim before squeezing the trigger.

R700 LTR $48,000

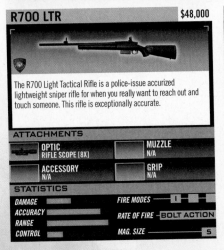

The R700 Light Tactical Rifle is a police-issue accurized lightweight sniper rifle for when you really want to reach out and touch someone. This rifle is exceptionally accurate.

ATTACHMENTS

OPTIC RIFLE SCOPE (8X)		MUZZLE N/A	
ACCESSORY N/A		GRIP N/A	

STATISTICS

DAMAGE	FIRE MODES	I
ACCURACY		
RANGE	RATE OF FIRE	BOLT ACTION
CONTROL	MAG. SIZE	5

AWM $51,000

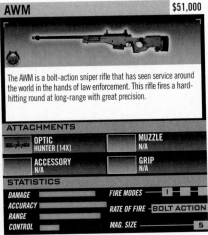

The AWM is a bolt-action sniper rifle that has seen service around the world in the hands of law enforcement. This rifle fires a hard-hitting round at long-range with great precision.

ATTACHMENTS

OPTIC HUNTER (14X)		MUZZLE N/A	
ACCESSORY N/A		GRIP N/A	

STATISTICS

DAMAGE	FIRE MODES	I
ACCURACY		
RANGE	RATE OF FIRE	BOLT ACTION
CONTROL	MAG. SIZE	5

.300 KNOCKOUT
OPERATOR ASSIGNMENT 2

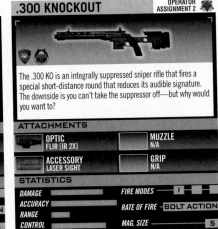

The .300 KO is an integrally suppressed sniper rifle that fires a special short-distance round that reduces its audible signature. The downside is you can't take the suppressor off—but why would you want to?

ATTACHMENTS

OPTIC FLIR (IR 2X)		MUZZLE N/A	
ACCESSORY LASER SIGHT		GRIP N/A	

STATISTICS

DAMAGE	FIRE MODES	I
ACCURACY		
RANGE	RATE OF FIRE	BOLT ACTION
CONTROL	MAG. SIZE	5

SEMI-AUTO RIFLES

Also known as Designated Marksman Rifles (DMRs), these rifles bridge the gap between assault rifles and sniper rifles, offering impressive stopping power while maintaining respectable rates of fire and reload times. These rifles are best deployed when engaging targets at intermediate to long ranges in situations when a higher rate of fire is more important than precision and damage. Their size makes these rifles somewhat cumbersome when operating in close quarters, so consider switching to a sidearm when entering structures and other confined spaces.

> The SOCOM 16 for the police and the PTR-91 for the criminals are very effective guns at almost any range. I like using the ACOG 4x for this gun, and on bigger maps, the TA 648 scope works perfect. The extended magazine allows you to stay in one area longer unless teaming up with a an enforcer teammate who supplies ammo. In which case, laser light is a better choice. A heavy barrel and the stubby grip are good choices as well.
> —Diego Teran, Quality Analyst

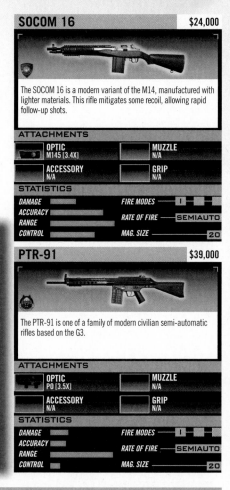

SOCOM 16 — $24,000

The SOCOM 16 is a modern variant of the M14, manufactured with lighter materials. This rifle mitigates some recoil, allowing rapid follow-up shots.

ATTACHMENTS

OPTIC M145 [3.4X]	MUZZLE N/A	
ACCESSORY N/A	GRIP N/A	

STATISTICS

DAMAGE	FIRE MODES I
ACCURACY	RATE OF FIRE SEMIAUTO
RANGE	
CONTROL	MAG. SIZE 20

SR-25 ECC — $40,200

The SR-25 Enhanced Combat Carbine is based on the AR-10 design, with a monolithic top rail. Lower recoil and semi-automatic operation allows for rapid shooting.

ATTACHMENTS

OPTIC ACOG [4X]	MUZZLE N/A	
ACCESSORY N/A	GRIP N/A	

STATISTICS

DAMAGE	FIRE MODES I
ACCURACY	RATE OF FIRE SEMIAUTO
RANGE	
CONTROL	MAG. SIZE 20

PTR-91 — $39,000

The PTR-91 is one of a family of modern civilian semi-automatic rifles based on the G3.

ATTACHMENTS

OPTIC PO [3.5X]	MUZZLE N/A	
ACCESSORY N/A	GRIP N/A	

STATISTICS

DAMAGE	FIRE MODES I
ACCURACY	RATE OF FIRE SEMIAUTO
RANGE	
CONTROL	MAG. SIZE 20

SAIGA .308 — $22,800

The Saiga family of semi-automatic rifles are a sport version of the AK-series rifles, intended for hunting and civilian use. This rifle mitigates some of the recoil, allowing for faster follow-up shots.

ATTACHMENTS

OPTIC PSO-1 [4X]	MUZZLE N/A	
ACCESSORY N/A	GRIP N/A	

STATISTICS

DAMAGE	FIRE MODES I
ACCURACY	RATE OF FIRE SEMIAUTO
RANGE	
CONTROL	MAG. SIZE 20

MACHINE PISTOLS

> Don't underestimate sidearms. The movement speed bonus can tip the odds your favor over even the strongest primary weapons. Try the professional with the MAC-10 in close quarters, the 93R at mid-range, and TEC-9 at long range, all while running Stealth Training to move with silent expertise. Your enemies won't know what hit them.
> —William Bordonaro, Quality Analyst

The professional's lack of close-quarter capability is addressed by these fully automatic and burst-fire machine pistols. Little more than standard handguns, these compact weapons are capable of spitting out rounds at a rapid pace. While the rates of fire are impressive, the harsh recoil makes it difficult to keep these weapons on-target. So unless you're engaging opponents at pointblank range, fire in quick bursts to manage muzzle climb. These weapons also have a tendency to burn through ammo fast, so keep them fully loaded at all times.

G18C — $0

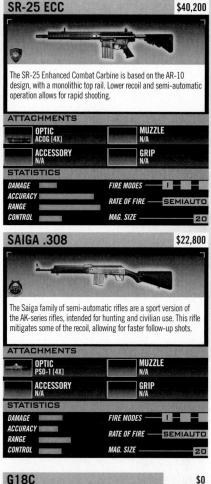

The G18C is a full-automatic pistol with a high rate of fire. It is difficult to control due to significant muzzle climb, but it spits out a lot of rounds.

ATTACHMENTS

OPTIC IRON SIGHTS	MUZZLE N/A	
ACCESSORY LASER SIGHT	GRIP N/A	

STATISTICS

DAMAGE	FIRE MODES I III
ACCURACY	RATE OF FIRE 900
RANGE	
CONTROL	MAG. SIZE 16

93R — $10,800

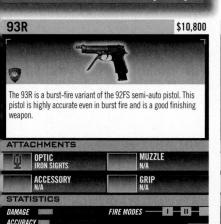

The 93R is a burst-fire variant of the 92FS semi-auto pistol. This pistol is highly accurate even in burst fire and is a good finishing weapon.

ATTACHMENTS

OPTIC IRON SIGHTS	MUZZLE N/A	
ACCESSORY N/A	GRIP N/A	

STATISTICS

DAMAGE	FIRE MODES I II
ACCURACY	RATE OF FIRE 900
RANGE	
CONTROL	MAG. SIZE 20

TEC-9 — $19,200

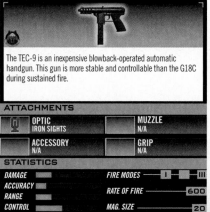

The TEC-9 is an inexpensive blowback-operated automatic handgun. This gun is more stable and controllable than the G18C during sustained fire.

ATTACHMENTS

OPTIC IRON SIGHTS	MUZZLE N/A	
ACCESSORY N/A	GRIP N/A	

STATISTICS

DAMAGE	FIRE MODES I III
ACCURACY	RATE OF FIRE 600
RANGE	
CONTROL	MAG. SIZE 20

MAC-10 — PROFESSIONAL ASSIGNMENT 2

The MAC-10 fires a .45 caliber round at a high cyclic rate. The high damage comes with short range and serious recoil to manage.

ATTACHMENTS

OPTIC IRON SIGHTS	MUZZLE SUPPRESSOR	
ACCESSORY STOCK	GRIP N/A	

STATISTICS

DAMAGE	FIRE MODES I II III
ACCURACY	RATE OF FIRE 1145
RANGE	
CONTROL	MAG. SIZE 15

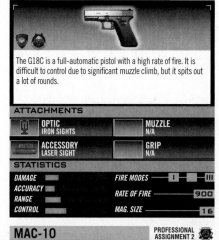

PROFESSIONAL GADGETS

LASER TRIPMINE $0

Explosive mine that detonates when the laser tripline is broken. Can be placed on any available surface in arm's reach. Can be disarmed by agents that spot it in time.

FIELD NOTES

These nasty little devices perform similar to claymores and are designed primarily as an anti-personnel mine. But in the right situation, they can also damage vehicles. These gadgets can be stuck to vertical or horizontal surfaces, after which they emit a visible green laser beam—enemy lasers appear as red. This beam extends approximately two meters from the gadget. If an opponent moves through this visible beam, the mine explodes. Unless you're playing on Hardcore mode, teammates do not trigger this device. These gadgets are best placed in tight quarters where opponents are less likely to notice the laser beam, such as around blind corners or in doorways. To limit the visibility of the laser, place these devices low, near the ground, below an opponent's line of sight. You can place up to two of these devices, but more can be retrieved from an enforcer's ammo box. If you spot an enemy laser tripmine, shoot it or use a grenade to detonate it.

> Keep your eye out for the red lasers of a trip mine! if you spot one before it's too late, it's easier to take it out with one well-placed shot from a pistol rather than an automatic weapon.
> —Ethan Solak, Video Editor

CAMERA $6,000

Camera which detects and reports enemy movement in a wide cone in front of the device. Don't underestimate the power of intel.

FIELD NOTES

These small, dome-shaped cameras can be stuck to any vertical surface and immediately report enemy movement within its 180-degree field of view. Enemy contacts appear as red triangles shown on each teammate's minimap. It's important to note that these cameras only detect movement. If an enemy is standing directly in front of a camera, and remains motionless, they are not shown on your minimap. But standing still is rarely an option in *Hardline*, so don't let this minor limitation dissuade you from purchasing this handy gadget. You can place up to two cameras at a time. But once placed, they can be retrieved and redeployed in new locations. Since the intel relayed by these cameras benefits your entire team, consider making the camera an early purchase for your professional. These devices prove invaluable during Crosshair and Rescue matches.

DECOY $25,800

Decoy noisemaker that projects fake player contacts on enemy radar and generates fake weapon sounds.

FIELD NOTES

The decoy is one of the most unique gadgets available, useful for luring opponents into ambushes. This device is essentially a small loudspeaker, emitting a loop of gunfire sounds. This generates phony contacts on the opposing team's minimap, potentially drawing them toward the decoy. You can use this to lure enemies into traps or to simply divert their attention away from more critical areas. You can only deploy one decoy at a time, but it can be retrieved and redeployed in new location—they can also be destroyed by enemies.

STEALTH TRAINING $48,000

Agents with stealth training have learned to move quietly. Footstep sounds are reduced, and actions like opening doors are quieter as well.

FIELD NOTES

By donning this hood, your professional gains a ninja-like appearance and demeanor, silently traversing the map while emitting little sound. Aside from the elite aesthetics of the hood, the benefits of this gadget are very subtle. But in modes like Rescue and Crosshair where the player counts are low and sound is very important, this gadget may just give you the edge necessary to flank your opponents or sneak past unnoticed. This is particularly beneficial when approaching enemies from behind for knife kills or non-lethal takedowns.

PROFESSIONAL TACTICS

☆ The professional works best at a distance. Use long-range sniper rifles to keep distance between you and your enemy, rendering their weapons nearly useless. However, it is best to stay hidden whenever you're not going for a kill shot because being spotted quickly draws a lot of attention to your position.

☆ Set up laser tripmines low on doorways, keeping them out of the direct line of sight from enemy foot-mobiles. If the enemy can't see it right away, there is a good chance they will trigger it, granting you an effortless kill and protecting your six.

☆ Stealth training is great on Rescue and Crosshair because opening doors and sprinting is incredibly loud and revealing when the enemy team is expecting you. Staying hidden is incredibly important but so is moving quickly. Being able to do both with a single gadget gives you a great advantage.

☆ Use the decoy to draw the attention of the enemy. This can be used as both a distraction or a deterrent. Deter the enemy from the VIP at an extraction that is not defended, or draw shooters to a location, luring them directly into your sights.

☆ Listen to your character's voice as he calls out when your camera spots an enemy. If you are able to sneak up to a key location to set up a camera, you can spot enemies that may be hiding out of your line of sight, behind cover. This gives you another set of eyes, allowing you to see things when no one else can.

☆ Because close-ranged combat is difficult with a sniper rifle, keep some distance between yourself and the enemy's objective, killing them before they know where you are.

WEAPON CUSTOMIZATION

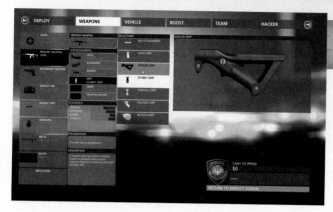

Study the weapon's stat bars on the right as you select different attachments to understand how each one affects performance

All primary and secondary weapons can be customized by adding a variety of attachments, improving their performance in specific ways. Attachments can be purchased from the loadout screen, but they're not available immediately. Each attachment has a kill threshold which must be met with the weapon you wish to modify. For example, before you can purchase the angle grip for the RO933 carbine, you must first score 90 kills with that weapon. The kill threshold for each attachment differs for each weapon. But you can purchase all attachments for a weapon by the time you've scored 100 kills with it.

To apply a new attachment, start by entering the loadout screen and selecting the owned weapon you wish to modify. Now choose what type of attachment you wish to add. There are four attachment categories: optics, accessories, muzzles, and grips. When you've selected an attachment category, you can now purchase the available attachments for the selected weapon. Some attachments may be locked, requiring you to score a specific number of kills with the weapon. But if the kill threshold has been met, you can purchase the attachment and add it to your weapon. Attachments cannot be shared across multiple weapons. For example, if you really like the compensator muzzle attachment, you need to buy it separately for each weapon. Before making your purchase, study the following tables to find the most beneficial attachments for your weapons, taking into account your style of play.

OPTICS

The optics in *Hardline* are divided into three major categories: close-range, medium-range, and long-range. Most firefights occur within 30 meters, making close-range optics more than adequate. When operating in large environments you may want to opt for greater magnification. The medium-range optics offer 3-4X magnification, ideal for intermediate-range engagements of 50-100 meters. The long-range optics are exclusive to the professional's bolt-action and semi-auto sniper rifles and benefit from 6-14X magnification. Equip these high-powered optics when engaging targets beyond 100 meters. Handguns have their own optics which function like miniaturized versions of the close-range red dot sights.

OPTICS

CLOSE RANGE

OPTIC	NAME	COST	DESCRIPTION
	Reflex (RDS)	$1,500	Red dot sight with a bright aiming point and clear sight picture for rapid target acquisition and tracking.
	Kobra (RDS)	$2,700	Russian reflex sight with a T bar reticle designed for CQB that keeps the point of aim clear.
	HOLO (1X)	$3,000	A holographic open sight for up to mid-range engagements. The reticle features a .65 MOA ring with a 1 MOA dot.
	Comp M45 (RDS)	$1,800	A modern close combat optic, the Comp M4S has a battery compartment located low on one side to power the red dot reticle.
	Micro T1 (RDS)	$3,000	A lightweight rugged red dot sight, the Micro T1 is a great choice for a short-range optic.
	SRS 02 (GDS)	$2,400	The SRS02 is a sealed reflex sight that takes up little rail space and has a green 1.75 MOA dot for aiming.
	PK-AS (1X)	$3,300	Russian unmagnified holographic sight with excellent light gathering capabilities and a clear field of view.
	IRNV (IR 1X)	$9,000	Infrared night vision scope that makes heat signatures visible in low light. Vulnerable to blinding effects.
	FLIR (IR 1X)	$16,800	Thermal sights with white hot on cold black view mode and 2X magnification. Very vulnerable to blinding effects.

MEDIUM RANGE

OPTIC	NAME	COST	DESCRIPTION
	M145 (3.4X)	$9,600	Fixed-power 3.4x Machine Gun Optic designed for medium- to long-range engagements.
	Prisma (3.4X)	$3,000	3.4x magnification with a cross and dot reticle. Best used in mid- to long-range fights.
	PO (3.5X)	$2,100	3.5x scope with a circle-and-dot reticle designed for medium- to long-range engagements.
	ACOG (4X)	$7,800	Fixed-power 4x Advanced Combat Optic Gunsight for use in bright to low light at medium-range.
	PSO-1 (4X)	$1,500	Fixed-power 4x Russian-made medium-range scope.

LONG RANGE

OPTIC	NAME	COST	DESCRIPTION
	TA 648 (6X)	$6,000	A 6x magnification self-luminous tactical rifle sight with ballistic drop compensator incorporated in the reticle.
	PKS-07 (7X)	$3,000	7x magnification Russian marksman daylight scope for engaging targets over long distances.
	Rifle Scope (8X)	$10,800	US-made 8x magnification rifle scope with ballistic drop compensator to aid in long range fire.
	Hunter (14X)	$1,200	High magnification 14x scope for accurate shooting in long range situations.

HANDGUNS

OPTIC	NAME	COST	DESCRIPTION
	Improved Iron Sights	$600	Replaces the standard iron sights with a set of rapid acquisition Improved Iron Sights for a clear sight picture.
	Mini (RDS)	$1,500	The Ruggedized Miniature Reflex sight is designed to be mounted on pistols. Allows for fast target acquisition and easy tracking.
	Delta (RDS)	$1,050	Compact 3.5 MOA red dot sight for handguns featuring a triangular reticle.

ACCESSORIES

These weapon attachments offer some helpful tactical enhancements. The canted iron sights and RDS are great additions to your weapon when using a medium- or long-range optic, offering secondary sight/optic with no magnification, ideal for close-range. The flash light and tactical lights come in handy in low-light environments, temporarily blinding your opponents. The laser sight gives your weapon better hip fire accuracy, allowing for tighter shot groups in close quarters. Some weapons aren't equipped with a stock by default, so consider adding one to increase control. If you're carrying a bolt-action sniper rifle, consider using the straight pull to stay on-target (zoomed in) while operating the bolt and chambering a new round. But the extended magazine remains the most popular accessory in this category, increasing the magazine capacity of your weapon. This varies from weapon to weapon.

ACCESSORY	NAME	COST	DESCRIPTION
	Canted Iron Sights	$600	Iron sights canted at a 45 degree angle for close-range target acquisition, even when equipped with a magnified scope.
	Canted RDS	$600	Mini red dot sight canted at a 45 degree angle for close-range target acquisition, even when equipped with a magnified scope.
	Extended Magazine	$6,000	Magazine with additional rounds for less frequent reloading. Adds a slight penalty to maneuverability.
	Flash Light	$1,200	Lights up dark corners. Especially blinding against IRNV and FLIR optics. Be careful as it can give your position away.
	Tactical Light	$1,500	Light automatically activated when you aim your weapon. Especially blinding against IRNV and FLIR optics. Can be toggled off for stealth.
	Laser Sight	$1,800	Bright red laser sight improves unaimed fire, making shots more predictable.
	Stock	$6,000	Adding a stock increases weapon control during rapid fire.
	Straight Pull	$4,800	Allows the shooter to stay in scope view when rechambering, allowing for better target following and shot observation.
	.338 Magnum	$100,000	Special .338 caliber Magnum ammunition. Increases effective range and damage against vehicles.

MUZZLES

By adding these attachments to your weapon's barrel, you can make slight adjustments in ballistic performance. Muzzle brakes and compensators are great for dampening a weapon's recoil. If you seek greater accuracy, attach a heavy barrel. Flash hiders reduce muzzle flash, making it easier to go unnoticed. The suppressors keep you off the minimap, but they also reduce a weapon's damage and range. The shotgun chokes modify the shot spread, improving their accuracy and lethality at range.

MUZZLE	NAME	COST	DESCRIPTION
	Muzzle Brake	$1,200	Reduces felt recoil, making the weapon more controllable in rapid fire.
	Compensator	$900	Reduces vertical recoil by venting muzzle gasses upwards, improving control at a cost to accuracy.
	Flash Hider	$600	Reduces or eliminates muzzle flash, making it easier to see the target and harder for enemies to observe the shot origin.
	Heavy Barrel	$3,300	Free floating heavy barrel improves aimed fire accuracy and slightly decreases recoil, but decreases maneuverability.
	Suppressor	$5,400	Sound suppressor that decreases the audibility of muzzle reports and does not show your position on the minimap. Also reduces bullet velocity and increases bullet drop.
	Full Choke	$3,900	Significantly tightens shotgun spread for improved accuracy, but has penalties for control and unaimed fire.
	Modified Choke	$4,200	Moderately tightens shotgun spread for improved accuracy, but has penalties for control and unaimed fire.

GRIPS

Some weapons can be equipped with foregrips, adding better control. The angled foregrip is best equipped on battle rifles. This reduces the recoil of the first shot, making follow-up shots much more accurate. The stubby grip works well on a variety of automatic weapons, making auto fire more accurate. Or attach the vertical grip, allowing for better control while moving and firing from the hip. This works well on carbines and SMGs when operating in close quarter environments.

GRIP	NAME	COST	DESCRIPTION
➤ ➤	Angled Grip	$3,000	Angled foregrip that positions the shooter's off-hand high on the centerline of the bore. Improves control by reducing first shot recoil.
▮ ▮	Stubby Grip	$1,200	The reduced length of this foregrip makes for a lightweight and strong point of control. Improves accuracy by reducing the rapid fire penalty and slightly increases maneuverability.
▮▮▮	Vertical Grip	$4,200	Vertical foregrip that provides greater stability when firing your weapon while moving. Also makes the weapon slightly more stable in unaimed fire.

SPECIAL WEAPONS

Instead of carrying a handgun as a sidearm, all classes can opt to equip one of these special weapons. These non-lethal weapons are available to all classes and factions, providing unique ways to neutralize and track the enemy.

T62 CEW — $21,000

The T62 CEW has short-range non-lethal takedown capability. Interrogate a stunned opponent to find out where his nearby teammates are.

FIELD NOTES

This is essentially a stun gun which fires two small metal darts into the target. The darts are tethered to the weapon via wires, allowing them to deliver an incapacitating jolt of electricity. Once a target has dropped to the ground, interact with their body to perform an interrogation. This reveals the locations of the target's teammates on the minimap for a limited time, giving your team a brief but significant advantage. But the T62 CEW is not a long-range weapon. For best results, use it when approaching opponents from behind and close within five meters before firing. Holster the weapon during firefights; you don't want to get into a gun fight with this weapon. The weapon comes equipped with 11 darts. More can be retrieved from an enforcer's ammo box.

TRACKING DART — $16,200

Fire and attach the tracking dart to enemy players and vehicles, spotting them in-world and on your minimap. This allows rockets to lock on to the target.

FIELD NOTES

A popular weapon from *Bad Company 2,* the tracking dart has made its return, offering a unique way to tag and track enemy targets. This is an air pistol loaded with tracking darts. When an enemy is tagged with one of these darts, they're immediately highlighted on the HUD, appearing as a red silhouette visible to your entire team, even when they're hiding behind cover. Their location is also permanently marked on the minimap. Tracking darts work equally well against infantry and vehicles. The dart inflicts minimal damage when striking opponents, but it's unlikely to be fatal unless the target has already suffered severe damage. The tracking dart is most effective against speeding vehicles as the darts allow rockets to home-in on the target. This works with the RPG and SMAW Battle Pickups, but not the Stinger. When you have one of these rocket launchers, aim toward the marked target to achieve a lock before firing. The rocket zooms-off toward the target, automatically making in-flight adjustments to zero-in on the tagged vehicle. This is a very effective and rewarding way to take down pesky enemy helicopters. The weapon is equipped with 11 darts, but you can retrieve more from ammo boxes.

SYNDICATE WEAPONS

OPERATOR: ARM ASSAULT RIFLE

MECHANIC: FMG9 SUBMACHINE GUN

ENFORCER: DOUBLE-BARREL SHOTGUN

PROFESSIONAL: .300 KNOCKOUT

Each class has one Syndicate weapon which cannot be purchased. Instead, these weapons must be unlocked. The criteria for unlocking each syndicate weapon remains a mystery. The developers want the *Battlefield* community to figure this out on their own. But if you keep playing the associated class, there's a good chance you'll unlock the Syndicate weapon! For starters, focus on completing the class-based assignments.

UNIVERSAL GADGETS

These gadgets are available to all classes and factions. You only need to purchase these gadgets once to make them available to all of your loadouts. It's a good idea to purchase these gadgets early so you can equip them across all classes.

GAS MASK	$4,800

The gas mask negates the effects of the gas grenade, and also blocks the effects of some environmental hazards.

FIELD NOTES

Given the popularity of gas grenades, particularly during Heist and Rescue, consider making the gas mask an early purchase. When worn, visibility through the mask is surprisingly good, with only some slight dark edges in the four corners of the HUD. The mask also has a darkened greenish tint, but you're unlikely to be blindsided due to these minor limitations. Needless to say, you should always wear one of these masks when carrying gas grenades. This allows you to enter gas-filled rooms and engage opponents while their vision is blurred and their health is low. The police and criminals use slightly different masks, but their performance is identical.

GRAPPLING HOOK	$9,600

Firing the grappling hook at a flat ledge creates a climbable grapple rope up to the top of the ledge. Ropes can be cut or shot to be destroyed.

FIELD NOTES

Grappling hooks offer a fast way to reach rooftops and other hard-to-reach locations. Although grappling hooks are available as Battle Pickups, it's never a bad idea to have one of your own so you don't have to scrounge around maps looking for one. When equipped, this gadget functions similar to a firearm. Take aim through the gadget's simple optical sight and point it toward a ledge. The optic has a reticle as well as rangefinder, showing the distance to the target. The grappling hook has a maximum range of 75 meters. When you target a suitable ledge, the reticle turns into a white bracket with a dot in the center. You can only fire the grappling hook when this reticle appears. Firing the device extends a rope from the ledge to the ground. Climb the rope as you would any ladder. But you're extremely vulnerable while climbing, so make sure the area is secure before interacting with the rope. The gadget comes equipped with four grappling hooks. But you can pick up lines by interacting with a deployed grappling hook, replenishing the gadget's ammo, and preventing opponents from using your ropes. More grappling hooks can also be retrieved from an enforcer's ammo box.

ZIPLINE	$13,200

The zipline creates a wire stretched between two points. Jump onto the zipline at any point to travel rapidly downwards. Disable enemy ziplines by severing the wire or taking out the supports.

FIELD NOTES

Ziplines are one of the fastest ways to move around a map, ideal for staging sneak attacks or making quick getaways. This crossbow-like gadget functions similar to the grappling hook. Aim through the crossbow's optic to find a suitable object to fire the wire into. The wire must be fired into an object at a lower elevation than your current position. When the reticle turns to a white dot surrounded by brackets, you can fire the wire. As the wire makes contact with your target, a metal support structure appears nearby. Interact with this support to zip down the wire. Alternately, you can jump up to grab the wire to begin your descent. The gadget comes equipped with four wires, but you can retrieve wires by interacting with the base of each support structure, or by adding ammo back to the gadget with ammo boxes. The zipline has a maximum range of 150 meters, allowing you to cover great distances in a matter of seconds. Look for opportunities to extend multiple ziplines across a map, moving from one rooftop to the next. Pay close attention to the angle of your wire. While shallow angles are acceptable, you move slower, making you an easier target for opponents. Steeper angles allow you to traverse the wire at high speeds.

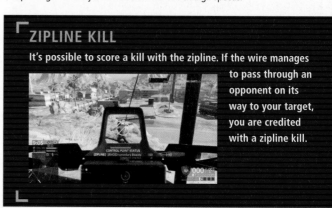

ZIPLINE KILL

It's possible to score a kill with the zipline. If the wire manages to pass through an opponent on its way to your target, you are credited with a zipline kill.

If you or a teammate have used the grappling hook to quickly get to a better vantage point, remember to crouch down next to the cable after everyone has finished climbing, then interact to pick up the hook. This helps cover your tracks so an enemy can't see that you've used it and where you went. You can use the grappling hook or a zipline as a decoy. Shoot the grappling hook to a higher level or the zipline to a lower level. Rather than using the hook or line, just hide somewhere nearby. As an Enemy investigates or begins climbing the grappling hook's line (or sliding on the zipline), engage in a surprise attack. Keep an eye out for any placed grappling hooks and ziplines. This may indicate where an enemy has recently traveled.
—Ethan Solak, Video Editor

STUNT DRIVER	$39,000

Stunt Driver equips any ground vehicle with a nitrous oxide boost, allowing the driver to accelerate quickly out of danger. In addition, drivers trained as stunt drivers take less damage when colliding with other vehicles or road hazards.

FIELD NOTES

If you spend a significant amount of time behind the wheel of cars and other ground vehicles, particularly during Hotwire, you should strongly consider purchasing the stunt driver gadget. It's not cheap, but when equipped, your vehicle is much faster and more durable. To initiate the gadget's nitrous oxide boost, hold down the sprint button/key and watch as flames spew from the vehicle's exhaust. Not only does this look cool, but the increased acceleration and speed is ideal for getting away from opponents or staging epic jumps. Launch nitrous-infused motorcycles off ramps to score some impressive jump bonuses. But use the nitrous sparingly, always when traveling along straight roads. Disengage it when attempting to make tight turns. There is no limit to how much nitrous you can use, so keep it active as long as you'd like. In addition to offering a nice speed boost, this gadget also reinforces your vehicle's chassis, reducing the amount of damage it takes from collisions. Collisions are common in Hotwire, so some additional durability is always welcome.

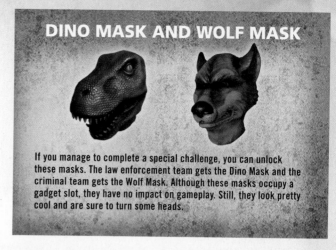

DINO MASK AND WOLF MASK

If you manage to complete a special challenge, you can unlock these masks. The law enforcement team gets the Dino Mask and the criminal team gets the Wolf Mask. Although these masks occupy a gadget slot, they have no impact on gameplay. Still, they look pretty cool and are sure to turn some heads.

LINE UP YOUR JUMP

Motorcycles cannot steer when the stunt driver's nitrous oxide is active. So line up those jumps before triggering the nitrous boost.

GRENADES

In *Hardline* there are several types of hand-thrown grenades available while customizing your character's loadout. By default, all classes begin with the M67 Frag grenade. But you can purchase more grenades from the loadout screen. Purchased grenades are shared across classes and factions. You only need to buy them once.

M67 FRAG — $0

High-explosive fragmentation grenade with a medium blast radius. Deals significant damage to infantry and vehicles.

FIELD NOTES

The M67 Frag is a standard-issue fragmentation grenade, available to all classes at the start of your multiplayer career. The M67 is most effective against infantry, but they can also inflict minor damage against light-skinned vehicles—just don't try taking out a counter attack truck with them. The M67 doesn't explode on impact. Instead, they tend to roll around until the timed fuse triggers the explosion. So keep this in mind when tossing an M67. They will bounce off surfaces and roll down slopes. Make a habit of tossing this grenade in buildings prior to entering, especially if you suspect an enemy presence. By default, you can only carry one of these grenades.

M18 SMOKE — $3,000

A timed fuse hand grenade that emits a concealing cloud of smoke. Smoke blocks spotting.

FIELD NOTES

Smoke screens created by these grenades are ideal for concealing squad movements when there is a lack of cover. Smoke is extremely helpful in high-traffic areas, obscuring the vision of your opponents. Or use smoke offensively to disorient opponents while picking them off through IRNV and thermal optics. You can only carry one smoke grenade, so make sure you deploy it in a good spot. The grenade disperses a large cloud of smoke which remains in-place for approximately 20 seconds.

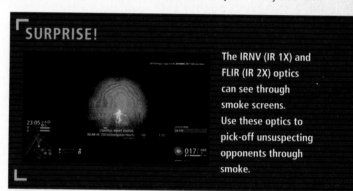

SURPRISE!

The IRNV (IR 1X) and FLIR (IR 2X) optics can see through smoke screens. Use these optics to pick-off unsuspecting opponents through smoke.

M84 FLASHBANG — $4,200

A timed fuse hand grenade that emits a concealing cloud of smoke. Smoke blocks spotting.

FIELD NOTES

The M84 Flashbang is a popular tactical aid deployed by SWAT and hostage rescue teams, serving as a deterrent while clearing rooms and performing dynamic entries in close quarter environments. In some respects, the flashbang is more effective than its more lethal counterparts, blinding opponents for approximately three seconds, leaving them vulnerable. The duration an opponent is blinded varies depending on their proximity to the device when it detonates. The direction an opponent is facing is also significant. If an opponent's back is turned, they aren't blinded as long. Toss flashbangs into rooms occupied by opponents just prior to rushing in and mowing down the opposition. This is an easy (but somewhat cheap) way to score knife kills too. By default, you can carry two flashbangs.

GAS GRENADE $4,800

Timed fuse grenades that emit a cloud of riot-control tear gas. Those affected by the gas suffer blurred vision, making it impossible to aim accurately, and are more susceptible to damage.

FIELD NOTES

New to *Hardline*, the gas grenade emits a faint, green cloud of tear gas, immediately blurring the vision of all within its wide radius. Prolonged exposure to gas also eats away at a player's health, including yours. When an opponent walks through a cloud of your gas, you see hit markers on the HUD, indicating an enemy is taking damage. Use this indicator as an early warning of an enemy's presence. You're equipped with a total of three gas grenades, allowing you to saturate wide areas (or multiple rooms) with gas. The gas lingers for approximately 30 seconds and has an effective radius of about 10 meters. The effects of gas can be completely negated by equipping the gas mask gadget which we recommend whenever you're carrying these grenades.

CAUTION

Be careful when deploying gas grenades around teammates who aren't equipped with gas masks. Gas injures teammates and can potentially kill them, penalizing you with a teamkill.

INCENDIARY DEVICE $6,600

Incendiary hand grenade which creates a pool of fire that can be used to temporarily block routes or flush enemies out of cover.

FIELD NOTES

Available exclusively to the police, these nasty grenades create a large fire, injuring (and potentially killing) anyone unlucky enough to be caught within its wide and persistent blast radius. During combat, the incendiary device is best deployed in tight choke points such as hallways, doorways, and stairwells, effectively halting the advance of opponents. The fire caused by the device keeps burning for approximately 10 seconds. Don't expect to score many kills with this device, as victims can often step outside its blast radius before suffering lethal injuries. Instead, use it primarily as a deterrent when defending choke points. You can carry a total of two incendiary devices. But think twice about running through the fire caused by these devices. Even when sprinting you can expect to lose more than 50% of your health. Purchasing the incendiary device for the police automatically unlocks the Molotov cocktail for the criminals.

MOLOTOV COCKTAIL $6,600

A breakable glass bottle containing a flammable substance such as gasoline, the Molotov cocktail is an impressive incendiary weapon. They are intended primarily to deny routes of access to opponents, rather than instantly destroy targets.

FIELD NOTES

This crude, yet effective grenade is the criminal team's answer to the incendiary device, and it functions in an identical fashion. Throw these grenades in tight quarters where opponents have a difficult time escaping the flames. Or when making an escape with loot, toss these behind you, preventing police from pursuing. Like the incendiary device, you're equipped with two Molotov cocktails. So consider purchasing these early to replace your M67 frag grenades. They're not as lethal, but they're much more effective when it comes to controlling foot traffic in tight quarters. Purchasing the Molotov cocktail automatically unlocks the incendiary device for law enforcement.

MELEE WEAPONS

If you've managed to sneak up on an opponent, instead of shooting them, consider performing a melee strike for a non-lethal takedown or an instant kill. Avoid using melee weapons during face-to-face confrontations as you're likely to get shot in the face as you swing your weapon like a crazed madman. It takes two hits from your melee weapon to take out an opponent with a frontal attack. But it's faster and safer to attack from behind. There are two categories of melee weapons in *Hardline*: blunt and sharp.

READY FOR ACTION

You can run faster while having a melee weapon (or secondary weapon) equipped.

BLUNT WEAPONS

By default, all players are equipped with a blunt weapon, carrying the police baton for law enforcement or baseball bat for the criminals. When attacking an opponent from behind, the blunt weapons allow for a non-lethal takedown. Your incapacitated opponent can then be interrogated, revealing the locations of their teammates on the minimap. More blunt weapons can be purchased, unlocked in Battlepacks, or earned by completing assignments. Although they look slightly different and have unique animations, all blunt weapons function the same way.

WEAPON	NAME	FACTION	COST/UNLOCK
	Police Baton	Law Enforcement	—
	Baseball Bat	Criminals	—
	Blackjack	Both	Battlepack Item
	Breaching Hammer	Law Enforcement	$1,000
	Collapsible Baton	Law Enforcement	$1,000
	Nightstick	Law Enforcement	Battlepack Item
	Gold Hammer	Law Enforcement	Complete Ground Vehicle Syndicate
	Gold Baton	Law Enforcement	Complete Air Vehicle Syndicate

WEAPON	NAME	FACTION	COST/UNLOCK
	Crowbar	Criminals	Battlepack Item
	Golf Club	Criminals	Battlepack Item
	Lead Pipe	Criminals	Battlepack Item
	Sledge Hammer	Criminals	$1,000
	Gold Golf Club	Criminals	Complete Black Hat Syndicate
	Gold Lead Pipe	Criminals	Complete Gun Syndicate
	Gold Sledge Hammer	Criminals	Complete Elite Player Syndicate
	Gold Crowbar	Criminals	Complete Water Vehicle Syndicate

SHARP WEAPONS

If you're not interested in interrogating your opponent, move in for the kill using a sharp weapon. These are mostly knives and bladed weapons designed for stabbing and slicing. Performing a melee strike from behind while using one of these weapons results in an instant kill. If performing a frontal attack, it can take up to two strikes to kill. And unlike *Battlefield 4*, there is no way to counter a frontal attack. With the exception of the criminal team's machete, there are no sharp weapons available for purchase. Instead, they must be retrieved from Battlepacks or earned by completing assignments.

WEAPON	NAME	FACTION	COST/UNLOCK
	Knife	Both	Battlepack Item
	Boot	Both	Battlepack Item
	Bowie	Both	Battlepack Item
	Carbon Fiber	Both	Battlepack Item
	Scout	Both	Battlepack Item
	Survival	Both	Battlepack Item
	Trench	Both	Battlepack Item
	ACB-90	Criminals	Battlepack Item
	Machete	Criminals	$1,000

WEAPON	NAME	FACTION	COST/UNLOCK
	Shank	Criminals	Battlepack Item
	Gold Knife	Both	Complete Gray Hat Syndicate
	Gold Boot	Both	Complete White Hat Syndicate
	Gold Scout	Both	Complete Game Mode Syndicate
	Gold Seal	Both	Complete Close Range Syndicate
	Gold Survival	Both	Complete Criminal Syndicate
	Gold Trench	Both	Complete Justice Syndicate
	Gold Machete	Criminals	Complete Progression Syndicate

BATTLE PICKUPS

Battle Pickups are unique weapons and gadgets found scattered about the battlefield. Battle Pickups are marked on the HUD and minimap with white icons. Interact with a Battle Pickup to retrieve it from the ground and then operate it like any other weapon or gadget. Battle Pickups are not part of your standard inventory. If you switch to a primary or secondary weapon, the Battle Pickup is dropped on the ground. You can always retrieve the Battle Pickup from the ground, so remember where you dropped it.

PICKUP	NAME	AMMO	DESCRIPTION
	M240B	200	The M240B is a belt-fed light machine gun equipped with two 100-round belts, a HOLO (1X) optic and a flash hider. The weapon hits hard, but exhibits harsh recoil. Fire in short bursts to keep the weapon on-target.
	MG36	200	The MG 36 light machine gun comes equipped with two 100-round drum magazines, a Comp M45 (RDS) optic, and a laser sight. The weapon performs much like an assault rifle, with less recoil (and damage output) than the larger M240B.
	RPG-7V2	2	This rocket launcher comes with two high-explosive rockets ideal for taking out enemy vehicles. Aim high when firing at distant targets, as the rocket tends to drop. The rocket can also lock on to targets marked with a tracking dart.
	MK153 SMAW	1	The SMAW fires a much more powerful rocket than the RPG-7V2, but you only get one shot. Still, one shot from the SMAW can take out any vehicle. The rocket travels at high speeds, giving it a flatter and more accurate trajectory than the RPG-7V2. It can also lock on to tracking dart-marked targets.
	FIM-92 Stinger	2	If enemy helicopters pose a problem, seek out one of these shoulder-fired anti-air missile launchers. Aim through the weapon's optic and wait until you get a lock before firing. One hit from a Stinger disables a helicopter—fire a second missile to destroy it.
	Grappling Hook	4	This grappling hook functions just like the gadget, only it doesn't occupy a slot in your inventory and you don't have to buy it. These are usually located in areas where you can gain a tactical advantage by climbing to a nearby vantage point.
	Zipline	4	Like the grappling hook, the zipline Battle Pickup functions just like the gadget, allowing you to benefit from its capability when you're loaded-down with other equipment. Look for it in elevated locations and use it to quickly access surrounding positions.
	Defibrillator	N/A	These defibrillators are stored in white, wall-mounted boxes marked with an AED sign. Interact with these boxes to retrieve the defibrillator inside and use it to revive downed opponents. Fully charge the paddles to restore a teammate to full health. Or use a full charge to kill an opponent.
	Ammo Locker	N/A	These lockers are located in secure areas and function similar to an ammo box, but you must interact with the locker to retrieve ammo. Ammo lockers only replenish bullets used by primary and secondary weapons. They do not supply grenades and gadget ammo.
	First Aid Box	N/A	Interact with these green, wall-mounted boxes to replenish your health. Each interaction increases your health by 20%. Keep interacting with the box until you've fully recovered.

VEHICLES

Vehicles are just one of the elements which sets *Battlefield* apart from its competitors. *Battlefield: Hardline* continues this rich tradition, offering a completely new take on vehicle combat. Whether driving a getaway car as a criminal or pursuing bandits as law enforcement, *Hardline* supplies plenty of quintessential *Battlefield* moments centered around its lineup of unique vehicles.

ARMORED SUV

LAW ENFORCEMENT: INTERVENTION SUV

CRIMINALS: ARMORED SUV

Lightly-armored vehicle providing moderate protection from small arms and explosives. Features a deployable weapon turret manned by an agent as well as gun ports for the passengers inside the vehicle. Bulletproof windows ensure the safety of agents inside.

VEHICLE PERFORMANCE

Acceleration	
Speed	
Maneuverability	
Armor	
Firepower	

VEHICLE OCCUPANCY

SEAT	POSITION	WEAPON	AMMO
1	Driver	None	—
2	Gunner	Roof Turret	Infinite
3	Passenger	Gun Port (Rear)	Infinite
4	Passenger	Gun Port (Side)	Infinite

ARMORED SUV CUSTOMIZATION

COUNTERMEASURE—UNLOCK CRITERIA: 10,000 POINTS

NAME	COST
Smokescreen	$11,200
Fire Extinguisher	$16,800

GUNNER PRIMARY—UNLOCK CRITERIA: 30,000 POINTS

NAME	COST
Minigun*	—
HMG	$10,000
M3M	$83,200

UPGRADES—UNLOCK CRITERIA: 20,000 POINTS

NAME	COST
Maintenance	$2,000
Counter Surveillance	$3,000
Reinforced Chassis	$26,800

UPGRADES—UNLOCK CRITERIA: 40,000 POINTS

NAME	COST
Gunner Aircooler	$2,950
Gunner Ammo Belt	$4,400
Gunner Proximity Scanner	$61,200

* = DEFAULT EQUIPMENT

FIELD NOTES

The armored SUV provides a good balance of protection and firepower, making it one of the most versatile vehicles in the game. Taking a seat in the gunner position opens a turret in the SUV's roof. Initially the turret is equipped with a rapid-firing minigun capable of traversing a full 360-degrees. While the minigun has a high rate of fire, it doesn't hit as hard as the slower firing HMG or M3M gunner upgrades. The gunner's left and right flanks are protected by two halves of the armored hatch. However, the gunner's head is vulnerable to attacks from the front and rear. When you can't safely cover all angles as the gunner, consider ducking back inside the vehicle and riding as a passenger. The two passenger positions are equipped with side-mounted gun ports, allowing you to fire a machine gun while protected behind the vehicle's bulletproof glass. While the armored SUV is resistant to small arms fire, it isn't invincible. Even the smallest caliber weapons inflict minor damage, accumulating over time. You can slowly restore the vehicle's health by keeping it out of danger for a short period of time. Alternately, ask a friendly mechanic to assist with a repair torch. However, all repairs must be conducted from the exterior of the vehicle as there are no passenger positions which allow access to troop kits.

VISCERAL TIPS

- The flaps on the SUV's hatch are bulletproof and can be used to protect the gunner from small arms fire.

- When taking heavy fire as an SUV gunner, quickly moving to an available interior seat can make the difference between life and death.

- Be aware of passengers in your vehicle when driving the armored SUV. Both the rear and side passengers can fire weapons so try to orient the vehicle accordingly.

DETAILS

For complete details on each weapon, countermeasure, upgrade, and optic, flip ahead to the Vehicle Customization section.

COUNTER ATTACK TRUCK

LAW ENFORCEMENT: **ARMORED RESCUE VEHICLE**

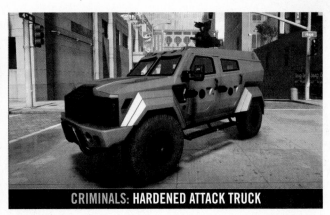

CRIMINALS: **HARDENED ATTACK TRUCK**

Heavy armored vehicle equipped with a mounted weapon system remotely operated from inside the cabin. Used in high-risk situations to provide firepower and protection from small arms. Equipped with bulletproof windows that ensure the safety of the agents inside.

VEHICLE PERFORMANCE

Acceleration	
Speed	
Maneuverability	
Armor	
Firepower	

VEHICLE OCCUPANCY

SEAT	POSITION	WEAPON	AMMO
1	Driver	AP MMG/Smoke Grenade Launcher	Infinite/3
2	Gunner	LMG Turret	Infinite

COUNTER ATTACK TRUCK CUSTOMIZATION

PRIMARY WEAPON—UNLOCK CRITERIA: 5,000 POINTS

NAME	COST
AP MMG*	—
HMG	$21,200
M3M	$83,200

SECONDARY WEAPON—UNLOCK CRITERIA: 10,000 POINTS

NAME	COST
Smoke Grenade*	—
Gas Grenade	$85,200

COUNTERMEASURE—UNLOCK CRITERIA: 20,000 POINTS

NAME	COST
Smokescreen	$11,200
Fire Extinguisher	$16,800

OPTIC—UNLOCK CRITERIA: 25,000 POINTS

NAME	COST
Zoom Optics*	—
IRNV Optics	$13,200
Thermal Optics	$48,000

UPGRADES—UNLOCK CRITERIA: 30,000 POINTS

NAME	COST
Maintenance	$1,000
Counter Surveillance	$1,500
Reinforced Chassis	$5,625
Autoloader	$14,800
Aircooler	$42,800

* = DEFAULT EQUIPMENT

GUNNER OPTICS—UNLOCK CRITERIA: 40,000 POINTS

NAME	COST
Gunner Zoom Optics*	—
Gunner IRNV	$13,200
Gunner Thermal Optics	$54,375

GUNNER UPGRADE—UNLOCK CRITERIA: 45,000 POINTS

NAME	COST
Gunner Aircooler	$2,950
Gunner Ammo Belt	$4,400
Gunner Proximity Scan	$61,200

FIELD NOTES

Built like a tank, no other vehicle has the combined armor and firepower of the counter attack truck. Both the driver and gunner have access to internally-operated machine gun turrets mounted on the vehicle's roof—the driver's turret has a smoke grenade launcher as an alternate fire mode. This allows both operators to engage hostile units from within the thick, armored shell of the vehicle without exposing themselves to incoming fire. All of this armor and firepower comes with a significant reduction in acceleration, speed, and maneuverability. This clearly isn't designed for high-speed chases. So instead of attempting to chase down opponents in faster vehicles, consider using the counter attack truck defensively, posting it near objectives or choke points. Although impervious to small arms fire, the vehicle is vulnerable to explosive attacks. So watch out for opponents armed with grenade launchers, breaching charges, and rocket launchers. Heavy weapons fired by armored SUVs, helicopters, and gunboats can also chip away at the vehicle's thick armor. The fire extinguisher countermeasure, maintenance upgrade, and a mechanic's repair tool are all good options for keeping the counter attack truck in the fight.

VISCERAL TIPS

- Wait for an ally to spawn into the gunner seat if you are driving the counter attack truck. The gunner is better equipped to deal with nearby enemies.

- Know your surroundings when driving the counter attack truck. It may be armored but its limited speed and mobility can leave it vulnerable to an enemy ambush.

- Smoke grenades combined with thermal optics can provide a great advantage for this vehicle.

MOBILE COMMAND CENTER

LAW ENFORCEMENT: **MOBILE COMMAND POST**

CRIMINALS: **SYNDICATE CREW CAB**

High-capacity armored transport vehicle. Creates an additional spawn position for the team. Agents in close proximity can replenish their health and ammunition. Provides protection against small arms, featuring bulletproof glass to keep its passengers safe.

VEHICLE PERFORMANCE

Acceleration
Speed
Maneuverability
Armor
Firepower

VEHICLE OCCUPANCY

SEAT	POSITION	WEAPON	AMMO
1	Driver	None	—
2	Passenger	None	—
3	Passenger	Gun Port (Side)	Infinite
4	Passenger	Gun Port (Side)	Infinite
5	Passenger	Gun Port (Side)	Infinite
6	Passenger	Gun Port (Side)	Infinite

MOBILE COMMAND CENTER CUSTOMIZATION

COUNTERMEASURE—UNLOCK CRITERIA: 10,000 POINTS	
NAME	COST
Smokescreen	$11,200
Fire Extinguisher	$16,800

UPGRADES—UNLOCK CRITERIA: 25,000 POINTS	
NAME	COST
Maintenance	$4,000
Counter Surveillance	$6,000
Reinforced Chassis	$15,000

FIELD NOTES

Think of the mobile command center as a miniature base on wheels, serving as a mobile spawn point for your entire team. Tactically, this is a very important vehicle and should be deployed near the front lines, allowing your team to spawn close to the action. This is ideal for exerting pressure on objectives. However, be wary of parking it too close to the action. Devious opponents may attempt to ambush your teammates as they exit the vehicle. It's better to keep this vehicle on the move, patrolling high-traffic areas while constantly dropping off teammates. When fully loaded, the mobile command center is an offensive powerhouse, with four side-mounted gun ports, each one fitted with a machine gun benefitting from unlimited ammo. Like the counter attack truck, the vehicle's armor repels all small arms fire. Explosives and heavy weapons mounted on vehicles still pose a threat—an added incentive to keep this vehicle on the move. The mobile command center isn't a fast or agile vehicle, so do your best to keep it on flat, paved surfaces. It has a tendency to tip over when traversing uneven terrain. Needless to say, you probably won't be scoring many jump bonuses in this heavy vehicle.

 VISCERAL TIPS

- Staying close to the mobile command center is generally a good idea as it replenishes both health and ammo for nearby teammates.

- This vehicle can be a very powerful weapon when fully loaded with two gunners on each side. Coordinate with your team to leverage the vehicle's full offensive potential.

- While the mobile command center can be defended on both sides, it is vulnerable from the rear. A good driver should know to orient the vehicle to make sure the passengers can properly defend the vehicle.

- Leaving the mobile command center in a strategic location can provide a significant tactical advantage. Look for a good place to hide the vehicle.

SEDAN

LAW ENFORCEMENT: **SQUAD CAR**

CRIMINALS: **SPORTS SEDAN**

Four-door passenger vehicle that can hold up to four agents. Passengers in the vehicle can move up and sit against the door to have a much improved attack angle.

VEHICLE PERFORMANCE

Acceleration	
Speed	
Maneuverability	
Armor	
Firepower	

VEHICLE OCCUPANCY

SEAT	POSITION	WEAPON	AMMO
1	Driver	None	—
2	Passenger	Troop Kit	—
3	Passenger	Troop Kit	—
4	Passenger	Troop Kit	—

SEDAN CUSTOMIZATION

COUNTERMEASURE—UNLOCK CRITERIA: 25,000 POINTS

NAME		COST
	Smokescreen	$11,200
	Fire Extinguisher	$16,800

UPGRADES—UNLOCK CRITERIA: 10,000 POINTS

NAME		COST
	Maintenance	$10,000
	Reinforced Chassis	$15,000
	LMG Armory	$75,600
	Anti-Armor Armory	$42,400
	Anti-Air Armory	$90,000

FIELD NOTES

The sedan is one of the most common vehicles available to both law enforcement and criminals—it's also a popular Hotwire vehicle. Since you'll likely be driving this vehicle often, consider investing in countermeasures and upgrades for the sedan early during your career. The LMG armory, anti-armor armory, and anti-air armory upgrades are particularly worthwhile, giving you access to a heavy weapon contained within the sedan's trunk. These weapons function just like their Battle Pickup counterparts, ideal for mowing down infantry, blasting enemy vehicles, or shooting down helicopters. Although the vehicle has no mounted weaponry, passengers are free to fire from the windows with their weapons and gadgets. It's possible to repair the vehicle with a repair tool while on the move. For a better view, lean out of the windows of the sedan. However, this leaves you exposed to incoming fire, so be ready to duck back inside the vehicle if you start taking damage. The sedan is not bulletproof and takes damage from all weapons. When engaging an enemy sedan, target the driver and passengers through the vehicle's windows. Killing the vehicle's occupants is more effective than trying to detonate the car with less precise gunfire.

SWITCH POSITIONS

If you're leaning out the window of a sedan, it's much faster to switch to another passenger position than it is to duck back inside the vehicle. Switching to a new seat instantly puts you back inside the vehicle, ideal for evading incoming fire.

COUPE

LAW ENFORCEMENT: POLICE INTERCEPTOR

CRIMINALS: MUSCLE CAR

Two-door passenger vehicle that can seat two agents. The passenger in the vehicle can move up and sit against the door to have a much improved attack angle.

VEHICLE PERFORMANCE

Acceleration	
Speed	
Maneuverability	
Armor	
Firepower	

VEHICLE OCCUPANCY

SEAT	POSITION	WEAPON	AMMO
1	Driver	None	—
2	Passenger	Troop Kit	—

COUPE CUSTOMIZATION

COUNTERMEASURE—UNLOCK CRITERIA: 25,000 POINTS	
NAME	**COST**
Smokescreen	$11,200
Fire Extinguisher	$16,800

UPGRADES—UNLOCK CRITERIA: 10,000 POINTS	
NAME	**COST**
Maintenance	$10,000
Reinforced Chassis	$15,000
LMG Armory	$75,600
Anti-Armor Armory	$42,400
Anti-Air Armory	$90,000

FIELD NOTES

Due to its speed and agility, the coupe is the perfect getaway car. Like the sedan, this is a very common car found throughout many maps and game modes. As a result, consider sinking some cash into the coupe's countermeasures and upgrades. The three armory upgrades give you access to an LMG, RPG, or Stinger in the coupe's trunk. With only one passenger position, the coupe lacks the offensive capabilities of the sedan. This requires a defensive mindset when driving. Use the smokescreen countermeasure to obscure the vision of opponents chasing you. The stunt driver gadget is also very effective when driving this car, greatly increasing the car's already impressive acceleration and top speed with a jolting nitrous oxide boost. Of all the four-wheeled vehicles, the coupe is best suited for aggressive, evasive driving. Look for ramps and other inclines to launch the car into the air, scoring some impressive jump bonuses.

 VISCERAL TIPS

- When taking heavy fire while sitting up on a transport vehicle's window sometimes the best thing to do is simply to get back inside the vehicle to get some protection.

- Want to sit on the window of a transport vehicle but the door has been destroyed? Simply repair the vehicle or ask a teammate for repairs to get a new door and get back up there.

- Transport vehicles equipped with a mobile armory upgrade can provide a significant tactical advantage. Defend them and make sure the weapon doesn't fall in the enemy's hands.

STREET MOTORCYCLE

LAW ENFORCEMENT: **POLICE MOTORCYCLE**

CRIMINALS: **STREET BIKE**

Highly maneuverable motorcycle that can seat two agents. Its combination of small size and high speed allows it to gain better access to crowded and tight areas.

VEHICLE PERFORMANCE

Acceleration	
Speed	
Maneuverability	
Armor	
Firepower	

VEHICLE OCCUPANCY

SEAT	POSITION	WEAPON	AMMO
1	Driver	None	—
2	Passenger	Troop Kit	—

FIELD NOTES

Deployed in urban areas, the street motorcycle packs a lot of power into a compact package. With unrivaled acceleration, this vehicle is perfect for rushing objectives during the opening moments of Conquest, Heist, Hotwire, and Blood Money matches. Its small size and agility allows it to access areas other vehicles can't—cut through narrow alleys, race up and down stairways, and leap great distances off ramps. The motorcycle is even small enough to fit in most elevators, allowing you to take your stunt driving to new heights. However, all of this mobility comes with one major drawback; the driver and passenger are completely exposed. As a result, its best to avoid high-traffic areas where you're likely to come under attack. There are no countermeasures or upgrades available for this vehicle, so you'll need to rely solely on raw speed and talent if you want to stay alive.

TOSSING CHARGES

Toss breaching charges when riding on the back of a motorcycle. This is a fun way to score some memorable kills, especially if you can stick a charge to a fully occupied enemy sedan or utility van.

OFFROAD MOTORCYCLE

LAW ENFORCEMENT: POLICE MOTORCYCLE

CRIMINALS: STREET BIKE

Dirt bike designed specifically for off-road. Can seat two agents and offers great traction and acceleration in steep or hilly terrain.

VEHICLE PERFORMANCE

Acceleration	
Speed	
Maneuverability	
Armor	
Firepower	

VEHICLE OCCUPANCY

SEAT	POSITION	WEAPON	AMMO
1	Driver	None	—
2	Passenger	Troop Kit	—

FIELD NOTES

The offroad motorcycle performs identically to the street motorcycle, but is usually deployed in rural areas. The enhanced suspension and traction make this motorcycle perfect for off-road travel, easily maneuvering over terrain that would wreck most four-wheeled vehicles—a good thing to remember when you're being chased by an enemy car. Make an effort to avoid congested roads. Instead, look for less-traveled paths along the perimeter of the map. This makes the offroad motorcycle ideal for staging flank attacks on distant objectives or for making quick, indirect getaways en route to an extraction point. As with the street motorcycle, there are no unlockable countermeasures or upgrades available for this vehicle. Just avoid racing headlong into a swarm of enemy units to prolong your lifespan.

HIT THE NOS!
Use the stunt driver gadget to give your motorcycle a sudden nitrous oxide boost. Initiate a boost before hitting a ramp or incline to score big jump bonuses.

UTILITY VAN

A commercial van capable of transporting up to five agents. The passenger side's sliding door and two rear doors can be opened too, allowing passengers to defend the vehicle.

VEHICLE PERFORMANCE

Acceleration	
Speed	
Maneuverability	
Armor	
Firepower	

VEHICLE OCCUPANCY

SEAT	POSITION	WEAPON	AMMO
1	Driver	None	—
2	Passenger	Troop Kit	—
3	Passenger	Troop Kit	—
4	Passenger	Troop Kit	—
5	Passenger	Troop Kit	—

FIELD NOTES

The utility van is a common civilian vehicle found on many maps, ideal for hauling your squad around. But despite the numerous defensive passenger seats, this van isn't designed for direct combat. Accumulative small arms fire and explosives can turn this van into a deathtrap, instantly killing everyone onboard. As a result, avoid driving a fully occupied van into danger. Passengers can open fire from the passenger side and rear of the vehicle. However, the driver's side is this vehicle's blind spot. Only the passenger in the second position can cover this side by hanging out their window and firing over the top of the van. So when attacking a utility van, pull along the driver's side and open fire, or slap a breaching charge on the side. Since passengers can access their troop kits, it's possible to use a repair tool while riding in the van, replenishing the vehicle's health. This is a critical tactic when a utility van is a Hotwire car. But unless playing Hotwire, use the utility van sparingly, transporting teammates from one location to another.

FUEL TANKER

A tanker truck designed for transporting fuel from refineries to gas stations. The truck's cab provides occupancy for one driver and one passenger.

VEHICLE PERFORMANCE

Acceleration	
Speed	
Maneuverability	
Armor	
Firepower	

VEHICLE OCCUPANCY

SEAT	POSITION	WEAPON	AMMO
1	Driver	None	—
2	Passenger	Troop Kit	—

FIELD NOTES

Carrying thousands of gallons of volatile fuel, the hulking fuel tanker is essentially a bomb on wheels. Dwarfing all other ground vehicles, this truck's mass is one of its biggest assets. Despite its sluggish acceleration, once this truck gets moving, it's difficult to stop it. Use the truck's mass and momentum to run other cars off the road or crash through blockades, sending vehicles, debris, and opponents flying through the air. The truck's flammable cargo makes it a juicy target for opponents, particularly those armed with explosive weaponry. With only one passenger positon and a slow cruising speed, the fuel tanker has limited defensive options. Grenades, rockets, and breaching charges can instantly detonate this vehicle. It can also explode due to accumulating damage from small arms fire. When the truck catches fire, get away as fast as possible. When the fuel tanker explodes, its lethality eclipses any explosive weapon in the game, instantly killing everyone within a wide blast radius. Consider booby-trapping one of these trucks with breaching charges and parking it near a high-traffic area to score multiple kills.

TRANSPORT HELICOPTER

LAW ENFORCEMENT: TRANSPORT HELICOPTER

CRIMINALS: EXECUTIVE HELICOPTER

High-capacity aircraft designed for ground support. Features mounted weapons and retractable doors on each side of the fuselage. Lightly armored to provide moderate protection against small arms fire and features bulletproof glass to keep agents inside the cabin safe.

VEHICLE PERFORMANCE

Acceleration	
Speed	
Maneuverability	
Armor	
Firepower	

VEHICLE OCCUPANCY

SEAT	POSITION	WEAPON	AMMO
1	Pilot	None	—
2	Gunner (Port)	HMG	Infinite
3	Gunner (Starboard)	HMG	Infinite
4	Passenger	Troop Kit	—
5	Passenger	Troop Kit	—
6	Passenger	None	—

TRANSPORT HELICOPTER CUSTOMIZATION

COUNTERMEASURE—UNLOCK CRITERIA: 10,000 POINTS

NAME	COST
IR Flares*	—
ECM Jammer	$30,000
Fire Extinguisher	$16,800

GUNNER PRIMARY—UNLOCK CRITERIA: 30,000 POINTS

NAME	COST
HMG*	—
Minigun	$60,000
M3M	$83,200

UPGRADES—UNLOCK CRITERIA: 20,000 POINTS

NAME	COST
Gyro Stabilizer	$1,000
Counter Surveillance	$1,500
Proximity Scanner	$61,200
Air Radar	$53,200

GUNNER UPGRADES—UNLOCK CRITERIA: 40,000 POINTS

NAME	COST
Gunner Aircooler	$2,950
Gunner Ammo Belt	$4,400

* = DEFAULT EQUIPMENT

FIELD NOTES

The transport helicopter is arguably the most valuable vehicle in each game mode where it appears. Given its speed and high-occupancy, this chopper is well-suited for dropping teammates at objectives and other frontline positions. Instead of worrying about landing, let your teammates bail-out and parachute down to the ground. In addition to serving as a transport, the helicopter is an impressive weapons platform, fitted with two side-mounted HMGs. These weapons can tear through enemy vehicles and personnel, giving teammates on the ground some much-appreciated offensive support. But these large, low-flying helicopters are likely to draw the ire of your opponents—heat-seeking Stingers, rockets, and small arms fire all pose a threat. If a Stinger launch is detected, an internal alarm sounds. Use this cue to jettison IR flare countermeasures to avoid getting hit. Don't get overconfident, though. Reduce altitude to avoid subsequent lock-ons by Stingers while your IR flares reload. Mechanics seated in the fourth or fifth crew positions can use their repair tools to conduct repairs, potentially keeping the helicopter airborne indefinitely.

VISCERAL TIPS

- When flying the transport helicopter always keep an eye on which side your gunners are and what weapon they are equipped with. Orient the aircraft accordingly to give them a good line of sight.

- When taking direct fire as a gunner or rear passenger inside the transport helicopter, try to move to the front passenger seat to get some protection.

- Leaving the rear passenger seats in the transport helicopter available for fellow mechanics to repair the vehicle can provide a strong tactical advantage.

ATTACK HELICOPTER

LAW ENFORCEMENT: PATROL HELICOPTER

CRIMINALS: ROGUE CHOPPER

Light patrol helicopter designed for reconnaissance as well as intervention. Features a fully customizable weapon system operated by the pilot as well as a gun turret for the passenger. Equipped with bulletproof windows to protect the agents inside from small arms fire.

VEHICLE PERFORMANCE

Acceleration	
Speed	
Maneuverability	
Armor	
Firepower	

VEHICLE OCCUPANCY

SEAT	POSITION	WEAPON	AMMO
1	Pilot	HMG	Infinite
2	Gunner	Minigun (Turret)	Infinite

ATTACK HELICOPTER CUSTOMIZATION

PRIMARY WEAPON—UNLOCK CRITERIA: 5,000 POINTS

NAME	COST
HMG*	—
Minigun	$60,000
M3M	$83,2000

UPGRADES—UNLOCK CRITERIA: 25,000 POINTS

NAME	COST
Gyro Stabilizer	$1,000
Counter Surveillance	$1,500
Proximity Scanner	$61,200
Air Radar	$53,200

COUNTERMEASURE—UNLOCK CRITERIA: 20,000 POINTS

NAME	COST
IR Flares*	—
ECM Jammer	$30,000
Fire Extinguisher	$16,800

* = DEFAULT EQUIPMENT

GUNNER OPTICS—UNLOCK CRITERIA: 40,000 POINTS

NAME	COST
Gunner Zoom Optics*	—
Gunner IRNV Optics	$13,200
Gunner Thermal Optics	$37,500

GUNNER UPGRADE—UNLOCK CRITERIA: 45,000 POINTS

NAME	COST
Gunner Aircooler	$2,950
Gunner Ammo Belt	$4,400
Gunner Proximity Scan	$61,200

FIELD NOTES

The attack helicopter makes few appearances in the game, but when it does, you should pay close attention. This agile, two-seat helicopter is packed with some impressive firepower, operated by the pilot and gunner. The pilot controls the two side-mounted HMGs. These weapons can be swapped out with twin miniguns or M3Ms. These fixed weapons aim in the same direction in which the helicopter is flying, requiring a skilled pilot to line-up accurate strafing runs. The chin-mounted minigun turret is operated by the gunner. Unlike the fixed side-mounted weapons, the turret can rotate and zoom-in on targets, allowing the gunner to engage targets in a wide arc around the chopper. While the turret's minigun can't be replaced, it can be customized with different optics and upgrades. Like the transport helicopter, the attack helicopter is vulnerable to small arms fire, rockets, and heat-seeking Stingers. Deploy IR Flares or other countermeasures to evade incoming Stingers. But unlike the transport helicopter, this chopper can't be repaired while in flight. So if you need to conduct repairs, find an isolated area of the battlefield (preferably near your team's deployment area) before landing and use a repair tool to patch-up any damage.

☠ VISCERAL TIPS

- Be aware of your primary weapon when flying the attack helicopter. Some weapons, like the HMG and M3M, are designed to fight vehicles, and others, like the minigun, to take down infantry more easily.

NO SAFETY FROM SNIPERS

The windows of the transport and attack helicopters are resistant to most gunfire. However, a professional armed with a bolt-action sniper rifle can penetrate these thick windows, striking (and potentially killing) occupants. Sniping helicopter pilots is a challenging but time-honored *Battlefield* tradition.

GUNBOAT

LAW ENFORCEMENT: **INSHORE PATROL VESSEL**

CRIMINALS: **SMUGGLER'S BOAT**

Fast and agile watercraft with four crew positions. Features mounted weapons on both sides of the stern.

VEHICLE PERFORMANCE

Acceleration	
Speed	
Maneuverability	
Armor	
Firepower	

VEHICLE OCCUPANCY

SEAT	POSITION	WEAPON	AMMO
1	Pilot	None	—
2	Gunner (Port)	HMG	Infinite
3	Gunner (Starboard)	HMG	Infinite
4	Passenger	Troop Kit	—

GUNBOAT CUSTOMIZATION

COUNTERMEASURE—UNLOCK CRITERIA: 10,000 POINTS	
NAME	COST
Smokescreen	$11,200
Fire Extinguisher	$16,800

GUNNER PRIMARY—UNLOCK CRITERIA: 30,000 POINTS	
NAME	COST
HMG*	—
Minigun	$60,000
M3M	$83,200

UPGRADES—UNLOCK CRITERIA: 20,000 POINTS	
NAME	COST
Maintenance	$670
Reinforced Chassis	$10,000
Proximity Scanner	$61,200

GUNNER UPGRADE—UNLOCK CRITERIA: 40,000 POINTS	
NAME	COST
Gunner Aircooler	$2,950
Gunner Ammo Belt	$4,400
Gunner Air Radar	$53,200
Gunner Proximity Scan	$61,200

* = DEFAULT EQUIPMENT

FIELD NOTES

The gunboats make their only appearance on Riptide, giving the police and criminals an opportunity to traverse the open ocean while targeting opponents with the vessel's port and starboard-mounted HMGs. These weapons make the gunboat an extremely dangerous threat, particularly to light-skinned vehicles like coupes and sedans racing along the shore. However, all of the gunboat's crew positions are completely exposed, making the pilot, gunners, and passenger vulnerable to incoming fire. Strafing runs by helicopters are particularly deadly. When targeting an enemy gunboat, try to pick-off the gunners first, as they pose the biggest threat. In addition to the exposed crew positions, the gunboat's light armor makes them susceptible to small arms fire. The boat's passenger, riding on the bow, can access their troop kit. This gives mechanics seated here the ability to conduct repairs on the boat with a repair tool. When piloting a gunboat be careful not to get too close to the shore or sandbars. If you accidentally run the boat aground, exit and strike the vessel with your melee weapon to *push* it back into the water.

AIRBOAT

A flat-bottomed watercraft designed for operation in extremely shallow waterways. Equipped with a minigun mounted on the bow.

VEHICLE PERFORMANCE

Acceleration			
Speed			
Maneuverability			
Armor			
Firepower			

FIELD NOTES

Found exclusively in the Everglades, the airboat is arguably the most unique vehicle in the game. The vessel is propelled by a large rear-mounted fan, allowing the airboat to skim across the surface of the water at impressive speeds. The airboat can even travel across land, albeit at much slower speeds. Use this capability to take shortcuts through the swamp. The airboat gets a nice offensive boost from the minigun mounted on the bow, ideal for engaging enemy personnel and vehicles. But like the gunboat, all of the airboat's crew positions are completely exposed making the pilot, gunner, and passenger vulnerable to incoming fire. Speed is the best defense, so keep moving to avoid giving your opponents the opportunity to score some easy kills. There are no customization options for the airboat, so be prepared to make the most out of the vessel's stock configuration.

VEHICLE OCCUPANCY

SEAT	POSITION	WEAPON	AMMO
1	Pilot	None	—
2	Gunner	Minigun	Infinite
3	Passenger	Troop Kit	—

VEHICLE CUSTOMIZATION

In *Battlefield: Hardline,* most of the vehicles can be customized utilizing unlockable upgrades, optics, countermeasures, and even weapons. The more you use a vehicle from a particular class, the more points you earn, unlocking access to different customization categories. Once a category is unlocked, you can then purchase a variety of enhancements through the same loadout screen you use to customize the classes. Most vehicles have multiple customization slots and you can assign one enhancement to each slot. Each enhancement costs money, so give some extra thought to each purchase. Here's a breakdown of all of the customization options. So before spending your money, use this information and analysis to best determine the most beneficial enhancements for your style of play.

WEAPONS

Some vehicles come equipped with mounted weapons, either assigned to a primary, secondary, or gunner slot. As points are accumulated with each vehicle, new weapons become available for purchase. Like the weapons associated with each class, these vehicle weapons have their own characteristics, with different rates of fire and damage output. But don't get too trigger happy. These weapons have a tendency to overheat. So fire in short, controlled bursts to prevent them from getting too hot.

AP MMG	MINIGUN	HMG

AP MMG

A medium machine gun equipped with high density armor-piercing rounds effective against agents and vehicles.

VEHICLE AVAILABILITY:

- **COUNTER ATTACK TRUCK (PRIMARY WEAPON)**

This is the default primary weapon equipped on the counter attack truck. Unlike the small-caliber weapons fired by infantry, this machine gun has enough power to damage all vehicles, including other counter attack trucks and mobile command centers.

MINIGUN

A fast-firing minigun effective against agents and vehicles.

VEHICLE AVAILABILITY:

- **ARMORED SUV (GUNNER PRIMARY)**
- **TRANSPORT HELICOPTER (GUNNER PRIMARY)**
- **ATTACK HELICOPTER (PRIMARY WEAPON)**
- **GUNBOAT (GUNNER PRIMARY)**

The rotating barrels of the minigun allow it to fire for prolonged periods of time without overheating, but it can still overheat, so don't get carried away. Combined with a blistering rate of fire, this is one of the most fearsome weapons available. However, it lacks the stopping power of the heavier .50 caliber HMG and M3M, requiring more hits against personnel and vehicles to produce lethal results. This is particularly evident when engaging heavily armored counter attack trucks and mobile command centers.

HMG

A .50 caliber machine gun equipped with high density rounds effective against armor.

VEHICLE AVAILABILITY:

- **ARMORED SUV (GUNNER PRIMARY)**
- **COUNTER ATTACK TRUCK (PRIMARY WEAPON)**
- **TRANSPORT HELICOPTER (GUNNER PRIMARY)**
- **ATTACK HELICOPTER (PRIMARY WEAPON)**
- **GUNBOAT (GUNNER PRIMARY)**

While this .50 caliber heavy machine gun has a relatively slow rate of fire, it hits hard, inflicting impressive damage against personnel and vehicles. Limit automatic bursts to three or four seconds. Otherwise the gun may overheat, making it inoperative for a few seconds.

M3M

A .50 caliber machine gun with a high rate of fire equipped with high density rounds effective against armor.

VEHICLE AVAILABILITY:

- ARMORED SUV (GUNNER PRIMARY)
- COUNTER ATTACK TRUCK (PRIMARY WEAPON)
- TRANSPORT HELICOPTER (GUNNER PRIMARY)
- ATTACK HELICOPTER (PRIMARY WEAPON)
- GUNBOAT (GUNNER PRIMARY)

It's not cheap, but this weapon addresses one of the major shortcomings of the HMG. It has a much higher rate of fire, increasing the damage output significantly. Furthermore, each round fired inflicts more damage against vehicles. If you're primarily targeting enemy vehicles, the M3M is superior to both the HMG and minigun.

SMOKE GRENADE

A grenade launcher that fires smoke grenades to conceal allies and block enemy line of sight.

VEHICLE AVAILABILITY:

- COUNTER ATTACK TRUCK (SECONDARY WEAPON)

Exclusive to the counter attack truck, the smoke grenade launcher is the vehicle's default secondary weapon. The launcher is fitted with a three-round magazine. Once expended, the magazine is automatically reloaded, taking several seconds. The time it takes for the launcher to be reloaded can be reduced by equipping the Autoloader upgrade. Use this launcher to saturate high-traffic areas with smoke, providing cover for your teammates while disorienting your opponents.

GAS GRENADE

A grenade launcher that fires tear gas grenades to disrupt the enemy.

VEHICLE AVAILABILITY:

- COUNTER ATTACK TRUCK (SECONDARY WEAPON)

Once you've acquired enough points with the counter attack truck, you can purchase gas grenades for the vehicle's secondary weapon. Just like their hand-thrown counterparts, these grenades emit clouds of tear gas, damaging and blurring the vision of those who aren't equipped with a gas mask. Exercise caution when using these grenades, because they can also affect your teammates.

COUNTERMEASURES

When properly deployed, countermeasures significantly increase the lifespan of your vehicle, either by preventing damage or by helping it recover from damage. Countermeasures aren't passive; they must be activated manually by the driver or pilot. Timing is critical when deploying a countermeasure, so be mindful of the proper cues, discussed below. Once deployed, all countermeasures are automatically reloaded. But this process takes time, leaving your vehicle vulnerable for several seconds.

SMOKESCREEN

Releases a thick cloud of smoke that visually obstructs the vehicle.

VEHICLE AVAILABILITY:

- ARMORED SUV
- COUNTER ATTACK TRUCK
- MOBILE COMMAND CENTER
- SEDAN
- COUPE
- GUNBOAT

Activate this countermeasure when making a getaway, deploying a barrier of smoke between your vehicle and any pursuers. But remember, smoke can be countered by opponents equipped with thermal and IRNV-based optics.

FIRE EXTINGUISHER

If your vehicle's on fire, the fire extinguisher can be deployed to put out any fires, bringing the vehicle back to a functional state, and let the vehicle start recovering from damage.

VEHICLE AVAILABILITY:

- ARMORED SUV	- COUPE
- COUNTER ATTACK TRUCK	- GUNBOAT
	- TRANSPORT HELICOPTER
- MOBILE COMMAND CENTER	- ATTACK HELICOPTER
- SEDAN	- GUNBOAT

Deploy this countermeasure when your vehicle becomes disabled due to heavy damage. The fire extinguisher puts out any flames, allowing the vehicle to return to an operable state. Take this as your cue to move the vehicle to safety or have an onboard mechanic conduct repairs.

IR FLARES

Infrared flare launcher that, when deployed, disrupts incoming missiles and breaks lock-ons.

VEHICLE AVAILABILITY:

- TRANSPORT HELICOPTER
- ATTACK HELICOPTER

For best results, wait until a missile has been launched before deploying IR flares. After flares have been deployed, it takes several seconds for new flares to be loaded, leaving your helicopter vulnerable to subsequent missile attacks. Reduce altitude and escape the area to prevent lock-ons.

ECM JAMMER

When activated, this countermeasure prevents targeting systems from locking on to you and disrupts any incoming missiles for a short time before it needs to be reloaded.

VEHICLE AVAILABILITY:

- TRANSPORT HELICOPTER
- ATTACK HELICOPTER

Like the IR flares, activate the ECM jammer once a missile has been launched. This not only prevents the missile from hitting your helicopter, but it also prevents your aircraft from being locked on for a few seconds, giving you enough time to fly to a safer area of the map. Once the ECM jammer is deactivated, it must be reloaded before it can be deployed again.

UPGRADES

Most vehicles have one upgrade slot and some have an additional gunner upgrade slot. Unlike countermeasures, upgrades are passive, requiring no interaction on behalf of the vehicle's crew. The benefits of upgrades are always active.

MAINTENANCE

Special attention to this vehicle's maintenance ensures that recovery from damage starts sooner.

VEHICLE AVAILABILITY:

- ARMORED SUV
- COUNTER ATTACK TRUCK
- MOBILE COMMAND CENTER
- SEDAN
- COUPE
- TRANSPORT HELICOPTER
- ATTACK HELICOPTER
- GUNBOAT

Maintenance increases the rate at which your vehicle recovers from damage. But your vehicle must no longer be exposed to incoming fire before recovery can take place. So get your vehicle to safety so auto-recovery can commence.

COUNTER SURVEILLANCE

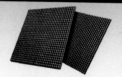

Take special care with this vehicle's heat and audio signatures to decrease the time your vehicle remains spotted by enemies.

VEHICLE AVAILABILITY:

- ARMORED SUV
- COUNTER ATTACK TRUCK
- MOBILE COMMAND CENTER
- TRANSPORT HELICOPTER
- ATTACK HELICOPTER

When this upgrade is applied, your vehicle only remains spotted for approximately two seconds, instead of the standard five seconds. This makes it much easier for your vehicle to avoid detection, minimizing your exposure on the enemy team's HUDs and minimaps.

REINFORCED CHASSIS

A reinforced, stronger vehicle chassis reduces the damage taken.

VEHICLE AVAILABILITY:

- ARMORED SUV
- COUNTER ATTACK TRUCK
- MOBILE COMMAND CENTER
- SEDAN
- COUPE
- GUNBOAT

This is a worthwhile upgrade for all applicable vehicles, slightly reducing the amount of damage a vehicle takes from weapons and collisions. But the increase in durability is very subtle, so don't get too overconfident.

PROXIMITY SCANNER

Scans the area around the vehicle and reveals enemy movement on the minimap.

VEHICLE AVAILABILITY:

- ARMORED SUV (GUNNER)
- COUNTER ATTACK TRUCK (GUNNER)
- TRANSPORT HELICOPTER (PILOT AND GUNNER)
- ATTACK HELICOPTER (PILOT AND GUNNER)
- GUNBOAT (PILOT AND GUNNER)

This upgrade functions like a radar, automatically highlighting nearby enemy units on the minimap. This is helpful for pilots and gunners alike, revealing the locations of enemy units. Glance back and forth between the minimap and HUD to identify, spot, and engage new targets. Spotting allows you to relay this information to your entire team.

AUTOLOADER

An enhanced mechanism that makes reloading faster.

VEHICLE AVAILABILITY:

- COUNTER ATTACK TRUCK

Exclusive to the counter attack truck, the autoloader increases the reload speed of the driver's grenade launcher, allowing them to deploy smoke and gas grenades at a faster rate.

AIRCOOLER

An enhanced mechanism that makes recovering from overheat faster.

VEHICLE AVAILABILITY:

- ARMORED SUV (GUNNER)
- COUNTER ATTACK TRUCK (DRIVER AND GUNNER)
- TRANSPORT HELICOPTER (GUNNER)
- ATTACK HELICOPTER (GUNNER)
- GUNBOAT (GUNNER)

When a machine gun becomes overheated due to prolonged automatic bursts, it becomes inoperative for a few seconds. This upgrade reduces the time it takes for the weapon to become operational again. Overheating is easily avoided by firing in short bursts. Consider choosing another upgrade for your vehicle.

LMG ARMORY

Outfits the vehicle with an LMG pickup for nearby allies.

VEHICLE AVAILABILITY:

- SEDAN
- COUPE

When applied to a sedan or coupe, this upgrade places a MG36 light machine gun in the trunk of the vehicle. Simply interact with the back of the car to retrieve the weapon from the trunk and go on a rapid-fire killing spree. The weapon is equipped with two 100-round magazines.

ANTI-ARMOR ARMORY

Outfits the vehicle with an anti-armor pickup for nearby allies.

VEHICLE AVAILABILITY:

- SEDAN
- COUPE

Like the LMG armory upgrade, this upgrade stows an RPG rocket launcher in the trunk of a sedan or coupe. Given the lack of anti-vehicle weapons in the game, this is a worthwhile upgrade, particularly when playing vehicle-heavy game modes like Conquest and Hotwire. You only get two shots with the RPG, so make them count.

ANTI-AIR ARMORY

Outfits the vehicle with an anti-air pickup for nearby allies.

VEHICLE AVAILABILITY:

- SEDAN
- COUPE

This upgrade places a Stinger anti-air missile launcher in the trunk of your sedan or coupe. If enemy helicopters are a problem, spawn into a sedan or coupe with this upgrade and retrieve the Stinger from the trunk. One hit from a Stinger is enough to disable a helicopter. Follow-up with second missile to destroy it.

GYRO STABILIZER

A system that tries to maximize maneuverability until repairs can be made. It is automatically activated when the aircraft is disabled.

VEHICLE AVAILABILITY:

- TRANSPORT HELICOPTER
- ATTACK HELICOPTER

This is perhaps the most valuable upgrade for helicopter pilots, significantly increasing the responsiveness of a chopper's controls when it becomes disabled. This often means the difference between crashing and keeping the helicopter airborne. If the opposing team is shooting a lot of Stingers, make sure you have this upgrade equipped.

AIR RADAR

Replaces the minimap with a radar display, highlighting airborne targets in a large radius around the vehicle.

VEHICLE AVAILABILITY:

- TRANSPORT HELICOPTER
- ATTACK HELICOPTER
- GUNBOAT (GUNNER)

If you're intent on hunting enemy helicopters, this may be a worthwhile upgrade. The radar which replaces the minimap makes it much easier to locate air targets. The radar scans the skies in a full 360-degrees, highlighting enemy air contacts. This makes it much easier to orient your vehicle (or guns) toward these airborne threats.

GUNNER AMMO BELT

An enhanced mechanism that improves rate of fire.

VEHICLE AVAILABILITY:

- ARMORED SUV (GUNNER)
- COUNTER ATTACK TRUCK (GUNNER)
- TRANSPORT HELICOPTER (GUNNER)
- ATTACK HELICOPTER (GUNNER)
- GUNBOAT (GUNNER)

This upgrade increases the cyclic rate of the gunner's weapon, essentially boosting its damage output. But the higher rate of fire comes with a couple of drawbacks. The weapon is less accurate and more prone to overheating. Fire in short, controlled bursts in an effort to keep the weapon on-target and cool.

OPTICS

Optics are only available for the counter attack truck and attack helicopter's camera-based gun turrets. By default, both vehicles come equipped with zoom optics. But as more points are earned with each vehicle, the IRNV and thermal optics become available for purchase, offering enhanced performance for low-light environments.

ZOOM OPTICS

Zooms the view to more easily spot and take out targets at greater distance.

VEHICLE AVAILABILITY:

- COUNTER ATTACK TRUCK
  (DRIVER AND GUNNER OPTICS)
- ATTACK HELICOPTER
  (GUNNER OPTICS)

This is the default optic applied to counter attack trucks and attack helicopters, offering a slightly magnified view through the turret's camera system—use the aim button/key to zoom. Zoom in the camera's view when engaging targets at great distances, allowing for greater precision.

IRNV OPTICS

Enhanced infrared night vision that will make heat signatures easily distinguishable at close to medium range.

VEHICLE AVAILABILITY:

- COUNTER ATTACK TRUCK
  (DRIVER AND GUNNER OPTICS)
- ATTACK HELICOPTER
  (GUNNER OPTICS)

In this night vision scope, cold and neutral objects appear green while warm objects appear in hues of yellow, orange, and red. This makes targets much easier to pick out, particularly in low-light or smoke-filled environments. However, the optic has limited range; infrared signatures of distant targets do not appear at all. This makes this optic most effective on small maps with limited lines of sight.

THERMAL OPTICS

A black and white night vision system that shows heat signatures across all ranges.

VEHICLE AVAILABILITY:

- COUNTER ATTACK TRUCK
  (DRIVER AND GUNNER OPTICS)
- ATTACK HELICOPTER
  (GUNNER OPTICS)

In this high-contrast black and white optic, active targets appear as stark white silhouettes. Like IRNV, this optic can also see through smoke screens and adverse weather conditions. But unlike IRNV, there is no range limitation of this optic—it can easily detect active targets at long ranges. But without a zoom function, engaging distant targets can still be problematic.

INTRODUCTION
BANK JOB
SWAT VS. THIEVES

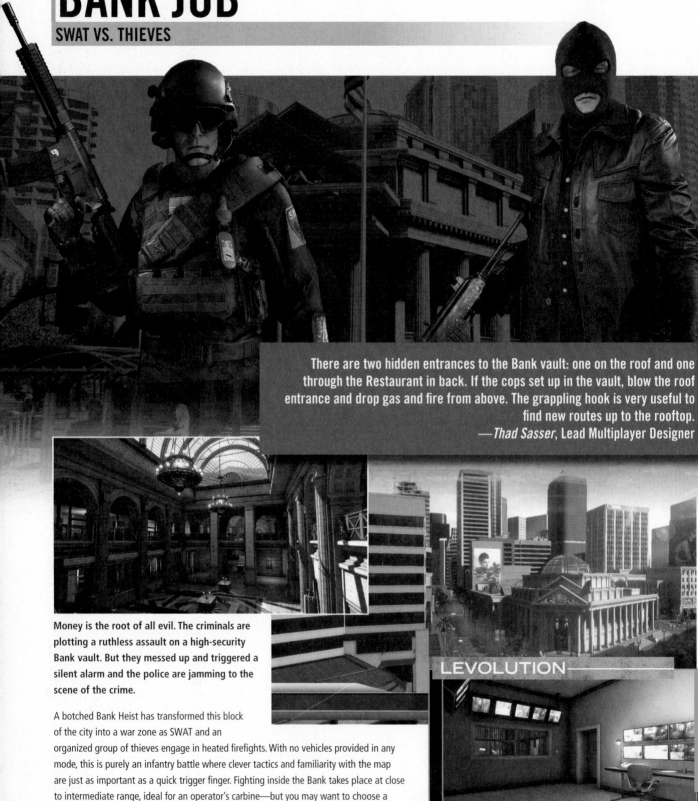

There are two hidden entrances to the Bank vault: one on the roof and one through the Restaurant in back. If the cops set up in the vault, blow the roof entrance and drop gas and fire from above. The grappling hook is very useful to find new routes up to the rooftop.
—*Thad Sasser*, Lead Multiplayer Designer

Money is the root of all evil. The criminals are plotting a ruthless assault on a high-security Bank vault. But they messed up and triggered a silent alarm and the police are jamming to the scene of the crime.

A botched Bank Heist has transformed this block of the city into a war zone as SWAT and an organized group of thieves engage in heated firefights. With no vehicles provided in any mode, this is purely an infantry battle where clever tactics and familiarity with the map are just as important as a quick trigger finger. Fighting inside the Bank takes place at close to intermediate range, ideal for an operator's carbine—but you may want to choose a mechanic's SMG or enforcer's shotgun when fighting it out around the Bank's vault. Prepare for longer range engagements when operating outside the Bank, particularly when engaging distant opponents from the rooftop or Parking Garage—battle rifles, DMRs, and sniper rifles are ideal for scoring such long range kills. Maintaining control of the Bank's roof is key in most game modes, so don't forget to bring along grappling hooks and ziplines.

LEVOLUTION

Open and close the various security doors around the vault to limit access to the opposing team. Take control of the security room and use the toggle switch to open and close the gates surrounding the vault door.

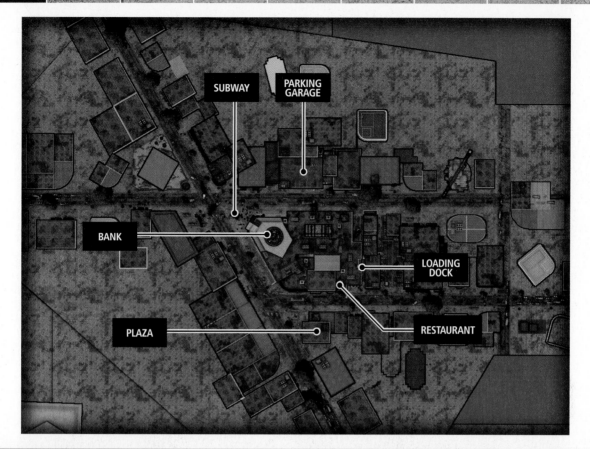

KEY LOCATIONS

BANK

The Bank is the centerpiece of this map, sporting an expansive and ornate lobby as well as a heavily secured vault. Climb to the Bank's rooftop for a great view of the surrounding locations, ideal for spotting and sniping opponents in the streets below.

PARKING GARAGE

This multilevel parking structure is located directly north of the Bank. Make your way to the top of this garage to engage opponents on the Bank's roof. You can also zipline over to the Bank, landing on its roof or entering through one of its second story windows.

LOADING DOCK

This secure area on the east side is where the Bank usually receives deliveries of cash and other valuables. While off-limits to customers, this "backdoor" offers direct access to the vault and security room, making it a popular route for criminals.

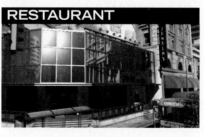

RESTAURANT

Big Eddie Spaghetti's ia a new eatery under construction. But sharing a wall with the Bank has made this Restaurant a prime target of criminals seeking to blast their way into the vault.

PLAZA

Located directly across the street from the Bank, this Plaza sees heavy action during Heist and Conquest modes. Don't loiter around here too long! Cover is limited, making you an easy target for opponents positioned on the Bank's roof.

SUBWAY

Isolated from the action in the map's center, this underground passage offers some refuge for those taking fire from the Bank. Regroup, resupply, heal, then move out!

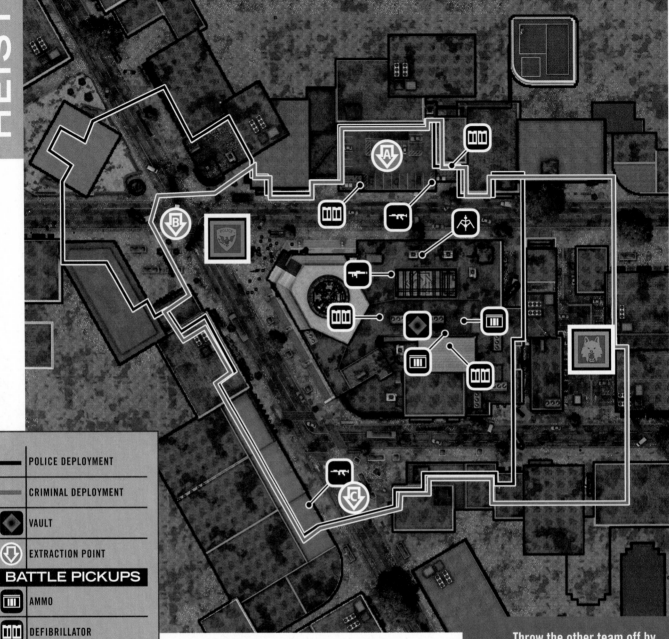

POLICE DEPLOYMENT

CRIMINAL DEPLOYMENT

VAULT

EXTRACTION POINT

BATTLE PICKUPS

AMMO

DEFIBRILLATOR

GRAPPLING HOOK

HEALTH

LMG

ROCKET LAUNCHER

STINGER

ZIPLINE

☆ With three potential entry points into the vault, SWAT has their work cut out for them in this high-intensity mode. Early in the round the police should send squads to cover all three breach points: at the vault door, the Bank rooftop, and the Restaurant. Maintaining control of the Bank's rooftop is crucial as it serves as a popular egress route for criminals attempting to reach one of the surrounding extraction points.

☆ While most criminals head directly for the vault door inside the Bank, it's important to take advantage of the two other breach points too. So in addition to attacking the Bank's interior, send at least a couple of squads to secure the breach points on the roof and in the Restaurant. Also, consider maintaining a presence on the roof's north side. From here you can fire down on police moving on the streets below as well as secure zipline routes for extraction.

> Throw the other team off by luring them with a Heist bag. Then make a beeline for the zipline on the roof and use it to go to the Parking Garage.
> —Brian Carden, Quality Analyst

> There are three entry points into the vault, it's a good idea to set traps for all three locations. Laser tripmines are good for this. With all points covered, even if the traps don't net a kill, the explosion will indicate which entry point the enemies are trying to breach.
> —Ethan Solak, Video Editor

★ This is a classic Bank Heist, and as expected, the loot is held within the Bank's secure vault. The primary breach point is the massive vault door, requiring criminals to drill their way through the door's lock system. Teams attempting to secure the vault door should take control of the adjoining security room. Activating the toggle switch inside the security room opens and closes the two cage-like doors, limiting access to the vault door. There are a number of narrower cage doors that can be manually opened and closed around the vault. Use these doorways as choke points to ambush unsuspecting opponents. Gas grenades and close-quarter weaponry rule supreme here, so make sure you're prepared for the fight.

> Throw gas in from the roof where the AC unit falls into the vault. Then enter and shoot.
> —David Price, Weapon Designer

★ Drilling through the vault door isn't the only option for the thieves. An alternative breach point is located on the rooftop, just above the vault. Placing charges here causes the roof to cave in, dropping an HVAC unit into the safe and killing anyone unlucky enough to be nearby. Another breach point is located inside the Restaurant. Plant charges on the wall behind the Restaurant's kitchen to blow a hole in the vault's south wall. Even if one breach has succeeded, the criminals should try to open all three routes to provide easier access to the Bank's vault.

★ There are three possible extraction points on this map, all surrounding the Bank. Extraction point (C), at the Plaza, is usually the easiest for the criminals to reach. They can escape through the Restaurant and cross the street, or zipline down from the roof. Ziplines also come in handy for scoring loot at the other two extraction points. From the roof of the Bank you can zipline across to the Parking Garage rooftop to reach extraction point (A). While extraction point (B), by the Subway entrance, is easy to reach by zipline too, it's also close to the SWAT team's deployment area, increasing the chance of a heavy law enforcement presence. The criminals are better off sticking to extraction points (A) or (C).

> As a cop, don't run directly through the main doors toward the vault. Take the time to flank down the north side of the Bank and engage the criminals from behind through the Loading Dock.
> —William Bordonaro, Quality Analyst

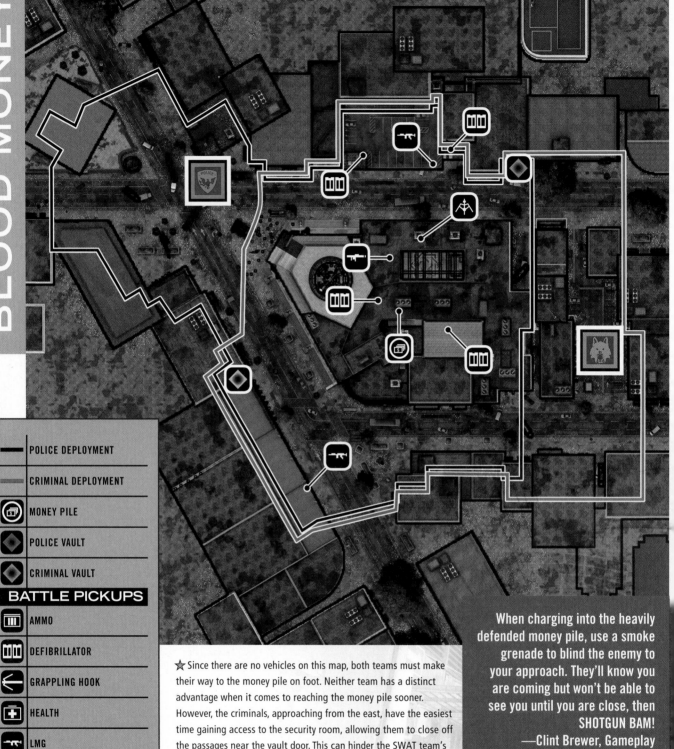

LEGEND

— POLICE DEPLOYMENT

— CRIMINAL DEPLOYMENT

MONEY PILE

POLICE VAULT

CRIMINAL VAULT

BATTLE PICKUPS

AMMO

DEFIBRILLATOR

GRAPPLING HOOK

HEALTH

LMG

ROCKET LAUNCHER

STINGER

ZIPLINE

☆ Since there are no vehicles on this map, both teams must make their way to the money pile on foot. Neither team has a distinct advantage when it comes to reaching the money pile sooner. However, the criminals, approaching from the east, have the easiest time gaining access to the security room, allowing them to close off the passages near the vault door. This can hinder the SWAT team's attempts to access the money pile.

When charging into the heavily defended money pile, use a smoke grenade to blind the enemy to your approach. They'll know you are coming but won't be able to see you until you are close, then **SHOTGUN BAM!**
—Clint Brewer, Gameplay Software Engineer

☆ The money pile is located within the Bank, just outside the vault room. This is a very small room with three entry points. If you're tasked with defending the money pile, it's difficult to determine where your opponents will appear. Therefore, professionals equipped with cameras and laser tripmines are essential for identifying and ambushing intruders. Gas grenades and flashbangs are equally effective in this small space. Think twice about hiding in the small wood-enclosed rooms nearby. Usually reserved for customers viewing the contents of their safety deposits boxes, the wood enclosures are easily shredded by gunfire and explosions.

☆ The SWAT team's vault is located in a small store on the west side of the map. With only one entry point, through the front door, this vault is relatively easy to defend. Defenders inside the store can seek cover behind the store's retail counter while scanning for incoming threats. This store is also easy to watch from the Bank's rooftop. But bring a weapon (and optic) with some decent range. Enemies moving in and out of this store are completely exposed unless they deploy a smoke grenade for concealment. If attempting to attack the law enforcement vault, approach with caution and toss grenades prior to entry.

☆ The criminals stash their cash in a similar store located on the map's north side. The large delivery truck parked outside the store provides some concealment and limits sight lines. As a result, the criminals are usually most successful when guarding their stash directly, hiding within the store and ambushing intruders. Defenders posted on the Bank's roof have a good view of potential attackers as they enter and exit the store. Attacking the criminal team's vault is extremely dangerous when properly defended. Always toss in gas grenades, flashbangs, or incendiary devices before entering.

> Watch out for incendiary and gas grenades at the money pile. You don't want someone stealing that loot off of your corpse that you worked so hard to collect!
> —Thad Sasser, Lead Multiplayer Designer

☆ The area around the money pile is an absolute death trap, with both teams taking heavy losses. Instead of jumping into the fray, consider working the periphery of the map, targeting opponents carrying money bags to their team's vault. The Bank's rooftop is the best place to watch each team's vault, but don't forget to scan your surroundings on a regular basis. Chances are you'll be sharing the rooftop with opponents. If you manage to neutralize an opponent carrying a money bag, parachute or zipline down from the Bank's roof to retrieve their money bag and score it for yourself.

> Don't just defend your team's stash from the inside; the Bank's roof has many good vantage points for both stashes.
> —Zachary T. Irwin, Quality Analyst

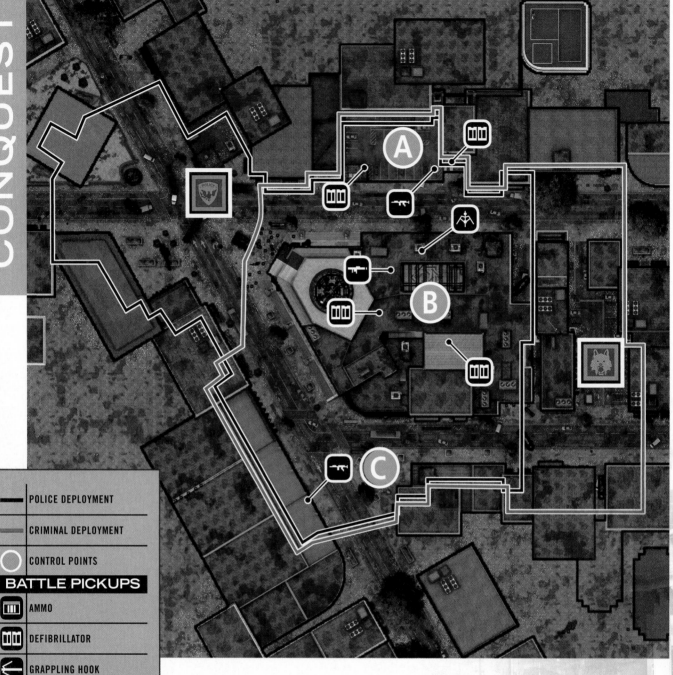

POLICE DEPLOYMENT

CRIMINAL DEPLOYMENT

CONTROL POINTS

BATTLE PICKUPS

AMMO

DEFIBRILLATOR

GRAPPLING HOOK

HEALTH

LMG

ROCKET LAUNCHER

STINGER

ZIPLINE

★ With only three control points up for grabs on this compact map, the law enforcement team needs to figure out where they're going to make their stand. Instead of rushing for the Bank (B), make a move for the Parking Garage (A) and Plaza (C) early during the round. While the Parking Garage (A) can be defended directly, it helps to have defenders posted on the Bank's rooftop when it comes to defending the Plaza (C).

Use the vault door to slow your opponents' access between the Bank and Plaza. Use the Bank's roof and ziplines to quickly get from point to point.
—Evan Champlin, Senior Multiplayer Level Designer

☆ The criminal team has a good chance of capturing the Bank (B) before SWAT can move into position. But don't just focus on this central control point. Grab the Plaza (C) as well. Utilizing the hole in the vault's wall, it's easy to transition from the Bank (B) and Plaza (C), moving through the Restaurant. By locking down these adjacent control points the criminal team has a good chance of holding out for a win.

☆ None of the control points in this Conquest match spawn vehicles. But that doesn't mean the control points are equal. Due to its central location, the Bank (B) is likely to see the heaviest action, switching hands multiple times throughout the course of the match. This is a good place to avoid unless you have the skills to mop-up at close range. The Plaza (C) is likely to change hands frequently too since it's rather exposed and vulnerable to attacks from the Bank's rooftop. The Parking Garage (A), on the other hand, is much more defensible. The control point is located on the garage's third floor, making it a bit difficult for attackers to approach unless they zipline across from the Bank's rooftop.

☆ Before deploying into a Conquest match, take into consideration what area of the map you'll be operating in. If you're going to be in the Parking Garage (A) or Plaza (C) consider spawning as an operator or professional and prepare to engage opponents on the Bank's roof or in the streets. If deploying near the Bank's (B) interior control point, the close quarter weapons of the mechanic and enforcer give you an edge. Although the Bank's rooftop offers no control point to attack or defend, operators and professionals can make a difference here especially when engaging traffic around the Parking Garage (A) and Plaza (C).

> If you are having trouble taking the control point in the Parking Garage, go to the roof of the Bank and fire across or use a grappling hook to climb up.
> —David Price, Weapon Designer

> Provide cover from the roof so teammates can hold the control points easier.
> —John Seefurth, Quality Analyst

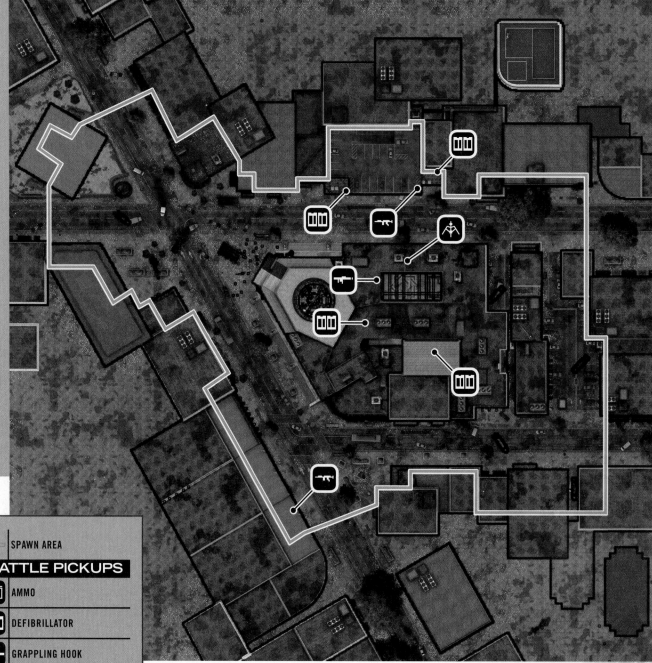

SPAWN AREA

BATTLE PICKUPS

Icon	Name
	AMMO
	DEFIBRILLATOR
	GRAPPLING HOOK
	HEALTH
	LMG
	ROCKET LAUNCHER
	STINGER
	ZIPLINE

★ Unlike most Team Deathmatch rounds, the action in Bank Job isn't restricted to a smaller section of the map. Almost the entire map is accessible, making it important to identify the hot zones. As usual, the interior of the Bank is often the site of the heaviest fighting. But if you're seeking to escape the chaos inside the Bank, steer clear of the city streets as they're most likely watched by snipers posted on the rooftops of the Bank and Parking Garage.

★ If your team is looking for a good location to defend, consider making a stand on the Bank's rooftop. From here your team can fire down on opponents in the streets below as well as engage opponents inside the Bank through the large skylight. This rooftop is massive, with three stairwell access points. Deploy laser tripmines and cameras to avoid getting surprised by sneaky opponents attempting to steal your team's base. Also, watch out for snipers and other threats attacking (and ziplining) from the Parking Garage to the north. If your team can manage to take control of the Parking Garage and the Bank's rooftop, you'll be well-positioned to take the lead.

☆ The elevated vantage points offered by the Bank's rooftop and Parking Garage make this a popular map for the operator and professional classes. Using high-powered rifles and optics, these classes can fire down on opponents racing about in the streets below. But if you prefer to dash around inside the Bank, consider spawning as a mechanic or enforcer—their SMGs and shotguns are ideal for the close quarter fighting within the Bank's corridors and offices. Mechanics seeking to keep their squad nearby should deploy a satellite phone in a low-traffic area, like the Bank's second floor offices and conference room.

☆ In most matches the action is centered around the Bank's interior and rooftop. If you're looking to avoid these risky areas, consider taking refuge within the Parking Garage while engaging opponents in the streets below or on the Bank's rooftop. If you want to get a little closer to the action while mitigating risk, consider patrolling the Loading Dock and adjoining corridors on the east side of the Bank. This is a great area to catch opponents off-guard as they sprint toward the high-action areas of the map.

> High ground is your friend. Always maintain control of the Bank's roof and the top of the garage. When the enemy has the upper ground, don't forget to use the grappling hook to circumvent their defenses.
> —Evan Champlin, Senior Multiplayer Level Designer

CROSSHAIR

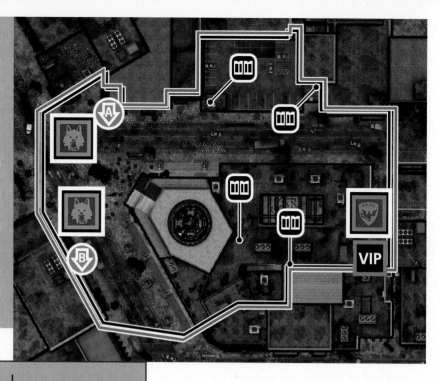

★ Starting off in the alley behind the Bank, the law enforcement team has a lot of ground to cover if they hope to get the VIP to one of the two extraction points before time expires. Of course, the other option is to hunt down and eliminate all the criminals. In any case, moving through the Bank's interior or along the Bank's rooftop offers the most cover. Avoid the northern street at all costs—you'll likely be cut down by criminals posted on the Parking Garage's roof.

★ For the criminals, this is a relatively large map with plenty of sneaky paths for the opposing team. It's best to take the high ground, watching the two extraction points from the Bank or Parking Garage's rooftops. While the middle ground gives the law enforcement team plenty of cover and concealment, they'll be completely exposed when moving into the street and making a move for either extraction point—this is your time to pounce. Consider posting one teammate near each extraction point to serve as a deterrent.

POLICE DEPLOYMENT

CRIMINAL DEPLOYMENT

EXTRACTION POINT

HOSTAGE

BATTLE PICKUPS

DEFIBRILLATOR

★ When defending as the criminals, play close attention to the stairway extraction points. Be ready to respond to attacks from the Bank's rooftop. This is a popular extraction route, so watch for incoming ziplines. If you do deploy teammates in the midfield, consider posting them on the Bank's rooftop in an effort to deter rapid zipline escapes. Even if the law enforcement team doesn't move across the Bank's rooftop, this elevated vantage point is perfect for covering either extraction point.

★ Armed only with a handgun, albeit a very powerful one, the VIP must let their teammates lead the way on this map.

Heading right out into the street might not be your best option as VIP—be sneaky! The roof is a great option if they're not expecting it, and if you bring a zipline all bets are off.
—Thad Sasser, Lead Multiplayer Designer

The long sightlines along the streets and around the extraction points make the VIP an easy target for enemy snipers. Paths leading through the Bank (or across its rooftop) are often the safest, offering decent cover and concealment. But exercise extreme caution when making a move for either extraction point. Consider deploying smoke grenades before crossing the street and rushing to the extraction points.

★ Careful gadget selection can make all the difference in these matches. Both teams should bring along grappling hooks and ziplines to quickly ascend and descend from the Bank's rooftop. The law enforcement team can benefit greatly from smoke grenades, which help conceal their advance toward either extraction point. The criminal team should consider booby trapping the extraction points with laser tripmines or breaching charges as a last ditch effort to prevent the VIP from escaping. To counter such booby traps, the law enforcement team should use frag grenades to detonate these devices before the VIP rushes down either stairway.

RESCUE

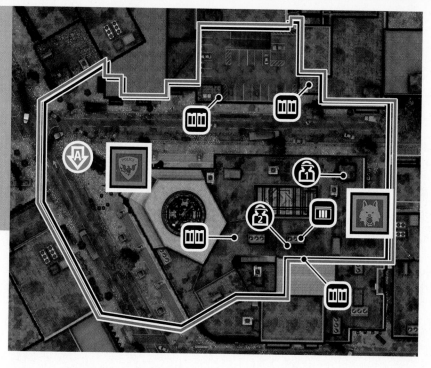

★ For the law enforcement team, speed is the key to entering the Bank before the enemy team can get set up. Entering the Bank is the easy part; reaching the hostages on the second floor is tricky. For best results, use the stairwell on the north side of the Bank. Avoid using the central stairways as they are completely exposed. Or get on top of the Bank and utilize the northeastern or southeastern stairwells to sneak up on the hostages. But keep an eye on the clock. Whichever path you take, you need to keep moving.

★ While the criminal team starts relatively close to each hostage, they must act quickly to secure them. With so many possible entry points, it's a good idea to establish your defenses around the hostages on the east side of the Bank. Be ready to cover the rooftop too. This is a popular escape route, particularly for law enforcement teams equipped with a zipline.

★ When it's your team's turn to defend the hostages, be careful not to spread your team too thin. The vaulted layout of this map makes it really easy to become separated from your teammates, allowing you to be easily overpowered by the incoming SWAT team. Instead, use two-man teams to guard each hostage while sending your fifth player to the rooftop to spot the opposing team. If you're not having success guarding the hostages directly, consider camping the rooftop and extraction point in an effort to stop the police from escaping with a hostage.

★ The hostages are located on the second floor of the Bank's east side. Hostage one is kneeling in the corner of a conference room on the east side while hostage two is held in an office along the southern side, only a few meters away. The green wall directly south of hostage one can be destroyed with explosives, ideal for catching SWAT in an ambush or for moving the hostage through the adjacent stairwell on the way to the rooftop. The office hostage two is held in is adjoined by several other offices to the west, providing the law enforcement team some much appreciated cover. It definitely beats moving through the exposed walkway outside the office.

★ Before the round begins make sure you're equipped with some beneficial gadgets. Criminals should deploy cameras and laser tripmines inside the two eastern stairwells, as these are often frequented by the opposing team either during entry or escape. Gas grenades are also effective when deployed inside the offices where the hostages are being held. The law enforcement team can benefit from ballistic shields, gas masks, flashbangs, and ziplines. After securing a hostage, get to the rooftop and zipline down to the extraction point for a quick escape.

> ing a ballistic shield to use on the top floor. Advancing down the hall with the shield up while crouched can be very effective when you're protecting a teammate who is a good shot.
> —Thad Sasser, Lead Multiplayer Designer

INTRODUCTION
THE BLOCK
SWAT VS. BANGERS

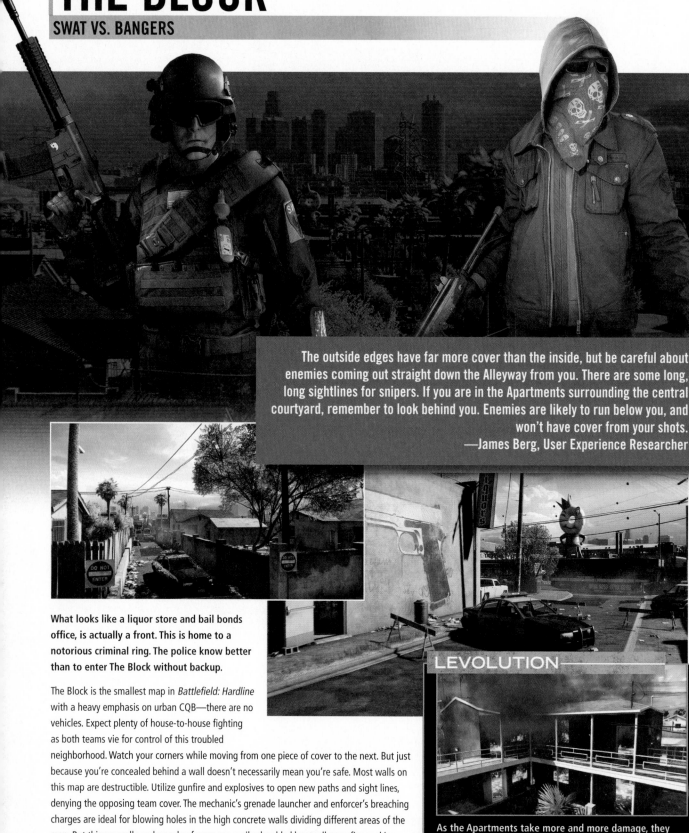

The outside edges have far more cover than the inside, but be careful about enemies coming out straight down the Alleyway from you. There are some long, long sightlines for snipers. If you are in the Apartments surrounding the central courtyard, remember to look behind you. Enemies are likely to run below you, and won't have cover from your shots.
—James Berg, User Experience Researcher

What looks like a liquor store and bail bonds office, is actually a front. This is home to a notorious criminal ring. The police know better than to enter The Block without backup.

The Block is the smallest map in *Battlefield: Hardline* with a heavy emphasis on urban CQB—there are no vehicles. Expect plenty of house-to-house fighting as both teams vie for control of this troubled neighborhood. Watch your corners while moving from one piece of cover to the next. But just because you're concealed behind a wall doesn't necessarily mean you're safe. Most walls on this map are destructible. Utilize gunfire and explosives to open new paths and sight lines, denying the opposing team cover. The mechanic's grenade launcher and enforcer's breaching charges are ideal for blowing holes in the high concrete walls dividing different areas of the map. But thinner walls and wooden fences are easily shredded by small arms fire, making each firefight a visual delight as the environment responds to each shot fired.

LEVOLUTION

As the Apartments take more and more damage, they eventually catch fire, spewing flames and smoke, adding an extra hazard to an already dangerous environment. The buildings eventually collapse, offering some sneaky areas to hide and crawl through.

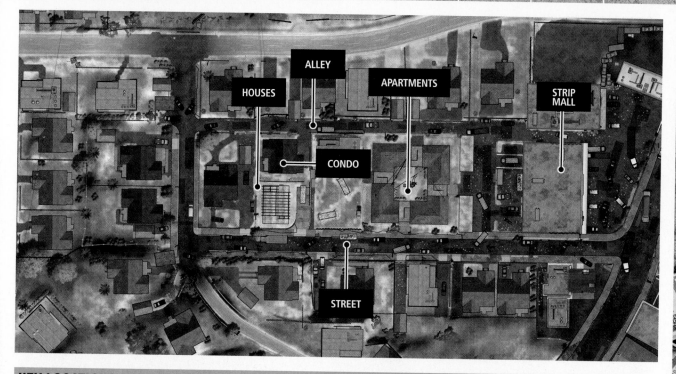

KEY LOCATIONS

APARTMENTS

Due to its central location, this small cluster of Apartments sees heavy action throughout all game modes. Use a grappling hook to reach the rooftops of these two-story buildings for a great view of the surrounding locations—but don't linger on these rooftops long, as there isn't much cover. In some game modes you can even find an RPG in the courtyard's playground.

STRIP MALL

This small Strip Mall is home to Knight Owl Liquors and E-Z Out Bail Bonds. A third storefront remains vacant, but is still accessible. Each business has a storage room on the west side. The vacant store and liquor store are accessible via large doors. Use the interior and exterior switches to open and close these doors, altering access and lines of sight.

HOUSES

This group of small, single-family homes on the west side of the map offers some great cover and concealment. Rush inside one of these Houses if taking fire from the Street, Alley, or Apartments. Unless you're carrying a shotgun or SMG, consider switching to your sidearm when hunting for enemies in these compact dwellings.

ALLEY

Stretching along the north side of the map, this Alley serves as a major east-west thoroughfare. While the cars and trucks parked in the Alley offer some cover, beware of snipers posted on the east and west sides. If you must move through this Alley, do so quickly, preferably while concealed by smoke grenades.

CONDO

Located between the Apartments and the Houses, this abandoned two-story Condo is a good midfield position. Peer through its second story windows to engage opponents rushing through the nearby Alley or vacant lot to the south. This is a good spot to place a satellite phone, allowing your squad to spawn close to the action.

STREET

Like the Alley to the north, this Street on the south side of the map, is another major east-west route. Given its width and sparse cover, the Street is often watched by sharpshooters, so be sure to leapfrog from one piece of cover to the next while advancing here.

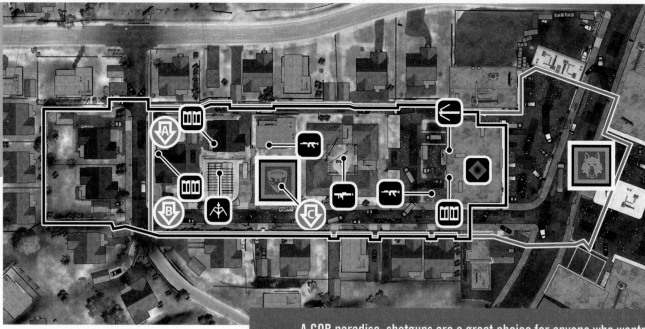

> A CQB paradise, shotguns are a great choice for anyone who wants to get up close and personal on this map. Grab a 44 Magnum and ask yourself one question: are you feeling lucky?
> —Aaron Broster, Quality Analyst

POLICE DEPLOYMENT	
CRIMINAL DEPLOYMENT	
◆	VAULT
⊕	EXTRACTION

BATTLE PICKUPS

Icon	Name
▥	AMMO
▥▥	DEFIBRILLATOR
⬅	GRAPPLING HOOK
✚	HEALTH
▬	LMG
▬	ROCKET LAUNCHER
▬	STINGER
⚓	ZIPLINE

☆ The law enforcement team begins this match with a major disadvantage—spawn far from the vault located in the bail bonds storefront of the Strip Mall. In most cases, the criminals will have planted at least one charge on the vault by the time the police arrive. Go into this match with some powerful close quarters weapons, like the mechanic's SMGs or the enforcer's shotguns. This gives you the best chance of chasing out the criminals and securing both the liquor store and bail bonds. An aggressive push during the early part of the match can make a huge difference. If you can't establish control of the vault, fall back to the west and secure the three extraction points, taking up positions in the Apartments, Condo, and Houses.

☆ Since you spawn in the Strip Mall's parking lot, reaching the vault isn't a big problem for the criminal team, but don't get overconfident. While the criminals can easily plant a charge on the vault before SWAT arrives, they need to babysit each charge for 30 seconds before they detonate. Keep the western entrances to each store closed, and be ready to ambush law enforcement as they pour through these narrow entrances. Expect plenty of close quarter fighting during the early moments of the round as both teams fight for control of the vault.

★ Bail bonds establishments are known for keeping plenty of cash on-hand. This has lured the bangers to hit the vault at the bail bonds store in the Strip Mall. By accessing the back room of the business, near the holding cell, criminals can plant a charge directly on the thick, metal doors leading into the vault. As the primary breach point, expect heavy action in this area with law enforcement attacking from the west and criminals approaching from the east. Both teams should attempt to hold this backroom, securing (and booby-trapping) the narrow eastern and western doorways.

★ Like most vaults, there's another way inside. In addition to attacking the primary breach point, the criminal team should also enter the liquor store's storage room and plant a charge on the northern wall, opening a new path into the bail bond store's vault. The law enforcement team should be prepared to shut down this flanking path, taking control of the liquor store's storage room as soon as possible. For best results, keep the large sliding door closed while attempting to lockdown this location and be prepared for attacks from both the east and west.

★ There are three possible extraction points and all of them are somewhat exposed, giving SWAT a good chance of ambushing the bag carrier before a chopper can swoop in for the score. Extraction point (C) is closest to the vault, but is located in the vacant lot, south of the Condo. Deploy smoke and use the storage containers if attempting to score here. Expect the police to be watching the point from the Condo. If you're tasked with running the bag to points (A) or (B), secure the house on the west side of the map before attempting to score. This house is a popular hiding spot for the law enforcement team, allowing them to cover both extraction points.

> Grab the MG36 LMG located behind the liquor store. This battle pickup's large ammo capacity and high rate of fire can be a game changer when attempting to secure the vault.

> Divide and conquer. It is crucial for both teams to control the 3 lanes. Use the Apartments to gain the high ground and cover your carrier as they approach the point.
> —Evan Champlin, Senior Multiplayer Level Designer

BLOOD MONEY

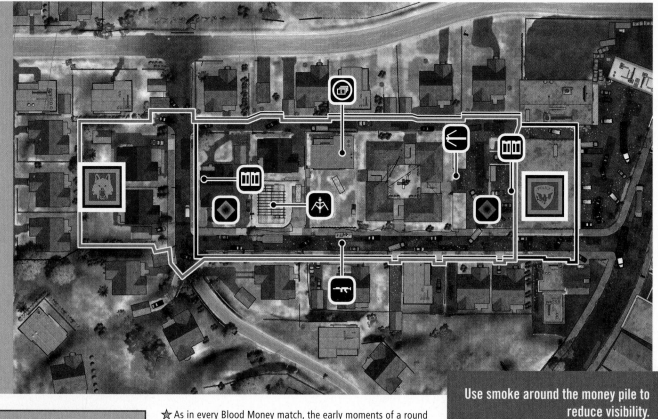

> Use smoke around the money pile to reduce visibility.
> —David Price, Weapon Designer

☆ As in every Blood Money match, the early moments of a round usually involve a mad dash for the money pile. Since this is a small map, with no vehicles, both teams are likely to arrive at the money pile at approximately the same time, leading to intense firefights around the Condo. But before rushing to your death, consider establishing control of the Condo's exterior first, controlling who enters and exits.

☆ The money pile is located on the first floor of the Condo. This structure is rather porous, with multiple entry points (including windows) on the first and second floors. But these are the only entry points; you can't use explosives to make a door of your own. However, the room in which the money pile is located is destructible. Shoot-up the interior walls to create new paths and lines of sight. Given the close-quarter nature of fights around the money pile, come prepared with a SMG, shotgun, or pistol. Grenades (of all types) are also very effective in this cramped, dark space.

▬	POLICE DEPLOYMENT
▬	CRIMINAL DEPLOYMENT
◉	MONEY PILE
◆	POLICE VAULT
◆	CRIMINAL VAULT

BATTLE PICKUPS

▥	AMMO
▦	DEFIBRILLATOR
←	GRAPPLING HOOK
✚	HEALTH
▬	LMG
▬	ROCKET LAUNCHER
▬	STINGER
⚓	ZIPLINE

☆ The SWAT team stores their cash in the armored truck parked behind the liquor store. When making a run for the vault, consider cutting through the Apartments. Or take to the Apartments' roof, via grappling hook, then zipline directly to the back of the armored truck. There are plenty of good hiding spots behind the liquor store where the police team can defend from. So if criminals are looking to steal from the police, they should avoid a direct assault. Instead, flank from the north or south, clearing out the area behind the liquor store before making a move for the armored truck.

☆ The armored truck in the map's southwest corner serves as the criminal team's vault. When running money back to this vault, cut through the house which is under construction, to the east, for a direct approach. But whether scoring loot or stealing it from this vault, it's much safer to hook-in from the north, cutting through the house adjacent to the armored truck. This indirect path allows you to sneak-up on opponents in the single-story house attempting to ambush you.

☆ With so much activity around the money pile, consider backing off and playing the midfield, gunning down runners and stealing their bags of cash. When playing as the police, consider patrolling the house under construction, located just east of the criminal team's armored car. This is the most direct route for the criminals and an easy place to score some kills. For the criminals, the Apartments are a great place to mow down opponents running back to their armored car behind the liquor store. The Apartments' second story windows are ideal for spotting enemy activity around the Condo and SWAT team's armored car.

Put Breaching Charges on your own vault so you can blow up any would-be thieves.
—Brian Paoloni, Quality Designer

Use the destruction to your advantage. Create lines of sight that allow you to cover the money pile from your side of the map.
—Evan Champlin,
Senior Multiplayer Level Designer

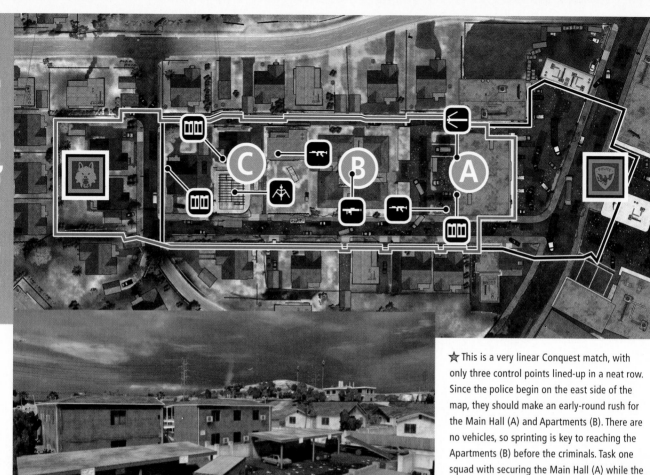

☆ This is a very linear Conquest match, with only three control points lined-up in a neat row. Since the police begin on the east side of the map, they should make an early-round rush for the Main Hall (A) and Apartments (B). There are no vehicles, so sprinting is key to reaching the Apartments (B) before the criminals. Task one squad with securing the Main Hall (A) while the rest of the team heads directly for the Apartments (B). Capturing and controlling the Apartments (B) early is the key to getting an early round drain on the opposing team's ticket count.

☆ The criminal strategy doesn't differ much from the police strategy. But instead of taking the Main Hall (A), the criminals should grab the Foreclosed House (C) with one squad while the rest of the team rushes to secure the Apartments (B). Once again, sprinting is key. Upon reaching the Apartments (B), secure the second floor and fire down on the opposing team funneling in from the east side.

> Use the grappling hook to get on top of roofs that others can't reach.
> —Brian Paoloni, Quality Designer

▬▬	POLICE DEPLOYMENT
▭▭	CRIMINAL DEPLOYMENT
◯	CONTROL POINTS

BATTLE PICKUPS

▥	AMMO
▦	DEFIBRILLATOR
⬿	GRAPPLING HOOK
✚	HEALTH
⌐	LMG
⌐	ROCKET LAUNCHER
⊢	STINGER
⩙	ZIPLINE

☆ Without a doubt, the Apartments (B) are the focal point of this Conquest match. But its central location isn't the only reason this control point is worth fighting for. The rooftops here are some of the highest points on the map, giving snipers an excellent view of the surrounding area. But there's no easy way to access these rooftops, so bring along a grappling hook to make your ascent. Even if you can't get to the rooftop, the second floor windows offer great vantage points. Also, don't forget the RPG battle pickup located on the playground in the courtyard. You only get two shots, so make them count. But remember, if the Apartments (B) get too hot, and your team is losing too many tickets, fall back and capture the Main Hall (A) and Foreclosed House (C) to secure the drain on the opposing team's tickets.

☆ Of all the Conquest matches in *Battlefield: Hardline*, this is one of the most frantic, requiring thoughtful loadouts and careful spawning. Chances are you'll be operating in a variety of close-quarter and intermediate range environments. This makes the operator class a safe bet, as their assault rifles and carbines are well-suited for any of these locations. But those tasked with defending the Main Hall (A) or Foreclosed House (C) may benefit from the close-quarter power of a mechanic's SMG or enforcer's shotgun. Given the fast-action of this match, playing as a professional can be tricky. But if you're up for the challenge, settle on a good DMR over a bolt-action rifle. You'll be grateful for the higher rate of fire.

> Flanking the enemy and capturing their point disrupts their game plan. Use the Alleys to maneuver up the Street and attack them from behind.
> —Evan Champlin, Senior Multiplayer Level Designer

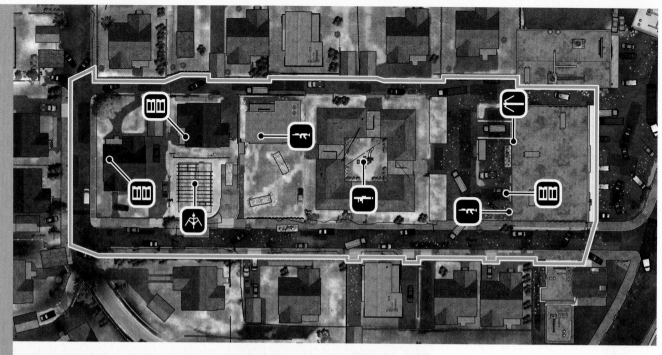

SPAWN AREA

BATTLE PICKUPS

![]	AMMO
![]	DEFIBRILLATOR
![]	GRAPPLING HOOK
![]	HEALTH
![]	LMG
![]	ROCKET LAUNCHER
![]	STINGER
![]	ZIPLINE

☆ The Block is a small map to begin with, and as a result, most of the map is accessible during Team Deathmatch. The only area that is off-limits is the parking lot on the east side of the Strip Mall. Make note of the MG36 LMG Battle Pickups behind the liquor store and at the Condo. These LMGs come with two 100-round magazines. The large magazines means you spend less time reloading, giving you a slight tactical advantage over your opponents. While operating these weapons avoid the urge of reloading after each kill. If you become skilled with this weapon you can score 8-10 kills without reloading.

☆ Given the small size of the map, there aren't many safe places to hole-up in. But if you want to lockdown one location, consider taking up positions in the Condo or Strip Mall. Both of these locations flank the Apartments, allowing you and your team to engage opponents in this high-traffic area. The Condo offers limited sightlines, but most of the exterior walls are solid, holding-up against small arms and explosives—the same can't be said of the Apartments. If hanging out in the Strip Mall, consider watching the Apartments from the back of the liquor store. But be mindful of opponents attempting to flank you from the bail bonds vault. There's a hole in the wall connecting the two businesses.

> Pick a weapon with a high ammo count that packs a punch, in a mode that encourages quick kills and deaths on the smallest map in the game—reloading is your greatest enemy.
> —William Bordonaro, Quality Analyst

★ The majority of engagements on this map take place at close to intermediate range. As usual, the operator is a safe bet here as their assault rifles and carbines can get the job done at any range. If you're brave enough to venture into the Apartments, consider bringing along a mechanic's SMG or an enforcer's shotgun. Though if carrying a satellite phone, the mechanic should consider deploying it in a safer location, like the Condo. Playing as a professional can be tricky due to the close quarter nature of the map. But these long-range specialists can find some opportunities by covering the Street and Alley, preferably with a fast-firing DMR. If playing as a professional, keep your fully-automatic sidearm at the ready when moving from one location to another.

★ Instead of locking down one location, consider roaming the map with your squad, overpowering your opponents with teamwork and oppressive firepower. A full five-player squad can experience great success patrolling areas like the Houses and Strip Mall. But it's best to avoid the action in the Apartments. Instead, bypass this hot zone by carefully moving along the Street to the south or the Alley to the north. Consider making regular sweeps of the liquor store and Condo so your squad can take advantage of the MG36 LMG Battle Pickups.

The outside edges have far more cover than the inside, but be careful about enemies coming out straight down the Alleyway from you. There are some long, long sightlines for snipers. If you are in the Apartments surrounding the central courtyard, remember to look behind you. Enemies are likely to run below you, and won't have cover from your shots.
—James Berg, User Experience Researcher

The VIP usually goes down one of the two side Alleys, but don't forget, you can grapple over the Houses too!
—Ben Gaciu, System Designer

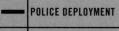

POLICE DEPLOYMENT

CRIMINAL DEPLOYMENT

EXTRACTION POINT

☆ The VIP and law enforcement team start the round near the Houses, on the west side of the map. During the early moments of the round consider taking temporary residence inside the Condo. This is an excellent place for the VIP to hide out while the rest of the team secures the area around the Apartments and Strip Mall. But the VIP should never be left alone; leave at least one team member to hang back and serve as a bodyguard. Also, consider booby-trapping the Condo with laser tripmines to further insulate the VIP from attacks. When your teammates have eliminated a majority of the opposing team, they can return to the Condo and resume escorting the VIP to one of the extraction points.

☆ The criminal team is tasked with preventing the VIP from accessing one of the two extraction points, both located at the Strip Mall. Extraction point A is located in the vacant store and extraction point (B) is in the liquor store. The opposing team is most likely to gain entry to each extraction point from the west, entering through the large doors behind each business. But it's important to note that the east side of the Strip Mall is accessible, allowing the law enforcement team to flank, entering from each building's front side. Extraction point (A) can also be accessed through a door on the building's north side. So when defending here, don't get tunnel vision, constantly staring off to the west. Consider deploying gadgets like cameras or laser tripmines to detect flank attacks.

★ As in all Crosshair matches, the criminal team faces the dilemma of either locking down the extraction points or aggressively attacking the law enforcement team in hopes of neutralizing the VIP. Both strategies have their merits on this map, so consider alternating your tactics to keep the opposing team on their toes. When locking down the extraction points, camp the parking lot behind the Strip Mall in an effort to ambush the VIP, but don't forget to watch the Street and Alley to prevent SWAT from sneaking up on you. When attacking, make an aggressive push toward the Apartments, hopefully catching the VIP and escorts off-guard as they near the Condo.

★ When escorting the VIP there are three distinct lanes on this map, each with their benefits and hazards. The flanking paths, along the Street and Alley, offer quick access to the extraction points, but provide limited cover. Bring along smoke grenades when advancing through these open areas. The center path, through the buildings, provides the most cover. But cover works both ways—what's cover for the VIP is a potential hiding spot for the criminals. In most rounds it's important to be reactive to the situation, taking the path of least resistance. So while you may start off going through the center of the map, it may be necessary to detour along the Alley or Street as you encounter resistance.

> As the law enforcement team, mix it up. Feint in a direction and quickly move to the opposite side to push forward behind the enemy. —Evan Champlin, Senior Multiplayer Designer

★ Whether attempting to escort or assassinate the VIP, both teams should rely on gadgets to keep tabs on the opposing team's whereabouts. Cameras, deployed by the professional, are extremely helpful here. Consider placing them near the Apartments to detect enemy movement. The decoy is equally effective, particularly for the law enforcement team, serving as a lure to draw criminals away from the extraction points. If you want a better perspective, bring along a grappling hook and climb to the roof of the Apartments or Condo. If you're feeling daring, consider ziplining from the apartment rooftops toward the extraction points for a quick escape as the VIP.

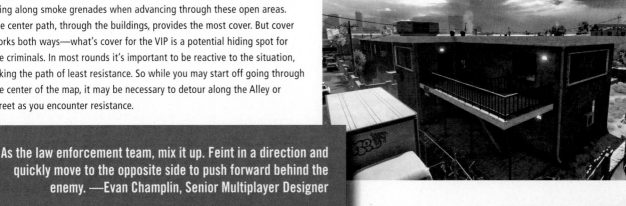

Pick a direction and move fast. This map is very narrow, and if you let the defense get established, you'll lose the important element of surprise.
—James Berg, User Experience Researcher

	POLICE DEPLOYMENT
	CRIMINAL DEPLOYMENT
🔒	HOSTAGE
⊕	EXTRACTION POINT

★ Starting across the Street from the Strip Mall, to the east, the law enforcement team must cover a lot of ground before reaching the two hostages. Since both hostages are located along the north side of the map, advancing down the Alley or cutting through the Apartments serves as the most direct routes, but they're also the most predictable. Instead, consider advancing along the Street, flanking the hostage locations from the south or west. This gives you the best opportunity to catch the criminals off-guard. Don't use the same route each time, though. Mix it up and keep the criminals guessing.

Don't forget to cover. Use the rooftops to gain an advantage.
—Evan Champlin,
Senior Multiplayer Level Designer

★ Since the criminal team starts near both hostages, they have just enough time to establish a perimeter before the SWAT team arrives. Keep one teammate posted near each hostage while the rest of the team fans out to the east, attempting to spot incoming opponents. Consider using a grappling hook to reach the roof of the Condo or Apartments for a better view of the area. But don't push too far to the east. Keep your defenses centered around the two hostage buildings.

★ Given the tight confines of both hostage buildings, locking down the interiors of each structure can be problematic for the criminals, making them vulnerable to incoming grenades. It's much safer (and effective) to engage the law enforcement team as they enter or exit each building. Or better yet, trap them inside one of the hostage buildings before launching your attack. Pour in gas grenades and flashbangs then open fire as they attempt to escape. Alternately, take up positions in the Apartments' second floor and engage the SWAT team before they expect it, attacking as they exit the Strip Mall. Or,

allow the opposing team to rescue a hostage then ambush them at the Strip Mall before they can reach the extraction point. Keep your tactics fresh each round to add a sense of unpredictability.

★ Both hostages are held in adjacent buildings on the west side of the map. Hostage one is located in the north bedroom of a single-story home. Instead of rushing into the house and clearing each room, consider busting in through the north window, adjacent to the Alley, for a quick rescue. Hostage two is held in the Condo, on the second floor bedroom. There are two stairways leading up to the second floor, one on the north side and one on the south side. The criminal team should consider booby-trapping both stairways with laser tripmines. This room can also be reached via zipline. Fire a zipline from the Apartments' rooftop into the Condo's eastern bedroom window to make a quick entry, bypassing any booby-traps on the two stairways.

★ Grenades are very effective for both teams when operating in the hostage buildings. The criminal team should keep the hostage rooms saturated with gas grenades to injure and disorient any SWAT players who aren't equipped with gas masks. Add in some smoke grenades to completely reduce visibility within each building. The law enforcement team shouldn't be shy about tossing in grenades around the hostages either. Frag grenades and incendiary devices won't harm the hostages, but they may kill or expose criminals. Outside, grappling hooks come in handy for reaching rooftops of the Apartments and Condo. Use these rooftop positions to scan for threats or setup zipline paths between the hostage buildings and extraction point.

> Make sure you don't put your breaching charges or laser tripmines too close to the hostages or they won't explode.
> —Brian Paoloni, Quality Designer

INTRODUCTION
DERAILED
SWAT VS. BANGERS

> Drop the train in the center to take away good sniping spots.
> —David Price, Weapon Designer

The industrial side of Los Angeles is home to many shady dealings. A criminal ring has set up shop in the warehouse and scrapyards, where they're trying to make money from illegal doings.

Derailed is vast and industrial. Even from the air it is impossible to see everything, so it really depends on teamwork and good communication to win a match on any mode. This map is a classic *Battlefield* map with a wide range of uses for each and every class. Balance your squad and it won't be a problem giving each of them a task to keep everyone alive and resupplied. Derailed is an all urban environment, catering to the inner police-chase driver in all players. Drive through the city or take a detour under the Tram Bridge and through the ravine. There are plenty of options when in a car; just don't get caught at a dead end not knowing how to get out. Break out the stunt driver gadget and get to work on this high octane, large scale blast of a map.

LEVOLUTION

Driving under the Tram Bridge? Get past it quickly because directly above you i a large explosive train car ready to collapse the entire bridge burning anything its vicinity. Just like any explosive item in *Battlefield: Hardline*, it only takes firir your weapon or a few explosives and the ready-made bomb is going to create a large display seen from across the map. Blowing up the bridge works well if your team is constantly getting pinned down by enemy sniper fire from here o if the other team is repeatedly driving their Hotwire vehicles under the bridge untouched. After the bridge is collapsed, the way is blocked and the vantage point gone, making this destructive environment piece a consciously tactical or

CONSTRUCTION YARD

SCRAPYARD

TRAM BRIDGE

CONSTRUCTION YARD

TRAIN DEPOT

LOGISTICS CENTER

KEY LOCATIONS

CONSTRUCTION YARD

The Construction Yard is a vastly open key location from the air, but once you're on the ground it's an entirely different story. Take cover behind silos, shipping containers, portable construction buildings, and all of the construction materials ready to take some fire. Keep to the nearest structure and don't let the enemy see you.

LOGISTICS CENTER

This key location fits the locale of the industrial zone in Los Angeles perfectly because it includes all aspects. The Logistics Center is located in its own small gated compound equipped with shipping trucks, shipping containers, a large warehouse, and a ton of boxes that all provide excellent cover. This key location is central to Derailed so it is close to everything on the map.

SCRAPYARD

The Scrapyard plays a small role in most modes on Derailed, but when it's in play it is extremely complex and useful to those who get to know it well. Here is where an array of smashed cars stacked one on top of another serves as an excellent path to escape from incoming vehicles. The buildings are great strongholds that provide a deadly crossfire ambush spot.

TRAIN DEPOT

The Train Depot is by far the largest key location on the map, surrounded by stationary vehicles, shipping containers, train cars, equipment, and a warehouse full of sharp turns and complex shooting lanes. This key location has it all and a great deal of it. Have someone constantly watching your back when traveling here. There's always the chance of missing a bad guy or two.

TRAM BRIDGE

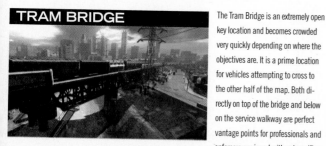

The Tram Bridge is an extremely open key location and becomes crowded very quickly depending on where the objectives are. It is a prime location for vehicles attempting to cross to the other half of the map. Both directly on top of the bridge and below on the service walkway are perfect vantage points for professionals and enforcers equipped with sniper rifles and battle rifles.

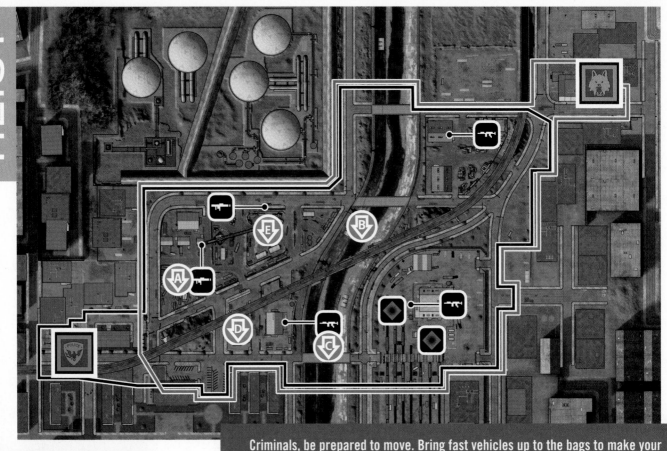

Criminals, be prepared to move. Bring fast vehicles up to the bags to make your getaway. Use the roof of the train yard to control the paths into the vaults.
—Evan Champlin, Senior Multiplayer Level Designer

━━━ POLICE DEPLOYMENT

━━━ CRIMINAL DEPLOYMENT

 VAULT

 EXTRACTION

BATTLE PICKUPS

 AMMO

 DEFIBRILLATOR

 GRAPPLING HOOK

 HEALTH

 LMG

 ROCKET LAUNCHER

STINGER

ZIPLINE

☆ You must maintain air superiority when playing as the police, adding a challenge that most Heist maps just do not have. Having a helicopter makes the criminals' job a whole lot easier, so destroy their chopper as quick and as often as possible. There are two objectives your team must protect, and neither one is within a direct line of sight of the other. You can try and split your forces on the initial defensive set up and surround each objective individually. However, use the Western Visceral Railroad Company main building as a hub for your forces to deploy at will. Bring a defibrillator with you and take advantage of the light machine gun battle pickup located nearby to

fend of incoming criminals. The LMG is great for taking down the enemy helicopter. It won't bring it down very quickly, but it will bring it down much faster than any other kit-based firearm. Keeping the criminals at bay without them setting any breach charges is obviously what is going to help you win the round. However, unlike Heist on many other maps, once the criminals have blown the doors on the train cars the rest of the round is well in their favor. If the train car doors get opened, it is a good idea to blow up the tram bridge, creating another obstacle for the criminals during their escape. It is important to note how far the extractions are from the cash pickups. As the police, you should have a few healthy vehicles at the ready because once the criminals begin their escape, it is incredibly difficult to catch them on foot. You better believe that they're going to make for a quick getaway.

★ Keep the helicopter in the air, healthy, and well manned with at least both gunners occupied and constantly fending off the enemy police helicopter and anyone with a rocket launcher. There aren't many opportunities in Heist where the criminals not only have fast getaway vehicles, but a helicopter to take the cash to the drop point. A good pilot on this mode/map combination doesn't go looking for the action, but constantly drops friendly bangers close enough to the objective to stay protected, giving them a leg up and keeping the pressure on the defending SWAT team. Good communication between your team's hacker and all squads creates great opportunities to breach, grab the cash, and head back away from the enemy deployment towards the friendly helicopter to take them to the least defended drop zone. Once your team has air superiority, take control of the train company building because it is the key location responsible for making both a safe breach and a safe first phase of a getaway.

★ Unfortunately for the criminals, there are two major breach points and no secondary breach points. Since they are not exactly right next to each other it is very possible to begin the breach process on one without the defenders of the other being able to respond in time without compromising the second objective. Each breach point is located in its own large red train car and can only be breached from the east side. Seeing that they are both on only one side, this makes attacking a little more difficult for the criminals and makes the adjacent building an even more important key location for this mode. The majority of the fighting happens before the breach; afterwards, it's a crapshoot.

★ Extraction heavily depends on a few different things: air superiority, major enemy occupancy, and friendly vehicles. Air superiority is extremely important because as long as there is an enemy helicopter fully equipped and strafing the streets, extractions like (B) and (C) are nearly impossible, however if your team owns the sky these extractions are close and easy to get to. Depending on where the majority of the enemy is, and if you have the vehicles to get there, extraction (A) is your best bet. (A) is located in the Construction Site and is covered on all sides with large dumpsters and buildings. If you set it up, you can park cars at the two entrances, buying your team a little extra time. Extraction (A) is the closest extraction to the police deployment, but because of how well guarded it is, it is still a prime location where teamwork and communication allows your squad to set up a good defense.

> **Utilize the vehicles for quick escapes.**
> —David Price, Weapon Designer

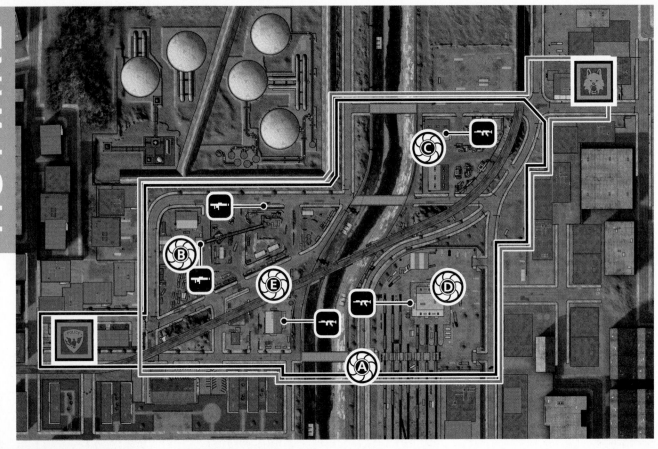

POLICE DEPLOYMENT
CRIMINAL DEPLOYMENT
HOTWIRE CARS

BATTLE PICKUPS

▦	AMMO
▥	DEFIBRILLATOR
←	GRAPPLING HOOK
✚	HEALTH
⚊	LMG
⚊	ROCKET LAUNCHER
⚊	STINGER
⚙	ZIPLINE

HOTWIRE CARS

VEHICLE		NAME
🚗	A	SPORTS SEDAN
🚚	B	FUEL TANKER
🚓	C	MUSCLE CAR
🚗	D	SPORTS SEDAN
🚐	E	UTILITY VAN

> Don't try to destroy vehicles with tripmines. It's a waste of your assets and won't work. Use the breaching charges instead.
> —John Seefurth, Quality Analyst

☆ At the beginning of a round of Hotwire on Derailed you want to capture the closest vehicle which are (B) and (E) for the police and (C) and (D) for the criminals. The police should note that objective E is the big explosive fuel tanker, meaning it is a better idea to go for (A) as soon as possible just because it's hard to tell really how long the fuel tanker can survive out on the streets. Knowing this, the criminals have a couple of choices in how to respond. The criminals can go for the tanker and hope that the police have totally abandoned the idea of controlling it. However, the better option is to go to Hotwire car A and, before attempting to capture it, form a defensive perimeter around it to defend the car from the police. If the criminals can successfully arrive on the scene and treat the car like it is a stationary position, it is easier to defend and keep the police off of the objective long enough for your team to bleed some tickets from the police for a small buffer. The good news for the police is that their deployment is slightly closer to (A) and if you don't hesitate when starting your round on this side, you can get there before anyone even knows that the game has started. Objectives (A) and (D) are the most valuable vehicles on this map, which is why the police must capture (A) as a priority. Both (A) and (D) are sports sedans, meaning they are not quite as quick as the muscle car, but they are still agile and they can carry two more people which translates to two more gunners launching grenades and shooting bad guys trying to blow up your car.

☆ The major crossroads are places that you should avoid as much as possible if you have any thought that there could be an enemy set up there. The main intersections, like the one dead center of the map right outside the Logistics Center, have about five major sightlines that look straight at it, meaning any one of them, or at worst all of them, could have an enemy waiting for your car ready to light it up and send you and your crew sky high. When driving anywhere on the map, use the mini-map on your HUD as much as possible because any sign of enemy movement should deter your vehicle. The muscle cars and sports sedans are fast and maneuverable, so they can avoid fire better than the others, but just a few key hits to the vehicle and it's done.

☆ The police may have a disadvantage when starting a round on this mode/map combination, but they definitely have the upper hand when it comes to battle pickup locations. In the Construction Site area there are two different rocket launcher pickups. This makes controlling the fuel tanker even scarier than normal, but if your team can get to the rocket launchers and use them for the enemy vehicles that cross the bridge, make them pay with a well-placed rocket to the chassis. On the same note, objectives (C), (D), and (E) all have light machinegun pickups near them. If you know the enemy is going to beat you to the Hotwire car, or you just want to sit and wait for them, pick up the LMG and turn the vehicles around you into Swiss cheese.

☆ Like in most situations on Hotwire, the helicopter is one of the most valuable vehicles because it can go anywhere and drop anyone off in locations required for tactical advantage. At the beginning of a round on Derailed, it is a little different. The helicopter is fast and can go straight to your destination, but with the ground you have to cover and the speed at which you have to do it, the motorcycle is extremely powerful. It is fast and can maneuver the streets of industrial Los Angeles with ease. Use the fast vehicles to get from point to point and stop the enemy from controlling Hotwire cars.

☆ Derailed is split into two clearly distinct halves separated by the large dry drainage system that runs down from north to south of the map. This is what splits up the "safe" driving areas. Each team is fairly safe driving on their half of the map because the dry ravine acts as a "no man's land" that is heavily policed by both sides and the attempt at crossing it is the biggest challenge for either side. The police should be driving around the Construction Site and Logistics Center as much as possible, if you must pass underneath the Tram Bridge do so quickly and get back to your half of the map because the driving bridge on the north side is deadly.

Using the river can be a good way of avoiding ambushes. Don't spend too much time down there. You may become an easy target for players wielding nearby battle pickups.
—Evan Champlin, Senior Multiplayer Level Designer

$10,000

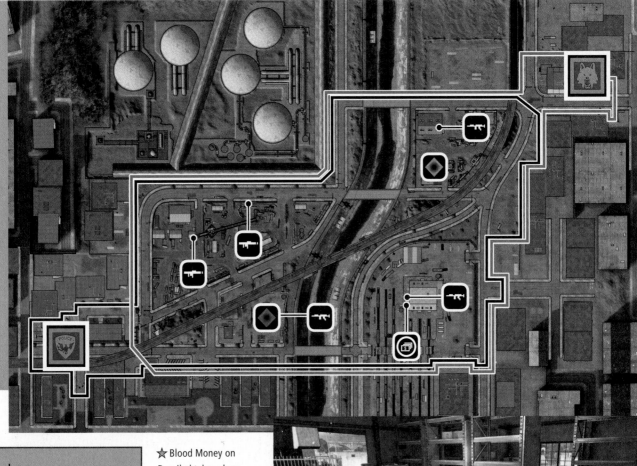

━━━	**POLICE DEPLOYMENT**
━━━	**CRIMINAL DEPLOYMENT**
	MONEY PILE
	POLICE VAULT
	CRIMINAL VAULT

BATTLE PICKUPS

	AMMO
	DEFIBRILLATOR
	GRAPPLING HOOK
	HEALTH
	LMG
	ROCKET LAUNCHER
	STINGER
	ZIPLINE

☆ Blood Money on Derailed takes place between the Logistics Center, Train Depot, and the Scrapyard, setting up a nice triangle which allows you and your team the decision on any tactic you wish to play. However, someone is going to have to rush the money pile at the beginning of the round, and the best way to do that is to first get someone on the roof of the Train Depot warehouse to fend off any enemies coming in from the distance. If you can spawn on this person or others spawn on you, it is a perfect location to drop down from the skylight right onto the money pile. This is a great place to drop a satellite phone because it's not quite on the money pile so it will stay safe, but it is extremely close, allowing your squad to drop right on to the money pile. Once your team is inside and has a good flow of money getting back to base, you want to set up defenses. Having someone on the roof at all times covers a major entrance, but you need a squad or two inside the warehouse covering each ground floor entrance. They are large and it is very easy to fit a small army of attackers through, making it difficult to defend.

☆ The money pile is located in the Train Depot which means it's off to the side of the center of the map, creating a large area of play to the north-west. It is important to keep your helicopter hovering and strafing the area around the Train Depot, adding another challenge to the enemy that further deters them from wanting to rush the money pile while your team takes all that they can.

☆ The police vault it located dead center in the middle of the Logistics Center, so just like defending the Train Depot, you can defend the police vault in the same fashion. You don't have to have someone guarding the roof, but finding a battle pickup and heading up there is a formidable way of fending off enemy vehicles attempting to steal from you. Attacking the police vault can be a little difficult to navigate because there is one main entrance. Drive up the ravine underneath the Tram Bridge and go around the Logistics Center, ending up in the back. From here you can see the open loading zone that is perfect for parking a vehicle close to and having all of your passengers load up on enemy cash before heading back to your base the same way.

☆ The criminal vault it located in the larger of the two buildings in the Scrapyard, a great location to defend from outside the building itself. Across the path is the second building in the Scrapyard that has a direct line to the vault and an upstairs office section that can be used as a guard tower because the windows can be shot out and used as cover when the enemy comes racing through the main gate. The only problem with holing up in the other building is that there is a staircase on the opposite side of the vault building that the enemy can access. This requires a guard or two holing up in the scrapped cars, watching the staircase and anyone breaking through the fences on this side. As long as there are friendly defenders in those two areas your team will at least have the entrances covered. However for added security you want to send the rest of the defending squad to pick off any that squeeze through the outer defenses. When attacking the criminal vault, the only reason you should attack from the front is if you have a fast vehicle that protects you from the incoming defender fire, so you can slip through and drive into the warehouse. The best and safest, but slowest, way to approach this vault is to take the ravine all the way around to the farthest side of the vault. Run your way to the building across from the vault to take out their defenders and place a satellite phone so that your squad can recoup there. From here, you can begin your attack on the vault and use the car you have parked in the back to make a quick getaway.

☆ The main ambush points on this map are going to be three points along the ravine that leads underneath the Tram Bridge, including the Tram Bridge itself. Unless the Tram Bridge has been blown up, it is a prime location for snipers to post up and kill anyone moving from the money pile back to their vault. This bridge is a little more useful for the criminal side since it is parallel with the escape route for the cops, but that's also why it is valuable to both sides. Along with the bridge, it is important to get through the ravine quickly and avoid everything in your path. It is one giant kill-box because of the elevated sides. Set up a barricade on the smaller bridge by the criminal spawn and use it to destroy any vehicles driving through the ravine attempting to attack the criminal vault or escaping with your money.

> **Hide on top of the office inside the warehouse to surprise the enemy.**
> **—John Seefurth, Quality Analyst**

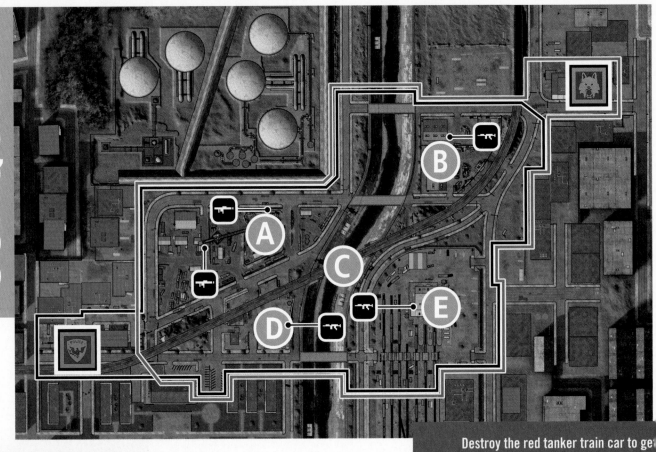

Destroy the red tanker train car to get easier access to objective B
—John Seefurth, Quality Analyst

▬▬	POLICE DEPLOYMENT
▬▬	CRIMINAL DEPLOYMENT
◯	CONTROL POINTS

BATTLE PICKUPS

	AMMO
	DEFIBRILLATOR
	GRAPPLING HOOK
	HEALTH
	LMG
	ROCKET LAUNCHER
	STINGER
	ZIPLINE

☆ Playing as the police, objectives (A), (C), and (D) are going to be the primary objectives that you want to take over. (A) and (D), the Construction Site and Logistics Center are going to be the easiest to get right at the start because they are close and the enemy cannot get there before you. However because they are so easy to capture, this doesn't mean they should be ignored or put off until (C) is captured. Objective (C) is incredibly valuable, but at least one squad each should be moving to capture (A) and (D) as quickly as possible to avoid any ticket bleeding that will come if they're not captured. The Tram Bridge is the central and most important key location because it is difficult to take over, but much easier to control. If the Tram Bridge is seeming too difficult to take after a couple of minutes of trying, go for (E). Taking the Train Depot from the criminals triggers a ticket bleed due to the fact that you control more points and it could draw some forces from (C) making it easier to take.

★ Playing on the criminal side isn't much different than the police, but based on your team's deployment both (A) and (E) are relatively the same distance away. After taking control of (B) you might make the decision to go for the Construction Site which could be heavily guarded, but could also create a distraction telling the other team that you might want the Construction Site more than the Tram Bridge. Doing this at the beginning of the round is the most effective because the other team is still trying to figure yours out. If taking control of (A) fails to distract the enemy from leaving (C) more open, don't worry. You can shoot the tanker on top of the bridge, killing anyone who decides to stick around. Wait for the bridge to fully collapse then move in to take the Tram Bridge because it is easier to reach and the police at this point are scrambling to decide which point they want to defend more, giving your team a major advantage.

★ The most valuable control points in Conquest are (A), (C), and (E) because they are central, and depending on the side you're on when you capture them, they have their backside facing your base for added defense. It is important not to forget (B) or (D) though. Even though they are considered the "gimme" locations due to their proximity to each team's base, sometimes the enemy team deploys in the middle of the map in order to defend those points and don't have anyone guarding the "gimme" control points. This situation is important to recognize because if you can weave through traffic or take the long way around to said points and take it over, it forces the entire team to draw their forces backward, opening up an opportunity for your team to begin their full frontal assault on the central control points.

★ The fortunate thing about Derailed is it lends itself extremely well to each and every class, but each has its own very large drawback. Bring out the big guns like the sniper rifles, battle rifles, and assault rifles when you're fighting out in the ravine or on top of any of the bridges, then equip your favorite shotgun or submachine guns when you're fighting inside the Train Depot, Scrapyard, or Logistics Center. The downside is, using these weapons in areas that they're not meant for could mean your downfall rather quickly. Don't forget that you can still play as an operator in a close-quarters situation to heal teammates and bring them back to life, but you want to equip a carbine instead of an assault rifle. The assault rifle is far more powerful at medium range, but the fire rate and close range accuracy of the carbine set serves you far better in the smaller areas.

> **Pesky snipers got you down? Destroy the fuel tanker on the rail bridge to take away their centralized high ground.**
> —Evan Champlin, Senior Multiplayer Level Designer

BATTLE PICKUPS

▬	POLICE DEPLOYMENT
▬	CRIMINAL DEPLOYMENT
▬	SPAWN AREA
	EXTRACTION POINT

BATTLE PICKUPS

🔲	AMMO
	DEFIBRILLATOR
	GRAPPLING HOOK
➕	HEALTH
	LMG
	ROCKET LAUNCHER
	STINGER
⚓	ZIPLINE

★ The setting in which Team Deathmatch takes place on Derailed is in the extended area of the Construction Site. This area lacks the giant buildings and grand strongholds that most TDM maps have, but contains smaller construction portables, equipment, and materials spread out all over the site. Use anything and everything you can find as cover, but stay on the move because cover won't keep you alive forever here.

★ There aren't many proper strongholds on Derailed due to the Construction Site being in the process of building new buildings and structures, but there are a couple of areas that can be well-guarded. The dumpsters on the far southwest part of the map are tall enough to provide good cover for a single squad. Use the dumpsters as sightlines and the pathways through the dumpster area as entrances and exits. These can serve as the pieces that need to be covered by your squad to hold it and keep your backs to the outside of the map. The dumpsters can only be held for so long because the area is vulnerable to lobbed grenades and grenade launchers. Set your satellite phone down and use it for as long as you can, but if it falls, move on to any one of the corners on the map as they are all formidable areas that you can hole up in for longer than the average player on this map.

★ Unlike most other modes on Derailed, Team Deathmatch calls for a closer ranged class loadout. Shotguns do fine here because there are a lot of corners that you should be using to surprise your enemies and covering to watch your squad's back, but carbines and SMGs are the weapons that serve best. These short- to medium-ranged weapons work best on Derailed

because most of the sightlines are rather long. Even though they do not stretch across the entire map, they stretch long enough for a shotgun to do very minimal damage. However if you're held up in the dumpsters or in the portable buildings, the shotgun does its job exactly how you want it to. This map is great for decoys and security cameras as well. There are so many corners in the areas around the west side of the map that a well-placed security camera gives you the notice that you need when you just can't cover every approach to your position.

★ Derailed is a high risk, fast-paced map on Team Deathmatch. There is no reason you shouldn't be worried about running into someone every few seconds or someone running into you, especially when you and your squad are on the move. There are lots of small pieces of cover here, so move from each piece to another and don't stay at a single one for very long. You will be found unless you move to a new area as quickly as you can. On Derailed it is a good tactic to use the leap frog method, just like SWAT would perform in a real life situation. With the use and communication of your entire squad, the man farthest away from the objective or point of interest that you are attempting to get to should move through the squad to the front of the squad toward the objective. Once the farthest member is at the front and has made some advancement he should stop and the next farthest member should copy the previous squad member's movement and then move past him to advance even further. Repeating this method advances your squad further and the moving squad member always has four players covering them while they are most vulnerable.

CROSSHAIR

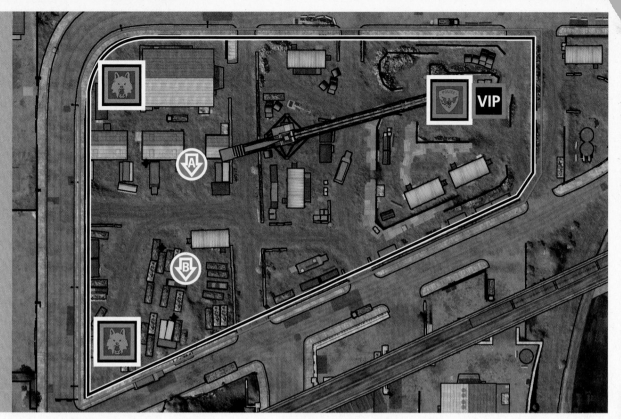

☆ Playing as the police, you have a great advantage on Derailed as long as you and your team take the approach slowly and carefully. Since Crosshair takes place in the Construction Site, there are tons of machines and buildings that you can use to cover your path and help with your plan to take the criminals by surprise. On the same note, this makes it very easy for the enemy to find hiding spots and prowl in the corners in between dumpsters and lying prone on top of roofs. Bring a decoy gadget with you to distract the enemy to one of the many paths available here. Since there are so many obstacles, it takes the enemy long enough to move and check out a distraction that if they fall for it, your team's VIP has an open lane to charge the extraction point. Place a teammate running the operator class in the two story building that's right in front of your deployment as an over-watch, but be careful because this position can be seen from the criminal deployment. Position the player up there but out of sight and stay in constant communication with everyone in your squad. If an enemy is spotted, the over-watch player can jump to the window quickly and take out the spotted enemy. When extracting, your team should occupy the building, splitting the two extractions to keep the VIP protected at all costs.

☆ As the criminals, it's best to find a hiding spot and stay there. Work and communicate with your team to set up the entire squad in strategic locations that can overlook both extractions and the major approaches so that your team doesn't get overwhelmed with incoming forces. Use the dumpsters near the B extraction and the roofs adjacent to the A extraction to protect each enemy objective. Staying close and keeping out of sight is key on Derailed because there are so many places to hide and the police don't have time to check them all. The only problem with using the roofs at A is that there is a two story construction portable near the police deployment that allows the police to have a vantage point that overlooks these roofs. If your team is going to use a roof, be prepared to take out this over-watch position in order to stay safe while hiding up there. In that same vein, you can use the grappling hook to climb any of the buildings. Just be aware that some of the roofs are rather short and if you're not positioned correctly you can be spotted from the ground level.

☆ On defense, Derailed is very much an all-out war when you attempt the rush tactic. It becomes less about which team has the better shooters and more about which team gets the luckiest and comes running around the corner before the enemy knows you're there. It is important to rush to a hiding spot and stay there simply because it is incredibly difficult to see which way the police are coming. Without a lot of sightlines straight to the extraction points, mechanics and enforcers should practice lockdown tactics.

☆ The best VIP routes on Derailed are along the outside perimeter of the map, specifically because of the pathway that leads horizontally across the middle of the map. Crossing this path is dangerous and getting caught here is close to guaranteed death. If you let the rest of your team cross the path safely, there is a good chance that it is safe for you and the VIP. However, a smart criminal will let them pass, wait for you to cross, then take you out. The outer perimeters minimize this risk because the visible access points to the road are in the middle. It is tougher to check both ways in a pinch than it is to check one, so make sure your back is to your base or out of bounds when crossing. In this map there are plenty of tight corners where laser tripmines and enemy players can be hidden. When out in the open move quickly, but in tight spaces move slowly and quietly because footsteps can be very loud, especially when running.

☆ Use the grappling hook to get to the roofs. Since you don't want to be there for very long, especially when attacking, zipline to the north or south side of the map bypassing the dirt road and avoiding as much danger as possible. When defending, be sure to carry the security camera with you and set it on the dumpsters and building walls to watch areas that you just don't have the bodies to cover at all times.

> **Smoke grenades can really help you make a getaway.**
> **—Brian Paoloni, Quality Designer**

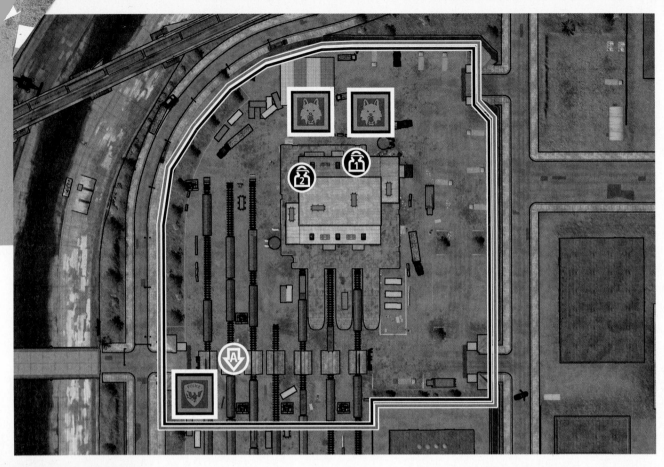

▬▬▬	POLICE DEPLOYMENT
▬ ▬ ▬	CRIMINAL DEPLOYMENT
🔲	HOSTAGE
⬇	EXTRACTION POINT

☆ Rescue takes place in the Train Depot key location on Derailed, making for an excellent "breach and clear" situation. The hostages and the criminals guarding them are held up inside the depot's main building which happens to be full of containers, shelving, boxes, and equipment. This doesn't make cover any more difficult to pay attention to when looking for defenders, but it does mean that the enemy could be anywhere and running in blind is sometimes your only choice. Use grappling hooks to get to the roof and drop in through the skylights, surprising the enemy. Or, take out a couple with a battle rifle before your team's ground forces come bashing down the door to clear out the rest and rescue

the hostages. It may seem like you have to deal with all of the enemies inside the warehouse, but remember that there are plenty of places to hide outside so that they can either catch you coming back out with a hostage or can take you out while you're paying attention to entering the building. It is a good idea to take the long way around the building to the backside where it is possible to surprise the criminals posted up outside. In fact, it is a good idea to make sure the outside is completely clear before any of your team members enters the warehouse. This secures that you don't get shot from behind and that your escape route is relatively safe.

★ When playing defense on Derailed, you must pay attention very closely to where the hostages are located. There is cover there, meaning the enemy can use this to conceal their approach even before starting the pick up on either of the hostages. In the larger part of the warehouse, it is good to have two players hidden in sight of the hostage while another is in the smaller hostage room barricading himself with tripmines or listening closely to footsteps coming around the corner. Right at the

> Law enforcement, use the access on the roof to your advantage. Scout the location and then attack from above. Flashbangs are your friend for those hidden corners.
> —Evan Champlin, Senior Multiplayer Level Designer

beginning it is good to send one of your teammates to the roof, hidden and watching for anyone that tries to climb up, rather than for what's going on down below. It's easy to get sniped while on the roof, so paying attention to only the roof for at least the first minute is important. After that first minute, it's okay to jump down and find a hiding spot outside the warehouse near the exit that you think they might come out of. This could be any of them, but you have to trust your gut and listen to where the action is happening. If the enemy is able to enter the building, it is far more important to retreat back to their extraction and try to catch the police as they exit the building instead of starting a firefight and risking killing one when there are two others ready to shoot you.

★ In the first round, it is a perfectly safe tactic to rush around the perimeter of the building and attempt to cut off any police going straight for the fast capture as they scramble to the closest entrance. This tactic should never be attempted twice in a row because if the opposing team expects the rush even one little bit, it could cost your entire team's lives before the first minute has passed. Derailed is wider than most Rescue maps, so it lends itself well to either the rush or the lockdown tactic. This map, more so than others, is all about adjusting to the current situation. If one enemy player has broken through your lockdown tactic it is important not to scramble. If the whole enemy team has broken through, whether they killed any of your team in the process or not, it is a good idea to get out of the defensive position and surround the building, ready to attack rather than attempting to hold your ground. Every situation is different, but as long as you use the train cars and shipping containers to conceal your movement, you can gain the upper hand at any moment.

★ Both hostages are being held inside shipping containers open on both sides. The first is located in the large main room of the warehouse and the other is in a smaller office type room. It is possible to cover both hostages from the large room, but you may want to at least set traps or be ready to surround the small room if you are going to leave it unguarded. When playing as the cops and going for these hostages, carefully peek inside to see if a criminal or two is sitting right next to the hostage. If there's no enemy there, use the cover of this container to move through it and check the other side for any hiding enemies before picking up the hostages. It's incredibly difficult to tell if there is someone on the other side of the open door, and it is important to check because, even though it is hard to see from back there, the enemy will be listening for you.

★ Grappling hooks and ziplines are your best friend when playing on this map. If you're the police and your team manages to pick up one or both of the hostages, there is a good chance that there are at least a few enemies right outside the exits waiting for you to leave. Try hooking the skylight above you and climbing to the roof because from there you can zipline in any direction, allowing you to safely land and put some distance between you and the enemies that were waiting for you. It is also good to equip a gas mask and throw gas grenades near the hostages. The shipping containers are incredibly slim and if there's a bad guy in there, you completely disorient him, giving you a grand opportunity to move in and take him out. Move fast because once he's gassed he will alert his friends.

> There are many entrances to the warehouse. Be aware of the roof and back doors.
> —David Price, Weapon Designer

INTRODUCTION
DOWNTOWN
SWAT VS. THIEVES

Destroy three out of the four crane anchors to trigger the crane Levolution.
—John Seefurth, Quality Analyst

The heart of Downtown Los Angeles is a jumping environment. The streets, the buildings, the cars—are all open to criminal deeds. The police have shut down the city center, and a heated confrontation is about to break out.

Traveling the streets of Los Angeles can get a little extreme; from the road rage in hotwire to the all-out firefights over the heist objectives, the true *Battlefield: Hardline* experience is happening Downtown. Downtown allows for all styles of play, the close quarters combat of the all the major buildings and the mid- to long-ranged firefights out on the streets keeps every class on their toes and more than just a small role to play in every mode. It's time to set your favorite class loadouts and get to work because Downtown is not going to control itself.

LEVOLUTION

As the fight heats up and the support of the large construction crane begins to give way, the crane has come crashing down taking out a huge chunk of one of the towers on its way down. Use the downed crane for an alternate route to key objective locations and tactical positions, but keep clear of falling debris as it will kill you without any chance of being revives.

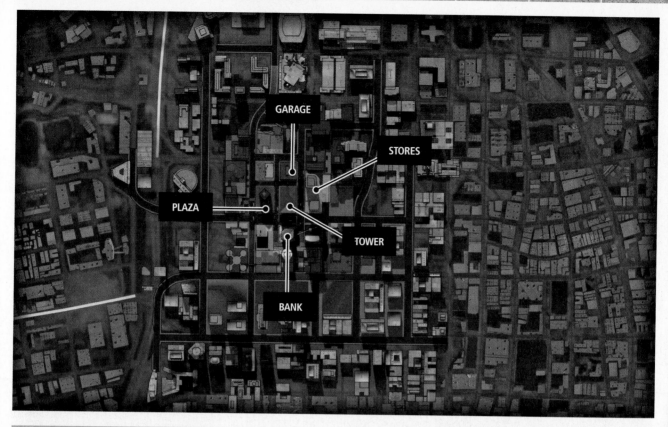

KEY LOCATIONS

GARAGE

The Garage has four separate floors, all of which lead to a tactical point. Use the roof as a vantage point to overlook both the Plaza and the Stores. The Professional strives on top of the Garage because he or she can use the sniper bolt action to kill at range and Laser Tripmines to protect their six.

STORES

The open air of the Stores area Downtown gives you and your team time to spread out and create multiple ambushes in this key location. With two levels and a hollowed out center, it is incredibly important to know where the enemy is hiding. The security camera and interrogation tactics are incredibly useful when defending this location. It is a good idea to take advantage of the battle pickups on this map and use them for the Stores because it quickly becomes a magnet for helicopters and vehicles attempting to attack this zone.

PLAZA

Drop in from the skyscraper adjacent to the Plaza to get the drop on any enemies that might be held up here. Cover is shallow, so be sure to go prone if you are under fire. If you have to retreat to the lobby of the building, do so quickly but be sure to watch your back from enemies using the elevators and moving street side.

BANK

If you're looking for a formidable stronghold for your team to set up, the Bank is the place you're looking for. With only a few entrances to the bank, you and your squad can lock down the major entryways and be able to retreat further in if the heat gets too hot. Holding both the bank floor and the parking Garage directly beneath it gives your team a safe fortress and alternate central deployment area for modes such as Conquest and Heist.

TOWER

The Tower is more specifically the penthouse in the larger of the interactive buildings. This penthouse is home to Blackstone Financial Services and is filled with offices and meeting rooms that serve as a great way to dive for cover and make a quick escape from enemy fire out the window down to the street level. Along with the roof access, there are multiple ways into the Tower, including the elevators. Stay keen to each one and control the tower for great tactical advantages.

> Climbing to the top of the Crane may seem like a great idea for budding Snipers, but with the amount of time this takes it may be wiser to take the elevator up to the top of a skyscraper instead. Keep an eye out for those Window Washer platforms!
> —Ethan Solak, Video Editor

169

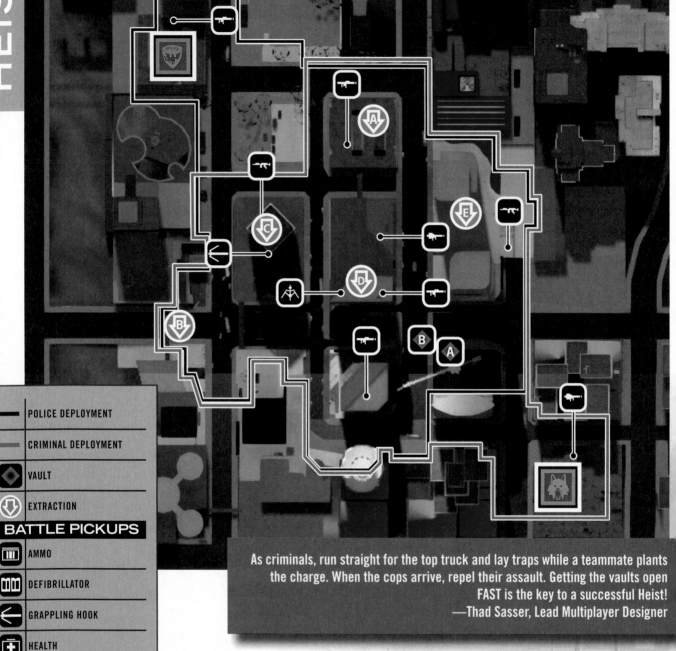

LEGEND

POLICE DEPLOYMENT

CRIMINAL DEPLOYMENT

◆ VAULT

⊗ EXTRACTION

BATTLE PICKUPS

AMMO

DEFIBRILLATOR

GRAPPLING HOOK

HEALTH

LMG

ROCKET LAUNCHER

STINGER

ZIPLINE

> As criminals, run straight for the top truck and lay traps while a teammate plants the charge. When the cops arrive, repel their assault. Getting the vaults open FAST is the key to a successful Heist!
> —Thad Sasser, Lead Multiplayer Designer

☆ The first two minutes of Heist on the police side are crucial. If your team gives the criminal side any time to get to the objectives and set a breaching charge before you get there it makes your job a whole lot tougher to pull off. It is key that you choose a vehicle deployment of some sort because with exception of the mobile HQ, all of the vehicles on this map are quick and you'll need them to cut off the enemy team. The helicopter provides for an excellent deployment point. Equipped with two machine guns, the police helicopter can defend itself in a pinch and the pilot can hover over any spot that needs defending and drop foot-mobiles on the battlefield by letting teammates deploy within. Even though the mobile HQ is the slowest vehicle in this mode, playing it in a prime location gives your team the upper hand when defending the cash. Parking the mobile HQ directly under the bridge that objective (B) is located on allows your team to deploy forces to defend objective (A) while the helicopter provides support for (B). Don't park the mobile HQ too far out in the open because even though you want to deploy close to the action, you don't want the vehicle being destroyed because the enemy has a direct line of sight to it.

★ On the criminal side, you and your team have to be careful. It is easy to lose a large chunk of tickets fast on this map, so stick to cover and try not to stay out in the open too long. Create cover by racing under the bridge if the majority of the police team is defending from atop the bridge. In the first seconds of the game, try planting the breaching charges at least on objective (B) and control that area as long as possible because if your team can keep the police distracted on the bridge, the second wave of attackers on your team can move in and set the breaching charge on (A) and have a little bit of extra time to prepare an escape plan. When placing your mobile HQ, park it on the east side of the construction site, at least at the start. Even though it isn't far from your original base, your deployment is still closer to the objectives than before. Parking the mobile HQ here also provides a deployment that can resupply the attackers on A with fresh reinforcements as they're defending.

★ Unlike most maps, Downtown has two completely separate Heist objectives with one primary breach point each and no secondary points. This means that each breach point is extremely essential and creates two very hot spots for both teams. Granted, the two objectives are close enough to each other to allow a single squad to protect both at the same time. However doing so causes that squad to be highly vulnerable sitting out in the open. The most optimal way to secure both packages before the time limit is up or the criminals run out of tickets is to pick up both packages simultaneously and run each to a different extraction point, thus spreading the police as thin as possible.

★ With two different primary locations it is easier for the criminals to gather at least one package, if not both. Because of how open this map is and how far apart each extraction is, the criminals must really coordinate in order to secure the package at their drop points. The easiest extraction, if available, is taking objective (A) to extraction (B). There is a motorcycle located in the construction site right next to the cash and a straight shot down the street under the bridge takes you right to the extraction. The toughest extraction is (C) because of the fact that it is located at the top of the Pacific Bank tower and if the police get there first, it is incredibly difficult to get past their line of defenses. Not to mention, you have to travel half-way across the map, up the elevator, and up a couple of flights of stairs just to get there. However, there is a clever path to this extraction point that requires the Tower key location. Travel up to the top of the Blackstone Tower and, from any of the top three floors, zipline to the extraction roof. If your squad coordinates using their own ziplines at the same time, catching the police off guard secures you a safe extraction.

Criminals, use your proximity to the vaults to ambush the responding Law Enforcement units. Have your teammates bring up a fast vehicle like the Coupe or Motorcycle to pick up the bag carrier immediately after the vaults are cracked.
—Evan Champlin, Senior Multiplayer Level Designer

Law Enforcement, be prepared to play defense. The Criminals can escape with the bags quickly if all of your teams resources are at the vaults.
—Evan Champlin, Senior Multiplayer Level Designer

Legend

	POLICE DEPLOYMENT
	CRIMINAL DEPLOYMENT
	HOTWIRE CARS

BATTLE PICKUPS

	AMMO
	DEFIBRILLATOR
	GRAPPLING HOOK
	HEALTH
	LMG
	ROCKET LAUNCHER
	STINGER
	ZIPLINE

HOTWIRE CARS

VEHICLE		NAME		VEHICLE		NAME
	A	MUSCLE CAR			D	MUSCLE CAR
	B	FUEL TANKER			E	SPORTS SEDAN
	C	SPORTS SEDAN				

★ The beginning in a round of Hotwire on Downtown is actually one of the more simple times on this mode/map combination. Each team should go for the two closest Hotwire vehicles. Because Downtown was made for hot pursuit and road rage, four out of five of the Hotwire vehicles are either coupes or sedans, making for slight differences in their advantages, but all are fast nonetheless. Taking off to your team's closest vehicles (A) and (C), or (D) and (E), for the law enforcement and criminals respectively, serves best for your team because you are able to start scoring as soon as you can, while the rest of your team uses the vehicles at your deployment area to chase down the enemy hotwire vehicles. While chasing down the quicker vehicles, the Tanker Truck (B) should not be forgotten. It may be big and it may be suicide driving too close to enemy gunfire, but it scores you just as many points as any other objective on the map. If you're feeling ambitious, go straight for the tanker and try to get it back to your team's half of the map before anyone else can get to it so you can stay protected for as long as possible. If you don't think you're going to make it there before the other team, why not blow it up? Odds are, if you're late then the enemy is undoubtedly nearby, giving you a grand opportunity for some easy kills. Because the Hotwire cars respawn quickly after being destroyed, you won't be waiting there too long before a new one appears and is ready for you to take it.

★ As with all Hotwire maps, the helicopter is going to be your team's best weapon against recovering enemy controlled objectives. Maneuvering the helicopter between the incredibly tall skyscrapers is extremely difficult, especially when chasing down enemy vehicles; so make sure your best pilot is flying. As long as there are always two gunners operating the side door machine guns, the helicopter is always the best vehicle available. Your base is also equipped with several fast vehicles that should be used to get to key locations as quickly as possible. Set up ambushes or cut off Hotwire vehicles and cause your opponents to lose control of the objectives for as long as possible.

> Zipline between rooftops to escape with the Heist bags in ways the cops won't think about!
> —Ben Gaciu, System Designer

★ When driving one of the Hotwire vehicles, it is always a good idea to stay away from the enemy's main deployment and when possible avoid driving directly under the main bridge in the center of the map. It's a great place for snipers to sit waiting for drivers to come screaming down the main street, creating an easy shot for them. So what do you do if you're avoiding these areas? Like most Downtown areas, this map is made of straightaways and sharp turns. Loop around your half of the map and make the very last turn you can before driving right by the enemy deployment. There is at least one turn that doesn't drive down the middle of the map and doesn't lead you straight to their base. Use the alternate, more dangerous, routes if needed because it's not impossible to survive as long as you're driving fast. There are also quite a few jumps, like the one at the top of the Garage, that allow you to bypass any roadblocks that are bottlenecking the major intersections.

> If the Cops shoot the helicopter enough it flies away before the Criminals can secure the loot.
> —Brian Paoloni, Quality Designer

★ As we mentioned before, the main bridge is an excellent place for snipers to set up and attempt to shoot anyone out of their cars driving directly under them. Your opponents have to drive straight toward you, so take the time to line up that perfect shot. There is some existing debris on the main bridge in the center of the map. This is useful for taking another car to set up in the middle of the road to cause enemy vehicles to either stop or come plowing in, forcing them to lose control over the objective that they currently control. If you're ready for a car to be stopped there, you can get up close and kill the driver and/or any passengers in the car to then commandeer it for your team.

★ There is a battle pickup inside almost every major building. Use these to destroy enemy Hotwire vehicles passing by or to quickly get around to a location you need. Use the light machine guns and rocket launchers at the ambush sites to destroy enemy vehicles much more easily. Use the zipline to put yourself in position to cut off the enemy if they get away from you alive.

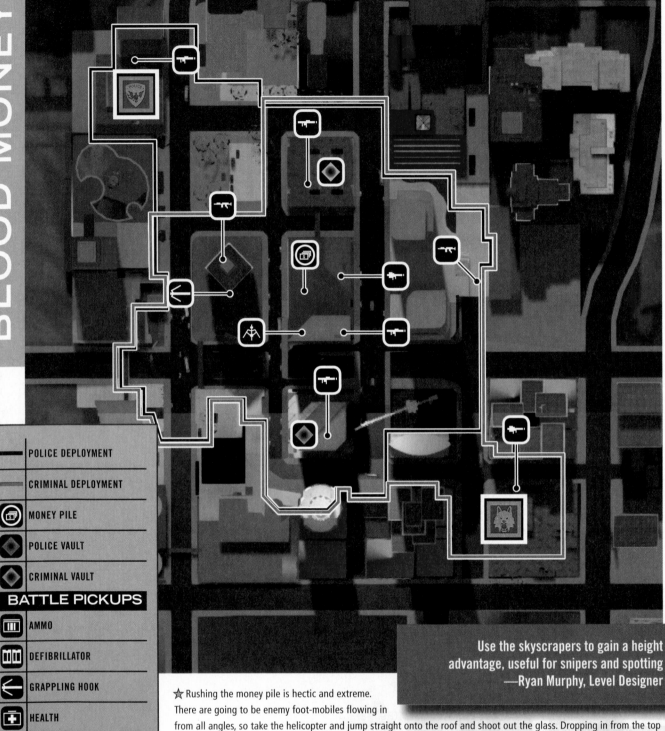

POLICE DEPLOYMENT

CRIMINAL DEPLOYMENT

MONEY PILE

POLICE VAULT

CRIMINAL VAULT

BATTLE PICKUPS

AMMO

DEFIBRILLATOR

GRAPPLING HOOK

HEALTH

LMG

ROCKET LAUNCHER

STINGER

ZIPLINE

Use the skyscrapers to gain a height advantage, useful for snipers and spotting
—Ryan Murphy, Level Designer

☆ Rushing the money pile is hectic and extreme. There are going to be enemy foot-mobiles flowing in from all angles, so take the helicopter and jump straight onto the roof and shoot out the glass. Dropping in from the top and surprising anyone who is stealing money gives you and your squad a large advantage. The building with the money pile is located on a multi-level platform that has entrances from two different street levels, so your squad must spread out and watch each other's back. This money pile is one of the toughest to defend in the game.

☆ Because the money pile on Downtown is so tough to defend, spread out and keep to the shadows both inside and outside the building. Push forward and use the roof, friendly vehicles, and anything you can get your hands on because holding this money pile is precious. Set up a defense zone outside the second floor entrance and make sure no one goes in or out of the building. There's a better chance of you and your squad surviving from the outside. Make sure your team is filtering people in to grab money and go. There's a good chance that the cash collectors won't survive if they're in there too long. Don't get greedy! Get in and then get right on out to head back to your vault quickly.

☆ Since the money pile is so difficult to defend simply due to the nature of the building it's located in, your strategy is going to be heavily predicated on defending your vault and attacking the enemy's. The police vault is an armored truck and it's located on the second floor of the Garage. There are a few entrances, one on the street level of the north side, the west side, and an entrance from the floor above the vault and below it. Watching the ramps leading above and below the vault truck is easier than watching the two street level entrances because they're much more difficult for the criminals to get to them. Don't neglect them though, as a good squad can sneak past any players not paying attention and sabotage their defenses. Rig some laser tripmines on the ramps because, more than likely, anyone entering this way is on foot or they are screaming in and alerting you to their presence really fast. Take advantage of the rocket launcher battle pickup located near the police vault to destroy any fast moving vehicles that can easily get away with a large amount of your team's money. Operators and professionals are best suited to handle the defense on the police side due to how large the Garage is and how it is better defended when you're far off in a corner, out of direct line of sight of the attackers.

> Law Enforcement, be prepared to play defense. The Criminals can escape with the bags quickly if all of your teams resources are at the vaults.
> —Evan Champlin, Senior Multiplayer Level Designer

☆ The criminal vault is also an armored truck and it's located in the basement parking Garage under the Bank. Unlike the police vault, there are fewer entrances to the basement, especially because there is no way to get to the vault from underneath. The tradeoff is fair however. Even though there may be fewer ways into the Bank's basement parking Garage, it is much easier to control the Bank and it provides the police an excellent home away from home deployment. With that being said, it is extremely important that your team protects the Bank in its entirety at all costs. You don't want to leave the vault completely unattended, but it is acceptable to split your team's forces up a little because it is still possible to protect the vault from the Bank. Playing an operator is extremely versatile since he or she can shoot at incoming enemies and rotate from upstairs to downstairs to defend against any targets that were missed on the first try. Use the rocket launcher battle pickup as a last resort to destroy anything with armor that could get away unscratched by small arms.

☆ On both sides there are similar ambush points when playing Downtown Blood Money; since there is one main road that leads to and from the money pile, try placing yourself on the other side of that street from the building that the money pile is in and wait for any targets trying to escape in the getaway car that is parked outside. Since there are multiple ways to get out of the building it's good to have a squad watching the alley way on the opposite side of the building than the main street; if the enemy tries to slip out the back and take the long route back home to try and trick you, you'll be waiting for them in their own bottleneck where they'll have nowhere else to run.

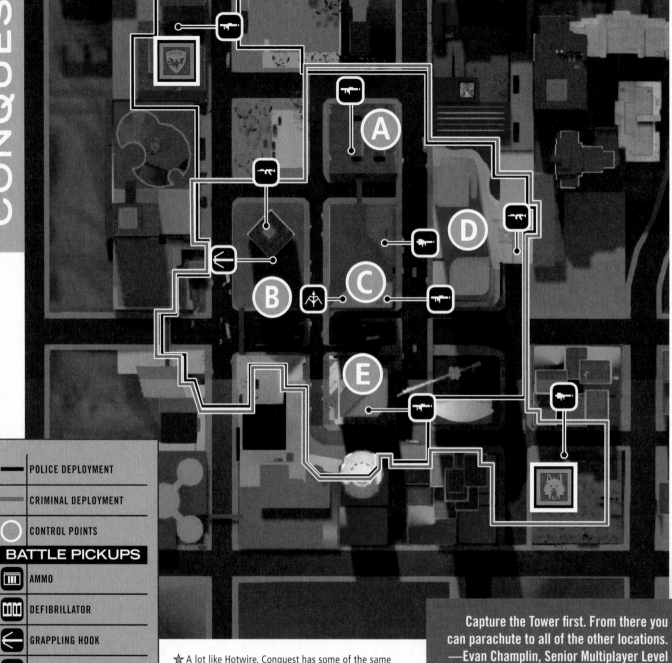

POLICE DEPLOYMENT

CRIMINAL DEPLOYMENT

CONTROL POINTS

BATTLE PICKUPS

AMMO

DEFIBRILLATOR

GRAPPLING HOOK

HEALTH

LMG

ROCKET LAUNCHER

STINGER

ZIPLINE

☆ A lot like Hotwire, Conquest has some of the same tactics, especially at the beginning of the round. For the police side you and your team must go for the two closest control points, (A) and (B), because starting the ticket bleed as early as possible is the name of the game. What's different about Conquest is (C) is far more important than any of the other control points on the map. Go for (C) first because it is the control point that is vulnerable on all sides, so capturing it fast and holding it as long as possible keeps your team in a strong position. Park the

> **Capture the Tower first. From there you can parachute to all of the other locations.**
> **—Evan Champlin, Senior Multiplayer Level Designer**

police mobile spawn point down the street from the Plaza towards the north. This is a great central place on the map between the triangle of the police's key control points. If any of the three major points becomes controlled by the criminals, your team should use the mobile spawn point to take it back as fast as possible.

> Avoid taking a direct route to Capture Point C. Rather than using the elevators in the lobby, head downstairs and take the elevators located in the parking Garage below. Beware however, as these elevators open behind you.
> —William Bordonaro, Quality Analyst

★ Playing as the criminals is very similar to playing as the police, especially because of how balanced Downtown is as a map. There is one extreme difference in how the criminals can gain the advantage in this mode/map combination. If your team is able to rush the Tower and keep enough forces there to capture the control point, the rest of the infiltration team can head to the roof and zipline to the next skyscraper. From here you can drop down to the ground floor using your parachute and take the Plaza by surprise. At the beginning of the round, park the mobile spawn point near the entrance of the Tower. Parking it here is not the best place to keep it, but you can use it to keep the pressure on C as long as possible, leaving the police without a clue on how to handle the backdoor take-over on the Plaza.

★ By far the most valuable control point is the Tower because it is dead center on the map and, once a team controls it, it's extremely difficult to take back due to how well it can be defended. However, this is where the attack helicopters come into play. If both attack helicopters are in the air they are going to have to fight over the air space, but once one of them is down the opposite chopper has full range on firing its miniguns straight through the penthouse of the Tower. If your team does not control the Tower, you need to gain air-superiority and take out all of the defenses or it's going to be a tough battle from here on. Even though C may be the most valuable control point, don't forget that if the majority of the team is defending it there won't be many bodies left to defend the others.

★ Due to the nature of Downtown, the map provides for all forms of combat, creating opportunities for all classes to shine and become equally useful. When defending the Stores, operators and mechanics are going to have the better primary weapons for the range of the mid-range to close-quarters firefights that break out here. Then, the Garage allows professionals and operators to put all of their gadgets to use, rigging traps for enemy foot-mobiles and healing wounded teammates once they've been dinged up by heavy incoming firepower and sniper rounds zipping through non-lethal body parts. Don't forget the enforcer, which is key when defending the Tower. With his wide spread shotgun, ballistic shield, and ammo box, he creates impenetrable blockades that not even a maniac with a light machine gun and body armor could get through.

> Don't forget about Capture Point C. Often whichever team controls C controls the match.
> —Ben Gaciu, System Designer

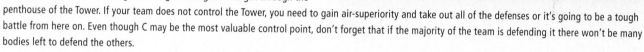

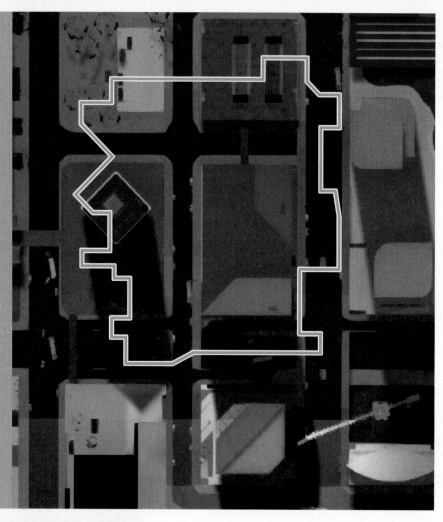

★ Team Deathmatch takes place in the busiest section of Downtown. Most of the action on this map happens between the Garage and the Bank with the Tower sitting right in the center of the fun. The two major streets are the lanes in which most of the sniping and mid- to long-range battle happens, so break out those 4x and 8x scopes for those shots that can only be made with the right optics. Most firefights happen around the atrium, which is the building in the middle with the glass roof and very wide open balcony, it is where the money pile in Blood Money is located and acts as the central location where both teams meet if they run straight toward each other after deploying.

★ If you and your team can successfully enter the atrium and set up defenses at every door, it acts as a formidable stronghold. The atrium is a large building and has plenty of room to set up laser tripmines and sabotage charges, not to mention very narrow doorways, so it is a great spot to hole up in, if your entire squad and maybe another is in there with you to cover all entrances. Another great stronghold is the very bottom floor of the Tower, also in the center of the map. The lower part of the Tower is at the lowest point on the map, but it is one of the only locations that has solid walls and a minimal amount of ways to get in. This parking garage not only has just a few ways to get in, but it is also much smaller than most locations so it only takes a single squad to protect it. If things get too hairy, be sure to escape out the main entrance to the street or up the elevators to the lobby of the Tower.

▬▬	POLICE DEPLOYMENT
▬▬	CRIMINAL DEPLOYMENT
▭	SPAWN AREA
⬇	EXTRACTION POINT

★ Like all modes, on Downtown there is a role for every class. However, with only a couple of areas to really be able to use the long range weapons like the bolt-action sniper rifles, keep the amount of professionals on your team to a minimum of two or three. Enforcers and mechanics really thrive in Team Deathmatch because unless you're on the street, the enemy is going to be right in your face with silenced P90s to keep their movements hidden and with double-barrel shotguns when breaking through doors looking for quick kills.

★ When you and your squad are on the move to either breach a stronghold or find one of your own, stay off of the streets as much as possible. The main streets are hunting grounds for snipers and operators equipped with assault rifles. There are plenty of hiding spots along these streets, so, if you need to, duck behind a car or in a bush to avoid being seen so that you can move on safely.

CROSSHAIR

☆ Playing as police, the three major lanes split up into quick and dangerous and extremely slow and safe. Heading up the north side of the map forces your team to move very slowly from cover to cover without being seen. There is an abundance of different forms of cover but they are all small and you must use them wisely so as not to get caught and pinned down by a storm of incoming fire. Choosing to lead your team south and through the construction site is much quicker. However, due to the amount of corners in the construction site, check every corner you pass by as each one is a good hiding spot for the defending side. The police's best bet is to split up and use smoke to cover each approach. The north street may be a little wide for a single smoke grenade, but two should cover enough to conceal your team's positioning on important cover spots where they have the advantage on ambushing the enemy if they get a little anxious. A single smoke grenade in the construction site covers most of it and allows you to move past defenders without them even noticing you were right in front of their face.

☆ When defending the enemy's approach from the criminal side, it is important to find a good hiding spot and stay there. Any movement after you've found your hiding place surely gives away your position and can get you killed very early in the round. The construction site is great for hiding in the shadows and corners of the sheet wall and behind the equipment. This is where you should listen very closely for footsteps and enemies jumping from ledges. Landing is very loud and allows you to pinpoint your opponent's exact location for you to call out to your team and strike when you have the advantage. Hiding in the construction site is mainly waiting for the enemy attackers to walk right into your sights, so be patient and get that perfect shot. Defending the north street is a completely different story. Carry an assault rifle or carbine for this side because your job is to watch all the way down the street for any movement whatsoever. The enemy has to move from cover to cover and you need a powerful and accurate shot if you're going to take them out without giving them a chance to fire back.

> Law enforcement, you have the high ground. Push into the objective areas and control the lanes before the criminals can climb into position.
> —Evan Champlin,
> Senior Multiplayer Level Designer

☆ It is best to use the lockdown method when defending on Downtown simply because it is a wide map without many choices to get back to the extractions if you're needed. Sometimes there is a great need for a rush on this map, especially since running back to your deployment then to the opposite extraction of the side you're on may take way too long. If you've pushed up farther than the halfway point on the map and you know your team has been killed on the other side, rush toward the enemy deployment and around to the other side, taking out any stragglers from behind and catching the VIP by surprise right before he escapes.

☆ The VIP has a large amount of cover at his disposal and should use it religiously. If you are the VIP and you decide to take the construction site route, have an escort move in front of you as he or she checks each corner. If by some chance your escort gets beat on the draw, you either have the chance to go for the kill since you know exactly where the enemy is or you must move around the defender and shoot him in the back for the same reason. If you decide to move along the north side, be sure to stay back until you know the coast is clear. It is too easy to spot the VIP on the north street because of how open it is, but if your team can lob a couple of smoke grenades to cover your approach to a closer cover, then use it and move quickly but try not to get boxed in.

> Don't let your VIP lead the way! Have them hang back so the rest of the team can engage the enemy first.
> —John Seefurth, Quality Analyst

☆ On defense, use the security cameras on the areas that you can't quite watch constantly. Even though there are only a couple of major avenues, there are plenty of smaller hallways and corridors that just can't be watched by only five players. When attacking, use the zipline to get from the bridge to the end of the construction site quickly to catch the enemy by surprise and steal a quick extraction.

 POLICE DEPLOYMENT

CRIMINAL DEPLOYMENT

HOSTAGE

EXTRACTION POINT

☆ Playing as the police on Downtown forces you to be a little more aggressive than most other maps when playing Rescue. Get to the atrium as fast as you can and scope out the hostage building adjacent to the Plaza. When you enter the atrium, stay alert because the criminals might have the same idea even though you can easily get there first. The atrium is a great holding point for most modes and Rescue is no exception. If you are able to take control of the atrium, you can scope out any criminals trying to advance due to impatience or repositioning and that is your time to thin their forces and strike. The hostages are located on opposite sides of the lobby from each other, so if you need to make a quick escape go for the closest hostage and book it back to the extraction. If you have a little time, about a minute or so, try taking the elevator to the top floor and zipline down to the extraction. Remember, if you can get to the top floor, so can the criminals. Don't go up there with your guard down.

★ Playing as the criminals on this mode/map combination can be easy if you and your team make good decisions. Playing defense on a map with roofs, wide open areas, and a place that the police can hole up in to give them an advantage is all about not giving away your position by any means. Keep a couple of teammates guarding the hostages either very close by or in a corner of the building, but the rest of your team should be spread out. If you like being outside and trying to catch any police attempting to enter through the front door, equip your operator class and sit on the far south end of the Plaza. There is cover there and you won't be seen by any police in the atrium. Go to the roof if the lower levels are not working for you. The police have a direct line to your roof from theirs via zipline, and if you are able to cut them off it could ruin their entire operation. If you are on the roof, be ready to parachute to the front of the building or to the extraction when the hostages are being picked up. Base jumping from the building gets you to the extraction much faster than they could on foot.

> The elevators can be a key route for escaping with the hostage. Parachute or zipline your way to safety!
> —Thad Sasser, Lead Multiplayer Designer

★ Downtown lends itself very well to both the rush tactic and the lockdown tactic. There are plenty of places to hide when attempting the lockdown tactic, including the roof, because even though you are spread out it doesn't take long to get back to the hostages. It is important that your team communicates which tactic you are performing because unless everyone is on the same page, any plan falls apart. The rush tactic is very available and works if the entire team knows where they're going. Being able to base jump from the roof to the atrium and dropping in on the police, or rushing straight for the atrium and hoping your team is able to take out those who decided to move into it allows your team a great advantage. Your team ideally should have the enemy outnumbered as long as there were no casualties. Your team also controls the middle ground which allows you quick access to any point on the map within seconds. If you see the police enter the hostage building, you can get there and kill them before they are able to pick up a hostage. If you see that one of the hostages has been taken, you can easily get to the extraction point much faster than the enemy and set up a defensive position for when they try to escape.

> Watch out for the atrium. It's a strong point for a weapon with good range. Take the hostage up the elevator and zipline or parachute out.
> —David Price, Weapon Designer

★ At the point in the round where the police can get to the hostages, the safest one is the hostage nearest your entry point, assuming you entered safely. The hostages are on opposite sides of the lobby from each other, so if you can get to one of them you have enough cover to pick him up if the other is being guarded.

★ Apart from the zipline that can take you from building to building or building to extraction, it is useful to carry the decoy, especially when attempting to distract the enemy while your team picks up the hostages. The camera is great on defense because you can set them up in a direction toward the hostages and be able to see the enemy attempt to pick up one before they even begin the process.

> Law enforcement, use the atrium roof to scout the building across the street. Don't forget about the elevators. Both teams have access to the roofs.
> —Evan Champlin, Senior Multiplayer Level Designer

INTRODUCTION
DUST BOWL
UNDERCOVER VS. BANGERS

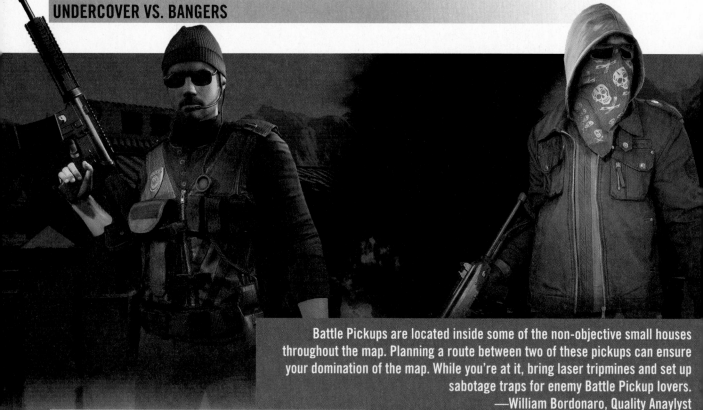

Battle Pickups are located inside some of the non-objective small houses throughout the map. Planning a route between two of these pickups can ensure your domination of the map. While you're at it, bring laser tripmines and set up sabotage traps for enemy Battle Pickup lovers.
—William Bordonaro, Quality Anaylyst

The small desert town of Joad is off the beaten path and well-known for meth trafficking problems. The cops have had enough and are on the scene to shut it all down.

Dust Bowl is one of the largest maps in *Battlefield: Hardline* offering a wide mix of gameplay opportunities across all seven game modes. Whether racing across the dusty terrain in a hotwired vehicle or escaping the Meth Compound with a bag of loot, the action here is never dull. Breathe in the wide open spaces of this small desert community and be sure to carry a big gun capable of reaching out and hurting someone. With some of the longest sight lines in the game, this is the perfect map for testing out those 4X and 6X optics. Assault rifles, sniper rifles, DMRs, and battle rifles are all very effective here, so choose your classes and loadouts carefully. To avoid getting dropped by a sniper's bullet or run down by a speeding vehicle, seek refuge in the town's houses and other structures. This is one map where you don't want to be caught out in the open.

LEVOLUTION

As the winds kick-up across this arid environment, a blinding dust storm materializes, limiting visibility for all; this is a particularly dangerous hazard for helicopter pilots. As the winds die down, the map is coated in a fine layer of dust.

KEY LOCATIONS

GAS STATION

Keep your distance from the gas pumps here; they explode when hit by grenades or small arms fire. The rooftop of the station is accessible via a ladder, but there's very little cover, so limit your exposure and don't stand still.

RADIO ANTENNA

Use a grappling hook to reach the central platform of the antenna. From here you have a commanding view of the nearby Motel, Gas Station, and Mine. Watch out for vehicles speeding along the nearby roads when moving out on foot.

WATER TOWER

Use a grappling hook (or helicopter) to reach the top of this popular sniping perch. But don't expect to go unnoticed. If you start taking fire, parachute or zipline to safety.

MINE

The Mine provides a large amount of temporary cover, but is highly destructible. Use the broken down rail cars to gain quick access to the roof for a great vantage point. Stick to the interior of the building and avoid being spotted.

METH COMPOUND

The rooftops and balconies of this compound offer a sweeping view of the map's central locations, ideal for spotting and sniping. Shoot the black explosive barrels inside the compound to open new pathways when you need to make a quick getaway.

MOTEL

As one giant kill-box; the Motel serves as a great ambush area. The upper floors of the Motel give players both an elevated advantage and cover to stay concealed until it is time to strike or to escape after being exposed. This central location also gives players a line of sight to most of the map.

▬▬	POLICE DEPLOYMENT
▬▬	CRIMINAL DEPLOYMENT
◆	VAULT
⬇	EXTRACTION

BATTLE PICKUPS

	AMMO
	DEFIBRILLATOR
	GRAPPLING HOOK
	HEALTH
	LMG
	ROCKET LAUNCHER
	STINGER
	ZIPLINE

> **Place Breaching Charges on the vault as a cop and blow up anyone that tries to break in.**
> —Brian Paoloni, Quality Designer

★ When playing as law enforcement, get to the vault at the Meth Compound as soon as possible. The transport helicopter is by far the quickest way to get teammates to the vault. Once on the ground, establish a perimeter around the vault while watching for Bangers approaching from the west. The Meth Compound's rooftop serves as a good vantage point for spotting incoming attackers.

★ The criminal team should pile into the executive helicopter and other high-capacity vehicles and make a beeline for the Meth Compound at the start of the round. Don't forget to utilize the syndicate crew cab as a mobile spawn point; park it near the meth compound so your team can apply constant pressure against the vault.

★ The vault is located in the Meth Compound's basement, just beneath the garage. The garage's floor serves as the primary breach point, allowing the criminals to blow a hole in the floor and access the vault from above. The garage door can be opened to provide easier access to this breach point. But defenders should keep the large garage door closed so they can ambush enemies charging through the two narrow doorways. The large garage door can only be opened from the inside, using the switch in the southwest corner.

> **Breach the money bag room from the garage and the basement in case the cops deactivate one of the charges.**
> —John Seefurth, Quality Analyst

☆ If the criminals gain access to the Meth Compound's basement, they can find a secondary breach point leading into the vault. Place charges on the corrugated steel door to blast your way in from the vault's east side. Initially, the basement can be accessed via two stairways within the compound.

> Blow up the basement for an easier escape. Use ziplines to get to the Motel quickly from the Meth Compound.
> —David Price, Weapon Designer

However, by detonating the black barrels along the basement's interior south wall, you can open up a new path leading outside the compound. The criminal team should open this pathway as early as possible, offering easier access in and out of the basement.

☆ Once the criminals have scored the loot, the easiest extraction points to reach are (A) or (E). Instead of hoofing it to these extraction points, consider exiting the hole in the basement's south wall and using a zipline to reach either nearby extraction point for a quick score. If extraction points (A) or (E) aren't available, you can still use ziplines to rapidly make your way toward the other points. Even if you're unlucky enough to get extraction point (D), you can still make a quick escape with ziplines. Zipline from the south side of the compound to the rooftop of the Motel. Then from the rooftop of the Motel, zipline again toward the Radio Antenna. In most cases, using ziplines is faster than relying on vehicles to make your escape. Whatever you do, try to avoid running the bag while on foot; you're much more likely to be gunned down or run over.

Shoot the black barrels in the Meth Compound's basement to tear a hole in the southern wall.

POLICE DEPLOYMENT

CRIMINAL DEPLOYMENT

 HOTWIRE CARS

BATTLE PICKUPS

AMMO

DEFIBRILLATOR

GRAPPLING HOOK

HEALTH

LMG

ROCKET LAUNCHER

STINGER

ZIPLINE

HOTWIRE CARS

VEHICLE		NAME
	A	FUEL TANKER
	B	UTILITY VAN
	C	UTILITY VAN
	D	SPORTS SEDAN
	E	SPORTS SEDAN

⭐ In the beginning of a round be sure to use as many vehicles in your spawn as possible and quickly spread your team out. There are many paths you can take, but charging straight for objectives (D) and (E) is the most useful when it comes to holding objectives for the maximum amount of time. (D) and (E) are sports sedans and driving them makes it much easier to avoid enemy fire because of their speed and agility.

⭐ On Dust Bowl, each team starts with the faster vehicles *Battlefield: Hardline* has to offer. Use the dirt bikes to cross the rough terrain of the desert and reach your desired location without many obstacles to slow you down. The transport helicopter for the police and the executive helicopter on the criminal side serve as the most important vehicles each team starts with. Use the helicopters as fast-moving, mobile deployments to take your team closer to each objective and use the left and right gunners to take down enemy control points to prevent the enemy from bleeding your team of tickets. The air space is very open on this map; use this to get from point to point quickly and avoid anti-air fire from Battle Pickups and sniper fire.

This map is big enough to have areas away from the action, great places to gain points on a quiet drive.
—Brian Carden, Quality Analyst

Going for Hotwire vehicles closer to the enemy deployment can be very dangerous. However if you succeed in capturing those points, the enemy is pushed towards a greater challenge in capturing their first points.

☆ The map is made up of a small grid-like street plan, so driving the Hotwire Vehicles around the outermost perimeter gives you the longest straightaways and allows you to stay spread out. However, with a full game there are enemy foot-mobiles waiting for you to enter their kill-zones near their deployments, so keeping to your own team's half of the map and driving on that part of the grid allows you to keep your vehicle intact longer. Be ready to shift to a different section of the grid if your area gets too hot.

☆ There aren't many roads on Dust Bowl that can't be avoided, so if you see a hazard or a roadblock ahead of you, make the first turn you see and keep moving. Keep your eyes peeled when driving up the two central roads in the middle of the map that lead to the Meth Compound because even when they look open, there are several Battle Pickups located in this area and one good shot by an enemy will tear your car to shreds. It is likely that there will be enemies on both sides of your car, making these two roads the most dangerous to travel.

☆ Controlling the Motel is a good tactic for Hotwire because it serves as a central point used for ambushing enemy vehicles and staying equidistant from objective deployment points. Use the ziplines that surround the Motel to get there quickly. There are two key pickups, an LMG and a rocket launcher, at both (D) and (E) that prove most valuable; Hotwire Vehicles are extremely vulnerable and claiming these weapons grants you a large advantage.

Road-kills are particularly fun and easy on this map. If you're getting road-killed a lot, try equipping Survivalist—it's a lifesaver!
—Thad Sasser, Lead Multiplayer Designer

▬▬	POLICE DEPLOYMENT
▬▬	CRIMINAL DEPLOYMENT
🔲	MONEY PILE
◆	POLICE VAULT
◆	CRIMINAL VAULT

BATTLE PICKUPS

🔲	AMMO
🔲	DEFIBRILLATOR
↖	GRAPPLING HOOK
➕	HEALTH
▬	LMG
▬	ROCKET LAUNCHER
▬	STINGER
⟁	ZIPLINE

> Disabling the hacker gas trap at the money pile is a good move if your Hacker is not on the ball.
> —Thad Sasser, Lead Multiplayer Designer

☆ When starting a round of Blood Money on Dust Bowl, you may notice that the objectives are set up in a triangle formation making it a tough choice whether to play the midfield or attack the money pile. If you choose to attack the money pile, the safest way to get there is by taking a vehicle up the outside road towards the back of the large house where the pile is stored. The money pile is located on the second floor of the house, so if you get there first take the quick route from the ground floor up the stairs. If you happen to get there a little late, get the drop on the enemy by using the grappling hook to get to the roof and take out the enemy attempting to gather the first score.

☆ Once you've gathered the cash, get to the roof and grab the zipline Battle Pickup. From the roof, you can see your team's vault no matter which team you're on. If you set the zipline as close to the drop point as possible, you can zip all the way down for a quick return.

☆ Looking down the road from the balcony that is directly east of the money pile you can see the police vault located in the house between the Mine and the Motel. Like most of the Blood Money vaults in *Battlefield: Hardline* this one is protected by cover on the side facing the money pile, but it is possible to send a zipline through the access door of the police vault. When defending this vault, it is possible to see the drop location from outside the door on the east side and staying right outside the house keeps you protected from attackers, but also keeps you close to your cash.

☆ From the roof you can look to the west and see the diner, where the criminal vault is located. If you aim the zipline right above the eastern door you can swiftly ride it straight into the criminal's vault. Just like the police vault, you can defend it from right outside the door, this time on the western side. However, this is where controlling the Motel becomes essential; you can cover your team while they run in the front door of the criminal vault and you can kill attackers running toward it.

> Use the roads less traveled to transport money back and forth. The main highway is typically well defended by both teams.
> —Evan Champlin, Senior Multiplayer Level Designer

☆ The Motel is extremely important on this map and this mode is just another example that proves it. Whichever team controls the Motel can move freely from their deployment to the money pile or the opposing team's vault under protection. Use the attack helicopters to clear out the Motel, but be aware of professionals shooting pilots out of their vehicles.

POLICE DEPLOYMENT

CRIMINAL DEPLOYMENT

CONTROL POINTS

BATTLE PICKUPS

 AMMO

DEFIBRILLATOR

 GRAPPLING HOOK

 HEALTH

 LMG

 ROCKET LAUNCHER

 STINGER

 ZIPLINE

☆ At the start of a round, the law enforcement team should make an aggressive aerial push to the west, utilizing their transport helicopter and patrol helicopter to assist in capturing the central control points, including the Radio Antenna (A), Motel (B), and Meth Compound (C). Players in slower moving ground vehicles can capture the Mine (D). With four control points under your control, hunker down and defend, bleeding the opposing team's ticket count.

> Find the Stinger Battle Pickups on the map and take out those choppers.
> —John Seefurth, Quality Analyst

☆ Like the police, the criminals should use their helicopters in the early moments of the round to gain a foothold on the map's central control points. In addition to capturing the three central control points, the criminals should also take control of the Gas Station (E). Establishing control of at least three control points is all it takes to begin draining the other team's tickets.

> **Ziplines can be really handy to move between control points quickly.**
> —Brian Paoloni, Quality Designer

☆ With the exception of a fuel tanker at the Motel (B) and a sedan at the Meth Compound (C), there aren't any other vehicles tied to holding the control points. Due to its central location, the Motel (B) usually sees the heaviest action and serves as a great spawn point for those seeking stay close to the fight. The rooms upstairs also offer decent vantage points of the surrounding area. Instead of grinding it out at the Motel (B), and losing tickets in the process, consider focusing on control points on the perimeter of the map. Sometimes holding the Motel (B) is simply too costly. The Meth Compound (C) to the north is a bit more defensible while offering a clear view of the map's central locations.

☆ Dust Bowl is a large map with some extremely long sight lines. As a result, the weapons offered by the operator and professional classes are well-suited for this environment. Mechanics and enforcers armed with SMGs and shotguns may have some success when fighting within the Meth Compound (C) and Mine (D). But these close quarter weapons are outmatched when moving beyond the confines of these locations. Enforcers are better off equipping the more versatile battle rifles in this game mode. Given the size of this map, ziplines are a very effective form of travel. When spawning at the Radio Antenna (A) or Meth Compound (C), ziplines can be used to quickly access the lower elevation control points in the map's center.

> **Shotgun use around the motel is crucial—especially during the dust storm!**
> —Ben Gaciu, System Designer

191

——	SPAWN AREA

BATTLE PICKUPS

	AMMO
	DEFIBRILLATOR
	GRAPPLING HOOK
	HEALTH
	LMG
	ROCKET LAUNCHER
	STINGER
	ZIPLINE

★ The action in this match is centered around the Meth Compound and Motel. Expect a healthy dose of close quarter firefights within these buildings as your team attempts to gain the upper hand. Due to its configuration and upper floor, the Motel is a popular hot spot and likely the site of the heaviest fighting. If you're looking to score some kills, this is the place to be.

> Utilize the high ground to dominate your enemy.
> —Evan Champlin, Senior Multiplayer Level Designer

★ Defensive minded teams should consider taking up residence within the Motel's eastern building. Stick to the second story rooms and engage opponents in the adjoining building to the west. This floor is relatively easy to lockdown thanks to its compact size. However, you must monitor for movement along the three stairways leading to the second floor. Consider placing cameras or laser tripmines near these stairways to prevent enemies from sneaking up on your team. If your team is working as one cohesive unit, consider expanding to the Motel's L-shaped western building. The western building offers better views of the surrounding area but is more difficult to defend due to its sprawling size. Still, if your team can manage to control both buildings at the Motel, you'll have a much better chance of coming away with a win.

★ Before choosing a class, decide where you'll be playing on the map. If you're going to be patrolling the interior of the Motel or Meth Compound, consider choosing mechanic or enforcer; their SMGs and shotguns are absolutely devastating in close quarters. But given the unpredictable nature of this mode and the relatively long sight lines of the map, the operator is the safest choice thanks to the versatility of their assault rifles and carbines. The professional class can find some success as sniper duels breakout between the Motel and Meth Compound, but they must be prepared to switch to their fully automatic sidearm when threats move to close range. In an effort to stay close to your squadmates, make sure you have at least one mechanic in your squad equipped with a satellite phone. This gadget is best deployed in one of the buildings on the periphery, away from the chaos erupting at the Meth Compound and Motel.

> Go from house to house for cover, instead of running out in the open.
> —Zachary T. Irwin, Quality Analyst

★ If you want to avoid the pitched battles at the Meth Compound and Motel, consider taking up positions in the small houses to the east or west. From these relatively quiet structures you can engage the cross traffic without drawing too much attention. Assault rifles or battle rifles equipped with suppressors offer enough range and power while keeping you off the minimap. But don't get comfortable in one house for too long. After scoring a few kills, move along to the next house. A well-organized squad hopping from house to house can score an impressive amount of kills while suffering minimal deaths.

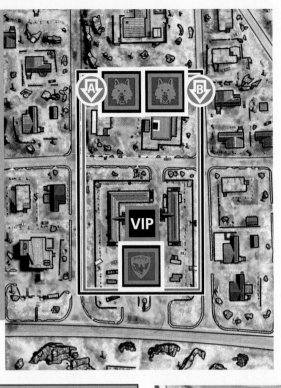

☆ When playing Crosshair on Dust Bowl as police, you are at a major disadvantage when trying to rush your team to an extraction. Take your time and try to get rid of a few bangers before moving too far ahead. Remember, there are only three minutes in each round so you have to move quickly after you've weakened their defenses. Your team make-up should consist of at least two operators and a professional. The professional is made to trap players, but the long range rifle is useful for scoping out the prospective extraction point.

☆ Dust Bowl has a slight advantage towards the criminal side because the criminal deployment is a little more elevated, and due to how open the map is, you can see the enemy advancing toward their objectives far before they see you. It is useful to have a couple of professionals and at least a couple of operators because of the range and firefights that often break out at the half way point just before the Motel.

☆ As with most Crosshair maps, there are two major strategies to defending the extraction points and not letting the VIP escape. Those two strategies fit this map as well. However because of the lack of cover near the street it is much safer to play the lockdown strategy and use the buildings near the criminal deployments as cover and protection from the charging police. However, there may be a situation that calls for the rush strategy, and the safest route is straight down the middle of the map towards the Motel. If you can use the Motel as cover, your team is able to ambush any of the enemies advancing past the Motel. If you can get across the street safely, keep to cover and be careful when advancing any further as you can expect to meet the enemy soon.

▬	POLICE DEPLOYMENT
▬	CRIMINAL DEPLOYMENT
🔒	HOSTAGE
⬇	EXTRACTION POINT

☆ As the VIP, you want to stay indoors until it's time to advance. If there are any enforcers on your team, it is advantageous to stay near them because any criminals that come hunting for you will be met by the close range shotguns and gadgets that keep you protected. If your team can manage to keep the criminals distracted, you might want to slip around the street side and use the walls of the buildings as cover while you make your way to the extraction.

☆ Use grappling hooks to get to the roofs of the Motel and the three-story building. Then use the zipline to get to tactical positions such as the corners of the Motel and the extraction points. If you can quickly get a zipline up, you are almost guaranteed an extraction due to the sightlines that appear from the Motel roof.

As law enforcement, use the Motel to your advantage. H
the enemy guessing by shifting fire f
window to wind
—Evan Champlin, Senior Multiplayer Level Desig

RESCUE

☆ The law enforcement team deploys on the east side of the map, near the Motel. The nearby diner serves as a good reconnaissance point to scan for enemy activity to the west. The windows along the west side of the diner offer a great view of both hostage buildings. Consider keeping at least one team member in the diner to spot enemies and provide covering fire while the rest of the team moves in to secure one of the hostages. Consider using a grenade to clear out the trees obscuring your vision.

☆ The criminal team deploys to the west of the Gas Station, where both hostages are being held. Given the distance between the spawn locations and the hostages, the criminals don't have too much time to establish a perimeter before the police arrive. For best results, get at least one team member next to each hostage while the rest of the team fans out. The rooftop of the Gas Station serves as an excellent overwatch position, ideal for spotting incoming cops approaching from the diner.

> As law enforcement, make sure the street is clear before attempting to cross. Cover your team from the Motel as they make their approach. Don't forget to utilize the zipline to quickly navigate across the open areas. When playing as criminals, use the limited access to the interiors to your advantage. Don't forget to bring your gas mask as the small space makes the Gas Grenade very effective.
> —Evan Champlin, Senior Multiplayer Level Designer

☆ When playing as the criminals, it's often easier to lockdown both hostage locations than it is to intercept the police. A full five-player team has adequate manpower to control both hostage locations; place two players in each garage, each covering one entry point. The fifth player can act as a rover or take to the rooftop to spot and engage incoming enemies.

☆ The hostages are located in the garages adjacent to the Gas Station. Hostage 1 is located in the garage to the north, while hostage 2 is held in the garage to the west. Each garage has two doorways which serve as potential choke points. When entering the garages the police team should perform simultaneous breaches to increase the chances of success, attacking from two different directions. The garage where hostage 2 is being held has two small rectangular windows on the north wall; tossing (or launching) grenades through these windows prior to entry can give the law enforcement team a significant advantage. There are no such windows in the garage where hostage 1 is being held, potentially making it a tougher rescue.

☆ Gas grenades are very effective in the tight confines of the two garages where the hostages are being held. As a result, both teams should be prepared to counter by wearing gas masks. A police team wishing to make a quick escape after securing a hostage should consider bringing along a zipline. Once a hostage is secured, climb to the roof of the Gas Station and fire a zipline into the concrete wall east of the extraction point for a quick escape.

> The hostages are fairly separated in this map; make sure you deploy your resources to defend both of them.
> —Thad Sasser, Lead Multiplayer Designer

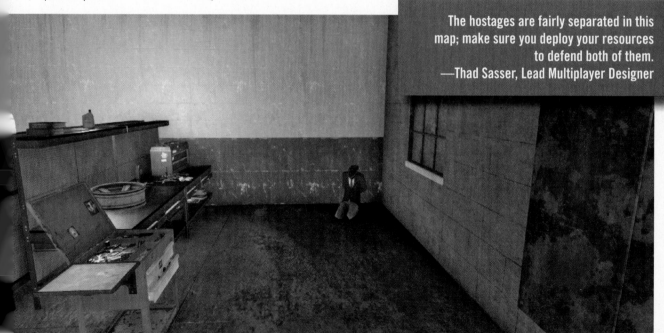

INTRODUCTION
EVERGLADES
UNDERCOVER VS. BANGERS

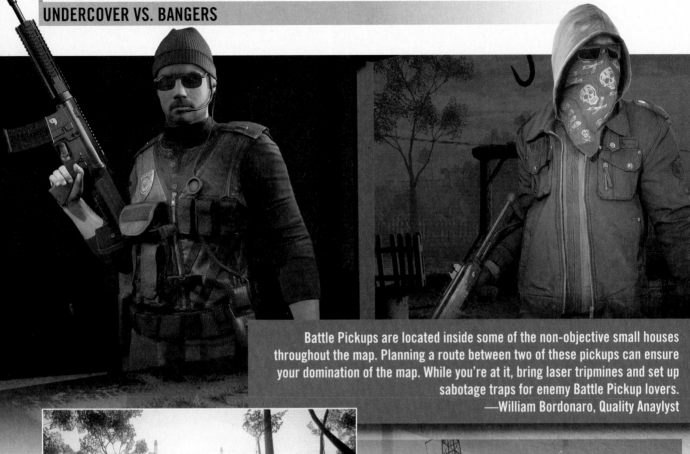

Battle Pickups are located inside some of the non-objective small houses throughout the map. Planning a route between two of these pickups can ensure your domination of the map. While you're at it, bring laser tripmines and set up sabotage traps for enemy Battle Pickup lovers.
—William Bordonaro, Quality Anaylyst

Florida is not all sand and beaches. Deep in the heart of the Everglades, a fracking site has turned into a battleground where cops and criminals wage war against each other.

As the sun rises over the Everglades, even the alligators rush for safety as undercover cops and bangers tear-up the dusty roads and shallow waterways, eager to exert control over this once pristine wetland. Whether you're breaking the law, or simply enforcing it, vehicles are essential for traversing the challenging terrain here. Don't let the narrow waterways fool you, most of these swamps are shallow enough to drive through. Be sure to watch out for enemy airboats patrolling these areas because their bow-mounted miniguns can chew up vehicles and personnel in a matter of seconds. When you're not cruising through the swamps, you can launch your vehicle off numerous ramps along the roadways to score easy jump bonuses. With miles of accessible roads and shallow canals, prepare yourself for some epic car chases.

LEVOLUTION

The three drilling towers in the middle of the fracking site can collapse independently. For each tower, interact with a button inside one of the adjacent second-floor offices. Doing this releases some natural gas at the base of the tower. Next, target the base of the leaking tower with explosives to trigger an explosion, causing the structure to come crashing down, and littering the facility with debris.

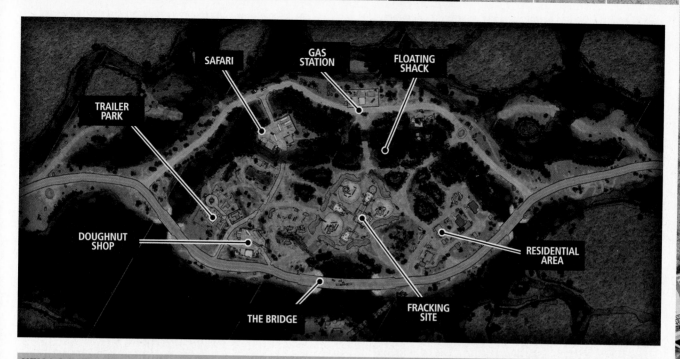

KEY LOCATIONS

FRACKING SITE

Firoco Energy has established this sprawling facility in the heart of the Everglades, consisting of two towering drill sites surrounded by clusters of prefabricated steel structures. The central platform of each drill site can be accessed via ladder, and offers a sweeping view of the map—making these ideal, but predictable, perches for snipers.

RESIDENTIAL AREA

This small neighborhood, west of the Fracking Site, consists of several single-story homes. The dirt roads cutting through this community often serve as detours for motorists seeking to get off the main highway. If helicopters become a problem, grab the Stinger anti-air missile Battle Pickup and clear the skies.

FLOATING SHACK

Sitting in the shadow of the Fracking Site, this rustic shack is a throwback to a fading lifestyle. The swampy water surrounding these structures is deep enough to slow foot traffic, but shallow enough for vehicles to drive through.

THE BRIDGE

Crossing the deep waters of the lagoon on the south side of the map, this large bridge serves as a major east-west thoroughfare. In some game modes, like Hotwire, the bridge is partially blocked by several wrecked vehicles. You can use the ramps here to jump over the wreckage or simply stick to the southern lane.

SAFARI

Before the energy industry moved in, tourism played a role in keeping the local economy afloat. Roadside tourist attractions like this allowed visitors to get a glimpse of the Everglades' indigenous wildlife. Now the parking lot of this abandoned convenience store serves as a truck depot for a major shipping company.

GAS STATION

The gas station on the north side of the map serves as the vault during Heist Mode, making it hotly contested area for both teams. But don't neglect this location during other game modes. Grab the LMG Battle Pickup here for a boost in firepower. Or, you can score a jump bonus by racing across one of the two small ramps to the west.

DOUGHNUT SHOP

It may look a bit run-down, but Joshie's Doughnut Shop is still open for business. Two trucks filled with Frostbite Cola have just arrived. Or maybe you just want to ambush traffic moving along the nearby road? The RPG Battle Pickup that is offered here is great for taking out enemy vehicles.

TRAILER PARK

Located on the far west side of the map, across the street from the Doughnut Shop, this small trailer park is the site of some heated action during Rescue. With a mix of structures, shipping containers, and abandoned vehicles, the Trailer Park offers enough cover for some intense firefights.

197

▬▬	POLICE DEPLOYMENT
▬▬	CRIMINAL DEPLOYMENT
	VAULT
	EXTRACTION

BATTLE PICKUPS

	AMMO
	DEFIBRILLATOR
	GRAPPLING HOOK
	HEALTH
	LMG
	ROCKET LAUNCHER
	STINGER
	ZIPLINE

★ When playing as law enforcement, get to the vault at the Gas Station as quickly as possible—the cars and motorcycle at the team's deployment area offer the best speed for rushing this area. Don't neglect the other vehicle's at your team's base, however. Get the mobile command post close to the Gas Station to give your team a spawn point near the action. Surround the Gas Station with your team's two intervention SUVs. The miniguns on these vehicles are ideal for fending off attacks by the criminals. Consider parking vehicles directly in front of the Gas Station's three entry points, limiting the criminal team's access to the building's interior. However, the criminals are likely to breach at least one of the gas station's entrances. When this happens, consider hiding a few teammates inside the building and saturate the interior with gas grenades to disorient any would-be attackers.

★ As in all Heist matches, the criminal team should waste no time rushing to the Gas Station and setting charges on all four of the breach points. Don't forget to bring some of your team's vehicles there as well. The armored SUVs are particularly useful for establishing a perimeter around the Gas Station while teammates set charges. Your team's mobile command center (or satellite phones) is essential for maintaining a spawn point close to the Gas Station. Consider creating a blockade of your team's vehicles on the east side of the building to prevent the law enforcement team from meddling with your charges. Be sure to keep at least a couple of vehicles nearby to serve as getaway vehicles—the armored SUVs are ideal for carrying money bags to the extraction points.

> When playing as a criminal, run to the east side of the gas station and pick up the LMG. Remain on that side of the building, Cops will run right past you, directly for the vault to get a disarm. Little do they know, you have a perfect sight line of their backs while protected in the corner of the building.
> —William Bordonaro, Quality Analyst

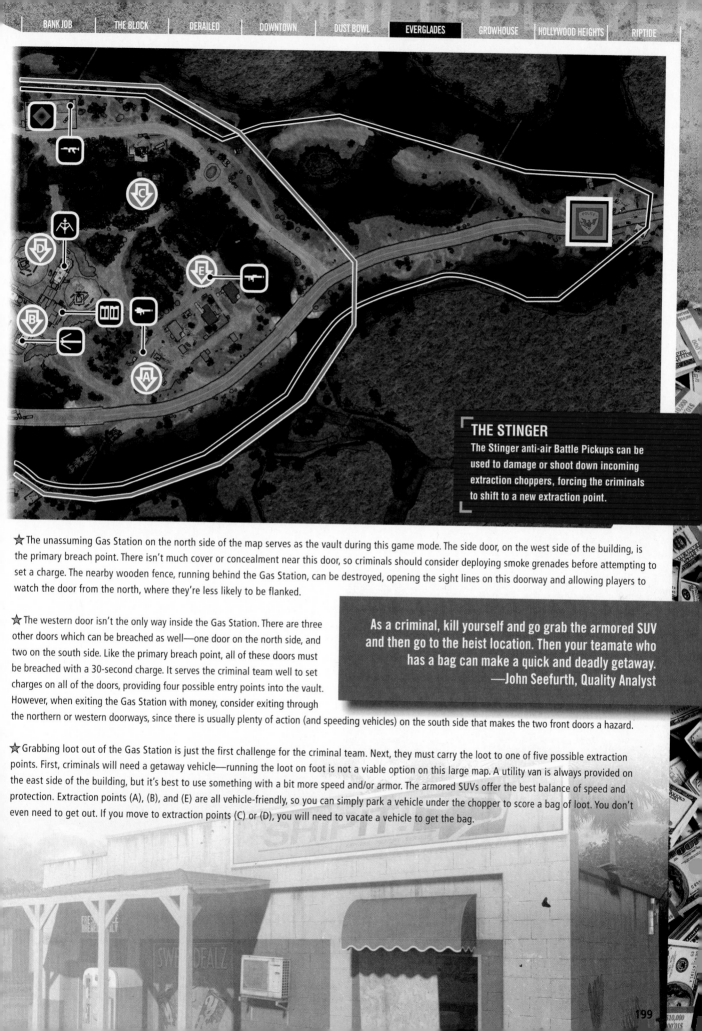

THE STINGER

The Stinger anti-air Battle Pickups can be used to damage or shoot down incoming extraction choppers, forcing the criminals to shift to a new extraction point.

★ The unassuming Gas Station on the north side of the map serves as the vault during this game mode. The side door, on the west side of the building, is the primary breach point. There isn't much cover or concealment near this door, so criminals should consider deploying smoke grenades before attempting to set a charge. The nearby wooden fence, running behind the Gas Station, can be destroyed, opening the sight lines on this doorway and allowing players to watch the door from the north, where they're less likely to be flanked.

★ The western door isn't the only way inside the Gas Station. There are three other doors which can be breached as well—one door on the north side, and two on the south side. Like the primary breach point, all of these doors must be breached with a 30-second charge. It serves the criminal team well to set charges on all of the doors, providing four possible entry points into the vault. However, when exiting the Gas Station with money, consider exiting through the northern or western doorways, since there is usually plenty of action (and speeding vehicles) on the south side that makes the two front doors a hazard.

> As a criminal, kill yourself and go grab the armored SUV and then go to the heist location. Then your teammate who has a bag can make a quick and deadly getaway.
> —John Seefurth, Quality Analyst

★ Grabbing loot out of the Gas Station is just the first challenge for the criminal team. Next, they must carry the loot to one of five possible extraction points. First, criminals will need a getaway vehicle—running the loot on foot is not a viable option on this large map. A utility van is always provided on the east side of the building, but it's best to use something with a bit more speed and/or armor. The armored SUVs offer the best balance of speed and protection. Extraction points (A), (B), and (E) are all vehicle-friendly, so you can simply park a vehicle under the chopper to score a bag of loot. You don't even need to get out. If you move to extraction points (C) or (D), you will need to vacate a vehicle to get the bag.

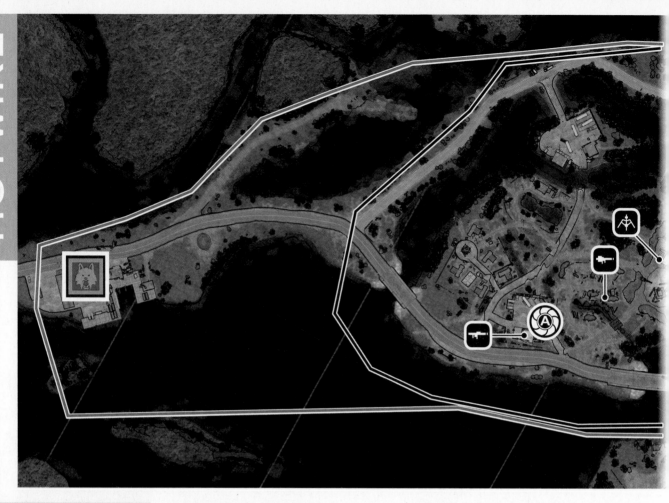

POLICE DEPLOYMENT

CRIMINAL DEPLOYMENT

HOTWIRE CARS

BATTLE PICKUPS

AMMO

DEFIBRILLATOR

GRAPPLING HOOK

HEALTH

LMG

ROCKET LAUNCHER

STINGER

ZIPLINE

HOTWIRE CARS

VEHICLE		NAME
	A	SPORTS SEDAN
	B	FUEL TANKER
	C	UTILITY VAN
	D	STREET BIKE
	E	SPORTS SEDAN

☆ In this chaotic Hotwire match both teams should attempt to maintain control of vehicles (A), (C), and (E). The fuel tanker (B) and street bike (D), are simply too vulnerable, making them difficult to control for extended periods of time. If these vehicles are empty, and your team needs them, give them a shot. The sports sedans (A and E) and utility van (C) aren't necessarily that much more durable, but they have the occupancy necessary to defend themselves. Try to keep a mechanic with a repair tool onboard to provide damage control while on the move. If your team can maintain control of cars (A), (C), and (E) for the duration of the match, you stand a good chance of winning the round.

> Go for the Jump on the bridge it's FUN!
> —David Price, Weapon Designer

☆ On Everglades each team maintains an ample supply of vehicles at their deployment areas, ready to chase down the Hotwire vehicles. Each team has two sedans, two coupes, one off-road motorcycle, one airboat, and one transport helicopter. The helicopter and motorcycle are perfect for rushing the Hotwire vehicles early during the match. Get the coupes and sedans on the road too, so they can be used to chase down enemy-held Hotwire vehicles. The airboat is great for patrolling the waterways—use its minigun to ambush enemy vehicles cutting through the swamps or racing across the bridge. While the surface vehicles are helpful, the transport helicopter will always be the MVP of your team, so keep it in the air as long as possible. Watch out for incoming Stingers. Instead of flying high, swoop low to the ground in an effort to break line of sight of opponents attempting to lock-on with a Stinger.

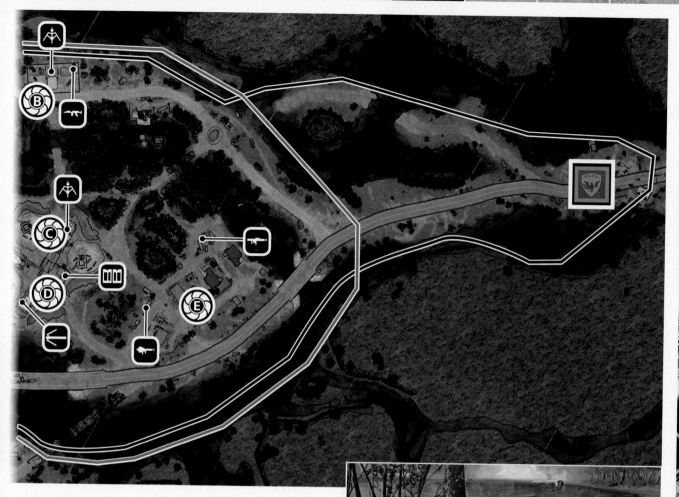

☆ Most players instantly recognize the racetrack-like oval formed by the paved roads running along the perimeter of the map. While this route is extremely popular—allowing for high speeds and several jump bonuses—it's also likely to be watched by opponents eager to spring an ambush. Instead of sticking to this route, consider making detours through the map's center, racing along the interior dirt roads and waterways. Most of the waterways are shallow enough to drive through. Consider looping around the waterways by the Floating Shack and Safari areas to stay off the more congested roadways.

☆ In Hotwire, the bridge to the south is partially blocked by a multi-vehicle accident involving a semi-truck. This makes it one of the most dangerous chokepoints on the map, often the site of explosive ambushes. Expect breaching charges, laser trip mines, and other explosive weapons here. In other words, avoid this bridge at all costs, particularly when driving a Hotwire vehicle. You should also be mindful of the RPG battle pickups located near the Doughnut Shop and residential area. Speeding through any of these areas can be exceptionally dangerous.

☆ Get familiar with the Battle Pickup locations on this map, since these powerful weapons can help give your team the upper hand. The Stingers are particularly helpful for keeping the opposing team's transport helicopter out of the sky. You should also focus on grabbing one of the RPGs and ambush vehicles at the blockade on the bridge. If you haven't already, consider unlocking the anti-armor armory upgrade for the coupe or sedan and pull your own rocket launcher out of the trunk of your car.

> The semi wreck on the bridge is a very attractive location for players. Be careful every time you take a Hotwire vehicle along this route. A lot of the water can be driven through, but be on the lookout for minigun-wielding airboats.
> —Evan Champlin, Senior Multiplayer Level Designer

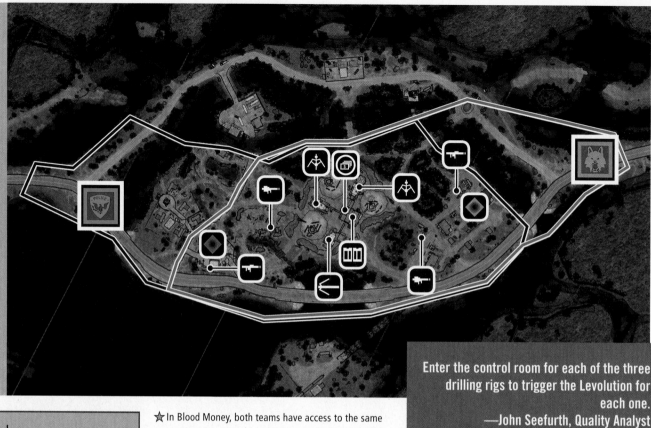

━━	POLICE DEPLOYMENT
──	CRIMINAL DEPLOYMENT
⊚	MONEY PILE
◈	POLICE VAULT
◈	CRIMINAL VAULT

BATTLE PICKUPS

▥	AMMO
▥▥	DEFIBRILLATOR
⟵	GRAPPLING HOOK
✚	HEALTH
⌐	LMG
⌐	ROCKET LAUNCHER
⌐	STINGER
⚓	ZIPLINE

☆ In Blood Money, both teams have access to the same types of vehicles. This gives both teams a shot of reaching the money pile at the Fracking Site during the first few seconds of the round. The transport helicopter provided at each team's deployment area is the fastest way to get teammates to the money pile—instead of landing the helicopter, simply circle around the money pile and let your teammates parachute to the ground. Don't forget to follow-up with supporting vehicles! Although slow, the counter attack trucks, provided at both deployment areas, are great for securing the area around the money pile.

☆ The money pile is located in the middle of the Fracking Site, situated in a narrow ground-level corridor. Expect heavy resistance here, as well as booby-traps. Before approaching the prize, toss a frag grenade into the corridor to detonate any breaching charges or laser tripmines. Even if you manage to grab some cash from the pile, take care making your exit—there may be snipers posted on the two drilling towers. Don't even think about moving the money back to your team's vault on foot. If you didn't bring a getaway vehicle of your own, hop into one of the two utility vans parked nearby to make your escape.

☆ The Doughnut Shop to the west serves as the vault for the law enforcement team—simply drop the loot next to the soda machines. A motorcycle spawns outside, offering quick transportation back to the money pile. There is also an RPG battle pickup offered here, giving defenders the chance to destroy incoming criminal vehicles. Consider bolstering the defenses of the Doughnut Shop by parking an armored SUV outside. This vehicle's roof-mounted minigun is the perfect deterrent. When attacking this area as criminals, consider deploying a satellite phone in one of the large semi-trailers located in the parking lot. This gives your squad a spawn point close to the opposing team's vault. The defending law enforcement team should also consider using this same tactic.

☆ Once they've scored some cash from the money pile, most players make a beeline directly for their team's vault, often dashing away on foot. Consider ambushing these bag carriers on the eastern and western outskirts of the Fracking Site. Law enforcement players should hide out along the swamp near the residential area, while criminals patrol the area east of the Doughnut Shop. Intercepting vehicles with bag carriers is a bit more problematic, since they may take a variety of routes back to their team's vault. Of course, you can always ambush them there, destroying their vehicles with rockets, breaching charges, or grenade launchers before they can score their cash.

☆ An armored truck in the residential area awaits deposits from the criminal team. Like the Doughnut Shop, there is a motorcycle spawn close by along with an RPG battle pickup. Defenders can keep a watchful eye on this truck from the confines of the nearby houses. However, it is best to park an armored SUV or a counter attack truck near this area, giving the criminal vault just a bit more defensive firepower. Law enforcement players attacking this area should move in hard and fast with vehicles of their own, overwhelming the defenders. If vehicles aren't available, sneak in through the houses and methodically clear the area before approaching the back of the armored truck, then use the motorcycle to make your getaway.

> **Use vehicles to raid the other team's vault.**
> —David Price, Weapon Designer

> **Airboats don't go fast off the water, but they do go—it still beats walking! There's always lots of cover for snipers to hide in, so make short runs between cover, don't stay exposed.**
> —James Berg, User Experience Researcher

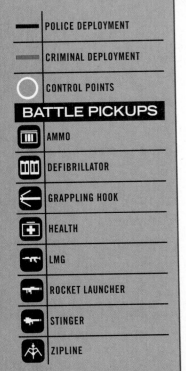

——	POLICE DEPLOYMENT
——	CRIMINAL DEPLOYMENT
◯	CONTROL POINTS

BATTLE PICKUPS

🔲	AMMO
🔲	DEFIBRILLATOR
🔲	GRAPPLING HOOK
🔲	HEALTH
🔲	LMG
🔲	ROCKET LAUNCHER
🔲	STINGER
🔲	ZIPLINE

★ Vehicles are key during the opening moments of the round, allowing both teams to quickly secure multiple control points. The law enforcement team should focus on securing the nearby Floating Shack (A), Fracking Site (B), and Residential Area (E). The two airboats provided at the team's deployment area are ideal for rushing the Floating Shack (A), while the transport helicopter and ground vehicles spread out among the Fracking Site (B) and Residential Area (E). Send the armored rescue vehicle to the Fracking Site (B), since you're likely to face the stiffest resistance there.

★ Starting on the west side of the map, the criminals should waste no time rushing the Doughnut Shop (D), Safari (C), and Fracking Site (B) control points. Use the two airboats to capture the Safari (C) control point while moving the transport helicopter and ground vehicles to the Doughnut Shop (D) and the Fracking Site (B). The armament of the hardened attack truck comes in handy when securing the Fracking Site (B).

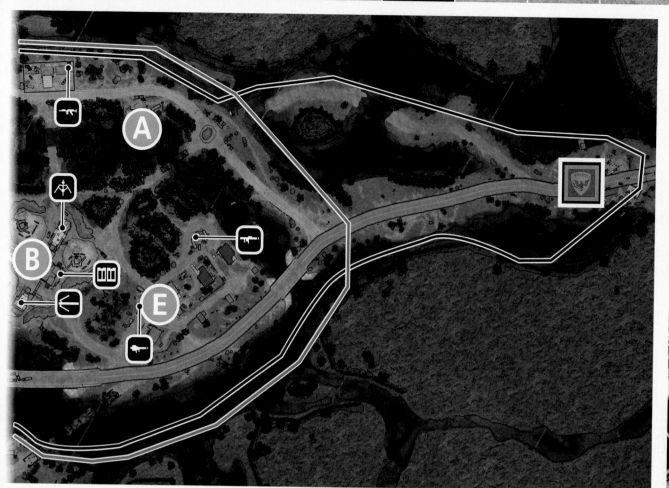

☆ All of the control points on this map spawn at least one vehicle, making it easier to expand control over this large map. But the Fracking Site (B) is the most valuable control point because it produces an attack helicopter. When crewed by a skilled pilot and a good gunner, the attack helicopter can be an absolute game changer on this map, picking off vehicles and personnel with ease. Given the heavy air traffic on this map, both teams should become familiar with the Stinger Battle Pickup locations at the Residential Area (E) and east of the Doughnut Shop (D). Alternately, equip the anti-air armory upgrade for the sedan or coupe and pull a Stinger of your own from the trunk of a car. With two transport helicopters and one attack helicopter in the air, suppressing the opposing team's air power can give your side a significant advantage.

☆ Everglades is a very large map, with many engagements occurring at intermediate-to-long range. As a result, consider choosing the operator or professional class and running with an assault rifle or DMR with at least a 4X optic—enforcers should opt for a battle rifle over a shotgun. Since the Fracking Site (B) is such a critical location, consider using a mechanic to deploy a satellite phone somewhere near this locale, securing a spawn point near the map's center for your squad. But don't get tunnel vison when fighting around the Fracking Site (B). If the action gets too heavy there, move out and capture one of the control points on the periphery—remember, you only need three control points to establish a drain on the opposing team's ticket count.

> The fracking towers are useful to gain a height advantage for sniping and spotting.
> —Ryan Murphy, Level Designer

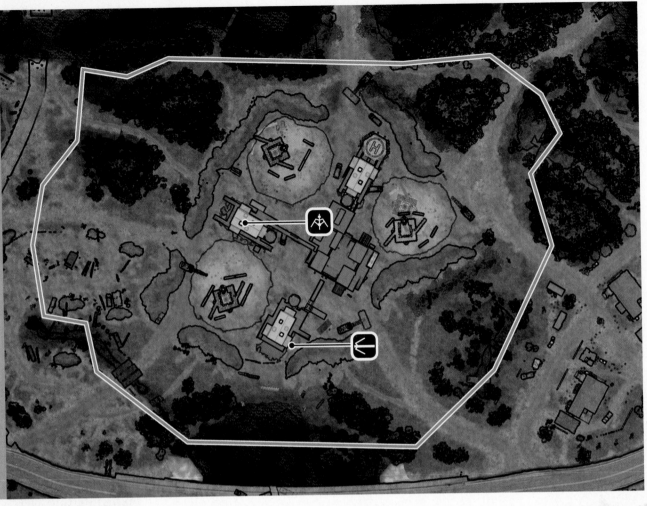

SPAWN AREA

BATTLE PICKUPS

AMMO

DEFIBRILLATOR

GRAPPLING HOOK

HEALTH

LMG

ROCKET LAUNCHER

STINGER

ZIPLINE

★ In Team Deathmatch, the action is restricted to the area around the Fracking Site. This sprawling industrial facility is the perfect playground for this mode, offering a dizzying mix of point-blank and long range engagements. Since you can't choose your spawn point initially, you need to enter this match carrying a weapon you're competent with at any range. Even if you just purchased a new weapon, consider spawning in with a weapon you have a bit more trigger time with—this is not the best environment to test out new gear.

★ The cluster of prefabricated steel structures in the center of the map offer excellent cover and concealment. However, there is no definitive stronghold here. If your team is looking to hold out at one location, consider occupying one of the second-floor structures building's access points— consider using laser tripmines to booby-trap stairways and catwalks. A mechanic's satellite phone can help your squad maintain its defensive position.

★ Versatility is key on this map, so spawn into the match ready to deal with threats at any range. This makes the operator a very popular class, since their assault rifles and carbines are well suited for this environment. However, the enforcer and mechanic can make their presence felt by hunting for prey in the map's center, blasting opponents with PDWs and shotguns. While the professional's gadgets are welcome on this map (particularly their cameras and laser tripmines), their sniper rifles and DMRs are best deployed when operating around the map's periphery—switch to your fully automatic sidearm when moving among the building's in the map's center. Also, avoid the urge of climbing one of the drilling towers. These locations offer great views of the map, but leave you completely exposed.

★ The bulk of the action on this map occurs in the center, as both teams engage at close range among the Fracking Site's building s. But make note of the map's outskirts. Patrolling the map's perimeter, and engaging action in the center, is much safer, allowing you to keep your back to the map's boundary. But when moving around the map's periphery, bring a weapon capable of engaging threats at intermediate-to-long range—assault rifles, battle rifles, sniper rifles, and DMRs are all effective. Don't just hold one position. Circle-strafe along the perimeter of the map while engaging opponents in the center. You may not score as many kills as those in the middle, but you'll probably die less too.

> The bridge is a great chokepoint for camping in any mode. Deploy as a Professional with laser tripmines and set them on the bottom and top of each ramp. They may look small and be designed for infantry, but two well-placed mines can take out a vehicle—especially when the driver beelines for an enticing jump bonus.
> —William Bordonaro, Quality Analyst

POLICE DEPLOYMENT

CRIMINAL DEPLOYMENT

EXTRACTION POINT

☆ As in Team Deathmatch, Crosshair takes place at the Fracking Site. Here, the law enforcement team faces the challenging task of escorting the VIP from the north edge of the facility to one of the two extraction points to the south. When the round starts, you should rush to the nearby structures, climbing to the second floor by the helipad. Keep the VIP secured in one of the buildings on the north side of the facility while the rest of the team cautiously pushes forward while scanning for criminals. The two drilling towers offer an excellent view of the extraction points. Climb the west tower for a good view of extraction point (A) or the east tower for an angle on extraction point (B). Though climbing these towers is risky as they're likely watched by the criminals.

When escorting the VIP, use the building interiors to navigate safely to the extraction points. Wait for the all clear and make your escape.
—Evan Champlin, Senior Multiplayer Level Designer

★ Like the law enforcement team, the criminal team should waste no time seeking cover among the prefabricated steel structures in the center of the map. Consider setting up defenses near the white, second floor structures on the west and south sides of the map. Both of these structures are close to the extraction points making them a good spot to ambush the law enforcement team. Keep an eye on the two drilling towers to the north and be ready to pick-off anyone climbing the ladder or using a grappling hook—law enforcement snipers may use these towers to spot and engage your team.

★ In most matches, the law enforcement team is likely to advance along the second floor catwalks in the middle of the map. When playing as the criminals, be ready to ambush your opponents on these narrow walkways. Move out quickly and try to pin down the police on the north side of the map, before they can branch out and make a move for either extraction point. Defending the extraction points is problematic, since there isn't much cover near the two police cars. If you want to camp the extraction points, do so from the second-floor white structures nearby.

★ The steel structures in the center of the map offer the best cover when escorting the VIP to one of the extraction points. However, you should avoid using the same path through these buildings each time. While the second floor walkways and catwalks offer the best visibility, they're also quite exposed. Instead, consider sneaking through the buildings on the ground floor. As you approach each extraction point, you may want to employ a zipline to reach the police cars—climb to the rooftops of the white buildings near each extraction point, then zipline down.

★ Given the close-quarter nature of the fighting around the central buildings, both teams can greatly benefit from grenades. The law enforcement team should deploy smoke grenades when crossing open terrain along the catwalks or around the extraction points. The criminals can make use of gas grenades and incendiary devices, cutting off access to the central catwalks. Use of cameras and decoys are also effective, helping detect and distract your opponents.

▬▬▬	POLICE DEPLOYMENT
▬▬▬	CRIMINAL DEPLOYMENT
🔒	HOSTAGE
⬇	EXTRACTION POINT

★ In Rescue, two hostages are held in the trailer park and it's up to the law enforcement team to rescue one of them. Speed is the key to getting the jump on the criminals. Instead of methodically moving down the center of the map and moving from house-to-house, consider rushing along the map's perimeter. Both the northern and southern edges of the map offer quick paths to the hostages, often allowing you to flank the unsuspecting criminals.

★ Like the police, the criminal team should utilize the northern and southern flanking paths to encircle their opponents. If you don't encounter police during your advance, consider camping the extraction point on the east side, placing breaching charges and laser tripmines near the squad car. Sometimes it's easier to ambush the police at the extraction point than it is to engage them near the hostages. Keep an eye on the north and south flanking paths, since they're likely to carry the hostage along one of these two routes.

As law enforcement, run down the north side of the map between the fence and the mangroves. Unless the criminals are savvy, that route seems like it would be out of bounds. If you follow the path all the way to the end of the fence, you will come out behind the criminals in perfect position to become the aggressor.
—William Bordonaro, Quality Analyst

★ When defending as the criminals, consider backing off from the hostages. Hiding inside the trailers, where the hostages are held, makes you vulnerable to incoming grenades. Instead, deploy gas grenades in each trailer and back away, watching each of them from a distance along the western edge of the map. This allows you to detect activity in the trailers, as well as monitor the flanking paths.

★ Each hostage is held in a trailer on the west side of the map. The trailers are nearly identical with two doorways—one on the east side and one on the west side. Given the quick and sneaky route on the north side of the map, law enforcement has the easiest time reaching hostage #2. But don't expect to run this route in each round, the criminal team will eventually catch-on. Fortunately, there's a similar flanking route on the south side of the map leading to hostage #1. However, the southern route offers less cover and requires a bit more time to travel.

★ This is a relatively small map, so if you're going to deploy gadgets, do so early. Enemy contact can occur within a few seconds, so make sure you're not fumbling with a gadget when you encounter your first opponent. The criminal team should deploy gas grenades, laser tripmines, and cameras near each hostage. Given the likelihood of booby-traps on each hostage trailer, police should bring along frag grenades to detonate these devices prior to entry. The frags won't harm the hostages. Police enforcers should also carry a ballistic shield, ideal for making aggressive pushes along the flanking paths.

Use the perimeter to navigate quickly to the hostages. However, you will need to be careful; there is not a lot of cover along the exterior fence. Smoke can be a very effective tool.
—Evan Champlin, Senior Multiplayer Level Designer

INTRODUCTION
GROWHOUSE
UNDERCOVER VS. THIEVES

The cops have located an illegal underground marijuana grow operation. Law enforcement raids the place, but the criminals aren't going down without a fight. After all, this is precious cargo for them.

Growhouse is one of the smaller maps in *Battlefield: Hardline,* bringing a whole new form of action to the Battlefield franchise. Everyone has a role in Growhouse; from the close ranged weaponry of the enforcer and mechanic, to the laser tripmines and sabotage bombs of the professional. Laser sights, incendiary devices, and gas grenades are very useful tools when playing this map because they allow you to check sharp corners quickly and block entire routes with a single item. Even though Growhouse is small, it is an extremely vertical map that provides cover to enemies above and below you. Keep your head moving and check every sightline before advancing too far. You don't want to be caught in a situation where you're squad is wiped out because the enemy wasn't directly in front of you.

LEVOLUTION

Located beneath the Merry Jane Cleaners' warehouse is a large contraband Growhouse. Like all of the maps in Battlefield: Hardline, Growhouse is extremely destructible. This is especially true in the case of the Growhouse itself. You can set the entire set of crops on fire, by using a grenade or by shooting the one of the gas tanks in the middle of the Growhouse, causing the Growhouse to become filled with smoke and blinding fire. This creates a large visual obstruction for all players in the area.

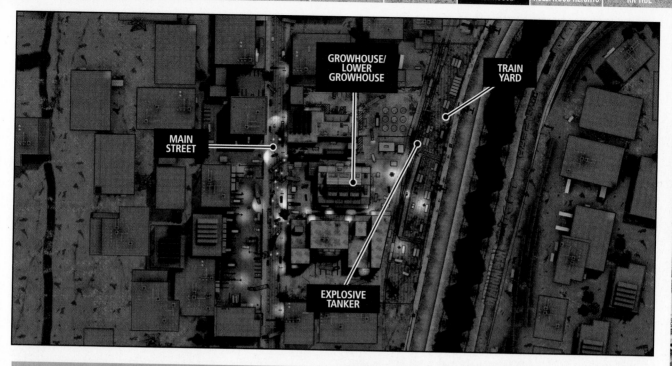

KEY LOCATIONS

TRAIN YARD

The Train Yard is surrounded by empty shipping containers and concrete barriers that are excellent forms of solid cover. Use the long firing lanes to keep your distance from this area when both attacking and defending.

MAIN STREET

The main street has several vantage points that can be used to protect this key location. Use the cars and shipping containers as cover and climb the buildings to cover each end of the street.

GROWHOUSE

The inside of Merry Jane Cleaners is one of the close-quarters sections of Growhouse, especially when the warehouse doors are shut. Keep your eyes on the roof and walkways, as there are a three different levels to the warehouse. All with their own advantage.

EXPLOSIVE TANKER

The Explosive Tanker right outside the Growhouse is a game changer. It is extremely dangerous and you should avoid the area immediately around it until it is destroyed. Once demolished, use it as the quickest shortcut to the Lower Growhouse. This Key Location is most important in game modes like: Heist, Crosshair, and Rescue.

LOWER GROWHOUSE

Beneath the cleaners warehouse is a hidden lair with many different entrances. Late in the game it is nearly impossible to cover every path to this part of the Growhouse, so choose your path wisely and make your time down in this area count.

LEVOLUTION

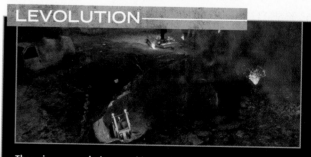

There is a second piece to this map's destructive environment; if you venture to the east side of Growhouse, you will notice a large Explosive Tanker on the railroad. Obviously, with enough damage, this tanker explodes and kills all players in its range. Destroying this tanker also creates a large hole in the street, opening up another avenue to the Growhouse.

> FLIR and Night-Vision scopes really shine on this map.
> —Jeff Zaring

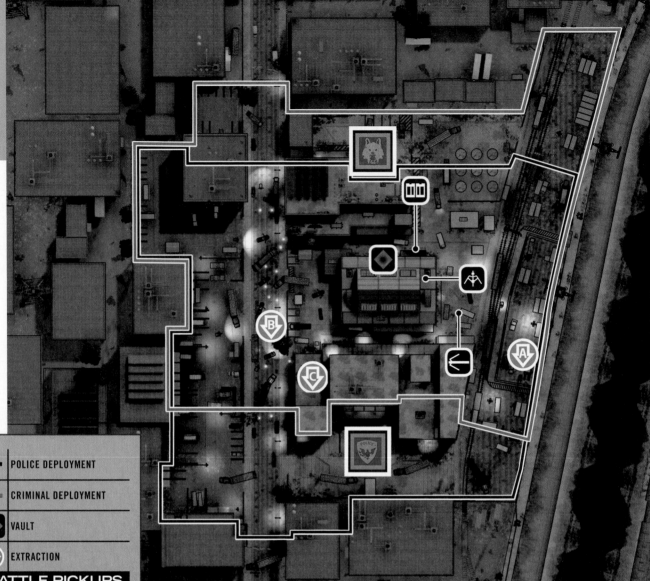

Legend:

— POLICE DEPLOYMENT

— CRIMINAL DEPLOYMENT

◆ VAULT

⊕ EXTRACTION

BATTLE PICKUPS

▥ AMMO

▦ DEFIBRILLATOR

◀ GRAPPLING HOOK

✚ HEALTH

▬ LMG

▬ ROCKET LAUNCHER

▬ STINGER

⋀ ZIPLINE

☆ As the defending team, law enforcement needs to watch three major points and has to get to each of them quickly. The fastest way to get to the main breach point is by entering through the warehouse door and heading inside the upper Growhouse. The enemy team deploys to the north. If your squad can set up a perimeter around the main breach point, you should be able to protect it. Be ready to shift your defense if the enemy opens the rollup door. If you choose to play a more offensive strategy, climb your way to the roof by using the grappling hook; from here you can cover the secondary breach point from above.

☆ When playing on the attacking team you have three options from the start; there are paths that lead east, west, and right up the middle. The eastern path takes you straight toward the police deployment area. You can see the large Explosive Tanker from this vantage point. Destroying this tanker early in the round has a high possibility of taking out an enemy squad or two. Take your entire squad to destroy this tanker as quickly as possible, but it also opens up an opportunity to breach a direct line to the money bags. This is the most dangerous route to the bags, but it is also the easiest breach point to open and serves to spread the cops' defense out thinner than they would probably like.

> There are multiple ways into the vault area. Search the perimeter for other points of access. Control what you open, don't allow the enemy to have better access that you.
> —Evan Champlin, Senior Multiplayer Level Designer

★ The primary breach point is inside the ground floor of the Growhouse. There's a ramp that leads downstairs on the north side of the warehouse and, since this is the primary breach point, it is probably the most protected entry point. If you can, find a way to the roof by using the grappling hook or the ladder on the west side of the building. You and your squad may be able to get the drop on the enemy while covering the rest of your team as they set the breaching charges.

★ There are three secondary breach points—one on the north side of the Growhouse, one on the south side, and part of the destructible environment is the Explosive Tanker that creates the opening to the third breach point and leads you directly to the duffle bags full of cash. While the Explosive Tanker may be the easiest to open, it is by far the hardest to enter because it is so close to the enemy deployment area. Possibly the best option is the northern breach because once you clear the surface defenses, your team should be able to hold it and drop a satellite phone to keep the pressure on.

★ Once you've grabbed the bags, extraction is heavily dependent on how many breach points your team has opened. The safest extraction is extraction (B). If you can retreat back through the northern breach point, have your team cover you while you follow the perimeter of the Growhouse towards the Main Street. If that extraction zone is too hot or not available, you may want to take one of the more dangerous routes like extraction (C.) Since this position is on the roof, it should be easier to defend during the helicopter phase. First, you should open the southern breach and quickly find a grappling hook to get to the top as quickly as possible. The alley is a kill-zone.

SMOKE SCREEN
Use the burning plants to deter any enemies defending the bags with special scopes.

Utilize infrared scopes to spot enemies easier, especially in the Growhouse basement.
—Brian Paoloni, Quality Designer

Don't forget to attack and defend the alternate vault entrances.
—Brian Mckelvey, Quality Analyst

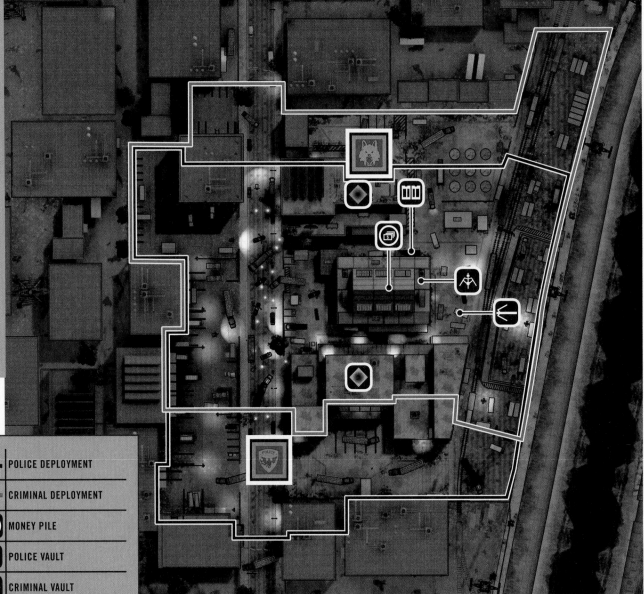

POLICE DEPLOYMENT

CRIMINAL DEPLOYMENT

MONEY PILE

POLICE VAULT

CRIMINAL VAULT

BATTLE PICKUPS

AMMO

DEFIBRILLATOR

GRAPPLING HOOK

HEALTH

LMG

ROCKET LAUNCHER

STINGER

ZIPLINE

★ Like in Heist, the money pile is right in the middle of the underground Growhouse, so it is important to use the environment and destructible obstacles to create as many paths from your team's deployment to the money pile as possible. Blowing up the big red tanker in the middle of the map provides an optional route for both teams, so if you're going to destroy it, make sure you take some enemies out in the process. Moving on ground level is the most dangerous path to the money pile because you can be seen from many different angles. However, this is the fastest route, so stay in cover and move quickly to be the first on the scene, then create a defense while you and your squad go for the first score of the game.

★ Once your team has a good control on the money pile, send squads to the major exits, like the loading ramp closest to the enemy deployment. Taking control and pushing your defenses a bit further than the money pile not only keeps your team safe while they're recovering cash, but gives them a chance to respond if the enemy breaks through the first line of defense, thus creating a second line. If your defense starts to break down and you know you're going to lose control of the money pile, shoot the gas tanks or throw a grenade near the plants. This gives you a little extra cover to escape with some money and disorients the enemy, delaying their defense.

> Control the money piles. Use the plants to sneak around silently taking down enemies.
> —Evan Champlin, Senior Multiplayer Level Designer

☆ Both the police vault and the criminal vault are in warehouses on opposite sides of the Growhouse from each other. They're near their team's respective deployments and since they are indoors they are extremely difficult to get into, let alone get out of safely, so make the decision to steal from your enemy very carefully. The difference between the two vaults are the roof locations. The police vault has roof access directly above the entrance to their vault, making a direct approach nearly impossible unless you start from afar and snipe their defenses before advancing. The criminal vault on the other hand, has a roof off to the side of the entrance, giving them a better defended defense nest, but less of an ambush opportunity for invading forces. You have to make an indirect approach and hug the walls of their vault to either slip by the defense or sneak up on them from behind.

> The center cash pile is great for grenade target practice. If you're there, make sure to crouch to make yourself less exposed. Each team's cash drop is exposed, with multiple access points. Be careful whether you're on offense or defense in that area.
> —James Berg, User Experience Researcher

☆ Playing the midfield on Growhouse is extremely intense and more than likely dictates the winner of Blood Money. The midfield on this map is more or less the entire ground level, but more specifically the Main Street and the Train Yard. Use the roof of the Growhouse to defend these two major areas from an elevated spot, making your field of view much wider than running around on the ground. You also want to use the shipping containers in the Train Yard as cover to defend the giant hole in the ground that may have been created by the ExplosiveTanker. The big hole in the ground is going to be a very hot location because it is a great shortcut to and from the money pile. If you are able to take down any enemies racing out of this spot, there's a good chance they are carrying a large amount of cash that you can grab and take straight to your team's vault for an easy score.

> The team vaults are close together, making it vital to protect your own vault.
> —Ben Gaciu, System Designer

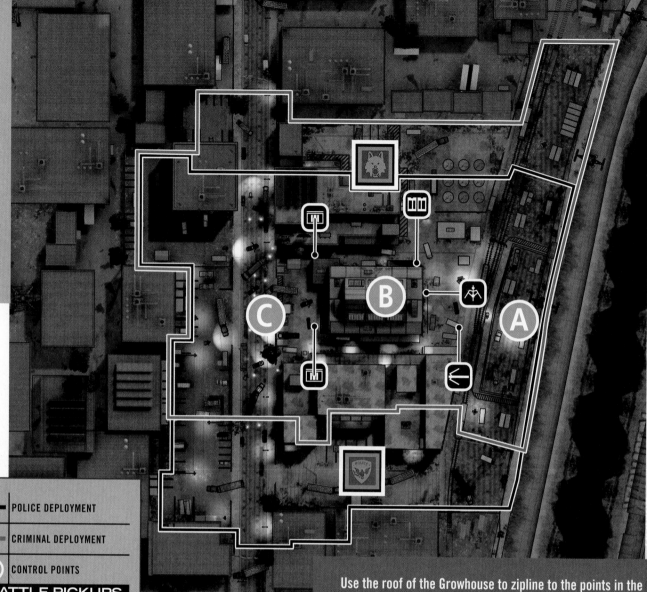

POLICE DEPLOYMENT

CRIMINAL DEPLOYMENT

CONTROL POINTS

BATTLE PICKUPS

AMMO

DEFIBRILLATOR

GRAPPLING HOOK

HEALTH

LMG

ROCKET LAUNCHER

STINGER

ZIPLINE

Use the roof of the Growhouse to zipline to the points in the open. Control the perimeter roofs when possible to prevent the enemy from capturing the open points.
—Evan Champlin, Senior Multiplayer Level Designer

★ Growhouse has no vehicle deployments, so you're going to have to run, walk, and crawl to your destination. Playing on either side, you are definitely going to want to take over the Growhouse, which happens to be (B). Starting on the police side however, you may want to split your forces. It is a little easier to get on the roof of the warehouse closest to your deployment, assuming your team has grappling hooks or you know exactly where the ladders are. From the roof, you can defend your side from any enemy presence on the Growhouse roof working to move towards you team's half of the map and attempting to flank any attackers on (B). You can also zipline down to the Main Street for a quick capture and a good start on bleeding the ticket count of the enemy team, as the battle for the Growhouse usually takes some time before either team has control over it.

★ The criminal side is a little bit different than the police. You still want the majority of your team attacking the Growhouse since it is prime real estate. However, since it is a bit more difficult to get to the roof of your team's closest warehouse, you may want to take your squad to the Train Yard. It takes your team much less time to get there and gives you a straight line of sight to the enemy roof where you and your squad can take out any enemy forces attempting to take the high ground on any conquest objective.

★ The control point (B), Upper Growhouse, is going to be the most valuable by far, simply because of the fact that your team can deploy there and attack either of the other control points without running through a barrage of bullets. However, you can't defend another control point unless you have another one to control, so if your team is going to control the Growhouse you also want to capture one of the others. (A) is the next most valuable since it is on a side of the Growhouse that is the most open and much more difficult to control from. Also, you don't want the enemy using the tanker entrance to flank your defenders. Be aware that the Upper Growhouse is only the most defensible if the majority of your squads are there to defend it. There are a lot of entry points and unless they are all defended, the enemy quickly swarms your location.

★ Growhouse is extremely close quarters, so enforcers and mechanics thrive here because of their primary weapons. Professionals equipped with sabotage and laser tripmines can narrow the playing field tremendously, making it difficult for the enemy to breach your defenses.

TANKER TIP
Use the Explosive Tanker to create a backdoor route to the Growhouse, but try not to kill any teammates in the process.

Destroy the red tanker train car to trigger the Levolution and access the grow room from the rear.
—John Seefurth, Quality Analyst

SPAWN AREA

BATTLE PICKUPS

AMMO	
DEFIBRILLATOR	
GRAPPLING HOOK	
HEALTH	
LMG	
ROCKET LAUNCHER	
STINGER	
ZIPLINE	

☆ Team Deathmatch on Growhouse does not change the layout of the map all that much from Conquest or Heist, but it does narrow a bit for a three lane structure that makes team play on this mode a little more organized. Calling out key locations such as the Main Street, Growhouse, and Train Yard provides valuable intel to your team because it gives them a lane to attack or keep away from that is highly specific and can be recognized as solid communication.

Smoke grenades and thermal scopes can give you that extra edge on this map. Drop some smoke on an objective to cover yourself and your teammates and see the enemy before they see you with a thermal optic, just don't forget the flash hider.
—Aaron Broster, Quality Analyst

✮ The stronghold for Growhouse is the underground growroom because, with minimal ways to get in, a squad or two can hold down choke points preventing anyone from coming in and flanking your team. Your squad may also want to hold down one of the other warehouses. If your squad is working alone, these warehouses have only a few entrances and since they are fully enclosed, there is no worry of getting shot from a distance. Keep your back to a wall and watch everything that comes around those corners.

✮ Sub-machine guns and shotguns are going to serve best on Growhouse Team Deathmatch especially if your squad holes up in one of the strongholds. An assault rifle may be more powerful and a tad more accurate at a distance, but up close there is nothing that beats a single well-placed shotgun blast or the rapid unload of a compact sub-machine gun. Remember to drop a satellite phone wherever your squad decides to set up your stronghold because nothing breaks your squad up worse than losing one member that can't get back to your location because he or she is pinned down outside.

✮ It is best to stay out of the wide open areas in the center of the Train Yard or the Main Street because, while the rest of the map is dark, these spots are lit up by a street light essentially calling you out to the enemy. Use cover and move slowly. There isn't an objective that your squad needs to rush to and running out to get a kill just to die right after nets your team back to zero.

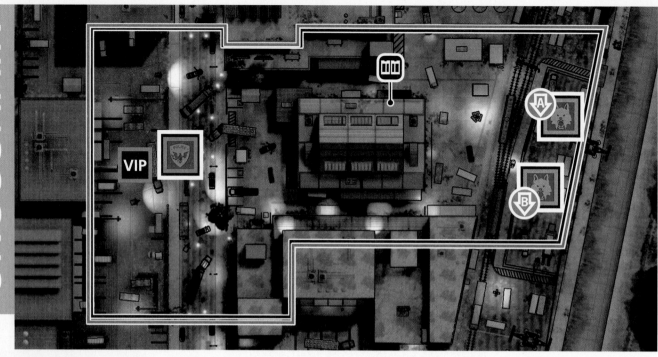

POLICE DEPLOYMENT

CRIMINAL DEPLOYMENT

HOSTAGE

EXTRACTION POINT

★ As with all Crosshair matches, no matter the map, the police have a slight disadvantage, so it's up to them to trick the criminals. Growhouse is no exception, however it is easier to slip away from the enemy with the use of cover and all of the tight spaces that the alleyways and shipping containers provide on this map. You want to get out of your team's deployment as quickly as possible and head to the outer perimeter of the Growhouse before beginning to slow down. It is imperative that you take your time and move from cover to cover on this map because the enemy is waiting for you around every corner. Get your better shooters to the roofs of the Growhouse and both the north and south warehouses because if your team can win the firefights that may happen up there, you have gained the upper hand. Without much time in each round, you must move quickly once your team has gained an advantage. Use the shipping containers and as many distractions as possible to set up blind spots and complicated ways for the enemy to find your VIP as he slips on by, straight to the extraction.

★ Playing on the criminal side is tricky on Growhouse because you have to coordinate heavily with the rest of your team on whether you want to spread yourselves out or pick a specific location to watch. Picking a specific location on this map is incredibly risky, but with the amount of cover that is provided you can stay hidden as the enemy passes you, giving you and your team a clear shot at their defenseless 6 o'clock. If you decide you don't want to take the huge risk of creating a singular ambush, there are some great spots to set up in order to watch each lane. Get two shooters to the roof of the Growhouse as quickly as possible. If they set up on your side of the roof and watch each side they can take out any snipers looking to clear a path for their VIP. Then your team should spread out the three on the ground, each watching one lane while keeping close to the deployment. There are many avenues the VIP can take, but they end up funneling to the three major lanes on the map.

★ In all Crosshair games, you want to change up your strategy from time to time. If your team feels like they have a handle on out-shooting the enemy they are more likely to branch out and rush the opposing team's deployment area. Growhouse makes the rush method extremely dangerous. With all the twists and turns, alleyways, and warehouses, the police can easily turn the tables on the criminals by finding their own hiding spots and playing their own form of defense.

★ Playing as the VIP, it helps to take the safest route and to have at least one bodyguard with you. The most concealed route is taking the underground path by running down the loading ramp and through the underground Growhouse. There are only a few exits and if the other team is smart they are watching those carefully, so choose wisely. Taking the paths along the northern perimeter provides enough cover and allows your teammates to create distractions on the south side, letting you to slip through.

★ Carrying a zipline and traveling to the roof in order to surprise the opposing team by zipping straight to one of the extractions can catch the criminals off guard and leave them no time to rush back and kill the VIP. From the criminal side, you may want to carry a sabotage bomb, laser tripmines, and gas grenades. This allows you to control which paths the enemy must take to get to their objective, or at the very least tells you where they are when they either trigger or disarm your equipment.

> As VIP, take the left roof from the start, explode the tanker, then backtrack through the Growroom and out of the crater to escape.
> —Jeff Zaring, Lead MP Map Designer

RESCUE

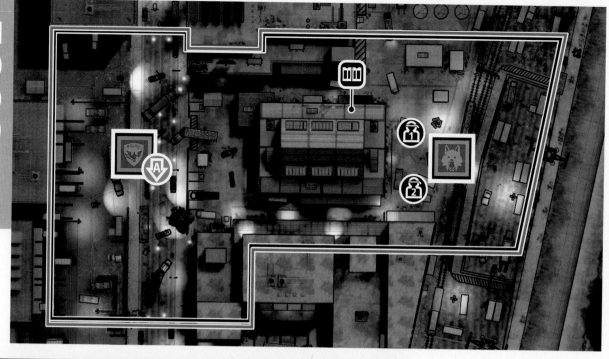

> **Team work is key, get a teammate with a riot shield to provide mobile cover while other teammates spot and return fire.**
> —Ryan Murphy, Level Designer

☆ Playing as police, you deploy on the Main Street where the extraction point is. Your job is to travel downstairs into the Growroom and retrieve at least one of the hostages and bring them back. It is a bit challenging getting to the hostages mainly because they are too near to each other.

Both are located in the Growroom and just on the other side of a pylon from one another. This means you have to get creative with the way that you enter and you need to work as a team to strike quietly in unison. The ideal way to win at least one round is by setting up your attack by having each member of your team breach the warehouse at a different location. From here, you should have one member shoot the tanker in the west until it explodes. Assuming the enemy defenders are near the entrance point that this explosion creates, they become disoriented, leaving them out of the fight for a few seconds. Meanwhile, the rest of the team breaches and clears the Growroom and the fifth member enters through the exploded hole in the ground, cleaning up the remaining foes.

> **Create an alternate path to the hostages by blowing up the fuel tank behind the warehouse.**
> —Ben Gaciu, System Designer

☆ As the criminals, you need to defend both hostages. Since the hostages are close by, your team should keep a tight perimeter around them because if the police team can get to one, then they can easily get to the other before you can. It is always good to have at least one scout roaming the wider perimeter for the chance of catching a couple of enemies in the act of preparing a breach plan. Keep as much of the building intact as possible because the fewer entry ways the enemy has, the better chance that you and your teammates are looking in the right direction when attackers approach.

☆ Normally it is a better tactic to stay close to the hostages and lock down the objective zone, keeping a tight lid on the situation. However, there are more ways into the Growhouse than there are to get back to the extraction zone. If the defending team moves as one and secures a perimeter around the extraction zone, it may be easier to protect than the hostages themselves. On that note, the police may want to give about thirty seconds before breaching and clearing the hostage room to see if any criminals come out looking for the attackers.

☆ The two hostages are very close together, so if the police team makes a successful grab of one of the hostages, it doesn't hurt to have a second team member grab the other and split up. In most maps, there is a good chance that one hostage may be under heavier guard than the other, but in this case if one hostage is clear the other might be clear as well. Split up and head in separate directions to increase your odds of making it to the extraction point.

☆ Timing is key in this map and mode combination. Since there are so many doors and walls covering the attackers' approach, the team needs to coordinate when breaching to keep the element of surprise. It is also extremely useful to have stealth on for the same reason. There may not be a criminal on the other side of that door, but he might be just around the corner waiting for that door-busting sound. If you open the doors quietly, you can get even closer to the enemy without them noticing.

> **As the criminals, make sure to place sabotage on the doors that enter the basement - you might get a kill, but you'll definitely know if an enemy comes through one!**
> —Thad Sasser, Lead Multiplayer Designer

INTRODUCTION
HOLLYWOOD HEIGHTS
UNDERCOVER VS. THIEVES

A mansion high in the Hollywood Hills looks ripe for a little crime. The criminals have started a wildfire in the nearby hills to distract the police. Do you think that'll work?

Hollywood Heights is deceivingly larger than most maps in *Battlefield: Hardline* due to the intricate mansion in the center of the map containing multiple floors, rooms, and a maze of walls that can be very confusing. From Heist mode to Rescue, Hollywood Heights forces teams to develop smart and well-planned strategies in order to win each fight. Equip your shotgun or submachine gun to bust down doors and take your enemy by surprise from above, below, and right to their face. This map has plenty of sabotage locations and Battle Pickups that give you and your team the advantage in any situation. Use the map's ups and downs to get an edge on the enemies as you and your team take this small neighborhood in the Hollywood Hills by force.

LEVOLUTION

Of course, **you can** blow giant holes through the walls of the mansion. Tear **your** way through the walls and into rooms whe the enemy **won't** be expecting you. However, there are cases where you must be stealthy and want to get around to the parts of the mansion that may not be accessible via destructio or any civilized means. In these circumstances, use the secret doors and high tech access points to get around covertly. Loo around the mansion for hand print recognition hardware and activate it to use the secret door that it's connected to. They'r all around the house so keep your eyes peeled.

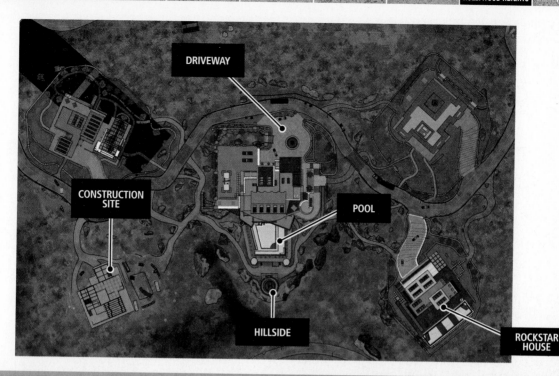

KEY LOCATIONS

DRIVEWAY

The Driveway is the main battleground before entering the mansion. It contains a wide open space, not much cover, and gives you a great view for figuring out a way to enter the mansion. This is the location where both teams are most vulnerable. With a straight shot to the garage and grassy green, you must be resourceful to survive and defend the Driveway successfully.

ROCKSTAR HOUSE

The Rockstar House has many rooms, a wide garage, and it's on a large luxurious lot. There are a ton of corners to hide behind and room to change position in a pinch. Players can move around when they need to, but the location also allows good players to show their talent when circumstances call for a quick reactionary shot to the enemy. Move around, adjust to your surroundings, but stay quiet. If the enemy can hear you, they can also blow holes through the walls to get to you.

POOL

The Pool is located right outside the back of the main section of the mansion and is illuminated more brightly than most places on this night map. In most modes, the pool is the central and most important key location on the map. It is the best way to get into the mansion and to catch anyone trying to escape from the upper floors. The solid walls of the pool rooms and large pillars holding up the overhead provide for excellent cover. Use them as much as possible and control the Pool for the biggest advantage.

CONSTRUCTION SITE

Hollywood Heights is where the rich come to enjoy their wealth. Celebrities love big, custom houses. The Construction Site calls for players to be accurate with their weapons and to trick their enemies with lure techniques and disorienting gadgets. Between the giant hole in the ground and the partially built frame of the house held up by wooden beams and a little bit of drywall, there is a great deal of cover, but none that should be trusted to last for very long. Most firefights result in cat and mouse games and outsmarting your enemy's movements while you appear behind them without them having the slightest suspicion. Take your time and survey the Construction Site before doing anything risky because it could be your final move.

HILLSIDE

Peering over the city from the Hollywood Hills, the Hillside is the lowest point on the map and serves several different uses in almost every game mode. The Hillside may seem like a difficult and invaluable control point, but with a helicopter spawning here on Conquest and the large cliff from the edge of the Pool, it is a useful spot and it's not impossible to defend. There is a small service room attached to the very end of the pool on the Hillside, it's tough and can take a beating so use it when you need to and beware of the sideways sightlines that point in this direction.

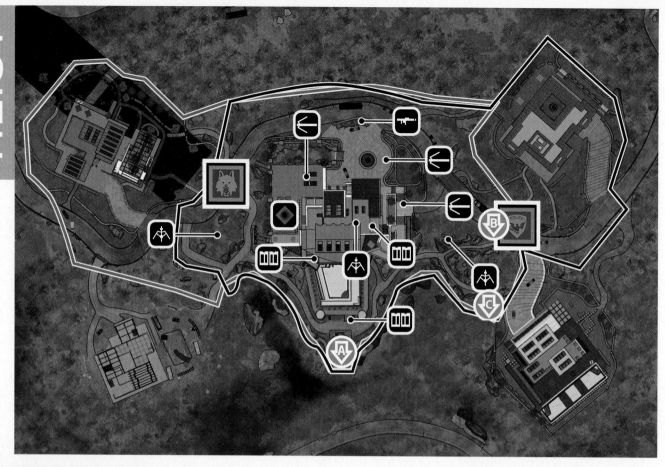

POLICE DEPLOYMENT

CRIMINAL DEPLOYMENT

VAULT

EXTRACTION

BATTLE PICKUPS

AMMO

DEFIBRILLATOR

GRAPPLING HOOK

HEALTH

LMG

ROCKET LAUNCHER

STINGER

ZIPLINE

★ When beginning a round of Heist on Hollywood Heights as the police, there are a few things you and your team must do. The main objective for the criminal team is the sculpture on the lawn of the mansion. Set up a perimeter around the lawn and use the house as a base of operations. Use satellite phones and sabotage charges to protect yourselves from enemies attempting to flank your defenders. This setup is important for the beginning moments of the round on Heist, but remember that there are other locations that the criminals can use to breach the vault. You and your squad need to be able to rotate to the secondary breach points before the enemy is able to plant the explosives or set up their drill, so don't bury yourself too deep inside the house. It is difficult to get out, especially when the enemy is on a full force attack.

★ As the criminals, you and your team must be resourceful and very opportunistic. There are several different ways into the money vault that aren't necessarily accessible by a single squad at the same time. If you notice the enemy team heavily defending one of the breach points, there is a good chance that one of the other two is a bit lighter on manpower. Because of this expensive layout and infrastructure, try not going to the same objective twice, or at least make sure that each breach point is being attacked equally and preferably at the same time. Overwhelming the enemy on Hollywood Heights is a strong tactic and when all three breach points are open, it is near impossible to defend the money bags for very long. Attack, attack, then attack some more! Keeping pressure on the enemy is never a bad idea as long as your team is coordinated. Don't forget, the attacking team has a ticket limit and should keep an eye on it from time to time.

> Use gas from the top entrance before you jump down.
> —David Price, Weapon Designer

★ The primary breach point to the vault on Hollywood Heights is located directly above the vault, adjacent to a sculpture in the mansion's lawn. This specific spot is right out in the open and, like most maps, it is not the best point to go for because it is the easiest for the police to defend. However, since it is the easiest to defend, if the criminals break the defense of this primary objective then it is the easiest to defend while the drill is doing its job breaking into the vault. Be aware that once this primary point is actually breached, the criminal team has one chance to enter and defend it or escape out the side before the police swarm it and it becomes extremely difficult to enter from the top side again.

★ There are two alternate breach points, classified as secondary breach points, but they are just as important as the primary. One breach point is located poolside on the flat open wall adjacent to the money vault. It is part of the wall that is on a ledge leading to the pool and can be defended from the other side of the walkway. There isn't a whole lot of room to defend this spot, so it is by far the easiest point to breach. The second breach point is on the other side of the lawn from the criminal spawn which means you should go around the lawn and enter through the Driveway. To get to this breach point, you must access the garage by either going through the house and opening up one of the secret passageways or by opening the garage with the security console. Once inside the garage, you can see the large empty space on the far wall, this is the third breach point and is a point that should be opened last once the criminal team is about to steal the packages because it creates a direct line to two of the extraction points.

★ Since there are only three possible extraction points, you can't be too picky about which one you to head for. Your best bet is to lead the path of least resistance. If you don't know where to go and extraction (A) is available, this is your best bet. Extraction (A) is furthest away from the law enforcement deployment and if you have a zipline equipped, exiting the money vault out the pool side and ziplining down to the helipad where (A) is located is the quickest way to capture a bag. If (A) is not available, both (B) and (C) are perfectly accessible. However you are going to require some back up. No matter which one your cash carrier chooses, the criminal team should use the hill and the roof of the mansion to defend these spots because they are the two high points and they overlook both positions rather well.

> Criminals, use gas and Molotovs to clear out any enemies inside the vault. Riot shields and shotguns can be very effective at gaining control of the vault room. Have your team focused on controlling the roof tops. If Law Enforcement gains control it will be a tough fight to the escape points.
> —Evan Champlin, Senior Multiplayer Level Designer

> Drop health packs in the vault area to help out your team.
> —Brian Paoloni, Quality Designer

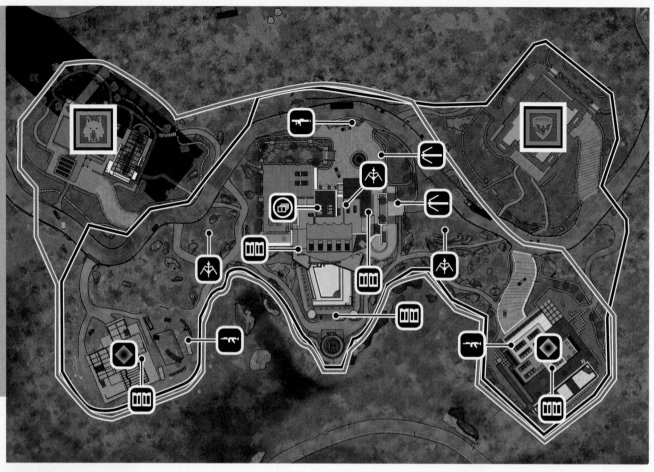

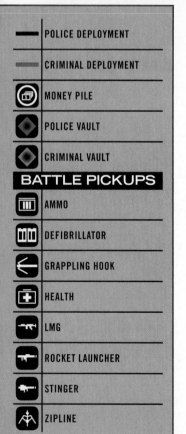

☆ When rushing the money pile, you have many different route options. The quickest route is not always the best. You want to get in and out as fast as possible, but heading straight from your team's deployment and through the front door is only going to cause problems. Instead, head around back to the Pool and watch the area across the Pool because it is much easier to clear. Head into the mansion where the money pile is located. There are no team air vehicles on Hollywood Heights so getting to the roof can be a small challenge unless your team takes control of the Hillside where the helicopter spawns. Equip a grappling hook and get to the roof quickly in order to cover your teammates as they make for a successful escape back to your base to return the cash they just collected. From the roof you have a few options. Drop down at any point around the perimeter of the mansion and take the path of least resistance to the money pile or drop down on enemy cash runners to steal their loot.

☆ The money pile is located on the bottom floor in the large entryway as you walk in the front door. Because the money pile is in the middle of the room, it can be protected from virtually anywhere within the mansion. When protecting the money pile, go up to the second floor and set up a sabotage charge on the nearest entrance in order to protect your blind side while you orient yourself towards the money pile and shoot anyone attempting to lay a finger on the cash. Remember, most of the walls inside the mansion can be shot through and broken down, so if you suspect the enemy is hiding in the other room, shoot him from the other side of the wall.

> Fight to the helicopter. Controlling it will bring you team a strong advantage. Use it to drop teammates on the enemies' vault roof.
> —Evan Champlin, Senior Multiplayer Level Designer

⭐ The Police vault is located in the main hallway of the Rockstar House. This key location can be accessed via the roof, so, just like the mansion, there are nearly unlimited ways to attack the police vault. This means there are also a wide variety of ways to defend it. With the amount of doorways and hallways inside the Rockstar House, set up sabotage charges and use the professional class to plant laser tripmines. Climb on top of the roof to protect your team's vault. When attacking, bring a shotgun with you to disarm these devices the explosive way.

⭐ The criminal vault is inside the Construction Site, which means it is not a good idea to defend your team's vault from inside the house. There are a few covered rooms that allow for some cover, but if the attackers even suspect that you're hiding in there, they quickly overwhelm your position. The best way to protect your vault is by hiding around the perimeter of the house and inside the unfinished pool. Most attackers go straight for the vault and attempt to steal your cash. Take advantage of this and hit them before they can even see your team's vault. When attacking, always think about how you should be defending that zone and use that mentality to protect yourself. Check the perimeter before moving in.

> Control the central money pile by hanging out on the ledge of the roof and shooting down into the main mansion, but watch your back, set up a laser trip mine to get anyone coming behind you while you are controlling the money pile.
> —Clint Brewer, Gameplay Software Engineer

⭐ Stay clear of the main road whenever possible. All the way along the main road are several ambush locations from the hill in front of the Rockstar House to the dip as you head towards the Construction Site. These two locations are dangerous and it is always a possibility that there is at least a full squad waiting to take down anyone who comes around the corner. These are also great ambush spots for the opposing team because it creates a wall that the other team just can't break through to either rush the money pile or bring the cash back to their own vault. However, the biggest ambush location is the Driveway because it is a central location and it is just outside the largest entrance to the mansion. Use the second floor balcony, the lawn, and the garage to ambush any enemy running through the Driveway and they won't stand a chance.

> Use the RPG near the cop car in the driveway to take out the helicopter.
> —Brian Paoloni, Quality Designer

BATTLE PICKUPS LEGEND

—	POLICE DEPLOYMENT
—	CRIMINAL DEPLOYMENT
○	CONTROL POINTS

BATTLE PICKUPS

	AMMO
	DEFIBRILLATOR
	GRAPPLING HOOK
	HEALTH
	LMG
	ROCKET LAUNCHER
	STINGER
	ZIPLINE

★ Each key location on Hollywood Heights has its own advantage, but sometimes there are priorities when your team is losing a location or needs one to give you an edge. Either side should make C, the Hillside, a priority. It spawns a helicopter as soon as you capture the point which is the only air vehicle on the map. Your next objective, or next preferred objective if the Hillside gets too hot is B, the Pool. It allows your team to deploy inside the house, providing a ton of cover for everyone nearby. Once you are able to take B and C, your team should already have D, the Rockstar House. This starts to bleed the enemy tickets, not to mention gives you the most important control points on the map. Since Hollywood Heights is so symmetrical and the three major points in the middle split the map directly in half, these tactics work equally for both sides. Most of the fighting takes place between A, B, and C. If you really want to throw the enemy off, try capturing the control point closest to their base.

★ The Hillside is the most valuable control point. It may be difficult to defend, but taking it early and granting your team the helicopter bonus gives friendlies the upper hand. If you can't take the Hillside, it is more than acceptable to settle for the Pool due to its durability and central location on the map. It provides a great deployment area and the entire mansion to keep the pressure on the two surrounding control points.

★ When choosing your classes and loadout, remember that, although most of the map is outdoors, you are still fighting in tight spaces and corridors. Equip carbines, shotguns, submachine guns, and, if you are going to use the hill between B and D, an assault rifle. At the beginning of the round, it is good use the operator class because it is versatile on the run and you aren't going to be setting up camp any time soon. Use gas grenades and carbines to secure your first control point and then move on to attacking the enemy, preventing them from capturing anything. The mechanic has a plethora of gadgets made for this map and the weapons to handle the range at which you regularly encounter enemies. Equipped with a shotgun, sabotage, and the armored insert, your mechanic is unstoppable. Create your own little fortress by barricading yourself in a room where you can respond to the closest control point at a moment's notice and make sure you don't get flanked by placing a sabotage charge on the doorways you aren't able to watch.

> Controlling the mansion roof will allow you to cover the routes to the other points with sniper fire. Watch out of the collapsing section of the mansion, you don't want to be caught in the wrong place at the wrong time.
>
> —Evan Champlin, Senior Multiplayer Level Designer

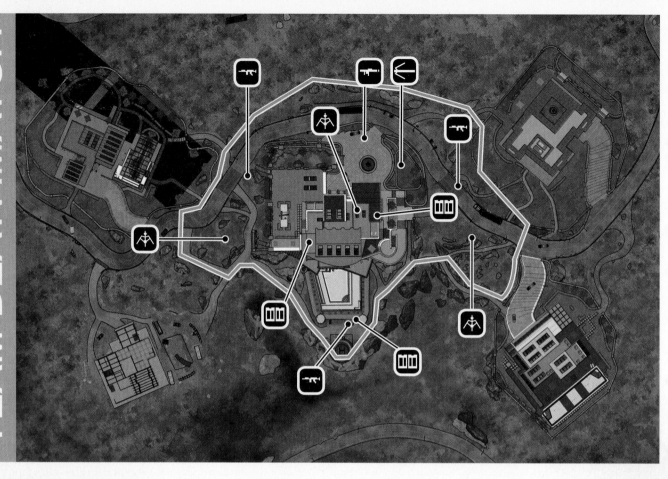

▦	SPAWN AREA

BATTLE PICKUPS

▥	AMMO
▦	DEFIBRILLATOR
⬅	GRAPPLING HOOK
✚	HEALTH
▬	LMG
▬	ROCKET LAUNCHER
▬	STINGER
⚹	ZIPLINE

★ Hollywood Heights is a map that fits the style of *Battlefield: Hardline* perfctly in both its size and stature. Getting rid of the outer four pieces of the full map, Team Deathmatch is set in the center part of the map. Team Deathmatch on Hollywood Heights is by far the most complex and deceiving when it comes to size and avenues a player can take to get from any one point to another. The map focuses around the mansion directly in the middle of the map with three different major levels to fight on: the bottom floor, the second floor, and the roof. Along with the mansion being the main focus of this mode/map combination, the Pool, the Hillside, and the Driveway are all fair game and important key locations when developing your strategy.

★ Unique to this map is the fact that at any location, there is some way for you to create a formidable stronghold to protect yourself and your squad as you rack up kills on the enemy team. The first and second floor are the main strongholds on this map, with its many walls and a manageable number of entrances your team can cover. It is large though, so it may take at least two squads to hold it properly. The roof is another possible stronghold. It is separated from the interior of the mansion, so it can be held exclusively from the first and second floor. Beware of grenades! An armored insert comes in

handy because you can shrug a distant grenade off while you attack the enemy that threw it and your squad mate heals you back to full health. The Pool, Hillside, the hill near the Rockstar House, and the dip near the Construction Site all have more than enough cover to create major chokepoints, allowing your squad to set up camp there. For this reason, keep a keen eye out for gadgets because attacking any location could drop you directly into a nest of bad guys.

★ Playing a mechanic or an operator on this map allows you the most versatility and ability to help our your squad when both on the move and setting up a stronghold. The mechanic's gadgets can protect your team while the operator's med kit and revive gadget brings the dead back to life if something bad happens. It is also a good idea to bring a grappling hook with you just in case an enemy squad decides to set up camp on top of the roof of the mansion and they are watching the stairs heavily. If you're on the roof and need a quick get away because you know you're about to be swarmed, use the Battle Pickups like the zipline or the rocket launcher to ditch your current area of operation or make some noise as a last resort.

★ When you're on the move and you're trying to find a new stronghold, attempting to get back to your squad, or just out hunting for enemies, the most important thing is to keep your eye out for enemy gadgets because there are potential spots everywhere on Hollywood Heights. Use the defibrillators on the walls if you're the last one alive and you don't have one on you. Your team will thank you and you can save a few tickets in the process. Remember to never turn a corner without your gun at the ready and your squad can breathe easy knowing that you have their backs, or that you died trying to protect them.

> FLIR and Night-Vision scopes are great on this map. Ziplines are also very useful.
> —Jeff Zaring, Lead MP Map Designer

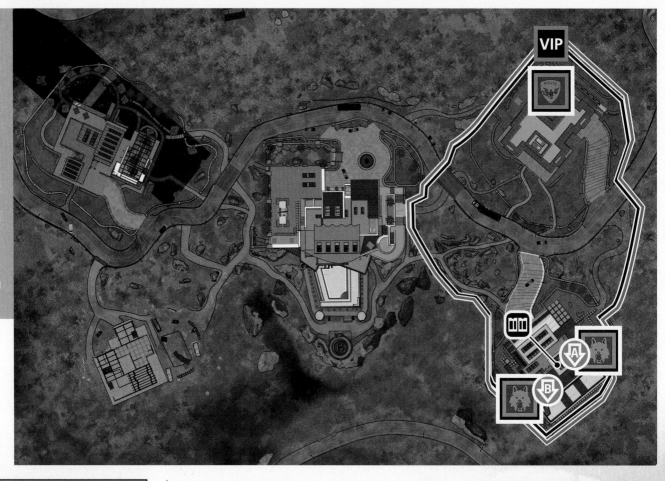

POLICE DEPLOYMENT

CRIMINAL DEPLOYMENT

EXTRACTION POINT

☆ Crosshair on Hollywood Heights takes place in the only section of the map that makes sense for extracting the VIP in this celebrity filled locale of *Battlefield: Hardline*, the Rockstar House. Playing as the police takes some quick and clean shooting in order to take the criminals down. Like all Crosshair maps, there are three major routes to the extraction points: two outside on the perimeters of the map and the massive house itself. The Rockstar House may be daunting from the outside because of its size, but even though there are many rooms, they are all fairly small, making it easy to know which one you are in. They are easy to clear, but you should clear the house slowly because there are criminals that enjoy hiding around sharp corners. Use the outside routes to secure the extractions while the rest of your team creates distractions inside the house. Equip an INRV and make sure there aren't any snipers because it is much easier to cover the VIP's approach from the outside-in rather than the inside-out.

☆ Playing as the criminals takes a mixture of classes in order to protect the extraction zones. It is important to watch the perimeters of the house, but you don't want to expose yourself to incoming cops as they come guns at the ready looking for you. Bring out the operators and professionals to watch the outer sections while the mechanics and enforcers shift toward a more offensive route inside the house. Indoors you must find a spot where you can get to the extraction quickly if the VIP slips by, but make sure your back is to a wall and you have a sightline that points toward one of the main routes from the front door. The kitchen is a prime location for this tactic.

Trip mines are lethal in the small hallways of the mans
—Ben Gaciu, System Desig

☆ Hollywood Heights is extremely hectic because it is tight, the sightlines are long and the walls are thin. Using the rush method can catch the opposing team off guard very easily because they cannot see you coming if you use the house as cover. Use the roof by attaching a grappling hook and running to the other side of the house to then drop down and attempt to flank the enemy. However, because of the corners and long sightlines it is a fairly simple set up when using the lockdown method. There is no reason that prevents you or your team from having eyes on the extraction points while staying hidden at the same time. Use the kitchen and dry pool to conceal yourself while you are able to peek at either extraction to make sure the VIP isn't close to it or for any clues left by the enemy that could tell you that they are planning to extract there. There isn't much time, but with how fast each team can reach the other side of the map, it won't take long to make the slow approach and rush the extraction when it's open. It is important that whichever method the you use, you are able to get to either extraction quickly in a pinch.

> **Shoot through the walls inside.**
> **—David Price, Weapon Designer**

☆ As it is always a good idea to use distractions, smoke screen covers, and false extractions in Crosshair, it is key to use them at the right time and in the right location. When you are the VIP, you don't want to have your team throw smoke directly on top of the extraction when using extraction (A). If the doors to the bedroom are closed, you don't have time to miss it and try to find it or have the smoke break the glass and make a noise that can be heard from the opposite end of the map. Instead, your team should throw the grenade just outside the bedroom because it allows you to find the extraction and it sets up a thick screen that the enemy cannot see through. However, you can at least see them come through it and protect yourself. Moving through the house as the VIP is very dangerous, but if taken carefully and you are able to avoid being spotted you are able to use the house and its many rooms as cover as you get close to both extractions before your team tells you which one is safe and which one is not. Always request a body guard and keep a little distance between you and him, stick to cover and let the house become your fortress.

☆ Gas grenades accompanied by gas masks are your best friends when playing on a map like Hollywood Heights. With small extractions and even smaller rooms that lead to them, a single gas grenade can both alert you and your team to enemies it affects and disorient them enough to breach and clear rooms without the risk of being shot from a distance. Using the roof is useful when you wish to rush to the other side of the map quickly, and the best way to do this is by using the grappling hook. Don't leave home without it.

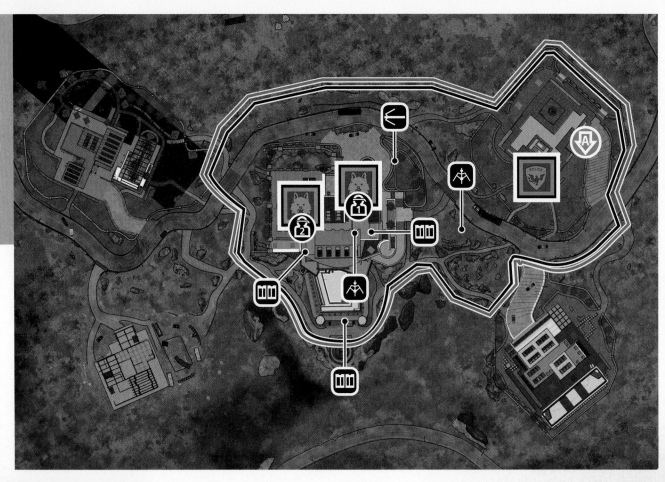

▬▬▬	**POLICE DEPLOYMENT**
▬▬▬	**CRIMINAL DEPLOYMENT**
🔒	**HOSTAGE**
⬇	**EXTRACTION POINT**

★ Playing as the police, you and your team should be ready to surround the objective and enter from all sides. Rescue on Hollywood Heights takes place between the villa where the police deploy and the giant mansion in the center of the map. The mansion is large because it is so big it creates a plethora of options for entering and clearing the hostage areas. However, it also allows the criminal team a great deal of options to hide and prepare for your arrival, so get to your breaching positions and make sure the rest of your team is ready before charging in. Keep your eye on the roofs. If the criminals make it up to the roof before you, they can see you from a mile out, making for an excellent sniper's nest, so it is important to be cautious while moving fast to avoid any surprises. Once your team is ready, breach the mansion and head to the second floor, where both hostages can be accessed. Your team can cover you from the second floor or by watching the major entrances while you and a partner grab the hostages and book it to the roof if you know it to be clear. From the roof, use a zipline to get straight to the extraction more quickly than anyone could get there on foot. If your team follows you down the zipline, you can set up a fast perimeter for anyone right on your heels attempting to stop you before the hostage is fully extracted.

★ Playing as the criminals leaves you more options than you can count. You can race to the roof and pick off the cops as they approach your stronghold. You can play the waiting game as they enter your already covered entryways. Or, your team can rush out and use the darkness as cover to create ambush sites and take out the undercover team as they walk right into your sights. There are plenty of different tactics your team can take, but it is extremely important that your team is all on the same page and agree on a single plan of action. If half of your team covers the entryways and the other half sets up ambushes outside, your defense falls apart. This often leads to entryways that are not covered properly and ambush areas which aren't wide enough to lockdown every escape route. Communicate with your teammates and use every member to the best of their ability. Be flexible and move about based on where your defense needs you most. It is possible to shoot through the walls inside the mansion so if you're going to try and hole up in one of the hostage rooms, be prepared to shoot back through them.

★ When your team is on defense, the most important thing is to make sure the cops don't rescue the hostages, but the second most important thing is to work together. Because of the complexity of Hollywood Heights, it is easy to spread your forces too thin and lose track of who is where and what is or is not being covered. Both the rush and lockdown tactics work well on this map, but neither one of them work very nicely if your team is not on the same page. Lock down the mansion by spreading out on each floor and watching the entrances like the doors and pool entrance. The lockdown method works, but is not flawless. Each teammate needs to be able to kill their target and then provide backup for any area that is breached. Do what you can to not give away your position too early and set laser tripmines and sabotage charges where you think they are most likely to trigger. Deterring the enemy from the larger entrances gives you the advantage of funneling an enemy into a narrower angle of fire allowing you to focus more on a specific area when defending. Or, rush out and create a perimeter around the mansion using the shadows and shrubbery as cover while you pick off each target as they move forward.

> Grab a hostage and zipline from the roof to the extraction point
> —John Seefurth, Quality Analyst

★ As with all Rescue matches, there are two hostages. On Hollywood Heights they are in two completely different rooms of the mansion, meaning your team needs to scope out the intended target before entering to determine which one is best or hedge your bets and go for both at the same time. Each hostage is in roughly the same location as the other, but on separate floors. The hostage on the first floor is located in the theater of the mansion northwest of the main entryway. The theater has a large wall on the entryway side that is highly penetrable, so sending one or two teammates upstairs while you unload on the room, revealing whether it is safe or not, lets them know whether they should cover you or go for the second hostage. The second hostage is located upstairs in the major living room behind a pillar in the middle of the room. Beware of the corners in this room. It is easy to forget about them and be caught by a defender as you are focused on capturing the hostage and getting the heck out of there. The hostage upstairs is the better grab if your escape tactic is to get to the roof and zipline down to the extraction, but the hostage downstairs is much safer when you know your team is outnumbered by defenders and you must make a quick decision.

INTRODUCTION
RIPTIDE
SWAT VS. THIEVES

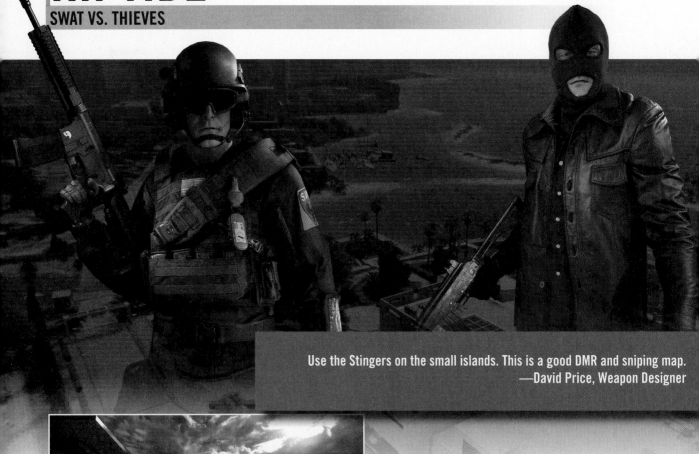

Use the Stingers on the small islands. This is a good DMR and sniping map.
—David Price, Weapon Designer

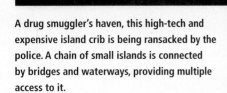

A drug smuggler's haven, this high-tech and expensive island crib is being ransacked by the police. A chain of small islands is connected by bridges and waterways, providing multiple access to it.

Stormy skies and choppy seas should be the least of your concerns in this exclusive seaside locale. SWAT units have swarmed a cartel stronghold triggering an all-out war, raging across seven intense game modes. Vehicles play a key role on this map, but don't let the lack of roads fool you. Due to the low tide, the sandbars on the northern and southern edges of the map can be accessed and traversed by ground vehicles, offering some unique flanking paths. Utilize vehicles as frequently as possible to safely transition from one location to another. When moving around on foot you take the risk of getting run over or sniped by an opponent on the Cartel Mansion's rooftop. Also, don't miss the opportunity to take a gunboat out for a spin—their side-mounted miniguns are perfect for taking out enemy vehicles and personnel.

LEVOLUTION

A hurricane is brewing offshore, bringing in high winds and sheets of rain. The dark clouds overhead decrease lighting significantly while the rain limits visibility. The hurricane is a timed event which only occurs in some of the game modes, like Heist and Conquest.

KEY LOCATIONS

CARTEL MANSION

Sitting on its own private island in the center of the map, this lavish mansion is the centerpiece of most game modes. The pristine, modern design touches of the mansion's interior don't last long once the bullets and grenades start flying. As one of the highest points on the map, the mansion's rooftop is a popular sniping perch.

VILLA

Although smaller than the neighboring Cartel Mansion, this Villa is no less spectacular when it comes to the finer touches of modern living, complete with its own swimming pool and tennis court. But the large floor-to-ceiling windows leave much to be desired for those seeking cover from incoming fire.

DOCK

The swanky Morgan Key apartments have their own Dock, allowing its residents to park their yachts within view of their front door. The central Dock is equipped with four fuel pumps and a large fuel tank. All of these objects are explosive, so be careful when operating nearby.

AIRPORT

Sporting a runway, helipad, and hangar, this small airfield is located a short distance from the Villa and Cartel Mansion. Speeding vehicles can cut through the hangar here to access the northern sandbar, a popular route during Hotwire matches.

STILT HOUSE

This rustic, rickety structure stands in stark contrast to the modern architectural designs of the neighborhood. Take to the top floor to monitor activity at the Cartel Mansion, or consider ambushing vehicles racing along the northern sandbar.

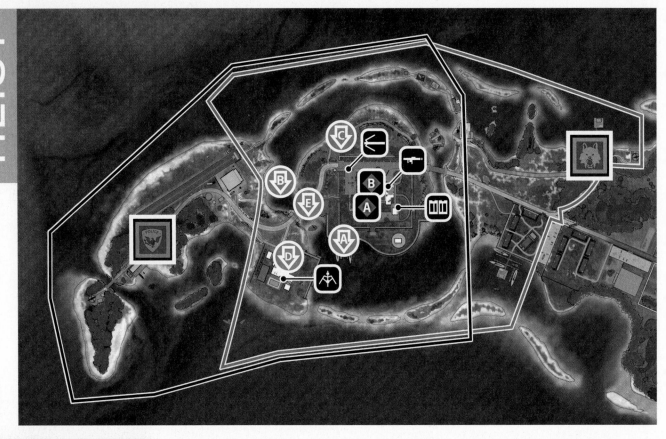

━━━	POLICE DEPLOYMENT
▬▬▬	CRIMINAL DEPLOYMENT
◈	VAULT
⊽	EXTRACTION

BATTLE PICKUPS

▦	AMMO
▥▥▥	DEFIBRILLATOR
⇐	GRAPPLING HOOK
✚	HEALTH
⌐╤─	LMG
⌐═──	ROCKET LAUNCHER
⌐━──	STINGER
⤒	ZIPLINE

⭐ Starting on the west side of the map, near the Airport, the law enforcement team must rely on their vehicles to rush the Cartel Mansion before the criminals can get away with the loot. In addition to transporting teammates to the vaults, the vehicles are essential for securing the area around the mansion. Surround the mansion with the armored SUV and two gunboats, using their miniguns to suppress enemy activity. Once you establish a perimeter, consider blockading the bridge on the west side of mansion to hinder criminal access. Also, don't forget to park the mobile command post somewhere nearby, giving your team a spawn point near the vaults.

⭐ Controlling the Cartel Mansion is the key for the criminal team. But locking down the island on which the mansion sits requires cooperation by the whole team. While one squad focuses on breaking into each vault inside the mansion, the rest of the team should use the team's vehicles to establish a perimeter, using the armored SUV and gunboats to engage approaching law enforcement vehicles from the west. Even before the vaults are breached, it's important to control access to the mansion's rooftop. From here the team can cover all approaches as well as the surrounding extraction points. Instead of racing away with the loot in a vehicle, consider ziplining down to the extraction points from the mansion's roof.

> Use the mobile command center to secure the drop off area and give your team an armored spawn point.
> —Ryan Murphy, Level Designer

☆ The primary vault (A) is located in the upstairs bedroom, in the mansion's west wing. This room is easily accessed via the nearby stairway, leading up from the den. However, due to the high-traffic on this side of the mansion, it's best to approach the bedroom from the second floor. Use one of the other staircases to the east, then enter the bedroom from the central living room. The bedroom is relatively large, and cover is as minimalist as the interior design. So when defending here, consider hiding in the nearby bathroom while using cameras and laser tripmines to detect enemy movement. The nearby stairway and eastern doorway are choke points, so look for opportunities to ambush opponents here.

☆ Cracking one vault isn't enough to gain access to both money bags. The second vault (B) is located downstairs, in the mansion's east den. There are three ways into this room: the stairway connecting to the bedroom, the southern doorway, and the northern window. With the exception of some flimsy furniture, there isn't much cover in this room. The large northern window poses another problem—the vault can be covered by vehicles parked outside. Whether attacking or defending, both teams should attempt to position their armored SUV on the north side of this room so the gunner can engage opponents moving around the vault.

ROCKET LAUNCHER
The SMAW rocket launcher Battle Pickup, in the mansion's third-floor office, can destroy any vehicle with one hit. Use it to help maintain control of the mansion.

☆ There are a total of five possible extraction points on this map, all surrounding the mansion. If the criminals are looking for a flashy way to make their escape, zipline down from the mansion's roof to any of the extraction points. You'll have an easier time deploying a zipline from the lower rooftops above the east and west wings. Ziplining is highly recommended when attempting to reach distant extraction point (D) by the Villa. Making a vehicle getaway is also an option. Use your team's armored SUV (or the nearby utility van) to reach the extraction points. When heading to extraction points (B), (C), (D), or (E), you can easily score the loot while within the confines of your vehicle. Unless riding a motorcycle, you'll probably need to exit a vehicle to reach extraction point (A).

As the criminals, use your mobile command center effectively. Park it in a location that is easily defensible and hidden.
—Evan Champlin, Senior Multiplayer Level Designer

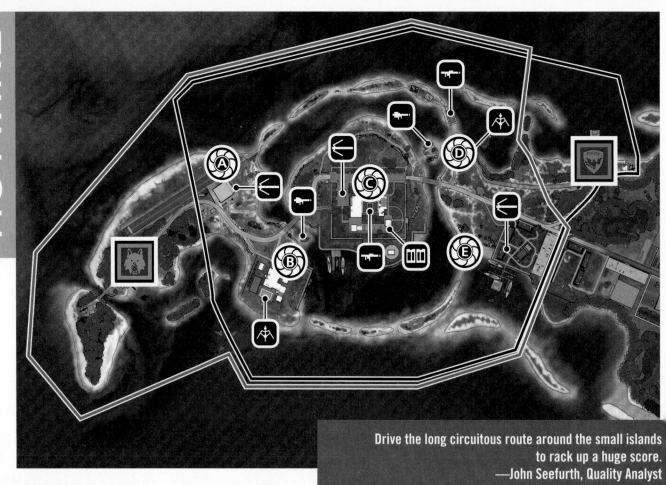

> Drive the long circuitous route around the small islands to rack up a huge score.
> —John Seefurth, Quality Analyst

	POLICE DEPLOYMENT
	CRIMINAL DEPLOYMENT
	HOTWIRE CARS

BATTLE PICKUPS

	AMMO
	DEFIBRILLATOR
	GRAPPLING HOOK
	HEALTH
	LMG
	ROCKET LAUNCHER
	STINGER
	ZIPLINE

HOTWIRE CARS

VEHICLE		NAME
	A	FUEL TANKER
	B	MUSCLE CAR
	C	SPORTS SEDAN
	D	SPORTS SEDAN
	E	MUSCLE CAR

☆ On Riptide, the five Hotwire vehicles are located at each of the five key locations. The sports sedans (C and D) are located at the Cartel Mansion and Stilt House. With four seats, the sedans offer enough positions to defend and repair the vehicle while on the move, assuming a mechanic is onboard with a repair tool. The muscle cars (B and E) aren't bad choices either; you can find them at the Villa and near the Docks. But with only two seats, the passenger has to decide whether to shoot back at opponents or conduct repairs. The fuel tanker (A), located at the Airport, is the least desirable of the Hotwire vehicles due to its slow speed and volatile cargo. Still, when in a pinch, capturing the fuel tanker can ease the drain on your team's ticket count.

★ Your team's vehicles are key to reaching and capturing the Hotwire cars on this map. Avoid running for these cars as you're likely to get run over, sniped, or strafed by an enemy helicopter. Each team has access to three sedans, a utility van, a street motorcycle, a coupe, and one transport helicopter. So when you're not driving a Hotwire vehicle, be sure to spawn back at your team's deployment area to grab one of these vehicles and give chase. Early during the round, use your transport helicopter to drop teammates near the Hotwire vehicles, then use its guns to engage enemy units.

> ### There are good driving routes along the sand bars.
> —David Price, Weapon Designer

★ When racing around the map in Hotwire vehicles, many players initially gravitate toward the central roads connecting the Docks, Cartel Mansion, and Villa. But there's a better route than these congested roads. Instead, consider racing around the map's perimeter, utilizing the southern and northern sandbars. For example, if you just hopped in muscle car (E) by the Docks, head west along the southern sandbar toward the Villa. From the Villa, turn north, racing through the Airport's hangar. Immediately after exiting the hangar, turn east to cross the northern sandbar. When you reach the Stilt House, head south, returning to the southern sandbar. By running this perimeter circuit you can maintain high speeds while avoiding the map's high-traffic center.

★ Unless you're boosting the sports sedan (C) parked outside the Cartel Mansion, consider the center of the map a "no-go" zone. The narrow bridges in the map's center are popular ambush points, often booby-trapped with laser tripmines and breaching charges. There is also less room to maneuver and maintain a consistent speed. For this reason, it's best to stay near the perimeter of the map, even if it means making tight circuits around one of the sandbars.

★ Maintaining access to the map's battle pickups can have a huge impact during the match. Use the Stingers, located near the Stilt House and Cartel Mansion, to shoot down the opposing team's transport helicopter, greatly increasing the survivability of your team's Hotwire vehicles. Also, make note of the two rocket launchers. One is located in the mansion and the other is located at the Stilt House. Instead of trying to ambush enemy vehicles directly with these rocket launchers, rely on tracking darts to achieve locks. This allows you to take out vehicles on the opposite side of the map.

> ### The tide is low so you can drive through most of the water.
> —Brian Paoloni, Quality Designer

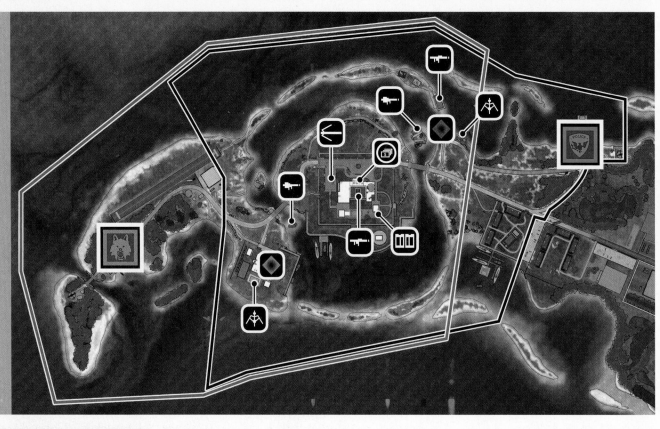

——	POLICE DEPLOYMENT
——	CRIMINAL DEPLOYMENT
🟢	MONEY PILE
◆	POLICE VAULT
◆	CRIMINAL VAULT

BATTLE PICKUPS

	AMMO
	DEFIBRILLATOR
	GRAPPLING HOOK
	HEALTH
	LMG
	ROCKET LAUNCHER
	STINGER
	ZIPLINE

★ In Blood Money, there is no shortage of vehicles supplied at each team's deployment area. Each team has access to a variety of ground vehicles, as well as a gunboat and a transport helicopter. Use these vehicles to rush the money pile at the Cartel Mansion in an effort to secure the area before the opposing team arrives. Vehicles are also essential for defending the money pile as well as each team's vault. Choose an armored vehicle, like the armored SUV or counter attack truck, and make regular trips between the money pile and your team's vault. These vehicles are also well-suited for attacking the opposing team's vault. In addition to the vehicles provided at the deployment areas, there are two utility vans parked near the mansion. If you've scored some cash and don't have a ride, hop into one of these vans to make your escape.

★ The money pile is located in the Cartel Mansion's northern foyer, offering quick access from the large driveway. But the large windows lining the north side of the foyer give vehicles outside a relatively clear view of the money pile. Consider parking an armored SUV or counter attack truck on the driveway, using their weapons to deny the opposing team access to the money pile. However,

parking any vehicle near the money pile makes it a tempting target for enemies equipped with explosive weapons—particularly if they grab the SMAW from the mansion's third-floor office. If defending the money pile directly, consider hiding beneath one of the two staircases on the east and west sides of the foyer. Players often rush toward the money pile without checking these two corners.

★ After retrieving cash from the money pile the law enforcement team must return it to their vault at the Stilt House. Simply drop your cash on the floor of the structure's lower level. The Stilt House's proximity to the water makes it easy to defend (and attack) with a gunboat. But instead of dropping anchor, keep moving. Otherwise your crew is vulnerable to snipers. Your team's counter attack truck is a better defensive option, allowing you to mow down all opponents without being exposed to small arms fire.

★ The armored truck parked at the Villa serves as the criminal team's vault. Defenders posted on the Villa's second floor have a good view of the truck, allowing them to ambush sneaky opponents attempting to steal some cash. Wait until they've begun stealing cash, then open fire or drop grenades down on them. But parking the team's counter attack truck or armored SUV nearby is even more effective, serving as an excellent deterrent.

> Control the mansion's roof to dominate the money pile. Also, use your helicopters effectively to ferry money carriers from vault to vault. A fully loaded helicopter can be a game changer.
> —Evan Champlin, Senior Multiplayer Level Designer

★ The two bridges on the east and west sides of the Cartel Mansion's island are critical choke points during this match, frequently traveled by vehicles from both teams. This makes them perfect ambush points. Simply drop some breaching charges along one of these bridges and wait for an enemy vehicle to drive across before springing your explosive trap. This is a great way to score multiple kills. If travel along these bridges becomes too dangerous, look for other ways to get to and from the money pile. Either board a gunboat or use ziplines to cross back and forth between your team's vault and the mansion.

> Go up ladders slowly in case an enemy put a trip mine at the top.
> —Brian Paoloni, Quality Designer

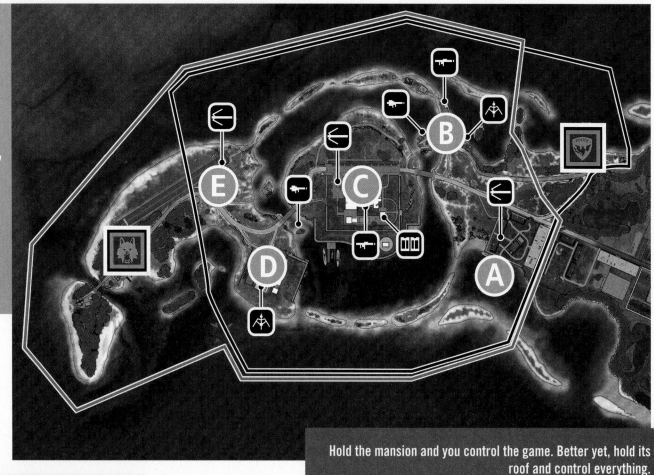

Hold the mansion and you control the game. Better yet, hold its
roof and control everything.
—William Bordonaro, Quality Analyst

━━━	POLICE DEPLOYMENT
━━━	CRIMINAL DEPLOYMENT
◯	CONTROL POINTS

BATTLE PICKUPS

	AMMO
	DEFIBRILLATOR
	GRAPPLING HOOK
	HEALTH
	LMG
	ROCKET LAUNCHER
	STINGER
	ZIPLINE

★ When playing as the police during Conquest, make an early round push to secure the three easternmost control points. Fill your transport helicopter and drop teammates at the Docks (A), Stilt House (B), and Cartel Mansion (C). Since the Cartel Mansion (C) is likely to see the heaviest action, waste no time moving your team's mobile command center to the central island. This gives your team a spawn point here, even if the criminals manage to capture the mansion. Once your team has captured at least three control points, lock them down by posting at least one squad at each location.

★ The criminals deploy on the west side of the map, making it easy for them to capture the Airport (D) and Villa (E) at the outset. But like the law enforcement team, the criminals should also make an aggressive early-round push to secure the Cartel Mansion (C). With a total of five control points up for grabs, capturing and holding a minimum of three points is necessary to begin draining the law enforcement team's tickets.

☆ As in most game modes, the Cartel Mansion (C) is the focal point of this battle—for good reason. In addition to offering an excellent rooftop sniping perch, the mansion also spawns an attack helicopter. When accompanied by the transport helicopter spawned at your team's deployment area, the attack helicopter can help your team control the skies, laying waste to enemy vehicles and personnel. However, the attack helicopter isn't indestructible. Watch out for Stingers. Stinger battle pickups are located near the Stilt House (B) and the Cartel Mansion (C). Use countermeasures and low-altitude flying to minimize your exposure to these missiles.

☆ On Riptide, snipers are always a threat, especially if the opposing team controls the rooftop of the Cartel Mansion (C). So when operating outside, along the mansion's perimeter, make sure you have a weapon capable of defending yourself. Sniper rifles, DMRs, and battle rifles equipped with 4X or 6X optics are all good choices. Engagement ranges reduce significantly when fighting in the mansion and Villa (E). Consider equipping a carbine, SMG, or shotgun for these close quarter firefights. Given the heavy vehicle traffic, get familiar with the battle pickup locations. There's an RPG by the Stilt House (A) and a SMAW on the Cartel Mansion's (C) third floor. The mechanic's grenade launcher is also effective for taking out vehicles.

SPAWN AREA

BATTLE PICKUPS

	AMMO
	DEFIBRILLATOR
	GRAPPLING HOOK
	HEALTH
	LMG
	ROCKET LAUNCHER
	STINGER
	ZIPLINE

★ Prepare for some intense close quarter firefights in and around the Cartel Mansion during Team Deathmatch. Although the mansion is rather large, it feels much smaller when occupied by two hostile teams. An extra sense of vulnerability is immediately realized as the mansion's interior is shredded by gunfire and explosives, leaving few intact pieces of cover. Use the interior's destructibility to your advantage, targeting opponents through pieces of furniture and even walls.

★ As in most game modes, the mansion's rooftop is a popular hangout for sharpshooters looking to pick-off opponents scurrying about on the grounds below. While this is a relatively secure spot to defend, players posted here aren't limited to engaging opponents on the perimeter of the map. Fire down through the skylight to target enemies in the mansion's living room. Just be ready to fend off attacks by opponents seeking to steal your perch. Place laser tripmines near the east and west ladder access points to deter such attacks.

★ Unless you're planning to camp the mansion's rooftop for the duration of the match, the mechanic and enforcer are the two go-to classes for this game mode. The mechanic's SMGs and enforcer's shotguns are ideal for chewing up opponents (and cover) during firefights inside the mansion. But don't overlook the importance of keeping a friendly operator nearby too. You'll need a few operators to heal and revive your teammates.

So if close quarter fighting isn't your forte, consider following around your squad with a first aid pack and defibrillator/adrenaline shot. You'll rack-up plenty of points just keeping your teammates healthy and on their feet. Gas masks and gas grenades are also very effective on this map.

★ If there's one place to avoid, it's the large first-floor living room on the south side of the structure. Although beautifully designed, this room is surrounded by second and third-floor walkways, making anyone on the bottom level extremely vulnerable to incoming fire and grenades. Make an effort to control the second floor walkways surrounding this room and catch your opponents in a deadly kill box below.

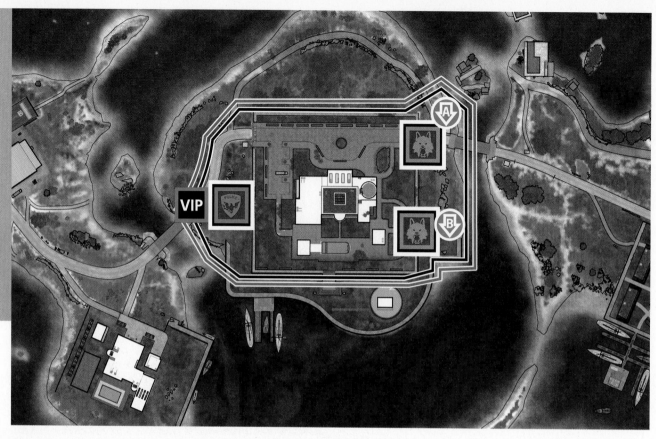

★ Once again, the Cartel Mansion is the site of the action in Crosshair, requiring the law enforcement team to escort the VIP through (or around) the mansion to one of the two waiting gunboats on the eastern shore. Sneaking along the north or south side of the mansion is risky, as there's little cover and you're likely to get hit by criminals firing from the rooftop. Instead, move through the mansion, offering the VIP more cover and concealment. The rooftop path is also effective, but is likely covered by the criminals. Bring a grappling hook and prepare for a fight.

POLICE DEPLOYMENT

CRIMINAL DEPLOYMENT

EXTRACTION POINT

The roof is a key location for both sides. If one side controls the roof, it can be a powerful advantage.
—Thad Sasser, Lead Multiplayer Designer

Lure the enemy away from the VIP by going the opposite direction and attracting them with the decoy or exposing yourself on the map by firing your non-suppressed weapon.
—John Seefurth, Quality Analyst

★ At the outset of the match, at least two players on the criminal team should rush the mansion's rooftop, utilizing the stairway near the helipad. From here they can monitor enemy movement along the rooftop and mansion's perimeter. The rest of the team should patrol the east side of the mansion in an attempt to intercept the VIP before they can reach one of the extraction points. It's up to the players on the rooftop to spot any movement around the perimeter, helping direct their teammates, on the ground, toward the VIP and the police escorts.

★ The area around the two extraction points is quite open, leaving defenders somewhat exposed. So instead of camping each extraction point, the criminal team should move closer to the mansion, ambushing the VIP and his escorts in the midfield, as they cross the eastern grounds of the compound. With the exception of some trees and shrubs, there isn't much cover on this side of the mansion, making it the perfect place to stage an ambush. Take up positions on the rooftop or areas to the north or south. You need to make your shots count. If the VIP manages to escape unscathed, they only have a short distance to sprint before they can reach either extraction point. Dropping some beaching charges near each extraction point may be a good insurance plan.

★ As in any Crosshair match, it's important for the law enforcement team to keep the criminals guessing. So even if you've managed to successfully run the same route twice in a row, change-up your approach. Instead of running across the roof each time, consider transitioning from the roof to the second floor before exiting on the mansion's east side. Or simply sneak through the first floor's rooms. But be careful when exiting the mansion, as there are likely criminals camping the eastern grounds. Deploy smoke to conceal your team's movements as you make your way to one of the extraction points.

★ Gadget selection is crucial for both teams. The law enforcement team needs at least one grappling hook, necessary for scaling the mansion's western wall and accessing the rooftop. A zipline can come in handy too for making a quick escape from the mansion's roof. When rushing through the mansion, consider leading the way with an enforcer's ballistic shield. The criminal team should deploy cameras on the east side of the mansion in an effort to detect the VIP. Laser tripmines and breaching charges are also effective when booby-trapping predictable routes, particularly the areas around the rooftop's ladders. Both teams can benefit from the use of gas grenades and gas masks. These can be a game changer during heated firefights inside the mansion.

As the VIP, run straight toward and up the ladder on the back of the mansion to take the high ground. From there you can cut through the second floor balcony or proceed to the roof, giving yourself the advantage over aggressive criminals.
—William Bordonaro, Quality Analyst

As law enforcement, equip DMRs and mid-range optics to control the outside lanes. Criminals may attempt to rush and catch you off guard.
—Evan Champlin, Senior Multiplayer Level Designer

—— POLICE DEPLOYMENT

—— CRIMINAL DEPLOYMENT

🔒 HOSTAGE

⬇ EXTRACTION POINT

⭐ In Rescue, the hostages are held in the Villa, both on the ground floor. Starting on the north side of the map, the law enforcement team should utilize indirect routes to approach each hostage. Instead of gaining entry on the north side, consider flanking from the south, where the criminals are less likely to expect an attack. Or bring along a grappling hook and take to the rooftop, gaining entry to the upstairs bedroom before making a move on the hostages downstairs. Also, don't underestimate the power of distraction. Use decoys or gunfire to draw the criminals away from the hostage your team is attempting to rescue. When making your escape, consider accessing the Villa's rooftop (through the upstairs bedroom) and ziplining down to the extraction point.

★ Regardless of which hostage the criminals spawn next to, they don't have much time to secure the Villa before the law enforcement team comes barging in. Therefore, don't waste any time deploying gas grenades around each hostage. They won't necessarily deter a rescue, but they damage and disorient any law enforcement players not equipped with gas masks. Incendiary devices and smoke grenades can also complicate things for the police, hindering and delaying their access to the hostages. While four teammates secure the hostages, the fifth player should head outside, toward the extraction point. If the law enforcement team manages to escape with a hostage, it's up to this player to prevent them from reaching the extraction point.

★ With so many access points into the Villa, it's difficult for the criminal team to predict where the police will enter, and the criminals don't have enough time to establish a solid perimeter on the building's exterior. This makes guarding each hostage location a viable strategy. However, if your team isn't having much luck withstanding the push from the opposing team, consider moving your defenses toward the extraction point. The black semi-truck parked to the north serves as a makeshift wall. Hide along the north side of this truck to get the jump on opponents rushing toward the extraction point. Or take to the Villa's rooftop and watch the extraction point from a distance.

★ Both hostages are held on the ground floor of the Villa. Hostage 1 is located in the large living room on the west side. This hostage is closest to the law enforcement team's deployment area, so criminal's should expect early-round attacks through the room's northern double doors. Hostage 2 is located in the kitchen, on the Villa's southeast corner. The north and south doorways aren't the only way into the kitchen. It's also possible to drop down through the skylight in the ceiling.

★ For the law enforcement team, this is a classic hostage rescue scenario requiring the careful deployment of gadgets and grenades to gain an upper hand. Expect heavy resistance in each hostage room, so be ready to deploy flashbangs to blind and confuse the criminals. Gas masks are a good choice as well, since the criminals are likely to saturate the hostage rooms with gas grenades. Lead the way to the hostage with a ballistic shield, giving your teammates mobile cover during entry. Finally, bring a zipline to make a quick escape from the Villa's rooftop. The criminals can benefit from gadgets too. In addition to booby-trapping the hostage rooms, plant laser tripmines in other high-traffic areas, like the upstairs bedroom. Also, use a grappling hook to gain quick access to the Villa's rooftop.

> The skylight on the kitchen roof is useful for getting the drop on the cops untying the hostage.
> —Ryan Murphy, Level Designer

GENERAL

EVENT	POINTS	DESCRIPTION
Avenger Bonus	25	Kill an enemy that recently killed a teammate
Draw Fire	1	Block damage with the Ballistic Shield
Drive By	25	Kill an enemy while in a vehicle
Driver Assist	75	Drive a vehicle while a passenger gets a kill
Driver Spawn Bonus	25	Have a teammate spawn in a vehicle you're driving
Enemy Killed	100	Kill an enemy
Equipment Destroyed	25	Destroy a piece of equipment
Explosive Destroyed	25	You destroyed an explosive
First Blood	100	Be the first player to get a kill in a match
Flashbang Bonus	25	A teammate kills an enemy who is flashed by your grenade
Grappling Hook Bonus	25	Have a teammate use a grappling hook
Headshot Bonus	25	Bonus score for a Headshot
Healing	10	Heal a teammate (given every tick while healing)
Interrogation Successful	50	Interrogate an enemy
Kill As HVT Bonus	25	You killed someone while the Hacker marked you as an HVT
Last Man Spawn	50	A squadmate spawned on you while you were the last man in the squad
Melee Bonus	25	Kill an enemy with a melee weapon
Mobile Ammo	25	A teammate takes ammo off of you
Mobile Healer	25	A teammate takes health off of you
Non-Lethal Takedown	25	You used a non-lethal weapon to take down an enemy
Passenger Assist	25	Be a passenger in a vehicle while another passenger or driver gets a kill
Payback	50	Kill your most recent killer
Ramming Bonus	50	You ram a vehicle which causes it to be disabled
Repairing	10	Repair a vehicle (given every tick while repairing)
Resupplying	25	Give a teammate ammo
Roadkill	25	Kill another player while driving a vehicle
Savior Bonus	25	Kill an enemy that's currently damaging a teammate
Shield Takedown	25	Kill an enemy with the Ballistic Shield
Spawn Beacon Bonus	25	A squadmate used your Spawn Beacon
Spot Bonus	25	Enemy is killed after you spotted them
Squad Avenger Bonus	50	Kill an enemy that recently killed a squadmate
Squad Grappling Hook Bonus	50	Have a squadmate use a grappling hook
Squad Healing	20	Heal a squadmate (given every tick while healing)
Squad Mobile Ammo	50	A squadmate takes ammo off of you
Squad Mobile Healer	50	A squadmate takes health off of you
Squad Order Bonus	50	You followed a Squad Leader's order
Squad Order Followed	25	Squad followed your order
Squad Repairing	20	Repair a squadmate's vehicle (given every tick while repairing)
Squad Resupplying	50	Give a squadmate ammo
Squad Savior Bonus	50	Kill an enemy that's currently damaging a squadmate
Squad Spawn On You	25	Have a squadmate spawn on you
Squad Spot Bonus	50	Enemy is killed by a squadmate after you spotted them
Squad Suppression Assist	50	Enemy is killed by a squadmate while you suppress them
Squad Vehicle Kill Assist	25	Be a passenger in a vehicle while another squadmate gets a kill as a passenger or driver
Squad Wiped	25	Kill the last member of the squad while other members are still dead
Squad Zipline Bonus	50	Have a squadmate use a zipline

EVENT	POINTS	DESCRIPTION
Suppression Assist	25	Enemy is killed while you suppress them
Target Marked	25	Mark a target with the Tracking Dart
Unanimous Support	5	As a Hacker, you have the support of all Squad Leaders
Vehicle Destroyed	50	Destroy a vehicle
Vehicle Disabled	50	Disable a vehicle so it catches fire
Zipline Bonus	25	Have a teammate use a zipline

HEIST

EVENT	POINTS	DESCRIPTION
Break In Denied	100	As law enforcement, kill a criminal while he's setting up a Heist break-in
Break In Successful	250	As a criminal, the Heist break-in you initiated is successful
Carrier Takedown	100	As law enforcement, kill the Heist Bag carrier
Carrier Takedown Assist	50	As law enforcement, damage the Heist Bag carrier before a teammate kills him
Disarm Denied	100	As a criminal, kill law enforcement while he's disarming a Heist break-in
Loot Carrier Savior	50	As a criminal, kill an enemy that's currently damaging the Heist Bag carrier
Loot Pickup	150	Pick up the Heist Bag
Loot Returned	500	As law enforcement, be close to the Heist Bag when it returns to its spawn point
Loot Secured	1,000	As a criminal, get the Heist Bag to the Helicopter
Loot Secured Assist	250	As a criminal, be close to the Helicopter when a teammate gets the Heist Bag to it
Vault Break In Initiated	150	As a criminal, initiate a Heist break-in
Vault Disarmed	250	As law enforcement, disarm the Heist break-in

BLOOD MONEY

EVENT	POINTS	DESCRIPTION
Cash Pickup	25	Pick up one stack of cash
Enemy Vault Grab	50	Grab cash from the enemy vault
Fully Loaded	150	Pick up the maximum amount of cash you can carry
Getaway Driver Assist	100	Give a teammate who has cash a ride back to your vault
Vault Defender	50	Kill an enemy while close to your vault

HOTWIRE

EVENT	POINTS	DESCRIPTION
Hotwire Cruising Bonus	10	Drive or be a passenger in a Hotwire car (given every tick)
Hotwire Takedown	250	Destroy a Hotwire vehicle
Hotwire Takedown Assist	150	Damage a Hotwire vehicle that is then destroyed by a teammate
Hotwired	50	Get a Hotwire car to capturing speed

CONQUEST

EVENT	POINTS	DESCRIPTION
Capturing	10	Awarded while within an enemy's Conquest Point capture radius (given every tick)
Conquest Capture	250	Capture a Flag in Conquest
Conquest Defense	25	Awarded when killing enemies in a friendly Conquest area
Conquest Neutralized	150	Neutralized a Flag in Conquest

CROSSHAIR

EVENT	POINTS	DESCRIPTION
Contract Kill Assist	250	Damage the VIP that is then killed by a teammate
Contract Killer	1,000	Kill the VIP
Escaped	1,000	Escape as a VIP
Guardian Angel	500	Kill an enemy while they're damaging the VIP
Survivor	500	Survive as law enforcement when the VIP escapes

RESCUE

EVENT	POINTS	DESCRIPTION
Hostage Defender	50	As law enforcement, kill a criminal near the Hostage
Hostage Denial	250	As a criminal, kill an enemy that's untying a Hostage
Hostage Lockdown	50	As a criminal, kill an enemy that's near a Hostage
Hostage Pickup	250	Pick up a Hostage
Hostage Rescue Assist	500	As law enforcement, be around the rescue zone when a Hostage is recued
Hostage Rescued	1,000	As law enforcement, rescue a Hostage

HACKER

EVENT	POINTS	DESCRIPTION
Agent Deployed Fast	25	Have a teammate spawn using the Fast Deploy you just gave them
Backdoor Camera Spot	10	An enemy is spotted by your Backdoor camera
Backdoor Gas Suppress	10	An enemy is gassed by your Gas System
Backdoor Pickup Used	50	A teammate picked up your Battle Pickup
Backdoor Transformer Flash	10	An enemy is flashbanged by your Transformer
Disabled Enemy Subroutine	25	Disable an enemy subroutine with a Trojan
Enemy Revealed	15	Reveal at least one enemy with GPS Spot
Friendlies Masked	15	You hid at least one teammate while using GPS Jam
Gas Suppression Assist	25	Have a teammate kill an enemy that's currently gassed by a Gas System backdoor
GPS Spotting Assist	25	Have a teammate kill an enemy while they're spotted by your GPS subroutine
Hacker Connection Severed	50	You disabled an enemy's Backdoor by giving a Trojan
Hacker Point Of Interest HVT Bonus	100	Have a teammate kill an HVT you marked as a Hacker
Jacked In	15	You took over a Backdoor
Rep Upgraded	50	Have a teammate accept a Hacker upgrade

MULTIPLAYER AWARDS

SERVICE STARS

CLASSES

	NAME	CRITERIA	TOTAL STARS	AWARD		NAME	CRITERIA	TOTAL STARS	AWARD
★	Bronze	10,000 Points	10	500 Points	★	Bronze	5,000 Points	10	500 Points
★	Silver	15,000 Points	10	1,000 Points	★	Silver	7,500 Points	10	1,000 Points
★	Gold	25,000 Points	100	2,000 Points	★	Gold	12,500 Points	100	2,000 Points
★	Bronze	10 Kills	10	500 Points	★	Bronze	15,000 Points	10	500 Points
★	Silver	15 Kills	10	1,000 Points	★	Silver	22,500 Points	10	1,000 Points
★	Gold	25 Kills	100	2,000 Points	★	Gold	40,000 Points	100	2,000 Points

COINS AND BOUNTIES

WEAPONS

	BOUNTY NAME	BOUNTY REQUIREMENT		COIN NAME	COIN REQUIREMENT
	Sidearm Bounty	Earn 50 Sidearm Coins		Sidearm Coin	Kill 4 enemies with any Secondary Weapon
	Assault Rifle Bounty	Earn 50 Assault Rifle Coins		Assault Rifle Coin	Kill 6 enemies with any Assault Rifle
	Sniper Rifle Bounty	Earn 50 Sniper Rifle Coins		Sniper Rifle Coin	Kill 6 enemies with any Sniper Rifle
	Battle Rifle Bounty	Earn 50 Battle Rifle Coins		Battle Rifle Coin	Kill 6 enemies with any Battle Rifle
	SMG Bounty	Earn 50 SMG Coins		SMG Coin	Kill 6 enemies with any SMG
	Shotgun Bounty	Earn 50 Shotgun Coins		Shotgun Coin	Kill 6 enemies with any Shotgun
	Melee Bounty	Earn 50 Melee Coins		Melee Coin	Kill 4 enemies with any Melee weapon
	T62 CEW Bounty	Earn 50 T62 CEW Coins		T62 CEW Coin	Neutralize 3 enemies with the T62 CEW

VEHICLES

	BOUNTY NAME	BOUNTY REQUIREMENT		COIN NAME	COIN REQUIREMENT
	Attack Helicopter Bounty	Earn 50 Attack Helicopter Coins		Attack Helicopter Coin	Kill 5 enemies with an Attack Helicopter
	Armored Vehicle Bounty	Earn 50 Armored Vehicle Coins		Armored Vehicle Coin	Kill 5 enemies with a CAT vehicle
	SUV Bounty	Earn 50 SUV Coins		SUV Coin	Kill 5 enemies with a SUV vehicle
	Watercraft Bounty	Earn 50 Gunboat Coins		Gunboat Coin	Kill 5 enemies with a Gunboat
	Transport Helicopter Bounty	Earn 50 Transport Helicopter Coins		Transport Helicopter Coin	Kill 5 enemies with a Transport Helicopter

GAME MODES

	BOUNTY NAME	BOUNTY REQUIREMENT		COIN NAME	COIN REQUIREMENT
	Heist Return Bounty	Earn 50 Heist Return Coins		Heist Return Coin	Return 2 bags in Heist
	Conquest Point Capture Bounty	Earn 50 Conquest Point Capture Coins		Conquest Point Capture Coin	Capture 2 points in Conquest
	Team Deathmatch Supremacy Bounty	Earn 50 Team Deathmatch Supremacy Coin		Team Deathmatch Supremacy Coin	Win a TDM match by doubling the enemy's score - match must end by score, not time
	Blood Money Bounty	Earn 50 Blood Money Coins		Blood Money Coin	Deposit 10 stacks of cash into your vault in Blood Money
	Conquest Supremacy Bounty	Earn 50 Conquest Supremacy Coins		Conquest Supremacy Coin	Win Conquest by depleting the enemy's tickets while having half of yours remaining
	Heist Grand Larceny Bounty	Earn 50 Heist Grand Larceny Coins		Heist Grand Larceny Coin	Capture at least 1 Heist bag and your team wins the match
	Heist Cop Supremacy Bounty	Earn 50 Heist Cop Supremacy Coins		Heist Cop Supremacy Coin	Win a Heist match as a cop without letting the criminals capture any bags
	Heist Criminal Supremacy Bounty	Earn 50 Heist Criminal Supremacy Coins		Heist Criminal Supremacy Coin	Win a Heist match as a criminal with at least 50% of your tickets remaining

	BOUNTY NAME	BOUNTY REQUIREMENT		COIN NAME	COIN REQUIREMENT
	Rescue Hostage Bounty	Earn 50 Rescue Hostage Coins		Rescue Hostage Coin	Successfully rescue a Hostage
	Rescue Lockdown Bounty	Earn 50 Rescue Lockdown Coins		Rescue Lockdown Coin	Kill 2 cops as they're in the process of freeing a hostage
	Rescue Cop Supremacy Bounty	Earn 50 Rescue Cop Supremacy Coins		Rescue Cop Supremacy Coin	Win a Rescue match as a cop with at least 3 of your teammates surviving
	Rescue Criminal Supremacy Bounty	Earn 50 Rescue Criminal Supremacy Coins		Rescue Criminal Supremacy Coin	Win a Rescue match as a criminal with at least 3 of your teammates surviving
	Crosshair Assassin Bounty	Earn 50 Crosshair Assassin Coins		Crosshair Assassin Coin	Kill the VIP
	Crosshair Cop Supremacy Bounty	Earn 50 Crosshair Cop Supremacy Coins		Crosshair Cop Supremacy Coin	Win a Crosshair match as a cop with at least 3 of your teammates surviving
	Crosshair Escape Artist Bounty	Earn 50 Crosshair Escape Artist Coins		Crosshair Escape Artist Coin	Successfully escape as the VIP
	Crosshair Criminal Supremacy Bounty	Earn 50 Crosshair Criminal Supremacy Coins		Crosshair Criminal Supremacy Coin	Win a Crosshair match as a criminal with at least 3 of your teammates surviving
	Blood Money Burglar Bounty	Earn 50 Blood Money Burglar Coins		Blood Money Burglar Coin	Capture at least 10 stacks of cash from the enemy's vault
	Blood Money Supremacy Bounty	Earn 50 Blood Money Supremacy Coins		Blood Money Supremacy Coin	Win Blood Money with at least double the money in your vault versus your enemy
	Hotwire Cruising Bounty	Earn 50 Hotwire Cruising Coins		Hotwire Cruising Coin	Earn a total of 500 points while driving or as a passenger in a Hotwire vehicle
	Hotwire Takedown Bounty	Earn 50 Hotwire Takedown Coins		Hotwire Takedown Coin	Destroy 3 enemy occupied Hotwire vehicles
	Hotwire Supremacy Bounty	Earn 50 Hotwire Supremacy Coins		Hotwire Supremacy Coin	Win Hotwire by depleting the enemy's tickets while having at least half of yours remaining

CLASSES

	BOUNTY NAME	BOUNTY REQUIREMENT		COIN NAME	COIN REQUIREMENT
	First Aid Pack Bounty	Earn 50 First Aid Pack Coins		First Aid Pack Coin	Earn 8 Heal bonuses
	Repair Tool Bounty	Earn 50 Repair Tool Coins		Repair Tool Coin	Earn 8 Repair bonuses
	Marksman Bounty	Earn 50 Marksman Coins		Marksman Coin	Perform a headshot from a distance of 250 meters or greater
	Satellite Phone Bounty	Earn 50 Satellite Phone Coins		Satellite Phone Coin	Have 3 Squad members spawn on your Satellite Phone
	Ammo Resupply Bounty	Earn 50 Ammo Resupply Coins		Ammo Resupply Coin	Earn 8 Resupply bonuses
	Revive Bounty	Earn 50 Revive Coins		Revive Coin	Earn 5 Revive bonuses

TEAM

	BOUNTY NAME	BOUNTY REQUIREMENT		COIN NAME	COIN REQUIREMENT
	Kill Assist Bounty	Earn 50 Kill Assist Coins		Kill Assist Coin	Earn 5 Kill Assist bonuses
	Avenger Bounty	Earn 50 Avenger Coins		Avenger Coin	Earn 2 Avenger bonuses
	Savior Bounty	Earn 50 Savior Coins		Savior Coin	Earn 2 Savior bonuses
	Spotting Bounty	Earn 50 Spotting Coins		Spotting Coin	Earn 4 Spot bonuses
	Ace Squad Bounty	Earn 50 Ace Squad Coins		Ace Squad Coin	Be a member of the best Squad
	MVP Bounty	Earn 50 MVP Coins		MVP Coin	Earn the highest combat score

GENERAL

	BOUNTY NAME	BOUNTY REQUIREMENT		COIN NAME	COIN REQUIREMENT
	Headshot Bounty	Earn 50 Headshot Coins		Headshot Coin	Earn 3 Headshot bonuses
	Interrogation Bounty	Earn 50 Interrogation Coins		Interrogation Coin	Perform 2 Interrogations
	Zipline Bounty	Earn 50 Zipline Coins		Zipline Coin	Earn 5 Zipline bonuses
	Grappling Hook Bounty	Earn 50 Grappling Hook Coins		Grappling Hook Coin	Earn 5 Grappling Hook bonuses
	Anti-Vehicle Bounty	Earn 50 Anti-Vehicle Coins		Anti-Vehicle Coin	Destroy any two vehicles
	Explosives Bounty	Earn 50 Explosives Coins		Explosives Coin	Kill 4 enemies with explosives
	Ballistic Shield Bounty	Earn 50 Ballistic Shield Coins		Ballistic Shield Coin	Deflect 100 points of damage with the Shield
	Camera Bounty	Earn 50 Camera Coins		Camera Coin	10 enemies spotted by your camera were killed while spotted
	Hacker Back Door Bounty	Earn 50 Hacker Back Door Coins		Hacker Back Door Coin	Capture 10 Back Door nodes
	Hacker GPS Jamming Bounty	Earn 50 Hacker GPS Jamming Coins		Hacker GPS Jamming Coin	Activate 15 GPS Jamming subroutines
	Hacker Point of Interest Bounty	Earn 50 Hacker Point of Interest Coins		Hacker Point of Interest Coin	Earn 500 points through the POI Kickback bonus
	Hacker Trojan Bounty	Earn 50 Hacker Trojan Coins		Hacker Trojan Coin	Activate 8 Trojan subroutines
	Hacker GPS Spotting Bounty	Earn 50 Hacker GPS Spotting Coins		Hacker GPS Spotting Coin	Activate 15 GPS Spotting subroutines
	Hacker Fast Deploy Bounty	Earn 50 Hacker Fast Deploy Coins		Hacker Fast Deploy Coin	Earn 500 points through the Agent Deployed Fast bonus
	Hacker Trace Bounty	Earn 50 Hacker Trace Coins		Hacker Trace Coin	Earn 500 points through the Trace Completed bonus
	Hacker Squad Upgrade Bounty	Earn 50 Hacker Squad Upgrade Coins		Hacker Squad Upgrade Coin	Earn 250 points through the Rep Upgraded bonus
	Hacker Overclock Bounty	Earn 50 Hacker Overclock Coins		Hacker Overclock Coin	Activate 5 Overclock subroutines

GAME MODE ASSIGNMENTS

	ASSIGNMENT NAME	PRE-REQ. 1	PRE-REQ. 2	PRE-REQ. 3	AWARD REQ. 1	AWARD REQ. 2	AWARD REQ. 3	PATCH REWARD
	Hotwire	Rank 10	Win 5 Hotwire Matches	—	50 Hotwire Cruising Coins	50 Hotwire Takedown Coins	—	Hotwire Assignment
	Conquest	Rank 10	Win 5 Conquest Matches	—	50 Conquest Capture Coins	50 Conquest Supremacy Coins	—	Conquest Assignment
	Heist	Rank 10	Win 5 Heist Matches	—	50 Heist Return Coins	50 Heist Grand Larceny Coins	—	Heist Assignment
	Conquest Capture Bounty	—	—	—	Collect the Conquest Capture Bounty	—	—	Conquest Capture Bounty
	Conquest Supremacy Bounty	—	—	—	Collect the Conquest Supremacy Bounty	—	—	Conquest Supremacy Bounty
	Heist Grand Larceny Bounty	—	—	—	Collect the Heist Grand Larceny Bounty	—	—	Heist Grand Larceny Bounty
	Heist Return Bounty	—	—	—	Collect the Heist Return Bounty	—	—	Heist Return Bounty
	Heist Cop Supremacy Bounty	—	—	—	Collect the Heist Cop Supremacy Bounty	—	—	Heist Cop Supremacy Bounty

ASSIGNMENT NAME	PRE-REQ. 1	PRE-REQ. 2	PRE-REQ. 3	AWARD REQ. 1	AWARD REQ. 2	AWARD REQ. 3	PATCH REWARD
Heist Criminal Supremacy Bounty	—	—	—	Collect the Heist Criminal Supremacy Bounty	—	—	Heist Criminal Supremacy Bounty
Hotwire Cruising Bounty	—	—	—	Collect the Hotwire Cruising Bounty	—	—	Hotwire Cruising Bounty
Hotwire Takedown Bounty	—	—	—	Collect the Hotwire Takedown Bounty	—	—	Hotwire Takedown Bounty
Hotwire Supremacy Bounty	—	—	—	Collect the Hotwire Supremacy Bounty	—	—	Hotwire Supremacy Bounty
Heist Winner	—	—	—	Unlock Gold Service Star 1 in Heist	—	—	Heist Winner
Conquest Winner	—	—	—	Unlock Gold Service Star 1 in Conquest	—	—	Conquest Winner
Hotwire Winner	—	—	—	Unlock Gold Service Star 1 in Hotwire	—	—	Hotwire Winner

WEAPON ASSIGNMENTS

ASSIGNMENT NAME	PRE-REQ. 1	PRE-REQ. 2	PRE-REQ. 3	AWARD REQ. 1	AWARD REQ. 2	AWARD REQ. 3	AWARD REQ. 4	AWARD REQ. 5	PATCH REWARD
Melee	Rank 20	Kill 10 Enemies With Blunt Weapons	Kill 10 Enemies With Knives	Steal 20 Patches from enemies	5 Melee Coins	5 Interrogation Coins	—	—	Melee Assignment
Battle Rifle 1	Purchase The Scar-h	Purchase The Sa-58	Purchase The Hk51	25 Battle Rifle kills	5 Battle Rifle Coins	—	—	—	Battle Rifle Assignment 1
Battle Rifle 2	Battle Rifle 1	1 Battle Rifle Weapon License Purchased	—	50 SCAR-H kills	50 HCAR kills	50 SA-58 kills	50 HK51 kills	25 Battle Rifle Coins	Battle Rifle Assignment 2
Assault Rifle 1	Purchase The Aks-74u	Purchase The M16a3	Purchase The Sg-553	25 Assault Rifle kills	5 Assault Rifle Coins	—	—	—	Assault Rifle Assignment 1
Assault Rifle 2	Assault Rifle 1	1 Assault Rifle Weapon License Purchased	—	50 AKM kills	50 M416 kills	50 G36C kills	50 RO933 kills	20 Assault Rifle Coins	Assault Rifle Assignment 2
SMG 1	Purchase The Ump-45	Purchase The Uzi	Purchase The P90	25 SMG kills	5 SMG Coins	—	—	—	SMG Assignment 1
SMG 2	SMG 1	1 SMG Weapon License Purchased	—	50 M45 kills	50 K10 kills	50 MPX kills	50 MP5K kills	20 SMG Coins	SMG Assignment 2
Sniper Rifle 1	Purchase The Sr-23	Purchase The Socom-16	Purchase The Ptr91	25 Sniper Rifle kills	5 Sniper Rifle Coins	—	—	—	Sniper Rifle Assignment 1
Sniper Rifle 2	Sniper Rifle 1	1 Sniper Rifle Weapon License Purchased	—	50 Scout Elite kills	50 SAIGA .308 kills	50 AWM kills	50 R700 LTR kills	20 Sniper Rifle Coins	Sniper Rifle Assignment 2
Shotgun 1	Purchase The 37 Stakeout	Purchase The Spas-12	—	25 Shotgun kills	5 Shotgun Coins	—	—	—	Shotgun Assignment 1
Shotgun 2	Shotgun 1	1 Shotgun Weapon License Purchased	—	50 870P kills	50 37 STAKEOUT kills	50 SPAS-12 kills	20 Shotgun Coins	—	Shotgun Assignment 2
Assault Rifle Ownership	—	—	—	Purchase 7 Assault Rifles to unlock Patch	—	—	—	—	Assault Rifle Ownership
Shotgun Ownership	—	—	—	Purchase 3 Shotguns to unlock Patch	—	—	—	—	Shotgun Ownership
SMG Ownership	—	—	—	Purchase 7 SMGs to unlock Patch	—	—	—	—	SMG Ownership
Battle Rifle Ownership	—	—	—	Purchase 4 Battle Rifles to unlock Patch	—	—	—	—	Battle Rifle Ownership
Sniper Rifle Ownership	—	—	—	Purchase 7 Sniper Rifles to unlock Patch	—	—	—	—	Sniper Rifle Ownership
Handgun Ownership	—	—	—	Purchase 6 Handguns to unlock Patch	—	—	—	—	Handgun Ownership

ASSIGNMENT NAME	PRE-REQ. 1	PRE-REQ. 2	PRE-REQ. 3	AWARD REQ. 1	AWARD REQ. 2	AWARD REQ. 3	AWARD REQ. 4	AWARD REQ. 5	PATCH REWARD
Automatic Pistol Ownership	—	—	—	Purchase 3 Automatic Pistols to unlock Patch	—	—	—	—	Automatic Pistol Ownership
Revolver Ownership	—	—	—	Purchase 3 Revolvers to unlock this Patch	—	—	—	—	Revolver Ownership
Assault Rifle Kill	—	—	—	Kill 1000 enemies between all Assault Rifles	—	—	—	—	Assault Rifle Kills
Shotgun Kills	—	—	—	Kill 1000 enemies between all Shotguns	—	—	—	—	Shotgun Kills
SMG Kills	—	—	—	Kill 1000 enemies between all SMGs	—	—	—	—	SMG Kills
Battle Rifle Kills	—	—	—	Kill 1000 enemies between all Battle Rifles	—	—	—	—	Battle Rifle Kills
Sniper Rifle Kills	—	—	—	Kill 1000 enemies between all Sniper Rifles	—	—	—	—	Sniper Rifle Kills
Handgun Kills	—	—	—	Kill 1000 enemies between all Handguns	—	—	—	—	Handgun Kills
Automatic Pistol Kills	—	—	—	Kill 1000 enemies between all Auto Pistols	—	—	—	—	Automatic Pistol Kills
Revolver Kills	—	—	—	Kill 1000 enemies between all Revolvers	—	—	—	—	Revolver Kills
Assault Rifle Bounty	—	—	—	Collect the Assault Rifle Bounty	—	—	—	—	Assault Rifle Bounty
Sniper Rifle Bounty	—	—	—	Collect the Sniper Rifle Bounty	—	—	—	—	Sniper Rifle Bounty
SMG Bounty	—	—	—	Collect the SMG Bounty	—	—	—	—	SMG Bounty
Battle Rifle Bounty	—	—	—	Collect the Battle Rifle Bounty	—	—	—	—	Battle Rifle Bounty
Shotgun Bounty	—	—	—	Collect the Shotgun Bounty	—	—	—	—	Shotgun Bounty
Melee Bounty	—	—	—	Collect the Melee Bounty	—	—	—	—	Melee Bounty
Explosives Bounty	—	—	—	Collect the Explosives Bounty	—	—	—	—	Explosives Bounty
Interrogation Bounty	—	—	—	Collect the Interrogation Bounty	—	—	—	—	Interrogation Bounty
Headshot Bounty	—	—	—	Collect the Headshot Bounty	—	—	—	—	Headshot Bounty
Marksman Bounty	—	—	—	Collect the Marksman Bounty	—	—	—	—	Marksman Bounty
Laser Tripmine	—	—	—	Kill 500 enemies with the Laser Tripmine	—	—	—	—	Laser Tripmine
Grenade Launcher	—	—	—	Kill 500 enemies with the Grenade Launcher	—	—	—	—	Grenade Launcher
Breaching Charge	—	—	—	Kill 500 enemies with the Breaching Charge	—	—	—	—	Breaching Charge
M67 Grenade	—	—	—	Kill 500 enemies with the M67 Frag Grenade	—	—	—	—	M67 Grenade
Incendiary Grenade	—	—	—	Kill 500 enemies with the Incendiary Grenade	—	—	—	—	Incendiary Grenade

MELEE ASSIGNMENTS

ASSIGNMENT NAME	AWARD REQ.	PATCH REWARD
Ballistic Shield Bashes	Kill 500 enemies with the Ballistic Shield	Ballistic Shield Bashes
Knife	Kill 100 enemies with the Knife	Knife
Boot Knife	Kill 100 enemies with the Boot Knife	Boot Knife
ACB-90	Kill 100 enemies with the ACB-90	ACB-90
Bowie Knife	Kill 100 enemies with the Bowie Knife	Bowie Knife
Carbon Fiber Knife	Kill 100 enemies with the Carbon Fiber Knife	Carbon Fiber Knife
Scout Knife	Kill 100 enemies with the Scout Knife	Scout Knife
Seal Knife	Kill 100 enemies with the Seal Knife	SEAL Knife
Survival Knife	Kill 100 enemies with the Survival Knife	Survival Knife
Trench Knife	Kill 100 enemies with the Prison Trench Knife	Trench Knife
Machete	Kill 100 enemies with the Machete	Machete
Shank	Kill 100 enemies with the Shank	Shank

ASSIGNMENT NAME	AWARD REQ.	PATCH REWARD
Nightstick	Kill 100 enemies with the Nightstick	Nightstick
Collapsible Baton	Kill 100 enemies with the Collapsible Baton	Collapsible Baton Assignment
Crowbar	Kill 100 enemies with the Crowbar	Crowbar
Sledgehammer	Kill 100 enemies with the Sledgehammer	Sledgehammer
Blackjack	Kill 100 enemies with the Blackjack	Blackjack
Lead Pipe	Kill 100 enemies with the Lead Pipe	Lead Pipe
Baseball Bat	Kill 100 enemies with the Baseball Bat	Baseball Bat
Breaching Hammer	Kill 100 enemies with the Breaching Hammer	Breaching Hammer
Golf Club	Kill 100 enemies with the Golf Club	Golf Club
Police Baton	Kill 100 enemies with the Police Baton	Police Baton
Interrogator	Interrogate 100 enemies	Interrogator

VEHICLE ASSIGNMENTS

ASSIGNMENT NAME	PRE-REQ. 1	PRE-REQ. 2	PRE-REQ. 3	AWARD REQ. 1	AWARD REQ. 2	AWARD REQ. 3	AWARD REQ. 4	AWARD REQ. 5	PATCH REWARD
Counter-Attack Truck Mastery	—	—	—	Unlock Gold Service Star 1 with Counter-Attack Trucks	—	—	—	—	Counter-Attack Truck Mastery
SUV Mastery	—	—	—	Unlock Gold Service Star 1 with SUVs	—	—	—	—	SUV Mastery
MSP Mastery	—	—	—	Unlock Gold Service Star 1 with MSPs	—	—	—	—	MSP Mastery
Sedan Mastery	—	—	—	Unlock Gold Service Star 1 with Sedans	—	—	—	—	Sedan Mastery
Coupe Mastery	—	—	—	Unlock Gold Service Star 1 with Coupes	—	—	—	—	Coupe Mastery
Gunboat Mastery	—	—	—	Unlock Gold Service Star 1 with Gunboats	—	—	—	—	Gunboat Mastery
Attack Helicopter Mastery	—	—	—	Unlock Gold Service Star 1 with Attack Helicopters	—	—	—	—	Attack Helicopter Mastery
Transport Helicopter Mastery	—	—	—	Unlock Gold Service Star 1 with Transport Helicopters	—	—	—	—	Transport Helicopter Mastery
Street Motorcycle Mastery	—	—	—	Unlock Gold Service Star 1 with Street Motorcycles	—	—	—	—	Street Motorcycle Mastery
Offroad Motorcycle Mastery	—	—	—	Unlock Gold Service Star 1 with Offroad Motorcycles	—	—	—	—	Offroad Motorcycle Mastery
Counter-Attack Truck Upgrades	—	—	—	Purchase all upgrades for the Counter-Attack Trucks	—	—	—	—	Counter-Attack Truck Upgrades
SUV Upgrades	—	—	—	Purchase all upgrades for the SUVs	—	—	—	—	SUV Upgrades

	ASSIGNMENT NAME	PRE-REQ. 1	PRE-REQ. 2	PRE-REQ. 3	AWARD REQ. 1	AWARD REQ. 2	AWARD REQ. 3	AWARD REQ. 4	AWARD REQ. 5	PATCH REWARD
	MSP Upgrades	—	—	—	Purchase all upgrades for the MSPs					MSP Upgrades
	Sedan Upgrades	—	—	—	Purchase all upgrades for the Sedans				—	Sedan Upgrades
	Coupe Upgrades	—	—	—	Purchase all upgrades for the Coupes			—	—	Coupe Upgrades
	Gunboat Upgrades	—	—	—	Purchase all upgrades for the Gunboats					Gunboat Upgrades Assignment
	Attack Helicopter Upgrades	—	—	—	Purchase all upgrades for the Attack Helicopters			—	—	Attack Helicopter Upgrades
	Transport Helicopter Upgrades	—	—	—	Purchase all upgrades for the Transport Helicopters					Transport Helicopter Upgrades
	Counter-Attack Truck Assault	—	—	—	Kill 500 players with Counter-Attack Trucks					Counter-Attack Truck Assault
	SUV Assualt	—	—	—	Kill 500 players with SUVs	—	—		—	SUV Assault
	GUNBOAT Assault	—	—	—	Kill 500 players with Gunboats					Gunboat Assault
	Attack Helicopter Assault	—	—	—	Kill 500 players with Attack Helicopters	—	—	—	—	Attack Helicopter Assault
	Transport Helicopter Assault	—	—	—	Kill 500 players with Transport Helicopters					Transport Helicopter Assault
	Armored Vehicle Bounty	—	—	—	Collect the Armored Vehicle Bounty					Armored Vehicle Bounty
	SUV Bounty	—	—	—	Collect the SUV Bounty	—	—	—	—	SUV Bounty
	Watercraft Bounty	—	—	—	Collect the Watercraft Bounty					Watercraft Bounty
	Attack Helicopter Bounty	—	—	—	Collect the Attack Helicopter Bounty	—	—	—	—	Attack Helicopter Bounty
	Transport Helicopter Bounty	—	—	—	Collect the Transport Helicopter Bounty				—	Transport Helicopter Bounty
	Anti-Vehicle Bounty	—	—	—	Collect the Anti-Vehicle Bounty	—	—		—	Anti-Vehicle Bounty
	Ground Vehicle 1	Sedan Bronze Service Star	Coupe Bronze Service Star	Msp Bronze Service Star	5 Armored Vehicle Coins	5 SUV Coins	—	—	—	Ground Vehicle Assignment 1
	Ground Vehicle 2	Ground Vehicle 1	SUV Silver Service Star	Cat Silver Service Star	25 Destroy enemy vehicles with a CAT	25 Destroy enemy vehicles with an Armored SUV	25 Roadkill bonuses	10 Armored Vehicle Coins	10 SUV Coins	Ground Vehicle Assignment 2
	Air Vehicle 1	Transport Helicopter Bronze Service Star	—	—	5 Attack Helicopter Coins	5 Transport Helicopter Coins	—	—	—	Air Vehicle Assignment 1
	Air Vehicle 2	Air Vehicle 1	Attack Helicopter Silver Service Star	—	25 Destroy ground vehicles with an Attack Helicopter	25 Destroy ground vehicles with a Transport Helicopter	25 Destroy helicopters with any other helicopter. In a round	—	—	Air Vehicle Assignment 2
	Water Vehicle 1	Gunboat Bronze Service Star	—	—	Watercraft Coins	—	—	—	—	Water Vehicle Assignment 1
	Water Vehicle 2	Water Vehicle 1	Gunboat Silver Service Star	—	25 Destroy vehicles with a Gunboat	20 Watercraft Coins	—	—	—	Water Vehicle Assignment 2
	Vehicle Destroyer	Rank 20	—	—	25 Destroy vehicles with an RPG	25 Destroy vehicles with a Stinger	25 Destroy vehicles with the Repair Tool	—	—	Vehicle Destroyer Assignment

ASSIGNMENT NAME	PRE-REQ. 1	PRE-REQ. 2	AWARD REQ. 1	AWARD REQ. 2	PATCH REWARD	REWARD 2
Mechanic Mastery	—	—	Unlock Gold Service Star 1 with the Mechanic	—	Mechanic Mastery	—
Operator Mastery	—	—	Unlock Gold Service Star 1 with the Operator	—	Operator Mastery	—
Enforcer Mastery	—	—	Unlock Gold Service Star 1 with the Enforcer	—	Enforcer Mastery	—
Professional Mastery	—	—	Unlock Gold Service Star 1 with the Professional	—	Professional Mastery	—
Mechanic Unlocked	—	—	Purchase all guns and gadgets with the Mechanic	—	Mechanic Unlocked	—
Operator Unlocked	—	—	Purchase all guns and gadgets with the Operator	—	Operator Unlocked	—
Enforcer Unlocked	—	—	Purchase all guns and gadgets with the Enforcer	—	Enforcer Unlocked	—
Professional Unlocked	—	—	Purchase all guns and gadgets with the Professional	—	Professional Unlocked	—
Operator 1	Operator Bronze Service Star	—	10 Assault Rifle kills	10 Heal teammates	Operator Assignment 1	—
Operator 2	Operator Assignment 1	Operator Bronze Service Star	25 Assault Rifle kills	5 Revive Coins	Operator Assignment 2	G17
Enforcer 1	Enforcer Bronze Service Star	—	10 Shotgun or Battle Rifle kills	10 Resupply teammates	Enforcer Assignment 1	—
Enforcer 2	Enforcer Assignment 1	Enforcer Bronze Service Star	25 Shotgun or Battle Rifle kills	250 Points of damage deflected with the Shield	Enforcer Assignment 2	Bald Eagle
Mechanic 1	Mechanic Bronze Service Star	—	10 SMG kills	5 Repair vehicles	Mechanic Assignment 1	—
Mechanic 2	Mechanic Assignment 1	Mechanic Bronze Service Star	25 SMG kills	10 Destroy vehicles with Sabotage	Mechanic Assignment 2	.410 Jury
Professional 1	Professional Bronze Service Star	—	10 Sniper Rifle kills	5 Laser Tripmine kills	Professional Assignment 1	—
Professional 2	Professional Assignment 1	Professional Bronze Service Star	25 Sniper Rifle kills	5 Camera Coins	Professional Assignment 2	MAC-10
Hacker 1	Hacker Bronze Service Star 5	—	—	—	Hacker Assignment 1	—
Hacker 2	Hacker Assignment 1	—	Hacker Silver Service Star 5	Upgrade to GPS Spotting version 5	Hacker Assignment 2	—

SYNDICATE ASSIGNMENTS

ASSIGNMENT NAME	PRE-REQ. 1	PRE-REQ. 2	PRE-REQ. 3	PATCH REWARD	REWARD 2
Gray Hat Syndicate	?	?	?	Hacker Grey Hay Syndicate	Gold Knife
Black Hat Syndicate	?	?	?	Hacker Black Hat Syndicate	Gold Golf Club
Operator Syndicate	?	?	?	Operator Syndicate	ARM
Enforcer Syndicate	?	?	?	Enforcer Syndicate	Double-Barrel Shotgun
Mechanic Syndicate	?	?	?	Mechanic Syndicate	FMG9
Professional Syndicate	?	?	?	Professional Syndicate	.300 Knockout

ASSIGNMENT NAME	PRE-REQ. 1	PRE-REQ. 2	PRE-REQ. 3	PATCH REWARD	REWARD 2
Ground Vehicle Syndicate	?	?	?	Ground Vehicle Syndicate	Gold Hammer
Air Vehicle Syndicate	?	?	?	Air Vehicle Syndicate	Gold Baton
Water Vehicle Syndicate	?	?	?	Water Vehicle Syndicate	Gold Crowbar
White Hat Syndicate	?	?	?	Hacker White Hat Syndicate	Gold Boot Knife
Game Mode Syndicate	?	?	?	Game Mode Syndicate	Gold Scout Knife
Close Range Syndicate	?	?	?	Close Range Syndicate	Gold Seal Knife
Criminal Syndicate	?	?	?	Criminal Syndicate	Gold Survival Knife
Justice Syndicate	?	?	?	Justice Syndicate	Gold Trench Knife
Gun Syndicate	?	?	?	Gun Syndicate	Gold Lead Pipe
Progression Syndicate	?	?	?	Progression Syndicate	Gold Machete
Elite Player Syndicate	?	?	?	Elite Player Syndicate	Gold Sledge Hammer

NOTE

The criteria for the Syndicate assignments are secret. But once these assignments are complete, you're rewarded with some unique weapons.

SQUAD ASSIGNMENTS

ASSIGNMENT NAME	PRE-REQ. 1	PRE-REQ. 2	PRE-REQ. 3	AWARD REQ. 1	AWARD REQ. 2	AWARD REQ. 3	PATCH REWARD
Squad Assignment	—	—	—	5 Squad Savior bonuses	5 Squad Avenger bonuses	Ace Squad Coin	Squad Assignment
Black Market Assignment	Zipline Purchased	Sabotage Tool Purchased	Grappling Hook Purchased	5 Explosives Coins	5 Zipline Coins	5 Grappling Hook Coins	Black Market Assignment
Cop Arsenal Assignment	Ballistic Shield Purchased	Armored Insert Purchased	T62 Cew Purchased	5 Interrogation Coins	5 T62 CEW Coins	5 Ballistic Shield Coins	Cop Arsenal Assignment
Clubs	—	—	—	Reach Rank 25	—	—	Clubs
Hearts	—	—	—	Reach Rank 50	—	—	Hearts
Diamonds	—	—	—	Reach Rank 75	—	—	Diamonds
Spades	—	—	—	Reach Rank 100	—	—	Spades
Jacks	—	—	—	Reach Rank 120	—	—	Jacks
Queens	—	—	—	Reach Rank 140	—	—	Queens
Kings	—	—	—	Reach Rank 150	—	—	Kings
Sidearm Bounty	—	—	—	Collect the Sidearm Bounty	—	—	Sidearm Bounty
Ammo Resupply Bounty	—	—	—	Collect the Ammo Resupply Bounty	—	—	Ammo Resupply Bounty

ASSIGNMENT NAME	PRE-REQ. 1	PRE-REQ. 2	PRE-REQ. 3	AWARD REQ. 1	AWARD REQ. 2	AWARD REQ. 3	PATCH REWARD
Ballistic Shield Bounty	—	—	—	Collect the Ballistic Shield Bounty	—	—	Ballistic Shield Bounty
Satellite Phone Bounty	—	—	—	Earn the Satellite Phone Bounty	—	—	Satellite Phone Bounty
T62 CEW Bounty	—	—	—	Collect the T62 CEW Bounty	—	—	T62 CEW Bounty
First Aid Pack Bounty	—	—	—	Collect the First Aid Bag Bounty	—	—	First Aid Pack Bounty
Revive Bounty	—	—	—	Collect the Revive Bounty	—	—	Revive Bounty
Repair Tool Bounty	—	—	—	Collect the Repair Tool Bounty	—	—	Repair Tool Bounty
Camera Bounty	—	—	—	Collect the Camera Bounty	—	—	Camera Bounty
Zipline Bounty	—	—	—	Collect the Zipline Bounty	—	—	Zipline Bounty
Grappling Hook Bounty	—	—	—	Collect the Grappling Hook Bounty	—	—	Grappling Hook Bounty
Kill Assist Bounty	—	—	—	Collect the Kill Assist Bounty	—	—	Kill Assist Bounty
Avenger Bounty	—	—	—	Collect the Avenger Bounty	—	—	Avenger Bounty
Savior Bounty	—	—	—	Collect the Savior Bounty	—	—	Savior Bounty
Spotting Bounty	—	—	—	Collect the Spotting Bounty	—	—	Spotting Bounty
Ace Squad Bounty	—	—	—	Collect the Ace Squad Bounty	—	—	Ace Squad Bounty
MVP Bounty	—	—	—	Collect the MVP Bounty	—	—	MVP Bounty
T62 CEW	—	—	—	Take down 500 enemies with the T62 CEW	—	—	T62 CEW
Sabotage	—	—	—	Kill 500 enemies using Sabotage	—	—	Sabotage
Cash Earner 1	—	—	—	Earn $1,000,000 while in-game	—	—	Cash Earner 1
Cash Earner 2	—	—	—	Earn $5,000,000 while in-game	—	—	Cash Earner 2
Cash Earner 3	—	—	—	Earn $10,000,000 while in-game	—	—	Cash Earner 3
Cash Spender 1	—	—	—	Purchase $100,000 worth of weapons, gadgets, and upgrades	—	—	Cash Spender 1
Cash Spender 2	—	—	—	Purchase $1,000,000 worth of weapons, gadgets, and upgrades	—	—	Cash Spender 2
Cash Spender 3	—	—	—	Purchase $5,000,000 worth of weapons, gadgets, and upgrades	—	—	Cash Spender 3
Cash Hoarder 1	—	—	—	Have $100,000 in your wallet at the end of any round	—	—	Cash Hoarder 1
Cash Hoarder 2	—	—	—	Have $1,000,000 in your wallet at the end of any round	—	—	Cash Hoarder 2
Cash Hoarder 3	—	—	—	Have $10,000,000 in your wallet at the end of any round	—	—	Cash Hoarder 3

NAME	DESCRIPTION	UNLOCK CRITERIA
GPS Jamming V1.0	Eliminate passive spotting by scrambling your team's GPS coordinates.	—
Trace V1.0	Reveal High Value Targets and enemy Hacker subroutines with an area scan.	—
GPS Spotting V1.0	Reveal enemy locations by gaining access to their GPS devices.	—
Squad Upgrade V1.0	Boost the Reputation of every Squad member to the next tier by upgrading their firmware.	—
Point of Interest V1.0	Highlight an important objective for one of your Squads through an AR overlay.	—
Fast Deploy V1.0	Decrease the deploy time for a Squad by rerouting traffic.	—
Trojan V1.0	Speed friendly interaction and slow enemy interaction; nullify enemy subroutines instantly.	—
Backdoor V1.0	Gain control of an automated in-world object by exposing a backdoor vulnerability.	—
Overclock V1.0	Decrease the cooldown on all subroutines. WARNING: some subroutines may overheat after use.	—
Overclock V2.0	V2.0 uses less active memory, increasing cooldown speed.	1 Hacker Bronze Service Star
Backdoor V2.0	V2.0 lowers the latency requirements of this subroutine, thus giving it a smaller cooldown time.	2 Hacker Bronze Service Stars
Trojan V2.0	V2.0 confuses administrative processes on interactions, allowing for a longer duration before being shut down.	3 Hacker Bronze Service Stars
GPS Jamming 2.0	V2.0 sends a stronger scramble signal, greatly increasing the affected area.	4 Hacker Bronze Service Stars
Point of Interest 2.0	V2.0 can run on the latest AR firmware, allowing the POI to last longer.	5 Hacker Bronze Service Stars
Fast Deploy 2.0	V2.0 scrambles the traffic controller's systems, leading to a longer duration before being purged.	6 Hacker Bronze Service Stars
GPS Spotting 2.0	V2.0 uses WiFi on GPS devices to echo the original signal, increasing the spotting area.	7 Hacker Bronze Service Stars
Trace V2.0	V2.0 sends multiple signals at different frequencies, which increases its duration and also displays Spawn Beacons.	8 Hacker Bronze Service Stars
Squad Upgrade 2.0	V2.0 reduces active memory, increasing cooldown speed.	9 Hacker Bronze Service Stars
Backdoor V3.0	V3.0 uses less active memory, reducing the cooldown further.	10 Hacker Bronze Service Stars
GPS Jamming 3.0	V3.0 refactors the code to run in parallel, making the cooldown faster and the duration longer.	1 Hacker Silver Service Star
Point of Interest 3.0	V3.0 unlocks the AR clock speed to recharge the cooldown faster.	2 Hacker Silver Service Stars
	V3.0 sends multiple shadow copies to	

NAME	DESCRIPTION	UNLOCK CRITERIA
Fast Deploy V3.0	V3.0 tracks satellite navigation systems, allowing for better traffic signal coordination and a greater decrease in return time.	6 Hacker Silver Service Stars
Trace V3.0	V3.0 adds a signal that displays any Trojans on an interaction placed by another hacker.	7 Hacker Silver Service Stars
Squad Upgrade V3.0	V3.0 optimizes many lists into a hashtable, further increasing cooldown speed.	8 Hacker Silver Service Stars
Backdoor V4.0	V4.0 batch processes commands, further lowering this subroutine's cooldown.	9 Hacker Silver Service Stars
GPS Jamming V4.0	V4.0 uses a signal amplifier, further increasing the area of affect.	10 Hacker Silver Service Stars
Point of Interest V4.0	V4.0 uses more of the AR battery for an even faster cooldown.	1 Hacker Gold Service Star
Trojan V4.0	V4.0 bypasses early detection systems and instead hacks the kernel inside an interaction, further increasing its duration.	2 Hacker Gold Service Stars
Overclock V4.0	V4.0 detects high heat areas and applies more coolant, reducing the number of subroutines that overheat.	3 Hacker Gold Service Stars
GPS Spotting V4.0	V4.0 amplifies the signal, further increasing the spotting area.	4 Hacker Gold Service Stars
Fast Deploy V4.0	V4.0 uses a more advanced routing algorithm to further decrease return time and cut cooldown time.	5 Hacker Gold Service Stars
Trace V4.0	V4.0 echoes signals off multiple radio towers, increasing its duration.	6 Hacker Gold Service Stars
Squad Upgrade V4.0	V4.0 decreases the effects of latency, speeding up the cooldown even more.	7 Hacker Gold Service Stars
Backdoor V5.0	V5.0 uses even less memory, greatly reducing cooldown.	8 Hacker Gold Service Stars
GPS Jamming V5.0	V5.0 reaches further while increasing the duration and speeding up cooldown time.	9 Hacker Gold Service Stars
Point of Interest V5.0	V5.0 hacks the AR kernel, allowing it the POI to last even longer on the HUD.	10 Hacker Gold Service Stars
Trojan V5.0	V5.0 refactors much of the code to run in parallel, greatly reducing cooldown for all uses.	11 Hacker Gold Service Stars
Overclock V5.0	V5.0 optimizes coolant application, leading to faster cooldown, higher clock speed, lower overheat time, and even fewer overheated subroutines.	12 Hacker Gold Service Stars
GPS Spotting V5.0	V5.0 optimizes for parallel architecture, decreasing the cooldown and dramatically increasing the duration.	13 Hacker Gold Service Stars
Fast Deploy V5.0	V5.0 is virtually invisible to an automated traffic controller, leading to a much longer duration before being purged.	14 Hacker Gold Service Stars
Trace V5.0	V5.0 interpolates positions with a more advanced algorithm, further increasing its duration.	15 Hacker Gold Service Stars
Squad Upgrade V5.0	V5.0 includes hardware-specific changes, yielding the fastest cooldown possible.	16 Hacker Gold Service Stars

SINGLE PLAYER
ACHIEVEMENTS / TROPHIES

The single-player Achievements / Trophies are fairly straightforward. Stay on the lookout for the episode specific awards and complete the campaign, including all extras, to earn them all.

GAME COMPLETION

The following are earned by completing the Prologue and 10 episodes. Finishing the game on Hardline difficulty is required to get all of them.

NAME	DESCRIPTION	TROPHY	XBOX POINTS	ORIGIN POINTS
On the Job	Complete the Prologue in single-player	Bronze	20	20
Pressure Applied	Complete Ep. 1: Back to School	Bronze	20	20
Bumpy Ride	Complete Ep. 2: Checking Out	Bronze	20	20
Deal? What Deal?	Complete Ep. 3: Gator Bait	Bronze	20	20
Good Guys	Complete Ep. 4: Case Closed	Bronze	20	20
You Probably Have Questions	Complete Ep. 5: Gauntlet	Bronze	20	20
Snow Blind	Complete Ep. 6: Out of Business	Bronze	20	20
Hollyweird	Complete Ep. 7: Glass Houses	Bronze	20	20

NAME	DESCRIPTION	TROPHY	XBOX POINTS	ORIGIN POINTS
From Their Cold, Dead Hands	Complete Ep. 8: Sovereign Land	Bronze	20	20
Some Damn Fine Fireworks	Complete Ep. 9: Independence Day	Bronze	20	20
Served Cold	Complete Ep. 10: Legacy	Bronze	20	20
Case Closed	Complete all single-player episodes on Officer difficulty	Silver	25	25
Super Cop	Complete all single-player episodes on Veteran difficulty	Silver	25	25
Blue Eagle	Complete all single-player episodes on Hardline difficulty	Silver	25	25

EPISODE SPECIFIC

Some Achievements / Trophies require completing specific tasks in Episodes 1, 5, 7, 8, 9, and 10. Stay on the lookout for the following as you play through the single-player campaign. Refer to the campaign chapter for full details on completing them.

NAME	DESCRIPTION	TROPHY	XBOX POINTS	ORIGIN POINTS
Motley Crew	Tag all criminals visible from the rooftop in Ep. 1: Back to School	Bronze	25	25
Their Own Medicine	Steal a T62 CEW from the back of a police cruiser in Ep. 5: Gauntlet	Bronze	20	20
Knock Knock	Blow up the meth lab in Ep. 5: Gauntlet	Bronze	20	20
Graceful Exit	Don't get spotted in Ep. 5: Gauntlet	Bronze	20	20
Hollywood Hideaway	Find Roark's hidden room in Ep. 7: Glass Houses	Bronze	20	20

NAME	DESCRIPTION	TROPHY	XBOX POINTS	ORIGIN POINTS
A Craftsman's Tools	Find your weapons in Ep. 8: Sovereign Land before instigating combat in the trailer park	Silver	25	25
Real Action Hero	Kill a criminal in Ep. 9: Independence Day from mid-air after escaping the penthouse	Silver	25	25
Dare Devil	Jump the dirt bike into the mansion grounds in Ep. 10: Legacy	Bronze	20	20
Social Climber	Find the hidden access to the mansion grounds in Ep. 10: Legacy	Bronze	20	20

THE COMPLETIONIST

Complete the extras, Case Files and Suspects with Warrants, in the single-player campaign to earn the following. Refer to the Episodes section of this guide to find out where to find them. Using non-lethal takedowns and completing the objectives will earn the expert score required to reach Expert Level 15.

	NAME	DESCRIPTION	TROPHY	XBOX POINTS	ORIGIN POINTS
	You're Getting Good at This	Reach Expert Level 5 in single-player	Bronze	20	20
	Almost an Expert	Reach Expert Level 10 in single-player	Silver	25	25
	One Good Cop	Reach Expert Level 15 in single-player	Silver	25	25
	Keep Digging, Detective	Complete any case file in single-player	Bronze	20	20

	NAME	DESCRIPTION	TROPHY	XBOX POINTS	ORIGIN POINTS
	True Detective	Complete 3 case files in single-player	Silver	25	25
	World's Greatest Detective	Complete all case files in single-player	Gold	50	50
	Bring 'em to Justice	Capture all warrants alive in single-player	Silver	25	25

STATS

Use Nick's various abilities and gadgets in single-player to earn the following. Once the player is capable of doing them, it does not take too long to complete each one.

	NAME	DESCRIPTION	TROPHY	XBOX POINTS	ORIGIN POINTS
	By the Book	Do a Non-Lethal takedown on 10 criminals in single-player	Bronze	20	20
	You Tazed Him, Bro!	Zap 5 criminals with the T62 CEW in single-player	Bronze	20	20
	Watched, Dawg	Identify 10 warrants with the scanner in single-player	Bronze	20	20

	NAME	DESCRIPTION	TROPHY	XBOX POINTS	ORIGIN POINTS
	Cape and Ears Not Included	Climb a total of 10 meters with the grapple gun in single-player	Bronze	25	25
	Fast Rope Expert	Travel a total of 90 meters with the zipline crossbow in single-player	Bronze	25	25
	Damn Thing Doesn't Work	Disarm 2 alarm boxes in single-player	Bronze	20	20

MULTIPLAYER

Face off against opposing players to earn these multiplayer Achievements/Trophies.

	NAME	DESCRIPTION	TROPHY	XBOX POINTS	ORIGIN POINTS
	The Big Score	Win 5 Heist and 5 Blood Money matches in multiplayer	Silver	25	25
	Electric Company	Take down 25 enemies with the T62 CEW in multiplayer	Silver	20	20
	Menz in the Hood	Kill 25 enemies with a MAC-10 and 25 with a sawed-off shotgun in multiplayer	Silver	25	25

	NAME	DESCRIPTION	TROPHY	XBOX POINTS	ORIGIN POINTS
	Gone Clubbing	Reach Rank 25 in multiplayer	Gold	50	50
	Hooked for Life	Purchase the grappling gun and zipline in multiplayer	Gold	50	50

PLAYSTATION PLATINUM TROPHY

Collect all of the Trophies, including Multiplayer, to earn this PlayStation 3/4 exclusive Trophy.

	NAME	DESCRIPTION	TROPHY
	Platinum Trophy	Collect all other Battlefield Hardline Trophies	Platinum

BATTLEFIELD HARDLINE

FREE SEARCHABLE AND SORTABLE EGUIDE

Go to www.primagames.com/code and enter the unique code
found at the back of this guide!

All the great information, tips, art, and more found in the print guide—all optimized for a second screen experience!

⭐ INTERACTIVE CONTENT

eGuides are fully searchable so you can jump directly to the content you want. Sortable tables enable you to compare items and display the
most relevant data.

⭐ ACCESS ANYWHERE

Responsive design optimizes your view for any size screen. Access your eGuide from your mobile phone, tablet, PC, or any web-enabled device!

⭐ STAY CURRENT

The enhanced eGuide is regularly edited to reflect changes and updates.

⭐ HIGH RESOLUTION

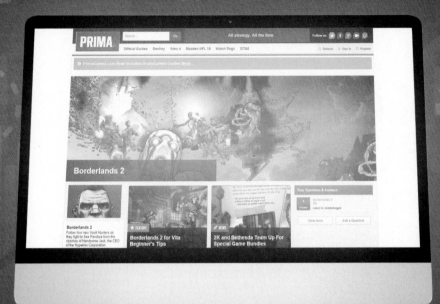

PRIMA OFFICIAL GAME GUIDE

Prima Games

An imprint of Random House, LLC, a Penguin Random House Company

3000 Lava Ridge Courte, Ste. 100

Roseville, CA 95661

www.primagames.com

Written by David Knight, Dan Herrera, and Michael Owen

ISBN: 978-0-8041-6360-6

PRIMA GAMES STAFF

VICE PRESIDENT AND PUBLISHER
Mike Degler

LICENSING MANAGERS
Aaron Lockhart
Christian Sumner

DIGITAL PUBLISHING MANAGER
Tim Cox

MARKETING MANAGER
Katie Hemlock

OPERATIONS MANAGER
Stacey Beheler

CREDITS

SENIOR DEVELOPMENT EDITOR
Jennifer Sims

BOOK DESIGNER
Tim Amrhein

PRODUCTION DESIGNERS
Julie Clark
Justin Lucas

BATTLEFIELD™

HARDLINE

FREE EGUIDE!

Go to www.primagames.com/code and enter this unique code to access your FREE eGuide!

H25M-TA8D-T2JV-YNG2

www.primagames.com